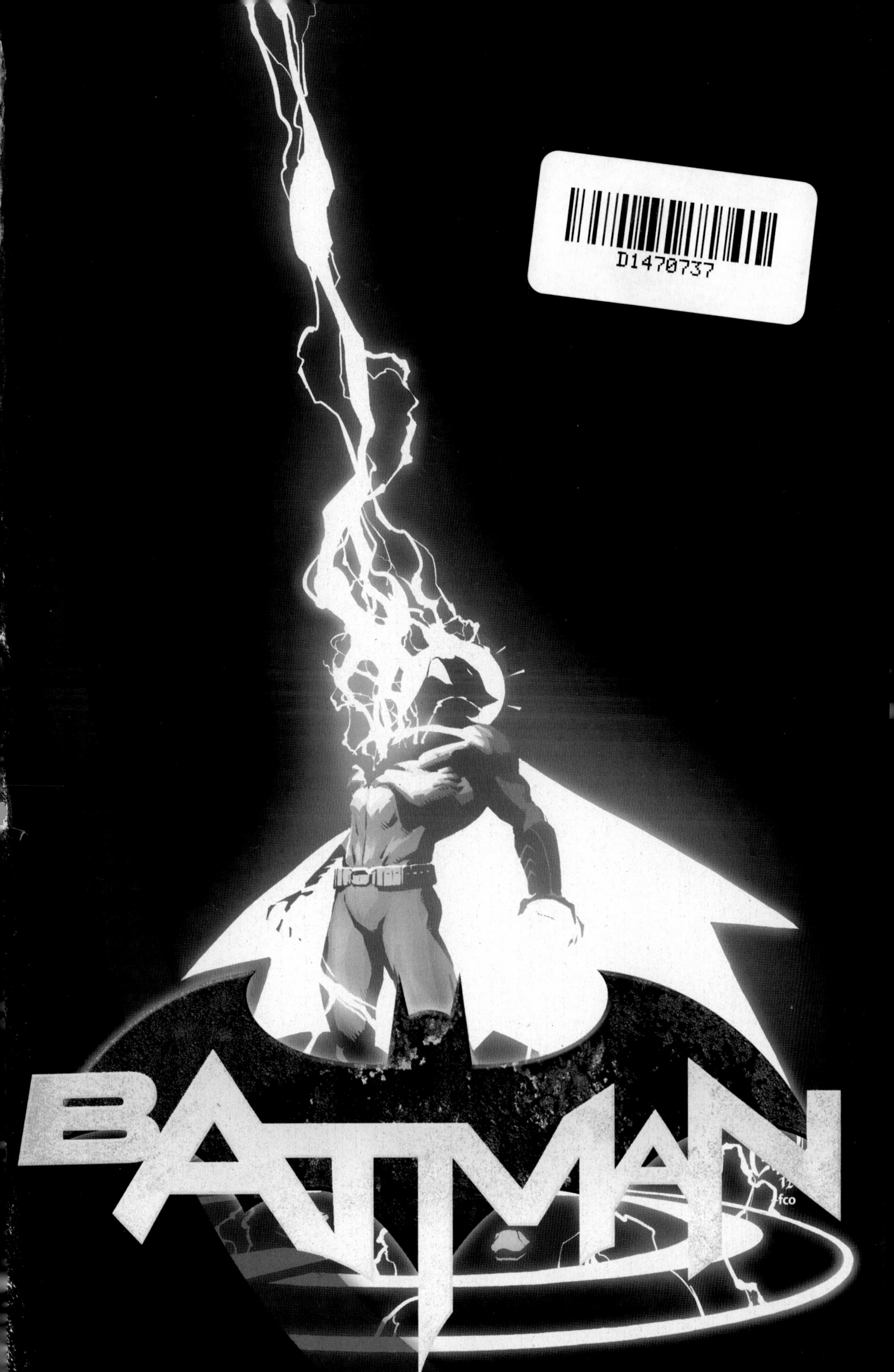
BATMAN

VOLUME 2 THE CITY OF OWLS

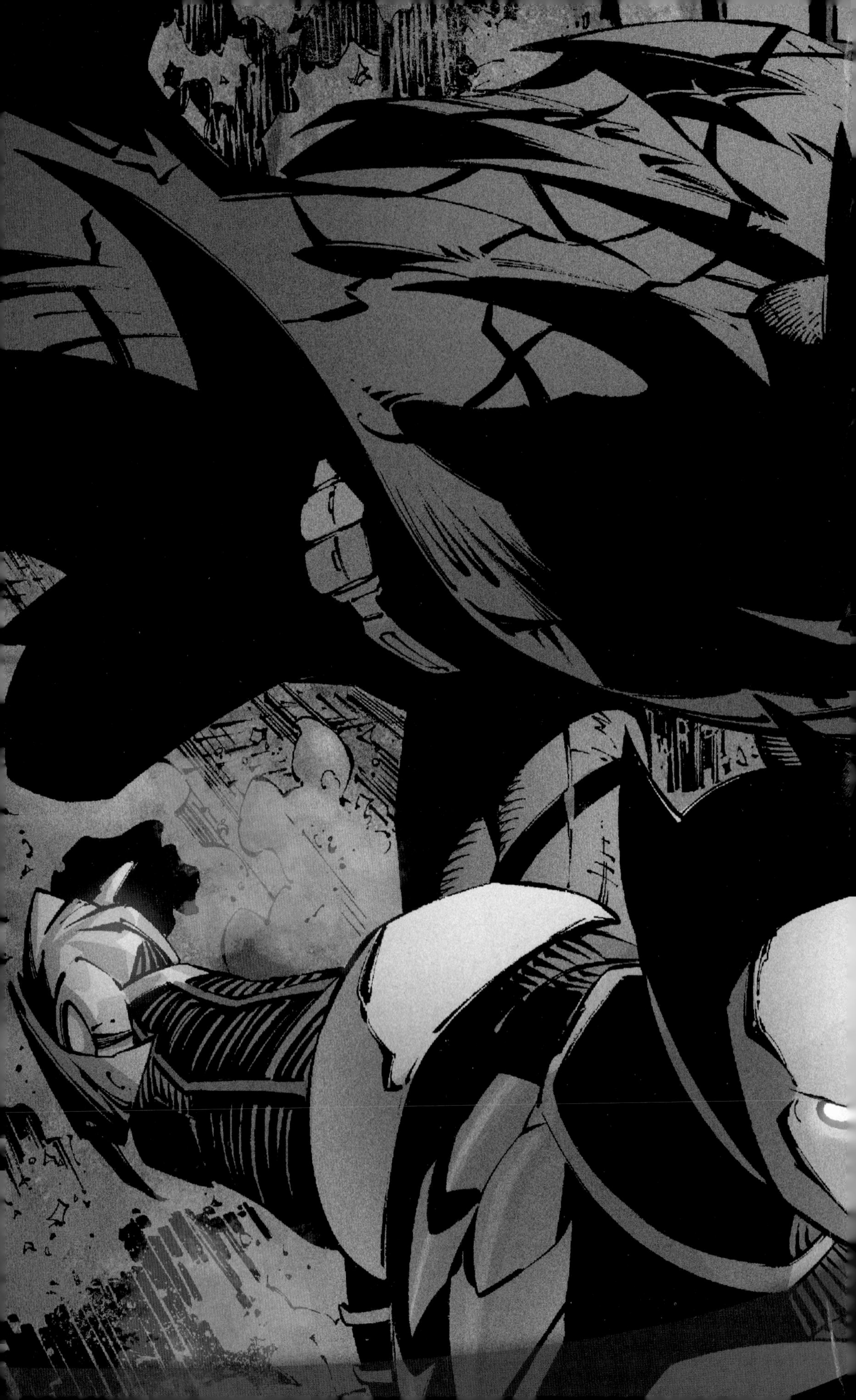

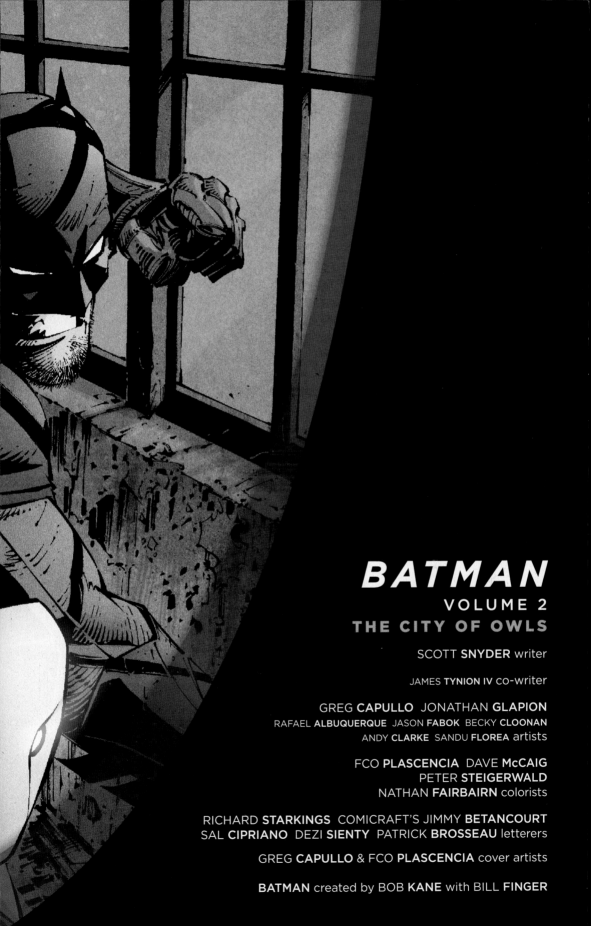

BATMAN
VOLUME 2
THE CITY OF OWLS

SCOTT **SNYDER** writer

JAMES **TYNION IV** co-writer

GREG **CAPULLO**   JONATHAN **GLAPION**
RAFAEL **ALBUQUERQUE**   JASON **FABOK**   BECKY **CLOONAN**
ANDY **CLARKE**   SANDU **FLOREA** artists

FCO **PLASCENCIA**   DAVE **McCAIG**
PETER **STEIGERWALD**
NATHAN **FAIRBAIRN** colorists

RICHARD **STARKINGS**   COMICRAFT'S JIMMY **BETANCOURT**
SAL **CIPRIANO**   DEZI **SIENTY**   PATRICK **BROSSEAU** letterers

GREG **CAPULLO** & FCO **PLASCENCIA** cover artists

BATMAN created by BOB **KANE** with BILL **FINGER**

MIKE MARTS Editor – Original Series KATIE KUBERT Assistant Editor – Original Series JEB WOODARD Group Editor – Collected Editions
PETER HAMBOUSSI Editor – Collected Edition STEVE COOK Design Director – Books ROBBIE BIEDERMAN Publication Design

BOB HARRAS Senior VP – Editor-in-Chief, DC Comics

DIANE NELSON President DAN DiDIO Publisher JIM LEE Publisher GEOFF JOHNS President & Chief Creative Officer
AMIT DESAI Executive VP – Business & Marketing Strategy, Direct to Consumer & Global Franchise Management
SAM ADES Senior VP – Direct to Consumer BOBBIE CHASE VP – Talent Development
MARK CHIARELLO Senior VP – Art, Design & Collected Editions JOHN CUNNINGHAM Senior VP – Sales & Trade Marketing
ANNE DePIES Senior VP – Business Strategy, Finance & Administration DON FALLETTI VP – Manufacturing Operations
LAWRENCE GANEM VP – Editorial Administration & Talent Relations ALISON GILL Senior VP – Manufacturing & Operations
HANK KANALZ Senior VP – Editorial Strategy & Administration JAY KOGAN VP – Legal Affairs THOMAS LOFTUS VP – Business Affairs
JACK MAHAN VP – Business Affairs NICK J. NAPOLITANO VP – Manufacturing Administration EDDIE SCANNELL VP – Consumer Marketing
COURTNEY SIMMONS Senior VP – Publicity & Communications JIM (SKI) SOKOLOWSKI VP – Comic Book Specialty & Trade Marketing
NANCY SPEARS VP – Mass, Book, Digital Sales & Trade Marketing

BATMAN VOLUME 2: THE CITY OF OWLS

DC Comics, 2900 W. Alameda Avenue, Burbank, CA 91505
Printed by Transcontinental Interglobe Beauceville, Canada. 5/5/17. Seventh Printing.
ISBN: 978-1-4012-3778-3

Library of Congress Cataloging-in-Publication Data

Snyder, Scott, author.
Batman. Volume 2, The City of Owls / Scott Snyder, Greg Capullo, Jonathan [sic] Glapion, James Tynion IV, Rafael Albuquerque, Jason Fabok.
pages cm
"Originally published in single magazine form in Batman 8-12, Batman Annual 1."
ISBN 978-1-4012-3778-3
1. Graphic novels. I. Capullo, Greg, illustrator. II. Glapion, Jonathan, illustrator. III. Tynion, James, IV, author. IV. Albuquerque, Rafael,
1981- illustrator. V. Fabok, Jay, illustrator. VI. Title. VII. Title: City of Owls.

PREVIOUSLY...

Batman had believed the Court of Owls was just a nursery rhyme. As a young boy, he'd even honed his detective skills trying to prove that they existed, but never found any proof that a secret, owl-obsessed cabal ruled Gotham City.

That was before the Talon, the Court's legendary assassin, tried to kill Bruce Wayne in the middle of his meeting with mayoral candidate Lincoln March. It took all of his wits and skills as the Dark Knight to survive the deadly plummet from the top of Old Wayne Tower.

Batman uncovered the Court's nests, hidden in secret floors of Wayne-constructed buildings, dating as far back as the 19th century. The Talon then captured the Caped Crusader and proceeded to hunt the Dark Knight through a labyrinth for the Court's sadistic amusement!

While trapped in the Court's maze, Batman discovered evidence of a long-standing rivalry between the Owls and the Wayne family—proof that they were responsible for the death of his great-great-grandfather, architect Alan Wayne. After a strenuous battle with the Talon, Batman made a harrowing escape—almost at the cost of his own life.

In defeat, the Court abandoned their champion. Upon examining his bested enemy, Batman made several shocking discoveries. The Talon he'd fought was William Cobb, Dick Grayson's great-grandfather. The Court recruited their killers from Haly's Circus, and they had intended to make Dick their next executioner! Even more disconcerting was that the reanimation process had endowed Cobb with metahuman regenerative abilities, which only extreme cold could suppress.

Now, the Court has unleashed their ultimate offensive. They have awakened all of the previous generations' Talons from suspended animation and set them loose on Gotham City! **And their first stop is Wayne Manor...**

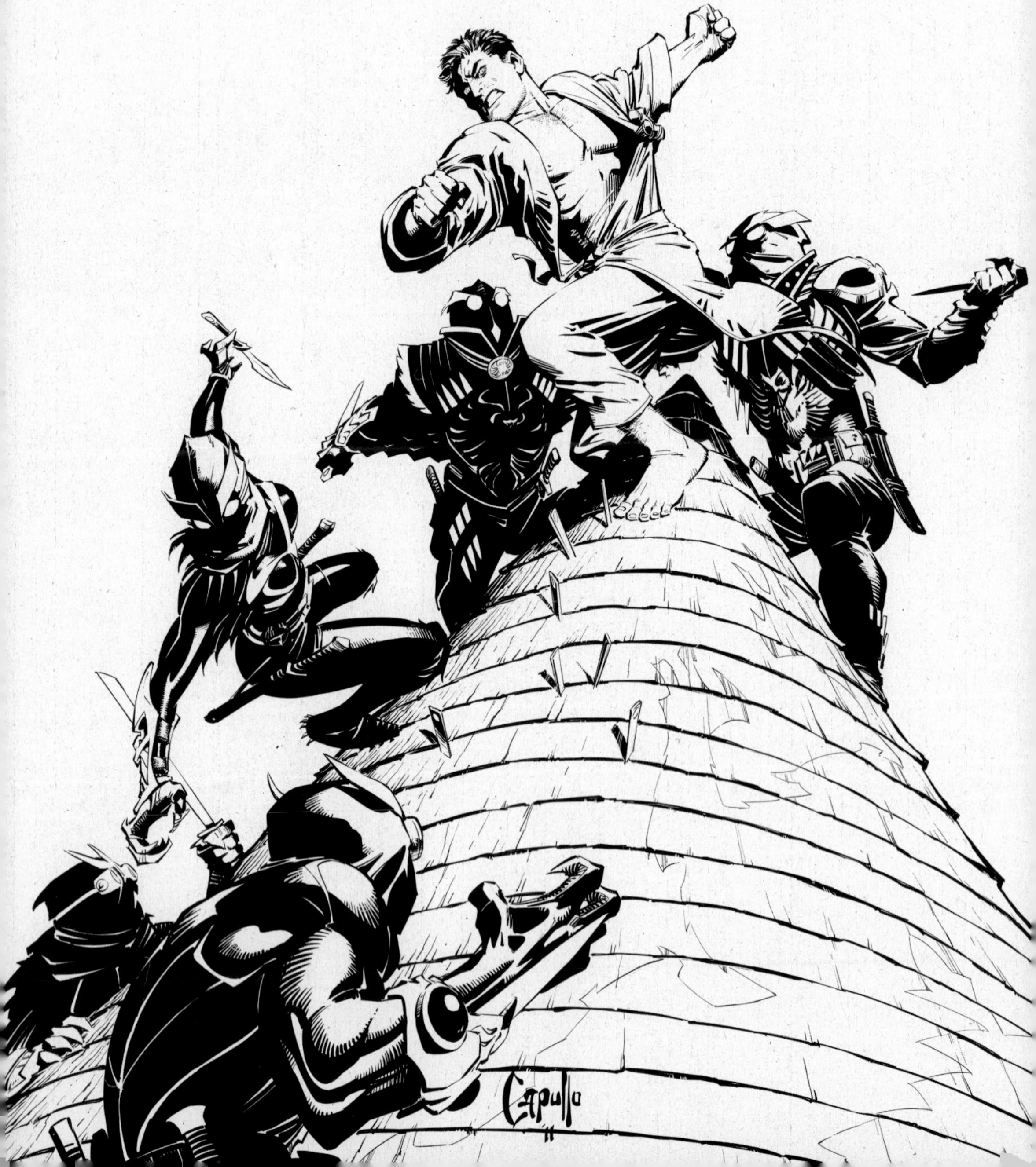
Capullo

ATTACK ON WAYNE MANOR SCOTT SNYDER writer GREG CAPULLO penciller JONATHAN GLAPION inker
THE CALL SCOTT SNYDER & JAMES TYNION IV writers RAFAEL ALBUQUERQUE artist
cover by GREG CAPULLO and FCO PLASCENCIA

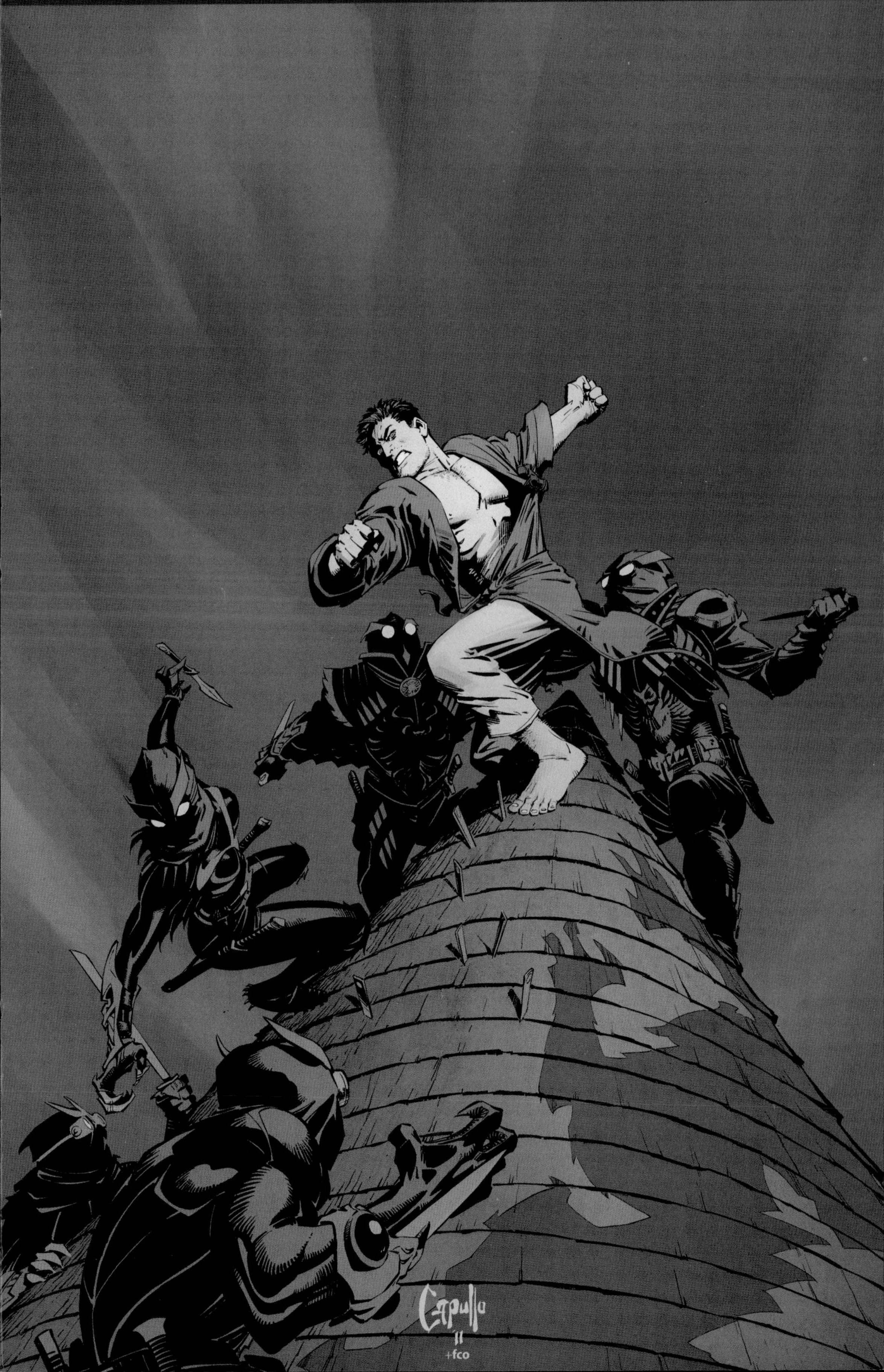
Capullo
'11
+fco

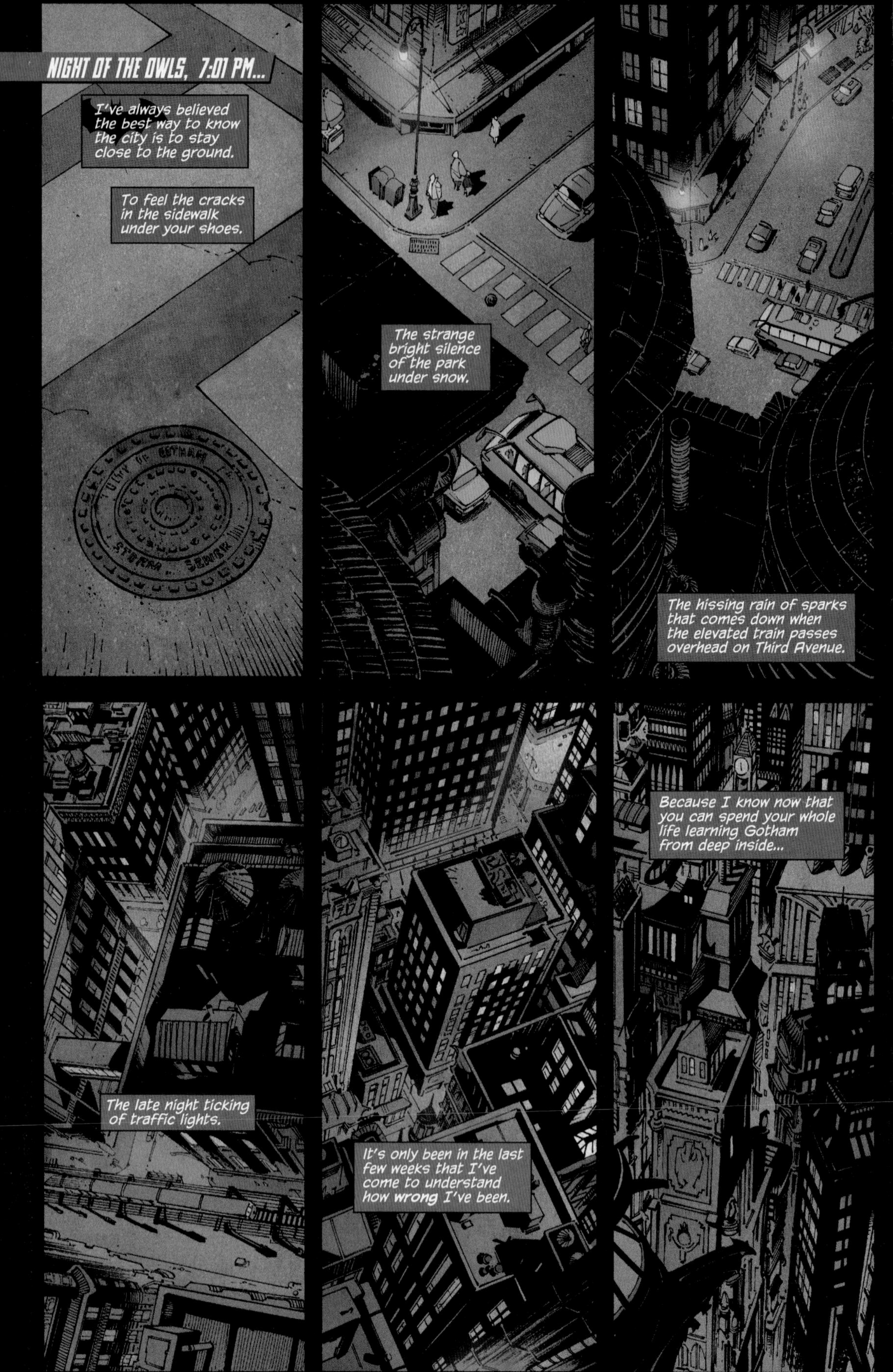
NIGHT OF THE OWLS, 7:01 PM...
I've always believed the best way to know the city is to stay close to the ground.
To feel the cracks in the sidewalk under your shoes.
CITY OF GOTHAM
STORM SEWER
The strange bright silence of the park under snow.
The hissing rain of sparks that comes down when the elevated train passes overhead on Third Avenue.
The late night ticking of traffic lights.
It's only been in the last few weeks that I've come to understand how wrong I've been.
Because I know now that you can spend your whole life learning Gotham from deep inside...

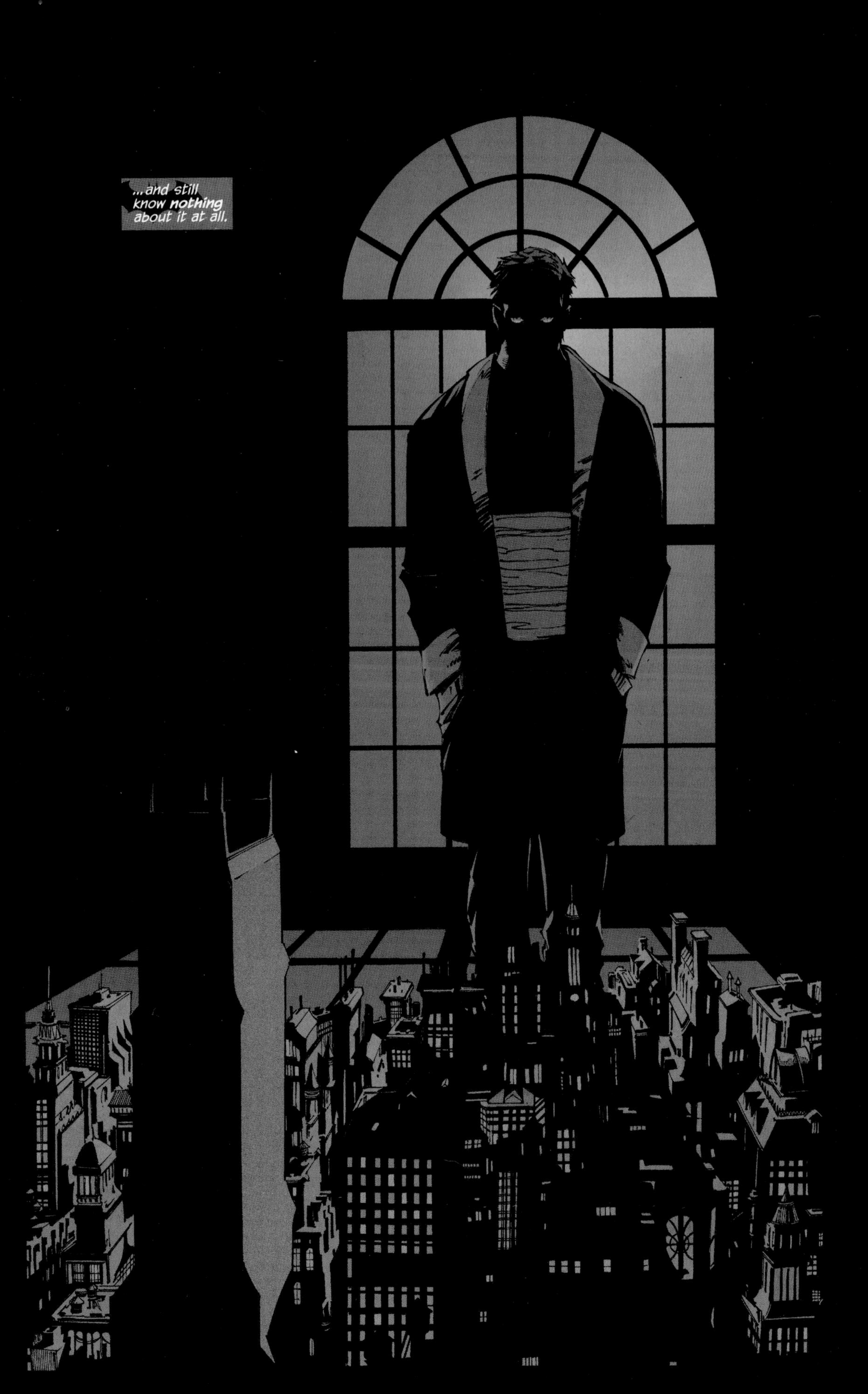
...and still know **nothing** about it at all.

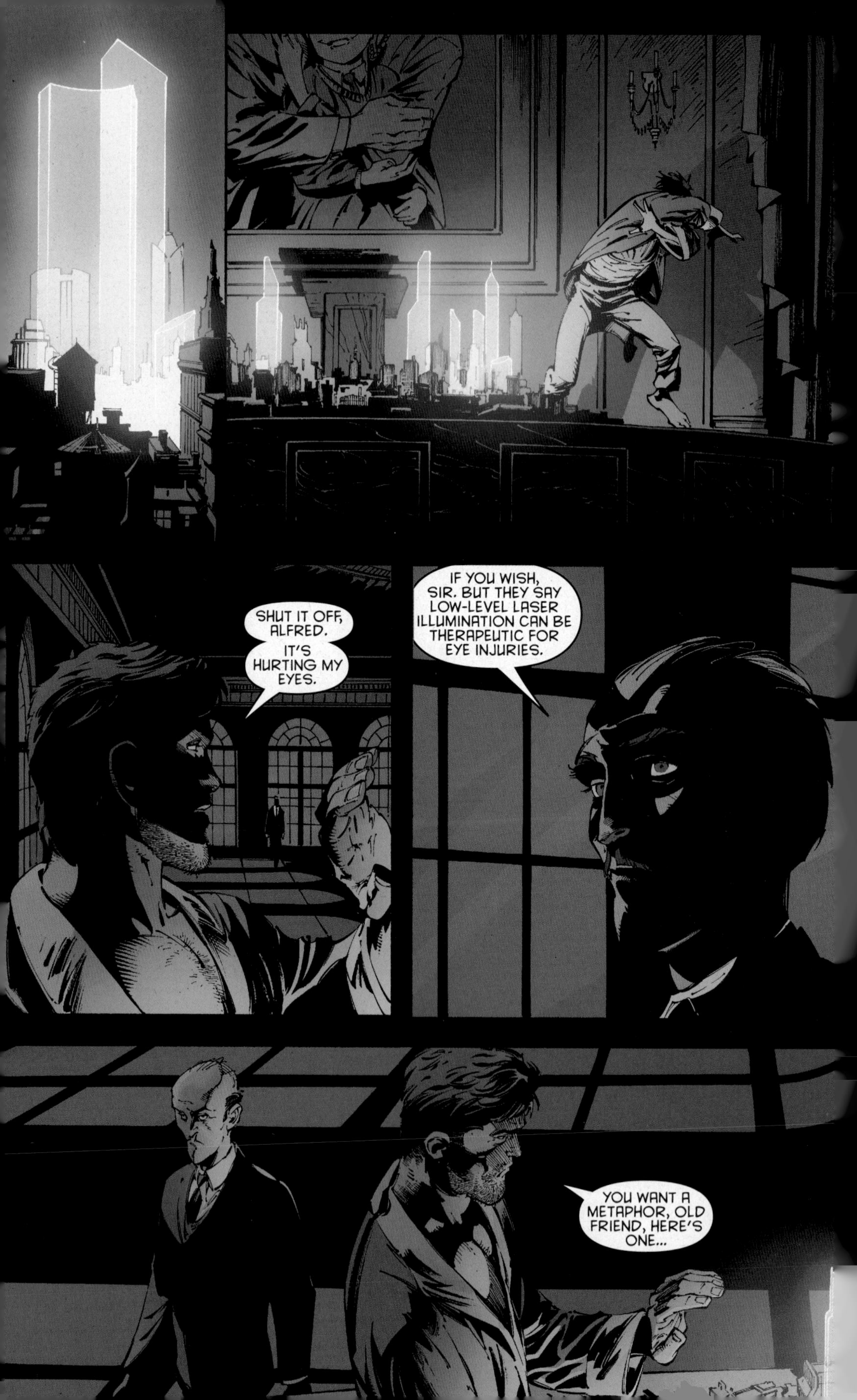

SHUT IT OFF, ALFRED. IT'S HURTING MY EYES.
IF YOU WISH, SIR. BUT THEY SAY LOW-LEVEL LASER ILLUMINATION CAN BE THERAPEUTIC FOR EYE INJURIES.
YOU WANT A METAPHOR, OLD FRIEND, HERE'S ONE...

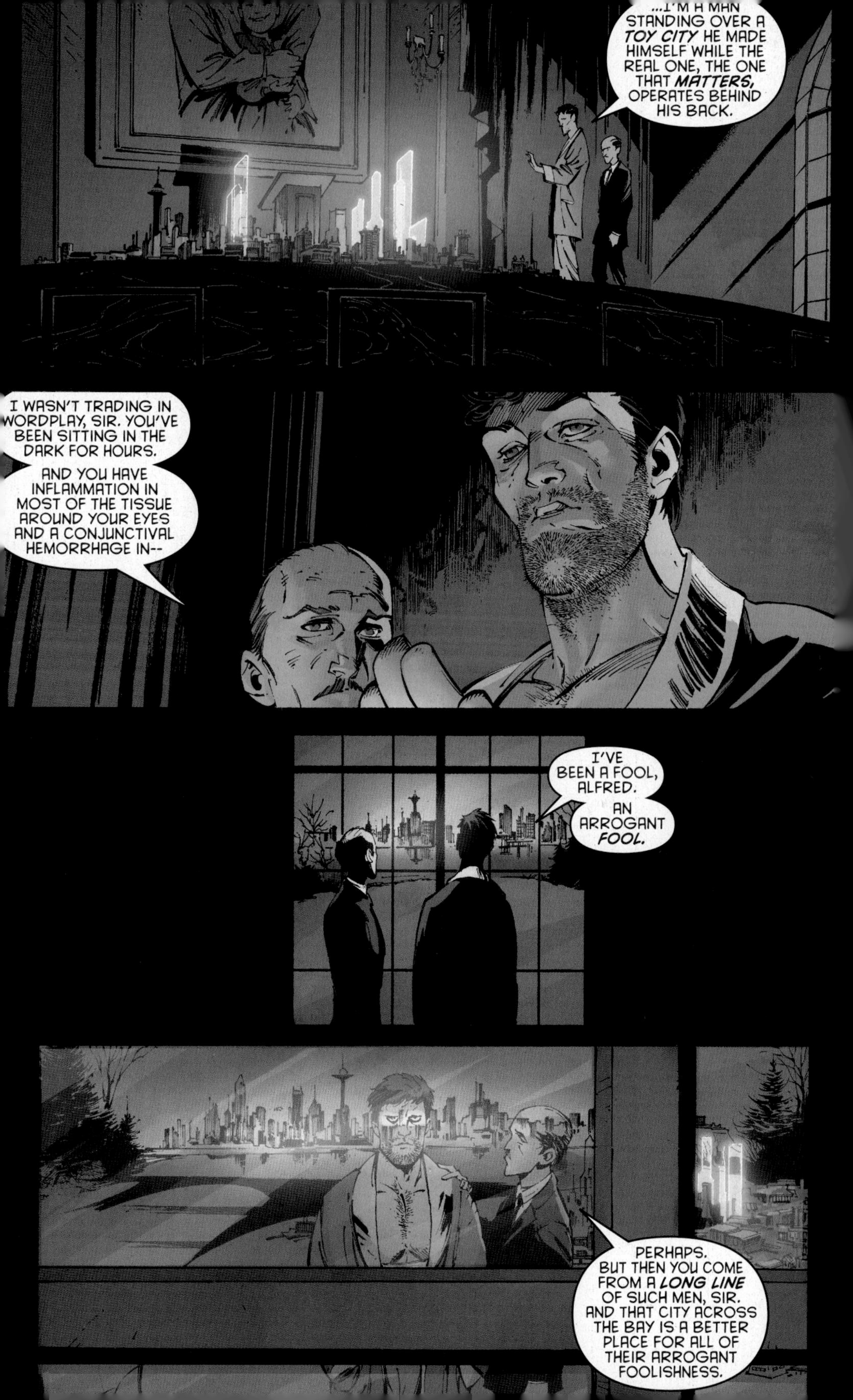

...I'M A MAN STANDING OVER A TOY CITY HE MADE HIMSELF WHILE THE REAL ONE, THE ONE THAT MATTERS, OPERATES BEHIND HIS BACK.
I WASN'T TRADING IN WORDPLAY, SIR. YOU'VE BEEN SITTING IN THE DARK FOR HOURS.
AND YOU HAVE INFLAMMATION IN MOST OF THE TISSUE AROUND YOUR EYES AND A CONJUNCTIVAL HEMORRHAGE IN--
I'VE BEEN A FOOL, ALFRED.
AN ARROGANT FOOL.
PERHAPS. BUT THEN YOU COME FROM A LONG LINE OF SUCH MEN, SIR. AND THAT CITY ACROSS THE BAY IS A BETTER PLACE FOR ALL OF THEIR ARROGANT FOOLISHNESS.

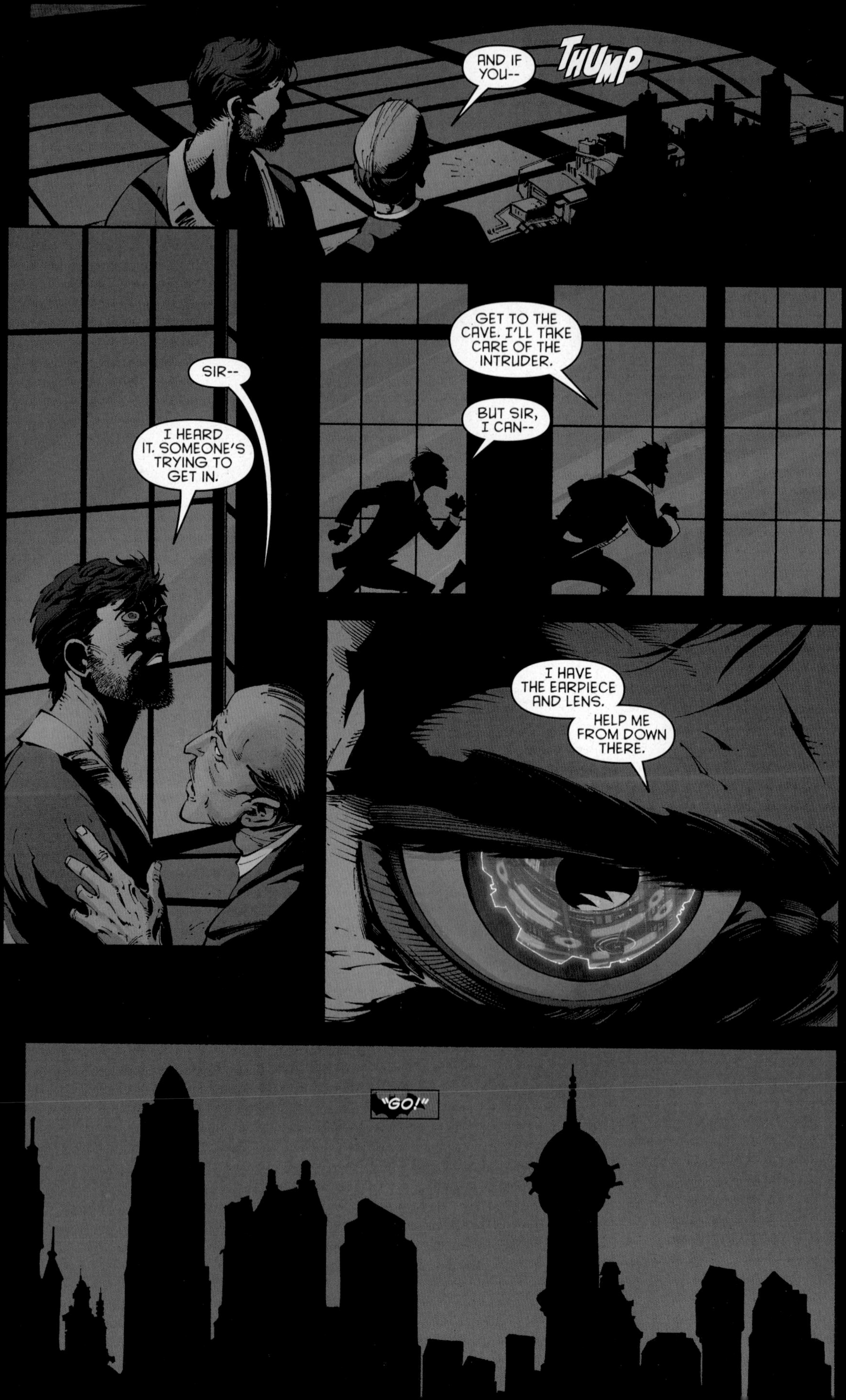
AND IF YOU--
THUMP
SIR--
I HEARD IT. SOMEONE'S TRYING TO GET IN.
GET TO THE CAVE. I'LL TAKE CARE OF THE INTRUDER.
BUT SIR, I CAN--
I HAVE THE EARPIECE AND LENS.
HELP ME FROM DOWN THERE.
"GO!"

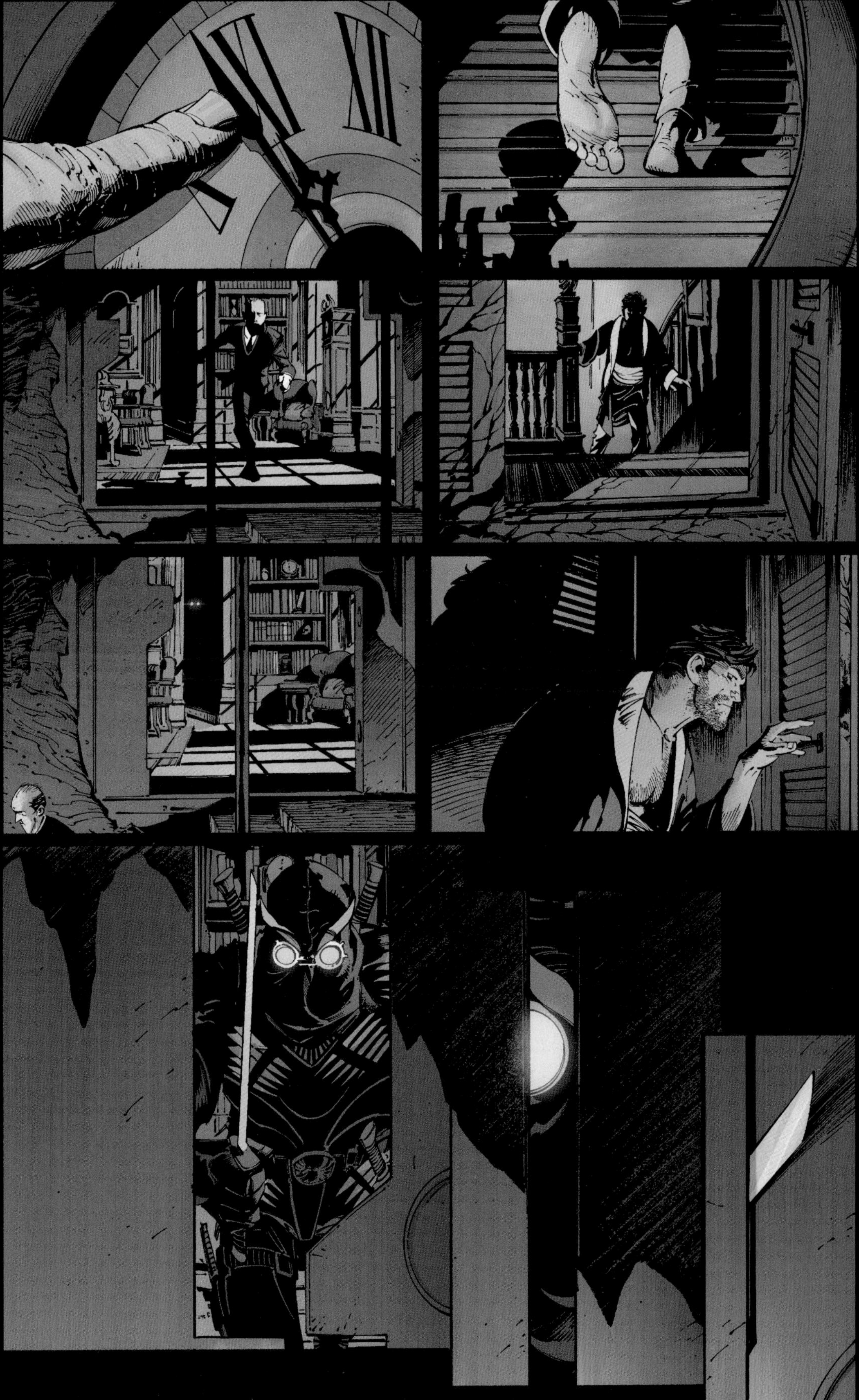

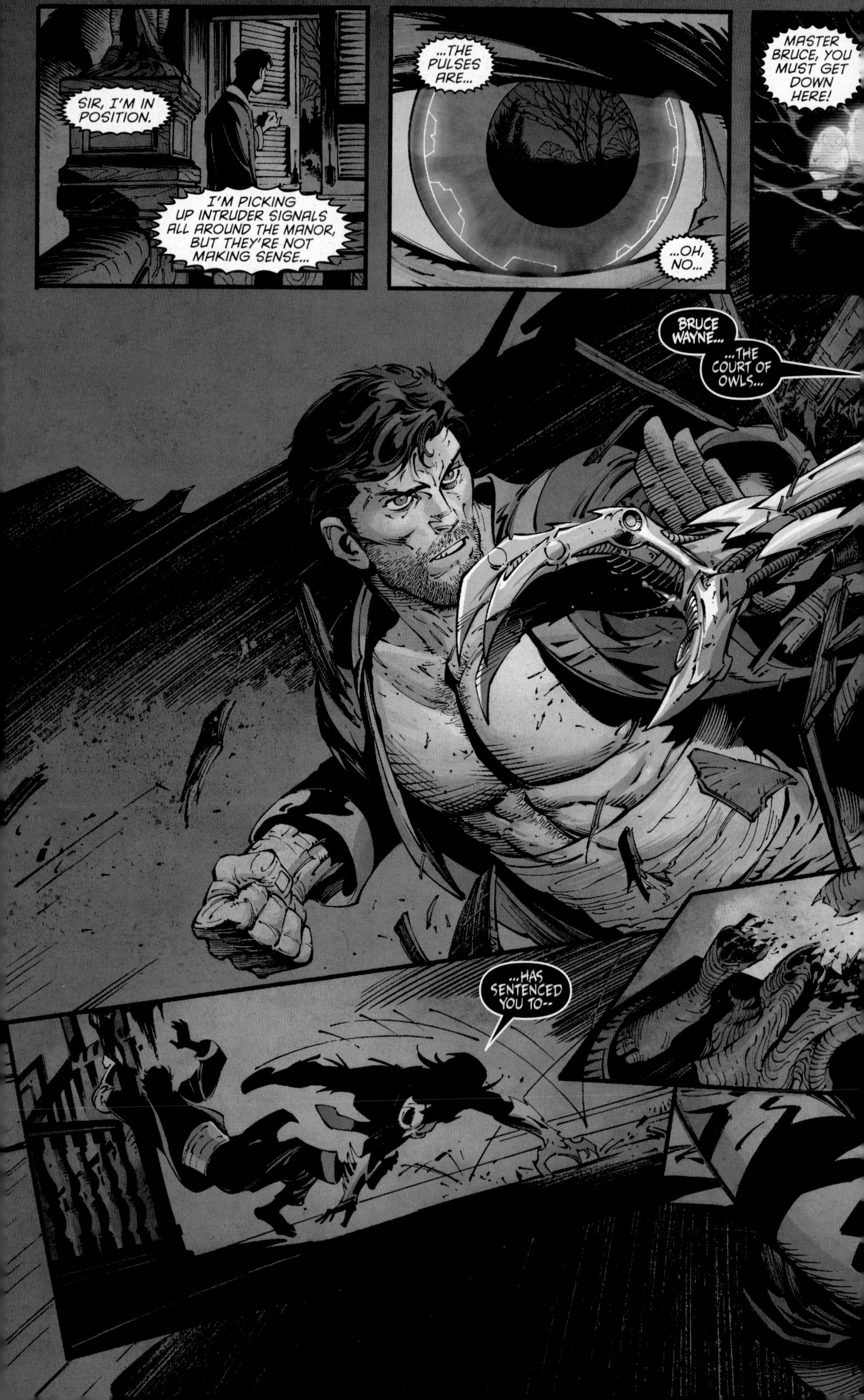
SIR, I'M IN POSITION.
I'M PICKING UP INTRUDER SIGNALS ALL AROUND THE MANOR, BUT THEY'RE NOT MAKING SENSE...
...THE PULSES ARE...
...OH, NO...
MASTER BRUCE, YOU MUST GET DOWN HERE!
BRUCE WAYNE...
...THE COURT OF OWLS...
...HAS SENTENCED YOU TO--

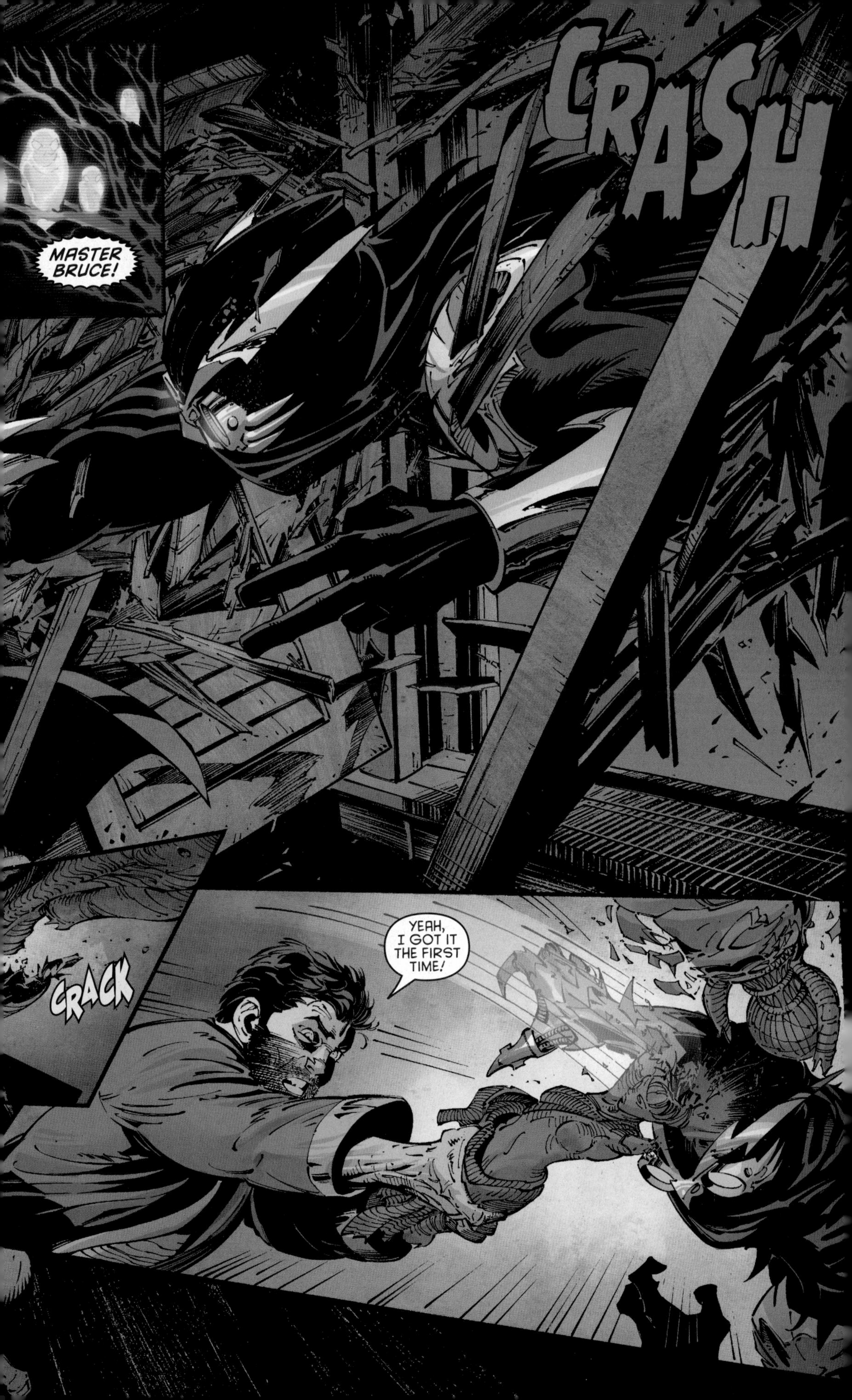
MASTER BRUCE!
CRASH
CRACK
YEAH, I GOT IT THE FIRST TIME!

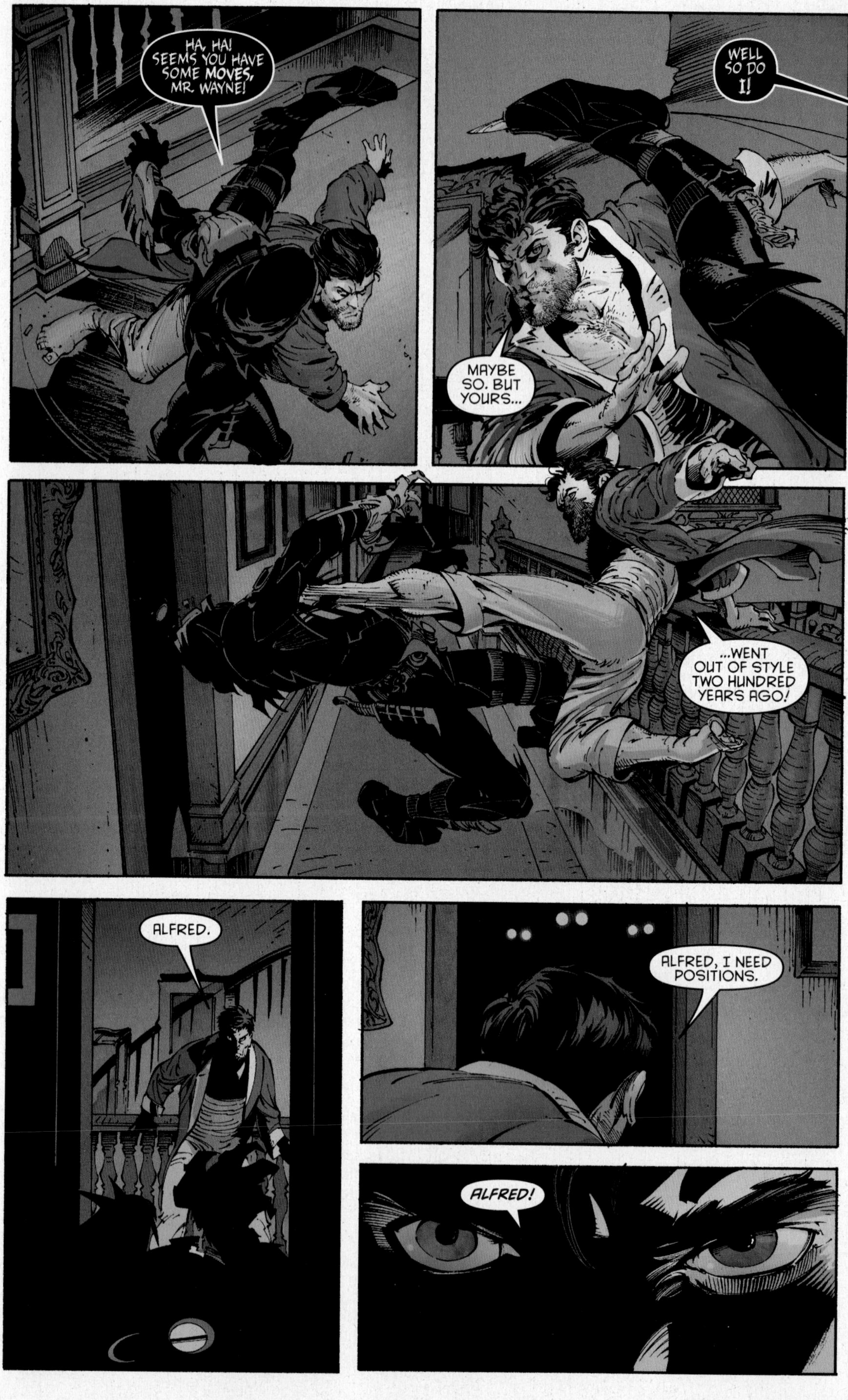

HA, HA! SEEMS YOU HAVE SOME MOVES, MR. WAYNE!
WELL SO DO I!
MAYBE SO. BUT YOURS...
...WENT OUT OF STYLE TWO HUNDRED YEARS AGO!
ALFRED.
ALFRED, I NEED POSITIONS.
ALFRED!

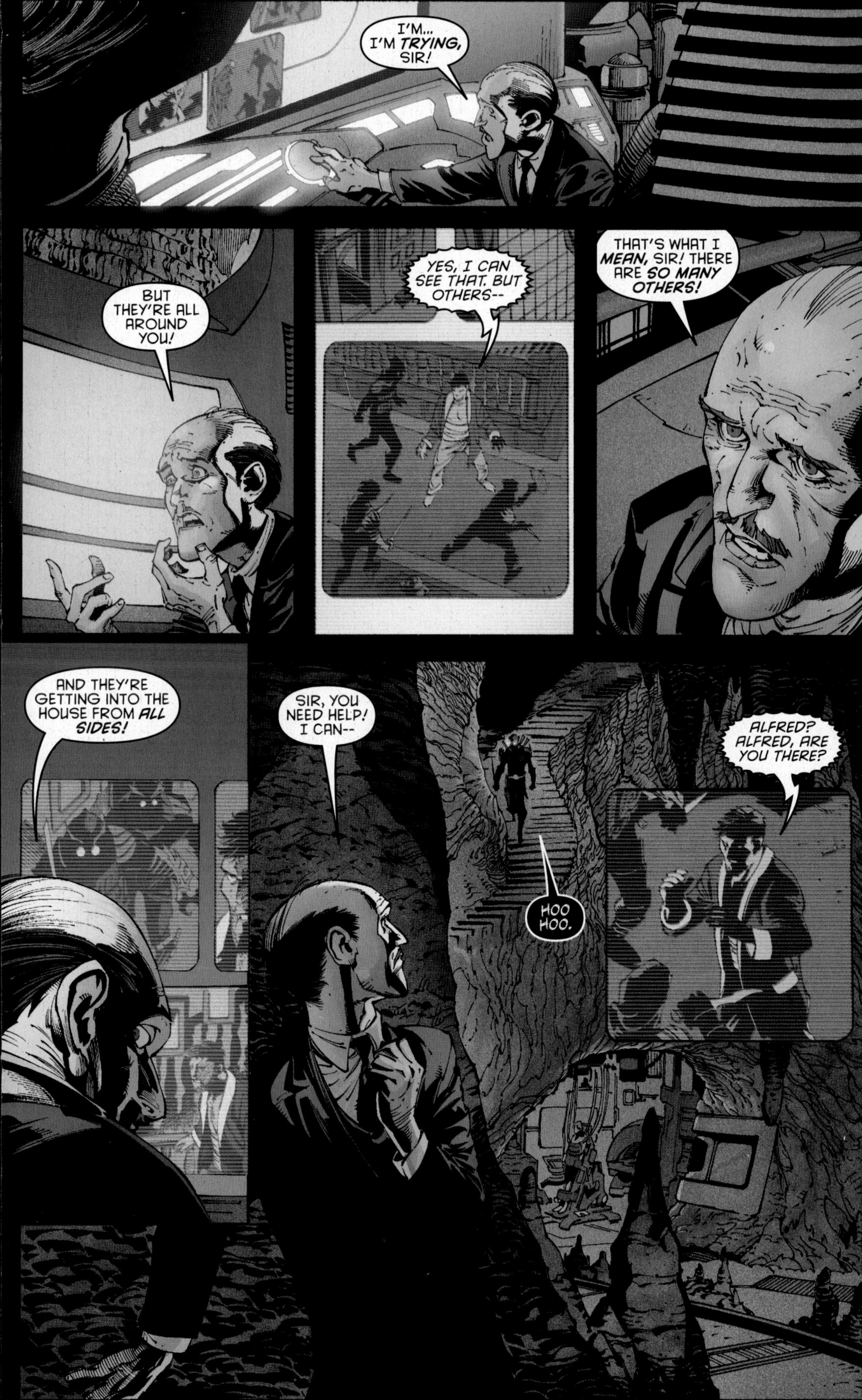
I'M... I'M *TRYING,* SIR!
BUT THEY'RE ALL AROUND YOU!
YES, I CAN SEE THAT. BUT OTHERS--
THAT'S WHAT I *MEAN,* SIR! THERE ARE *SO MANY OTHERS!*
AND THEY'RE GETTING INTO THE HOUSE FROM *ALL SIDES!*
SIR, YOU NEED HELP! I CAN--
ALFRED? ALFRED, ARE YOU THERE?
HOO HOO.

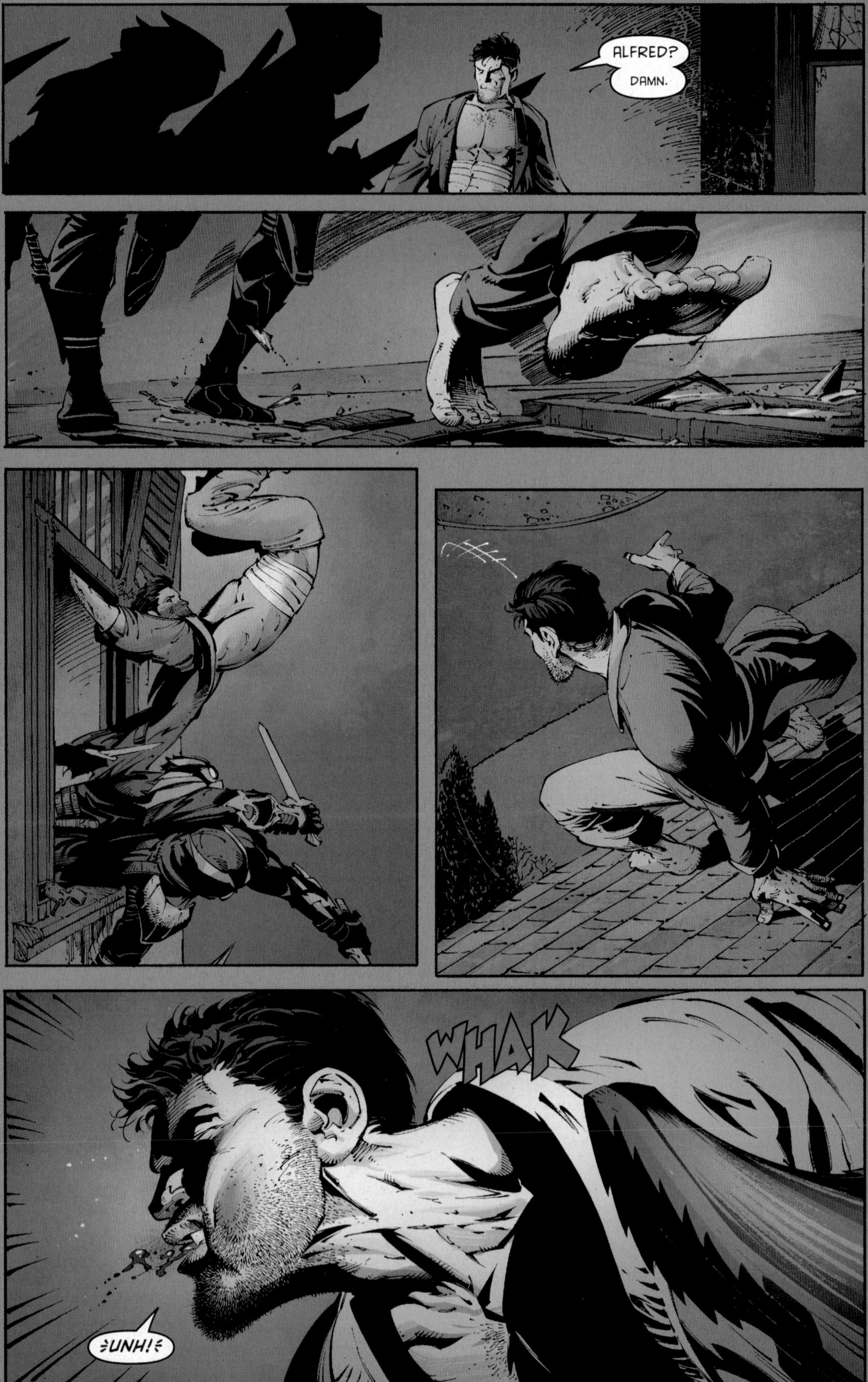
ALFRED?
DAMN.
WHAK
UNH!

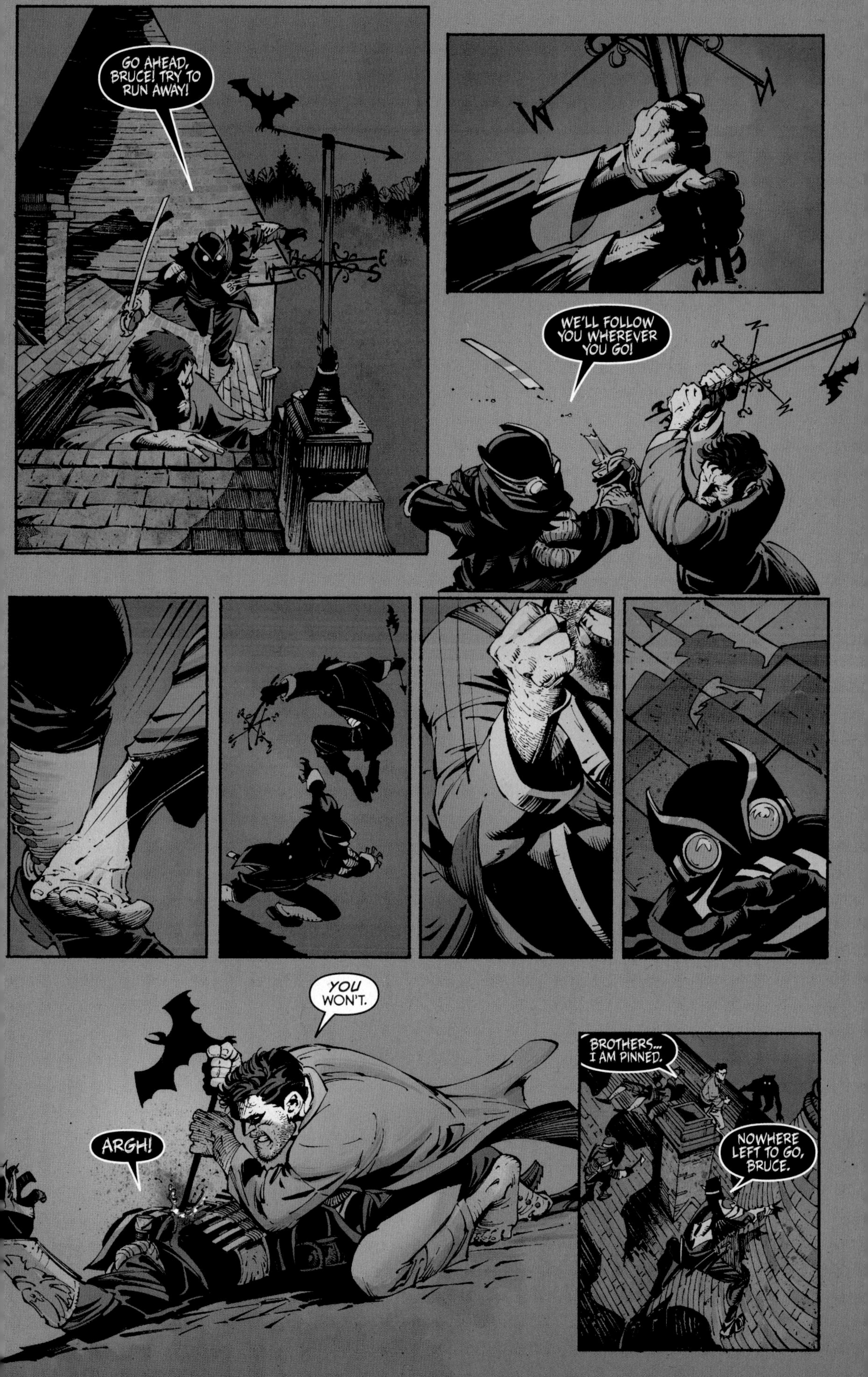
GO AHEAD, BRUCE! TRY TO RUN AWAY!
WE'LL FOLLOW YOU WHEREVER YOU GO!
YOU WON'T.
ARGH!
BROTHERS... I AM PINNED.
NOWHERE LEFT TO GO, BRUCE.

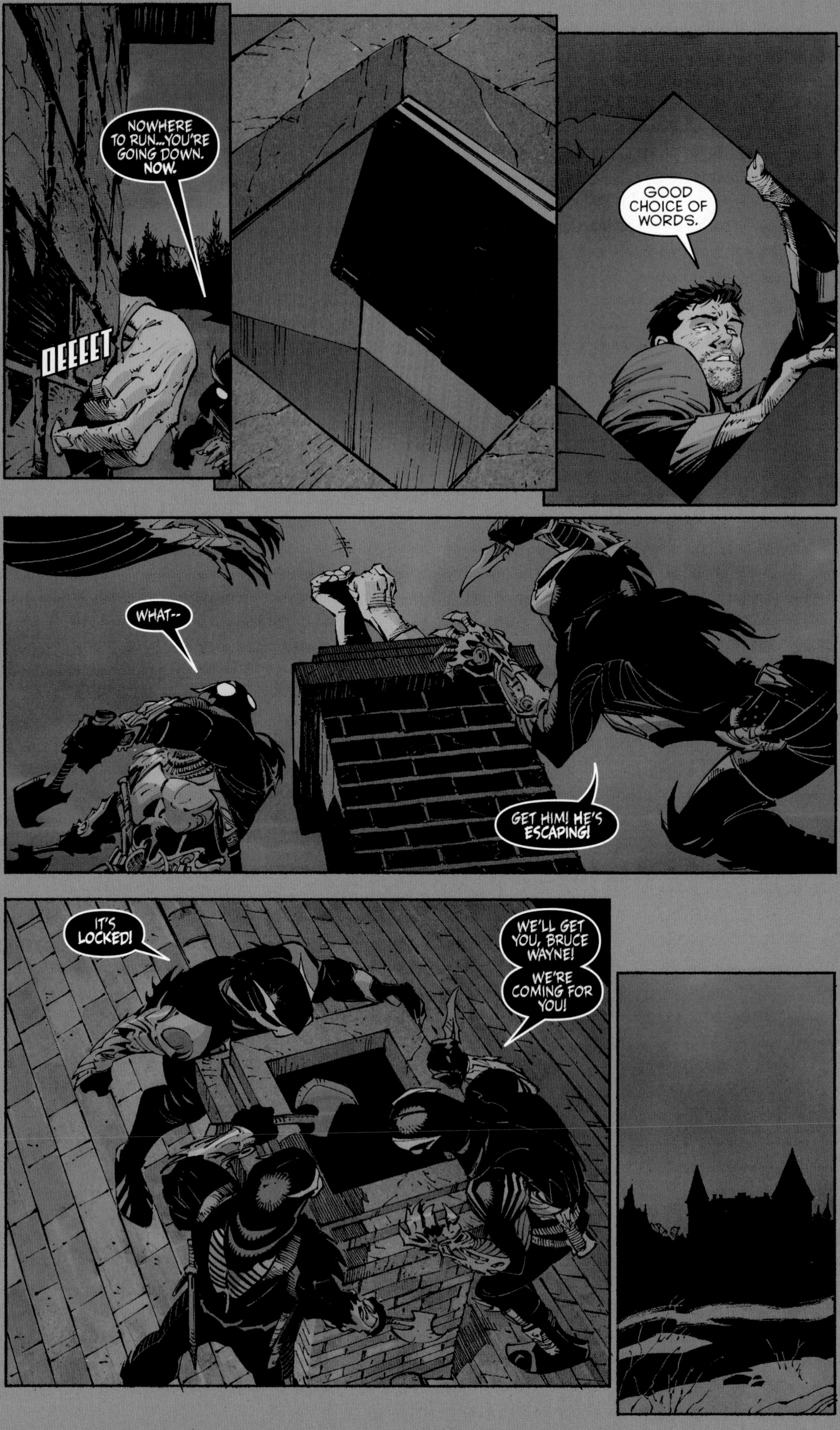
NOWHERE TO RUN...YOU'RE GOING DOWN. NOW.
DEEEET
GOOD CHOICE OF WORDS.
WHAT--
GET HIM! HE'S ESCAPING!
IT'S LOCKED!
WE'LL GET YOU, BRUCE WAYNE!
WE'RE COMING FOR YOU!

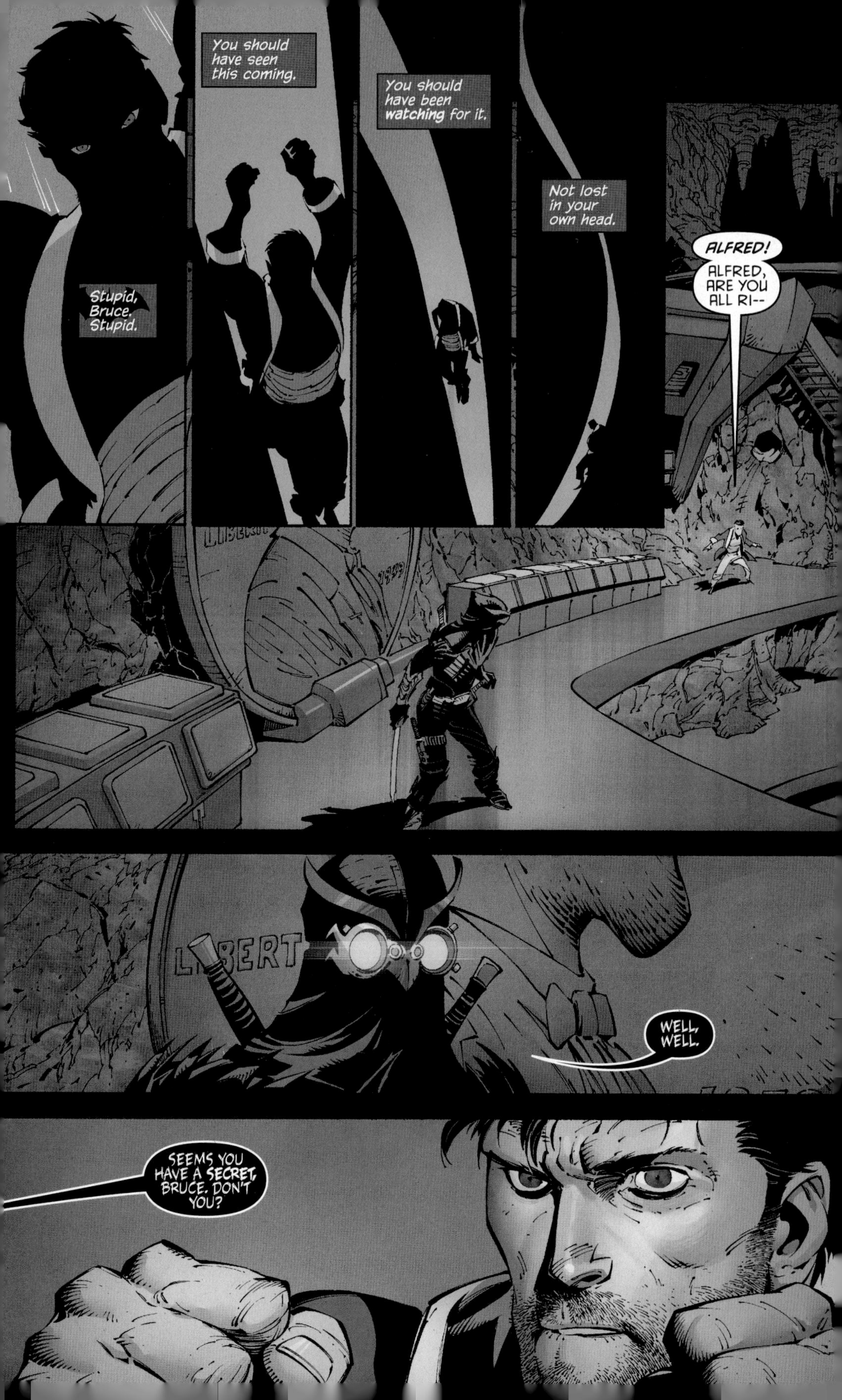
Stupid, Bruce. Stupid.
You should have seen this coming.
You should have been watching for it.
Not lost in your own head.
ALFRED!
ALFRED, ARE YOU ALL RI--
WELL, WELL.
SEEMS YOU HAVE A SECRET, BRUCE. DON'T YOU?

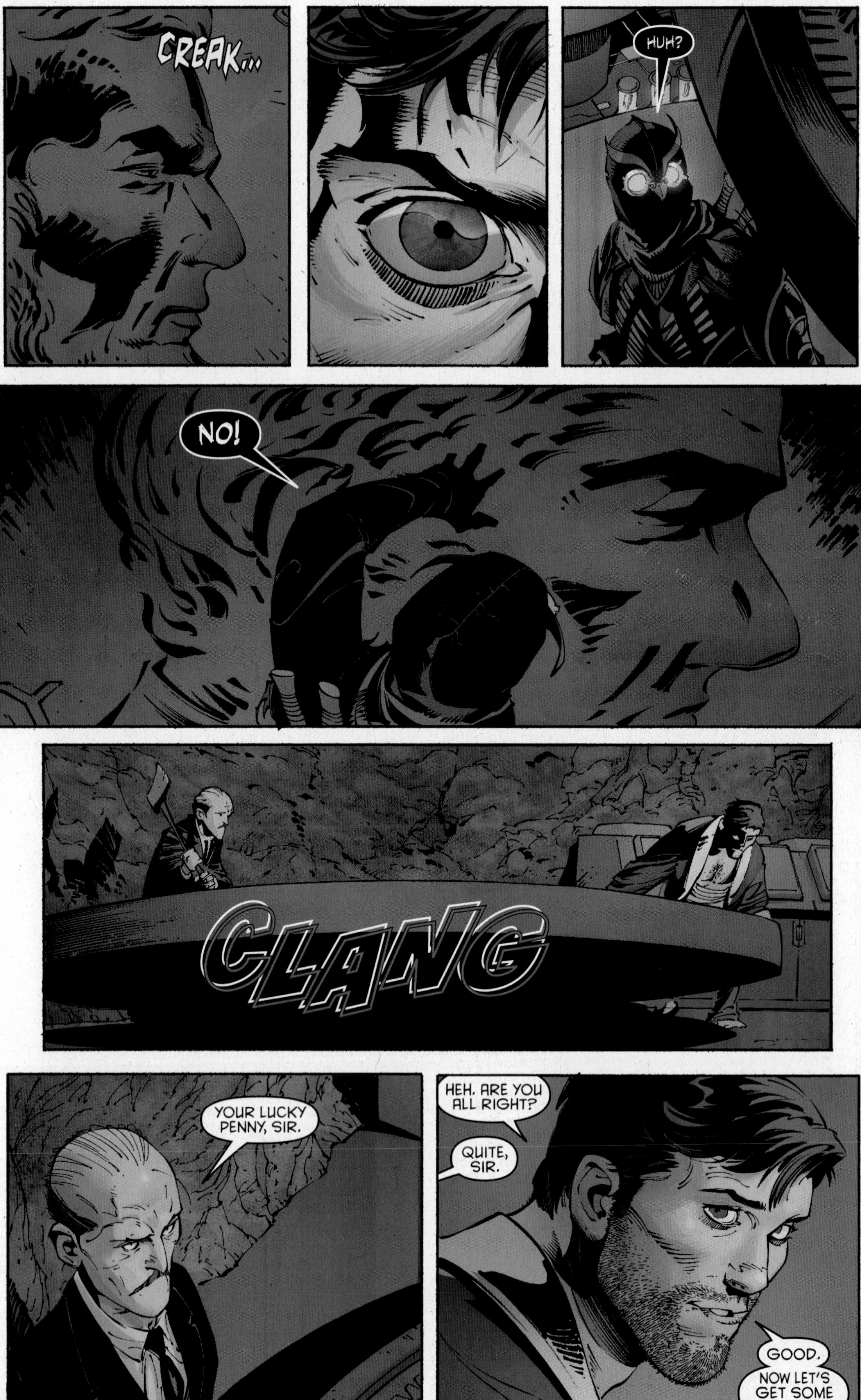

CREAK...
HUH?
NO!
CLANG
YOUR LUCKY PENNY, SIR.
HEH. ARE YOU ALL RIGHT?
QUITE, SIR.
GOOD. NOW LET'S GET SOME ANSWERS.

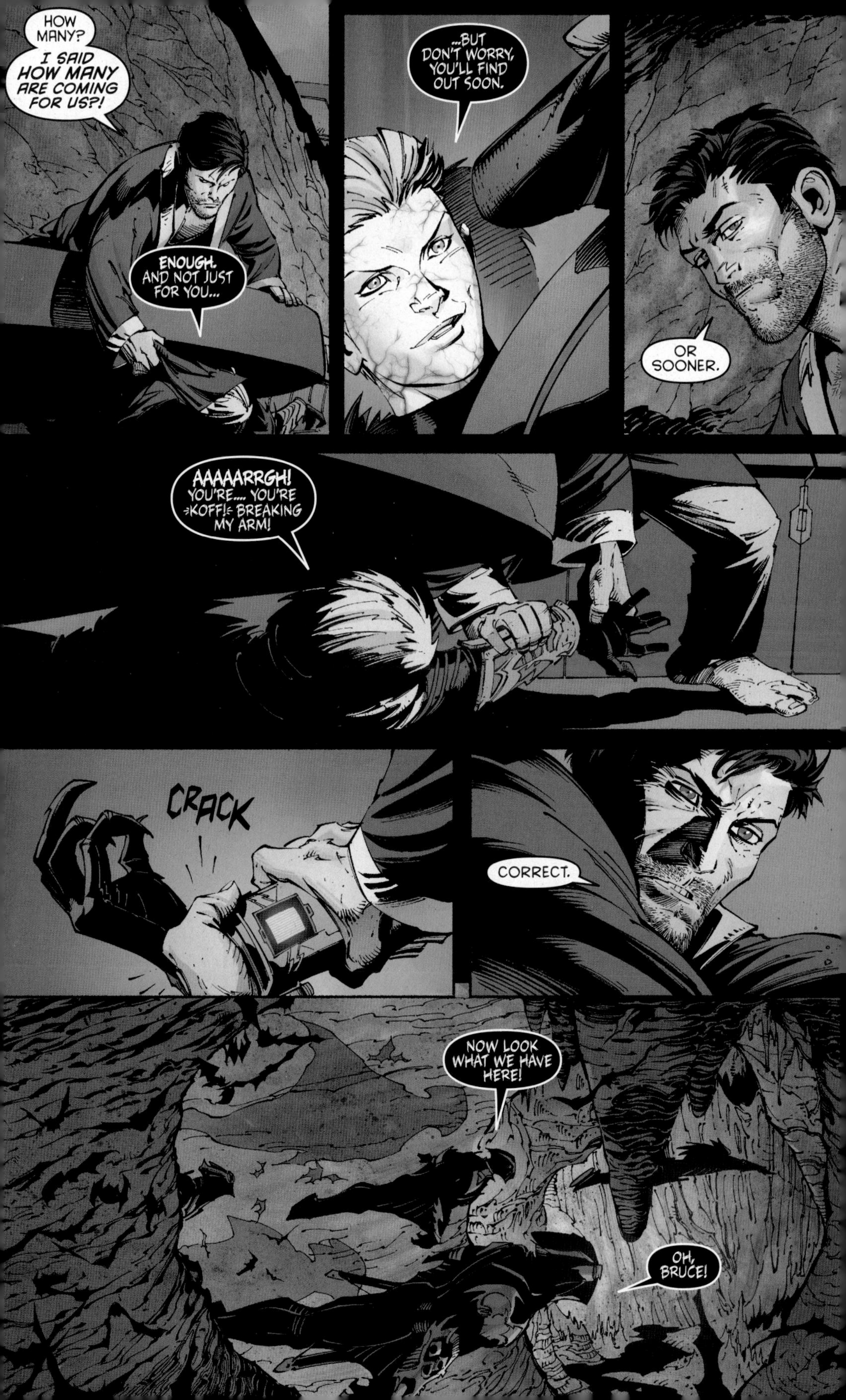
HOW MANY? I SAID HOW MANY ARE COMING FOR US?!
ENOUGH. AND NOT JUST FOR YOU...
...BUT DON'T WORRY, YOU'LL FIND OUT SOON.
OR SOONER.
AAAAARRGH! YOU'RE.... YOU'RE *KOFF!* BREAKING MY ARM!
CRACK
CORRECT.
NOW LOOK WHAT WE HAVE HERE!
OH, BRUCE!

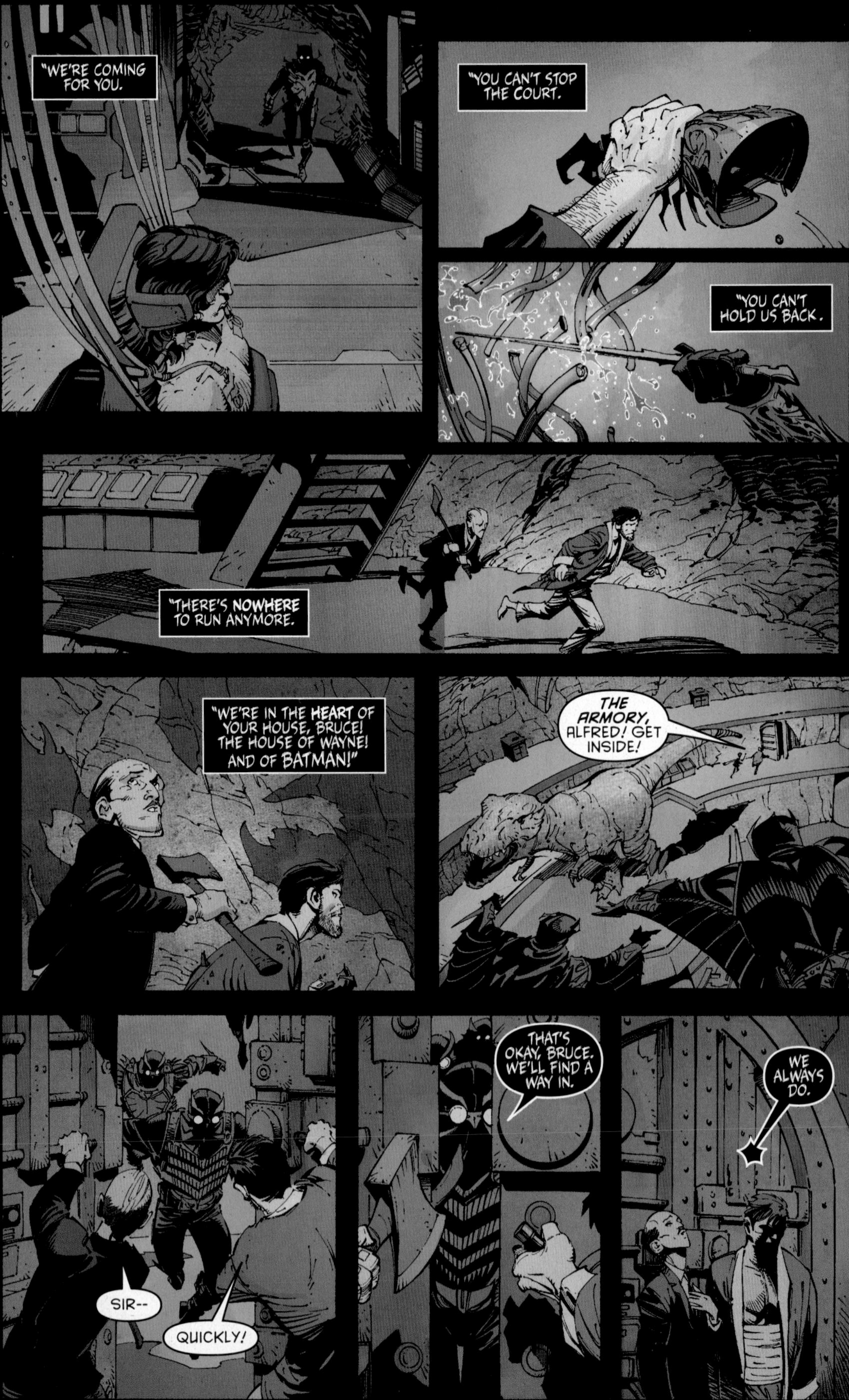
"WE'RE COMING FOR YOU.
"YOU CAN'T STOP THE COURT.
"YOU CAN'T HOLD US BACK.
"THERE'S NOWHERE TO RUN ANYMORE.
"WE'RE IN THE HEART OF YOUR HOUSE, BRUCE! THE HOUSE OF WAYNE! AND OF BATMAN!"
THE ARMORY, ALFRED! GET INSIDE!
SIR--
QUICKLY!
THAT'S OKAY, BRUCE. WE'LL FIND A WAY IN.
WE ALWAYS DO.

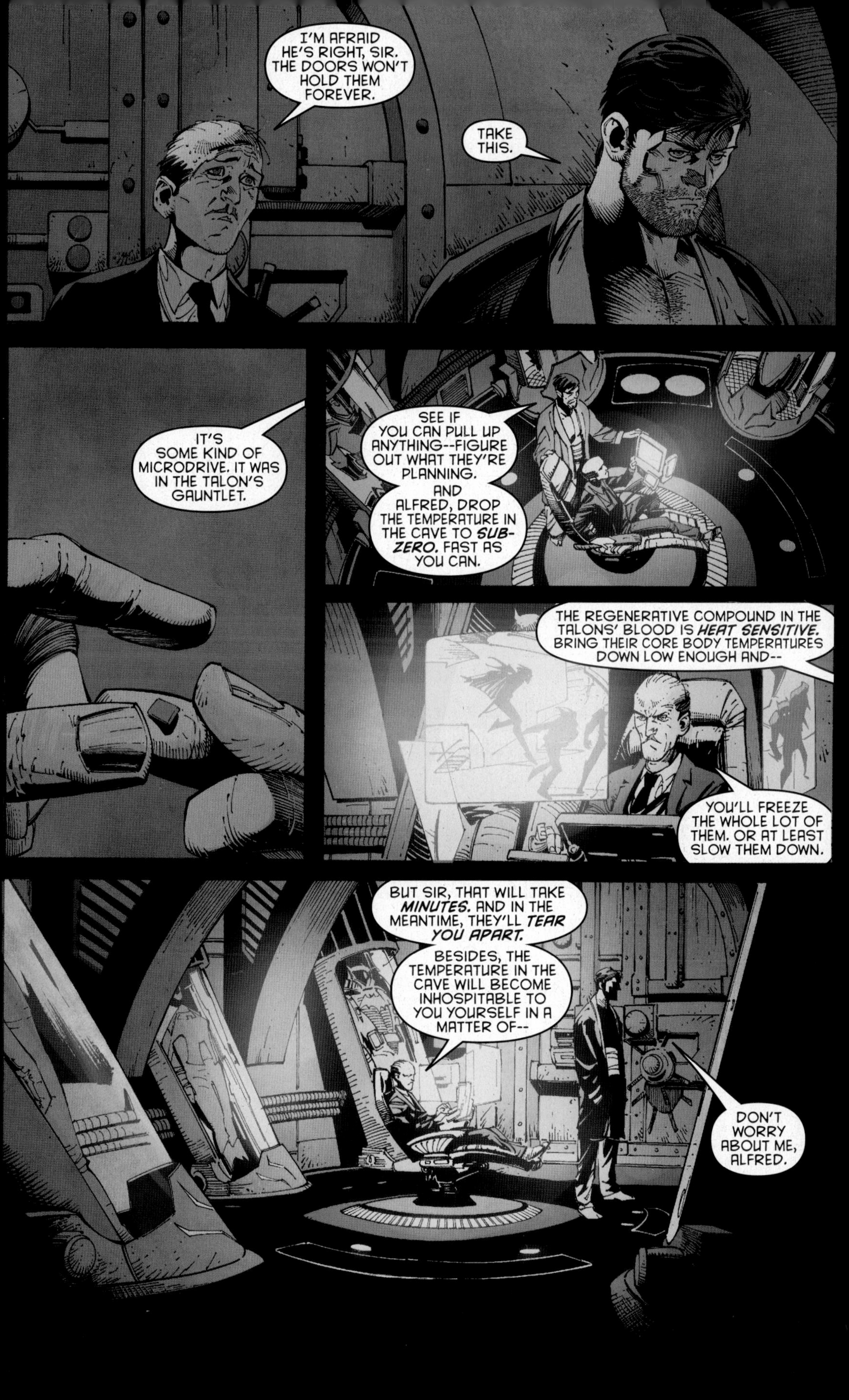
I'M AFRAID HE'S RIGHT, SIR. THE DOORS WON'T HOLD THEM FOREVER.
TAKE THIS.
IT'S SOME KIND OF MICRODRIVE. IT WAS IN THE TALON'S GAUNTLET.
SEE IF YOU CAN PULL UP ANYTHING--FIGURE OUT WHAT THEY'RE PLANNING.
AND ALFRED, DROP THE TEMPERATURE IN THE CAVE TO SUB-ZERO. FAST AS YOU CAN.
THE REGENERATIVE COMPOUND IN THE TALONS' BLOOD IS HEAT SENSITIVE. BRING THEIR CORE BODY TEMPERATURES DOWN LOW ENOUGH AND--
YOU'LL FREEZE THE WHOLE LOT OF THEM. OR AT LEAST SLOW THEM DOWN.
BUT SIR, THAT WILL TAKE MINUTES. AND IN THE MEANTIME, THEY'LL TEAR YOU APART.
BESIDES, THE TEMPERATURE IN THE CAVE WILL BECOME INHOSPITABLE TO YOU YOURSELF IN A MATTER OF--
DON'T WORRY ABOUT ME, ALFRED.

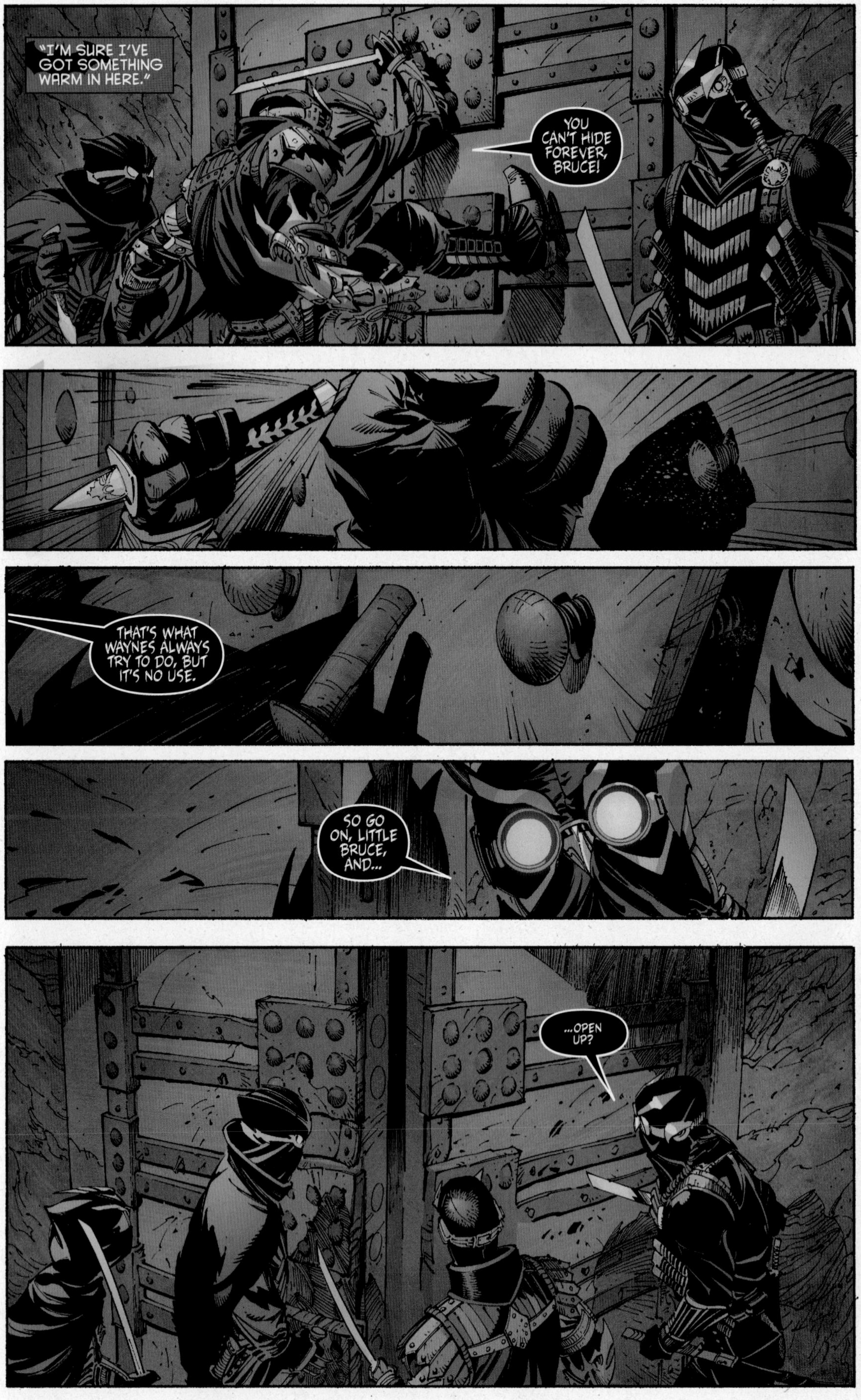
"I'M SURE I'VE GOT SOMETHING WARM IN HERE."
YOU CAN'T HIDE FOREVER, BRUCE!
THAT'S WHAT WAYNES ALWAYS TRY TO DO, BUT IT'S NO USE.
SO GO ON, LITTLE BRUCE, AND...
...OPEN UP?

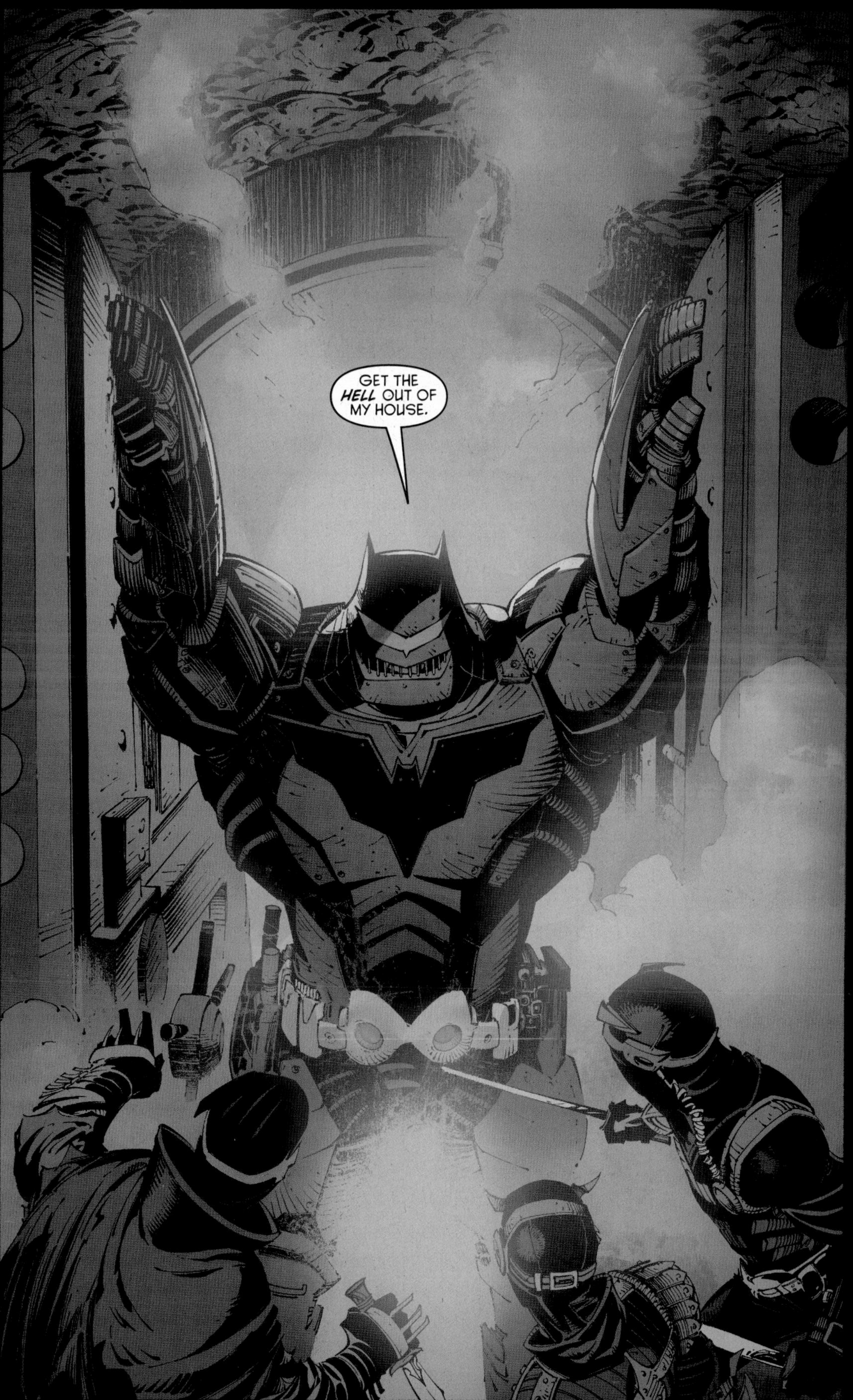
GET THE HELL OUT OF MY HOUSE.

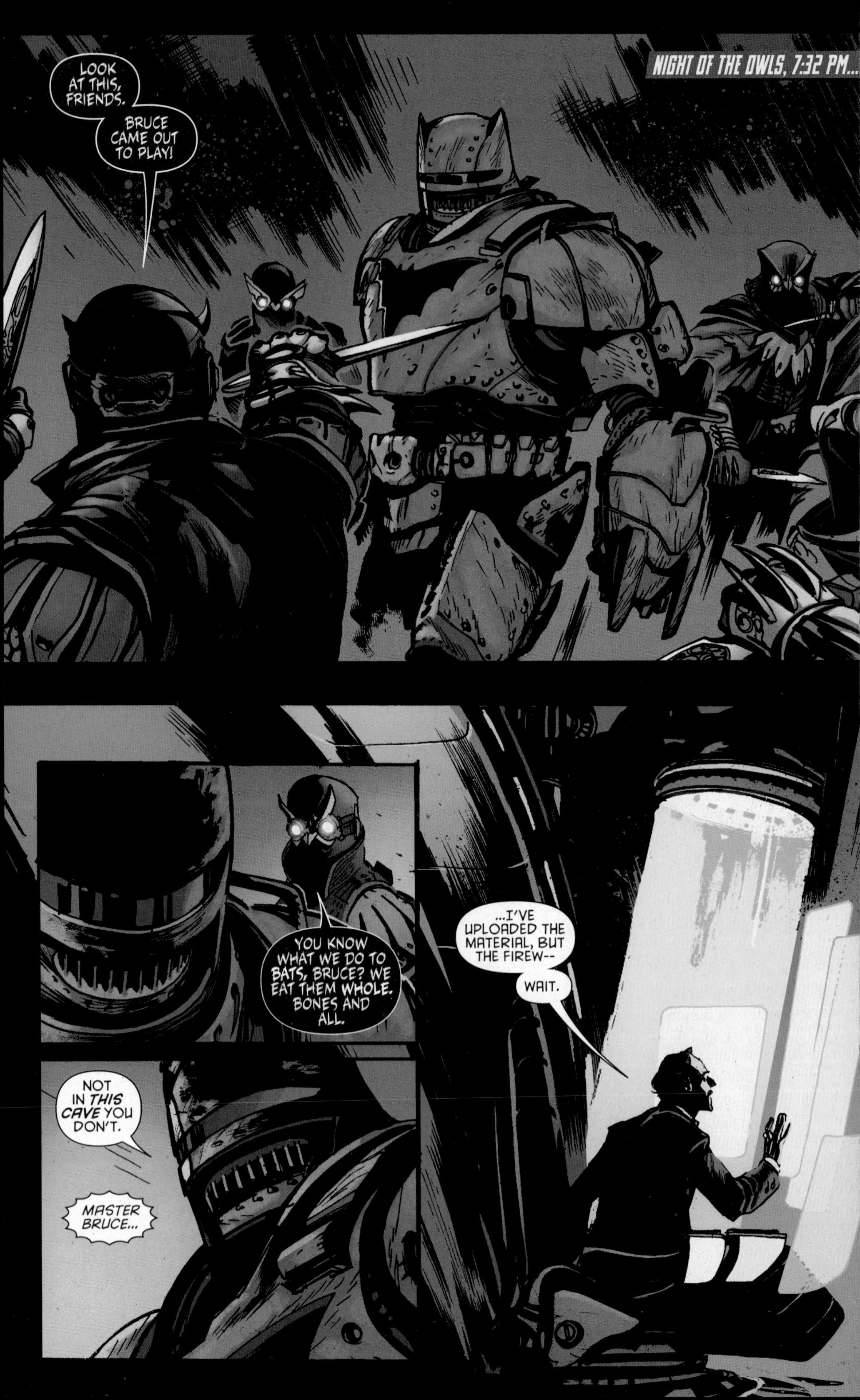
NIGHT OF THE OWLS, 7:32 PM...
LOOK AT THIS, FRIENDS.
BRUCE CAME OUT TO PLAY!
YOU KNOW WHAT WE DO TO BATS, BRUCE? WE EAT THEM WHOLE. BONES AND ALL.
...I'VE UPLOADED THE MATERIAL, BUT THE FIREW--
WAIT.
NOT IN THIS CAVE YOU DON'T.
MASTER BRUCE...

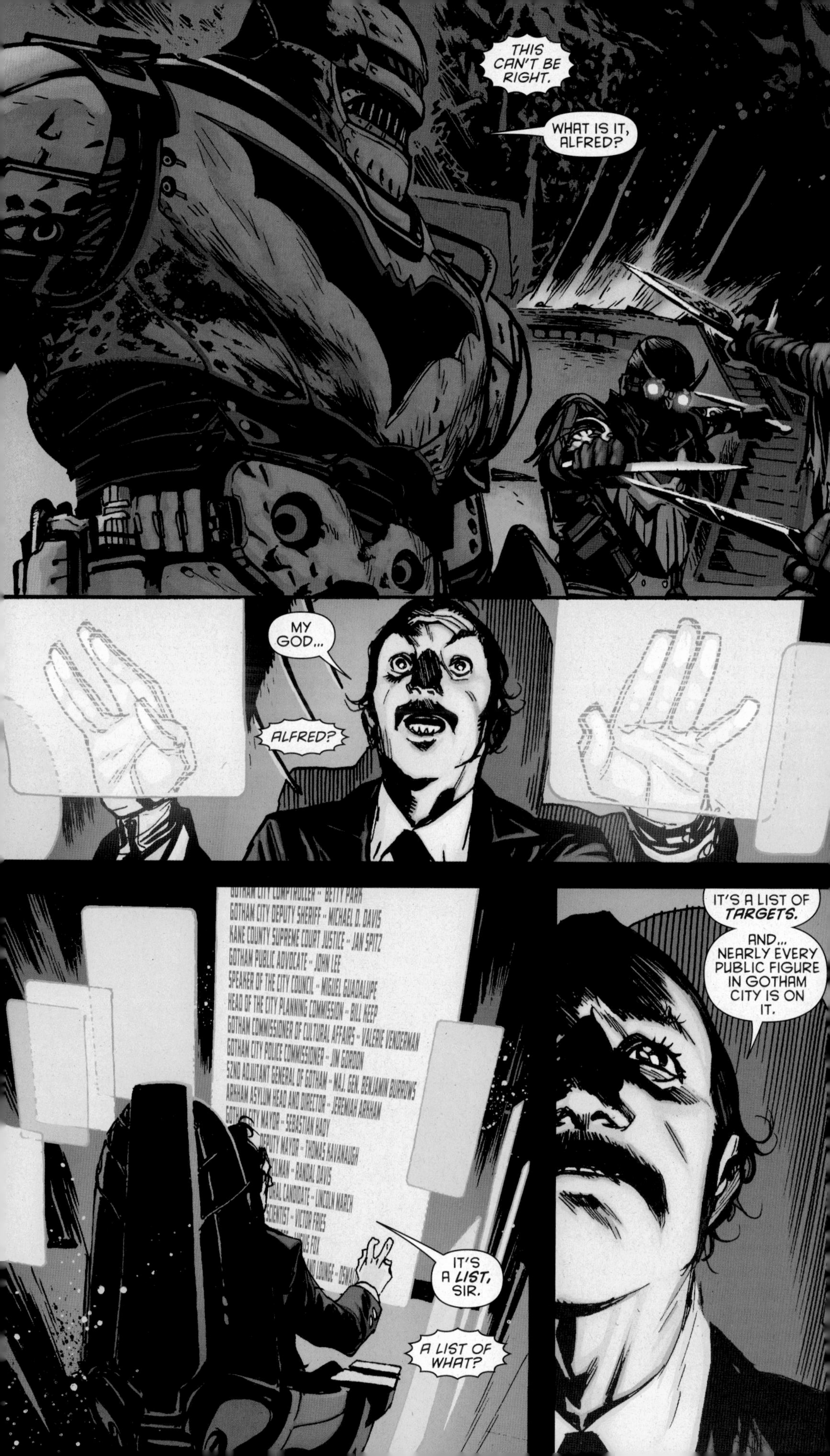
THIS CAN'T BE RIGHT.
WHAT IS IT, ALFRED?
MY GOD...
ALFRED?
GOTHAM CITY COMPTROLLER -- BETTY PARK
GOTHAM CITY DEPUTY SHERIFF -- MICHAEL D. DAVIS
KANE COUNTY SUPREME COURT JUSTICE -- JAN SPITZ
GOTHAM PUBLIC ADVOCATE -- JOHN LEE
SPEAKER OF THE CITY COUNCIL -- MIGUEL GUADALUPE
HEAD OF THE CITY PLANNING COMMISSION -- BILL KEEP
GOTHAM COMMISSIONER OF CULTURAL AFFAIRS -- VALERIE VENDERMAN
GOTHAM CITY POLICE COMMISSIONER -- JIM GORDON
52ND ADJUTANT GENERAL OF GOTHAM -- MAJ. GEN. BENJAMIN BURROWS
ARKHAM ASYLUM HEAD AND DIRECTOR -- JEREMIAH ARKHAM
GOTHAM CITY MAYOR -- SEBASTIAN HADY
DEPUTY MAYOR -- THOMAS KAVANAUGH
-- RANDAL DAVIS
-- LINCOLN MARCH
-- VICTOR FRIES
IT'S A LIST, SIR.
A LIST OF WHAT?
IT'S A LIST OF TARGETS.
AND... NEARLY EVERY PUBLIC FIGURE IN GOTHAM CITY IS ON IT.

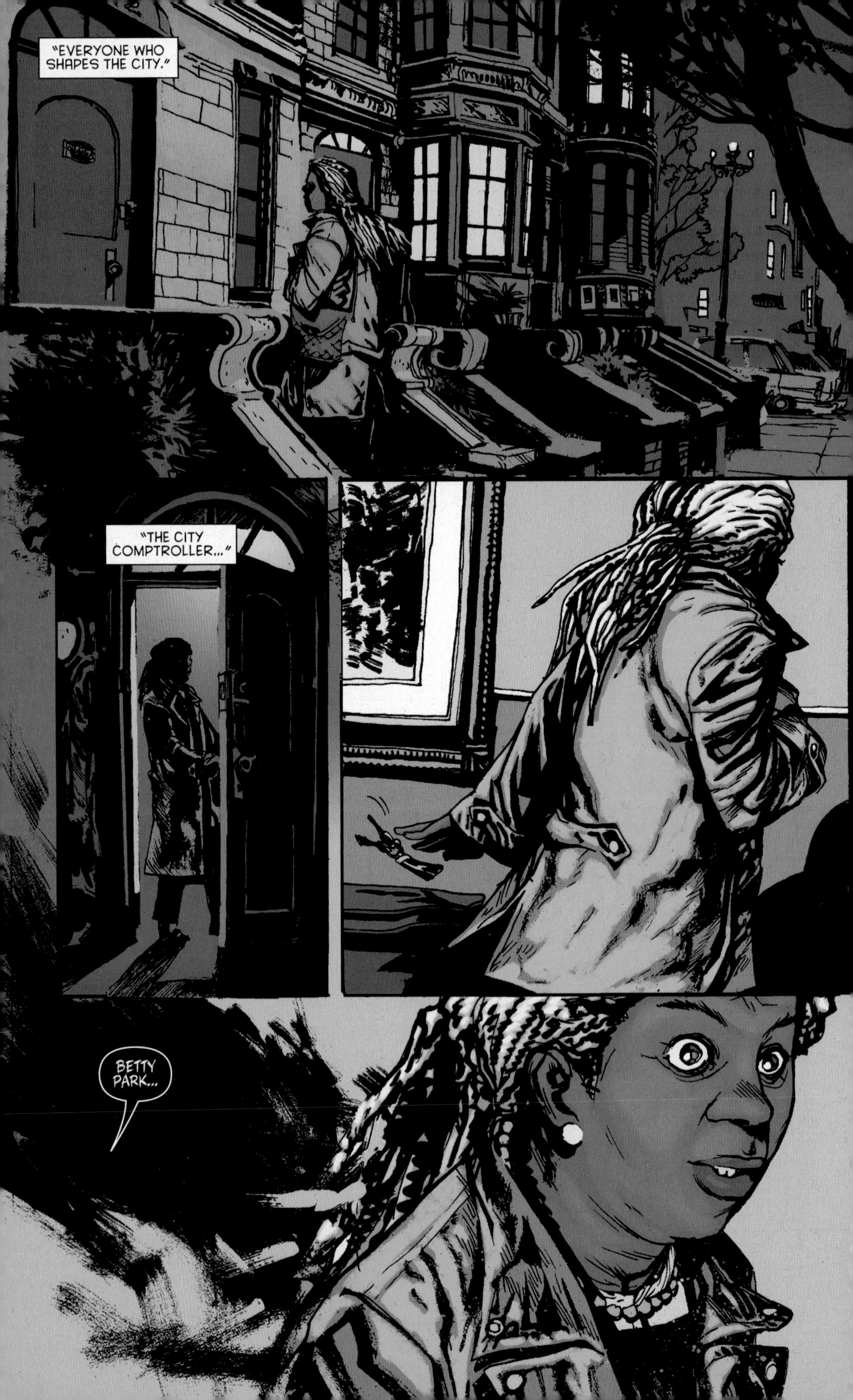
"EVERYONE WHO SHAPES THE CITY."
"THE CITY COMPTROLLER..."
BETTY PARK...

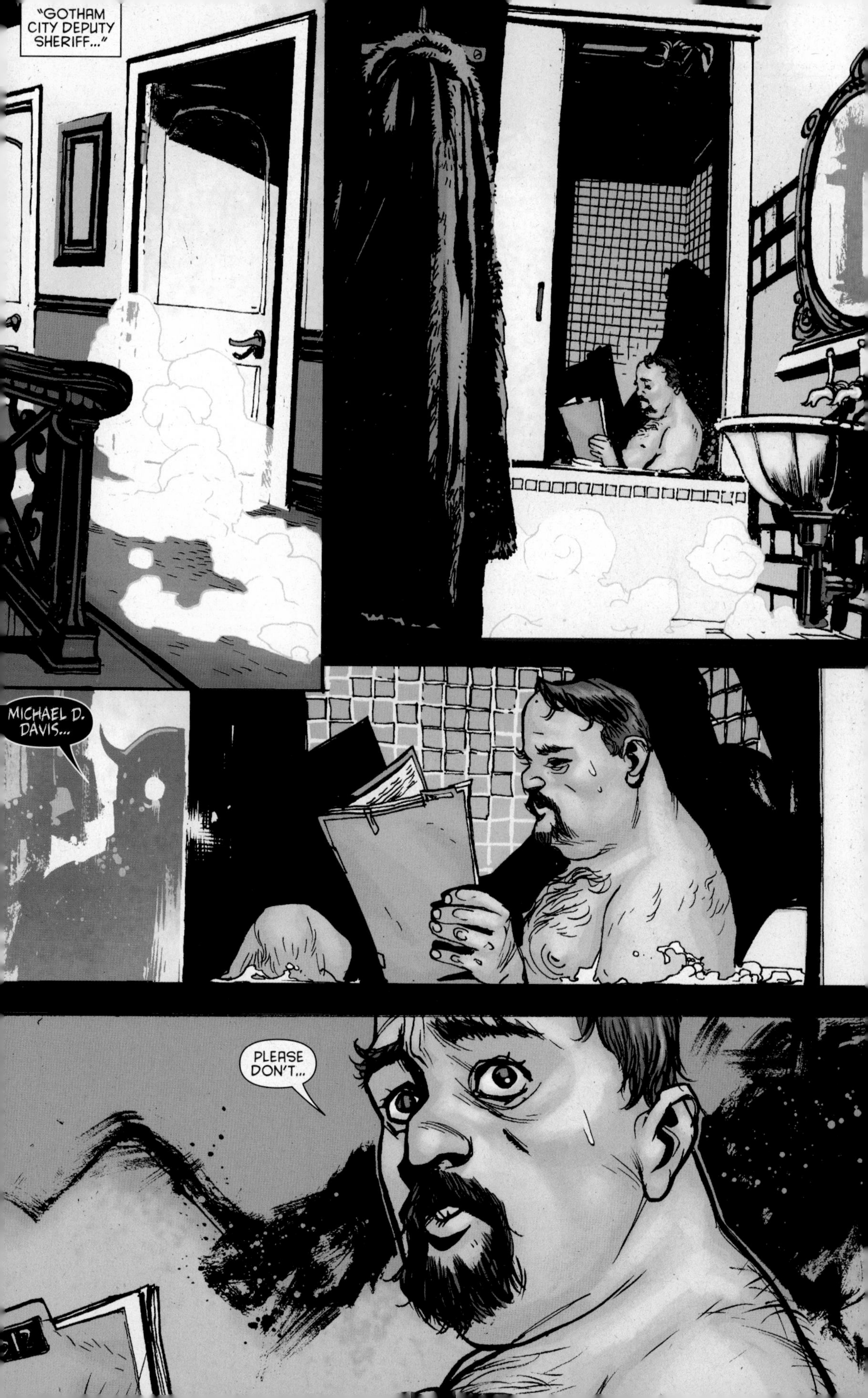
"GOTHAM CITY DEPUTY SHERIFF..."
MICHAEL D. DAVIS...
PLEASE DON'T...

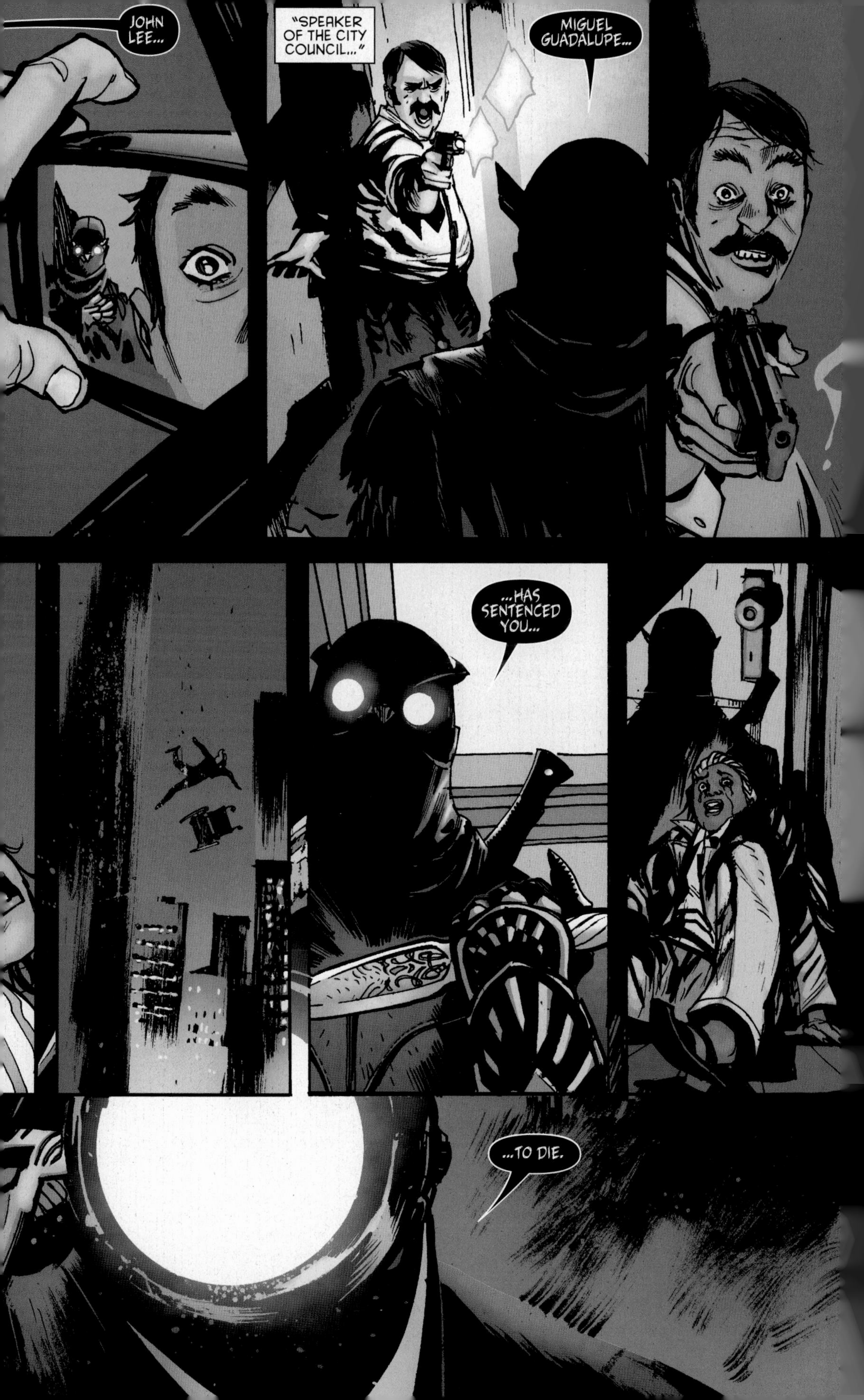
JOHN LEE...
"SPEAKER OF THE CITY COUNCIL..."
MIGUEL GUADALUPE...
...HAS SENTENCED YOU...
...TO DIE.

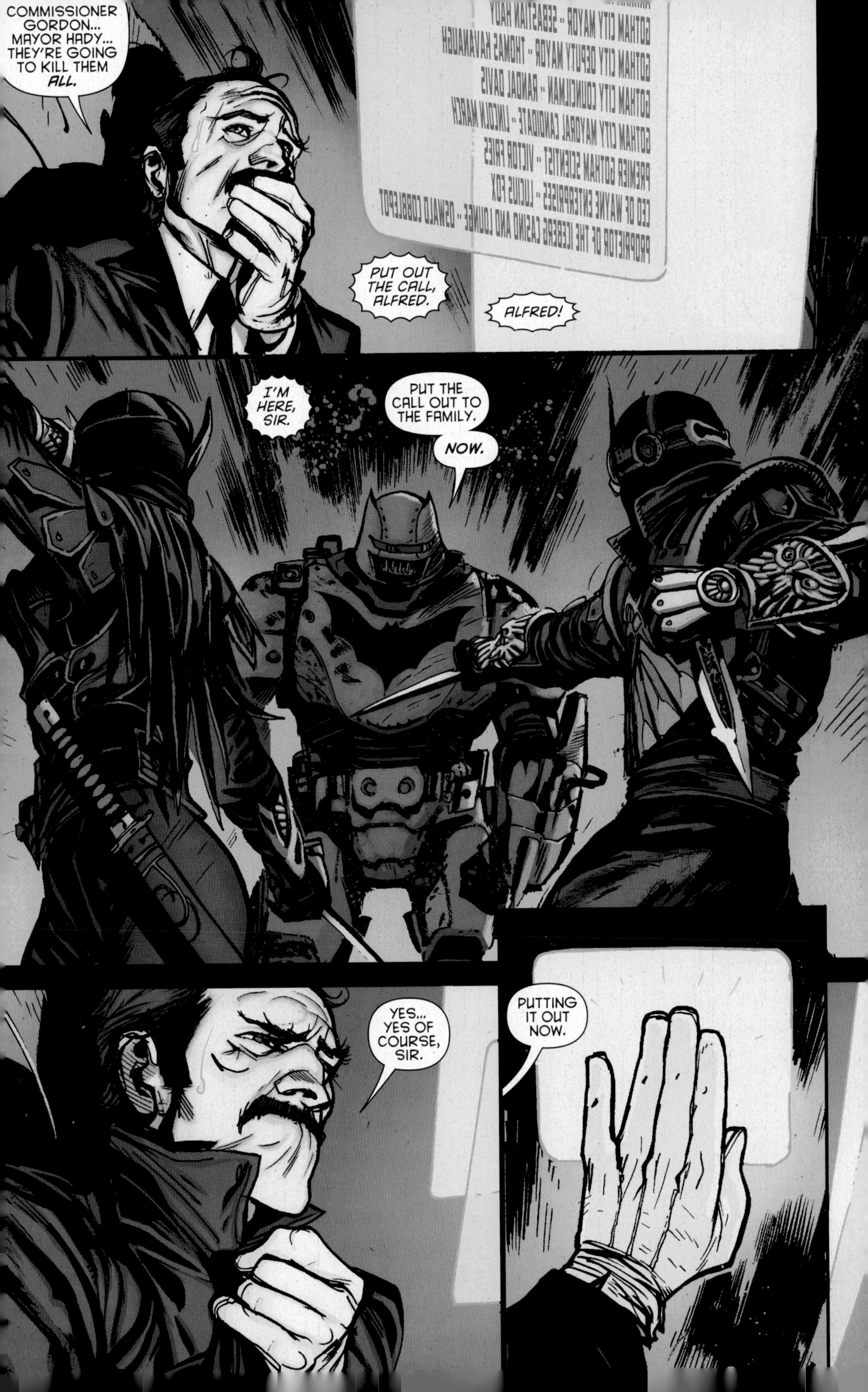
COMMISSIONER GORDON... MAYOR HADY... THEY'RE GOING TO KILL THEM ALL.
GOTHAM CITY MAYOR -- SEBASTIAN HADY
GOTHAM CITY DEPUTY MAYOR -- THOMAS KAVANAUGH
GOTHAM CITY COUNCILMAN -- RANDAL DAVIS
GOTHAM CITY MAYORAL CANDIDATE -- LINCOLN MARCH
PREMIER GOTHAM SCIENTIST -- VICTOR FRIES
CEO OF WAYNE ENTERPRISES -- LUCIUS FOX
PROPRIETOR OF THE ICEBERG CASINO AND LOUNGE -- OSWALD COBBLEPOT
PUT OUT THE CALL, ALFRED.
ALFRED!
I'M HERE, SIR.
PUT THE CALL OUT TO THE FAMILY.
NOW.
YES... YES OF COURSE, SIR.
PUTTING IT OUT NOW.

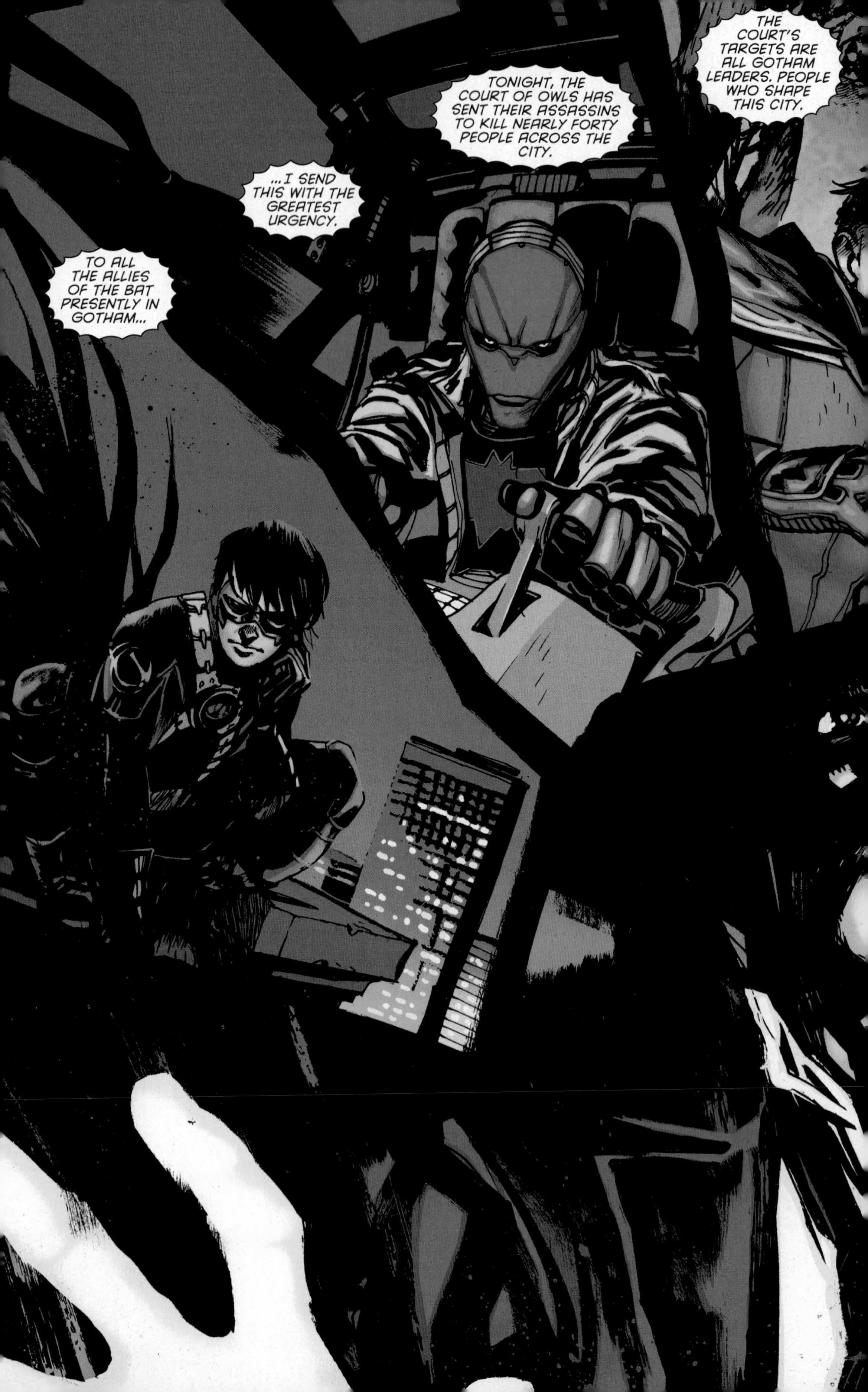

TO ALL THE ALLIES OF THE BAT PRESENTLY IN GOTHAM...
...I SEND THIS WITH THE GREATEST URGENCY.
TONIGHT, THE COURT OF OWLS HAS SENT THEIR ASSASSINS TO KILL NEARLY FORTY PEOPLE ACROSS THE CITY.
THE COURT'S TARGETS ARE ALL GOTHAM LEADERS. PEOPLE WHO SHAPE THIS CITY.

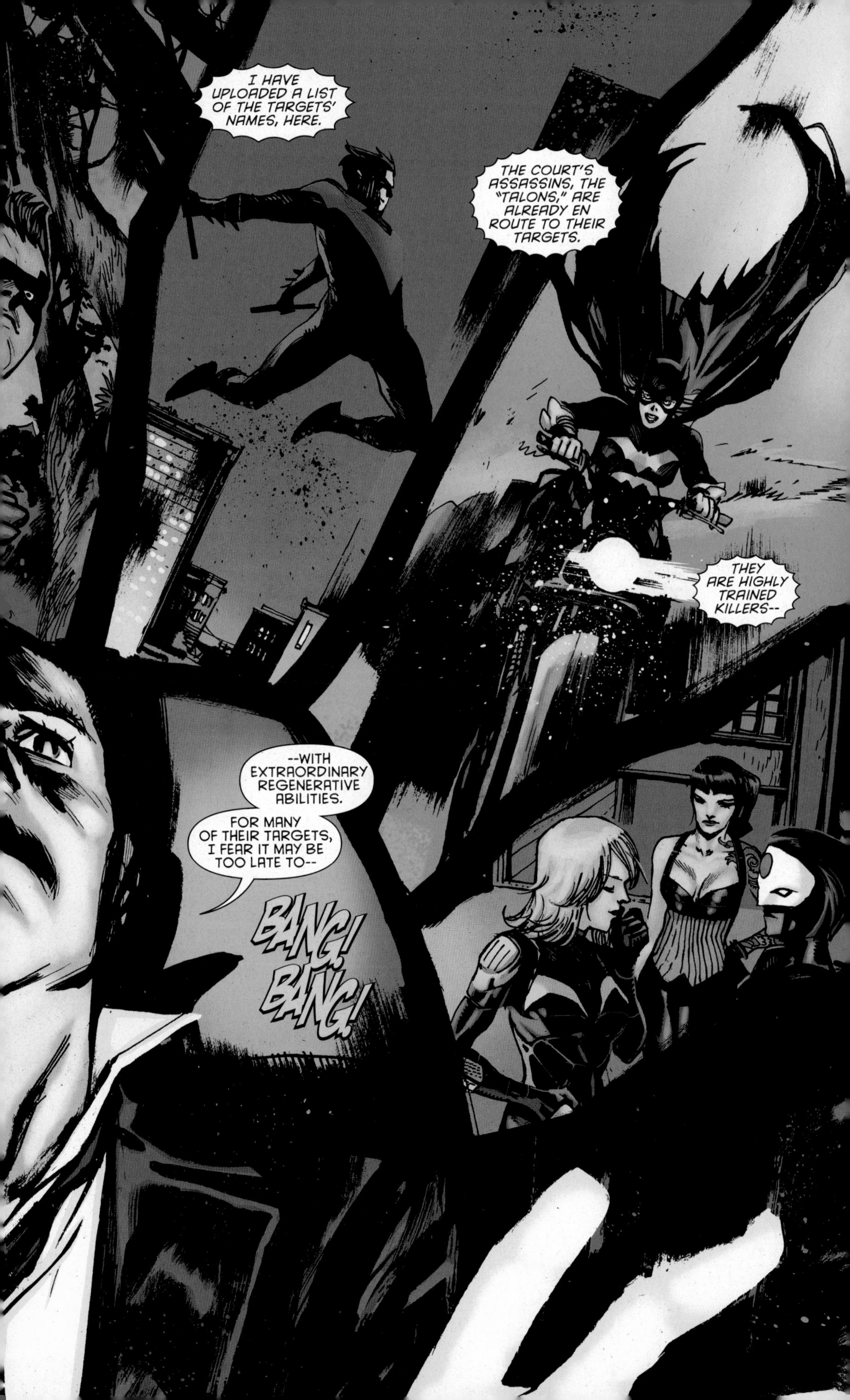
I HAVE UPLOADED A LIST OF THE TARGETS' NAMES, HERE.
THE COURT'S ASSASSINS, THE "TALONS," ARE ALREADY EN ROUTE TO THEIR TARGETS.
THEY ARE HIGHLY TRAINED KILLERS--
--WITH EXTRAORDINARY REGENERATIVE ABILITIES.
FOR MANY OF THEIR TARGETS, I FEAR IT MAY BE TOO LATE TO--
BANG! BANG!

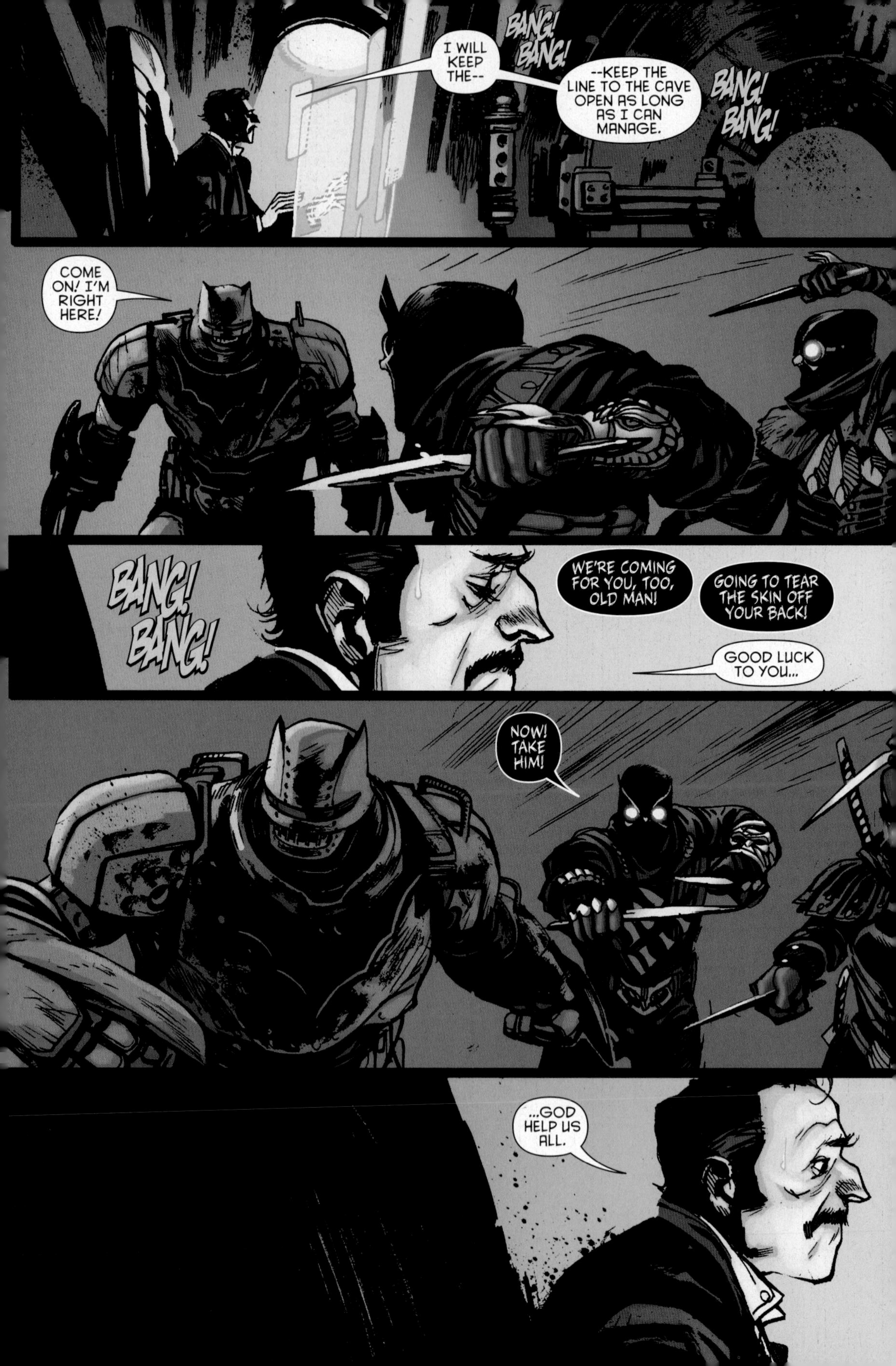
I WILL KEEP THE--
BANG! BANG!
--KEEP THE LINE TO THE CAVE OPEN AS LONG AS I CAN MANAGE.
BANG! BANG!
COME ON! I'M RIGHT HERE!
BANG! BANG!
WE'RE COMING FOR YOU, TOO, OLD MAN!
GOING TO TEAR THE SKIN OFF YOUR BACK!
GOOD LUCK TO YOU...
NOW! TAKE HIM!
...GOD HELP US ALL.

NIGHT OF THE OWLS

SCOTT SNYDER writer GREG CAPULLO penciller JONATHAN GLAPION inker

cover by GREG CAPULLO and FCO PLASCENCIA

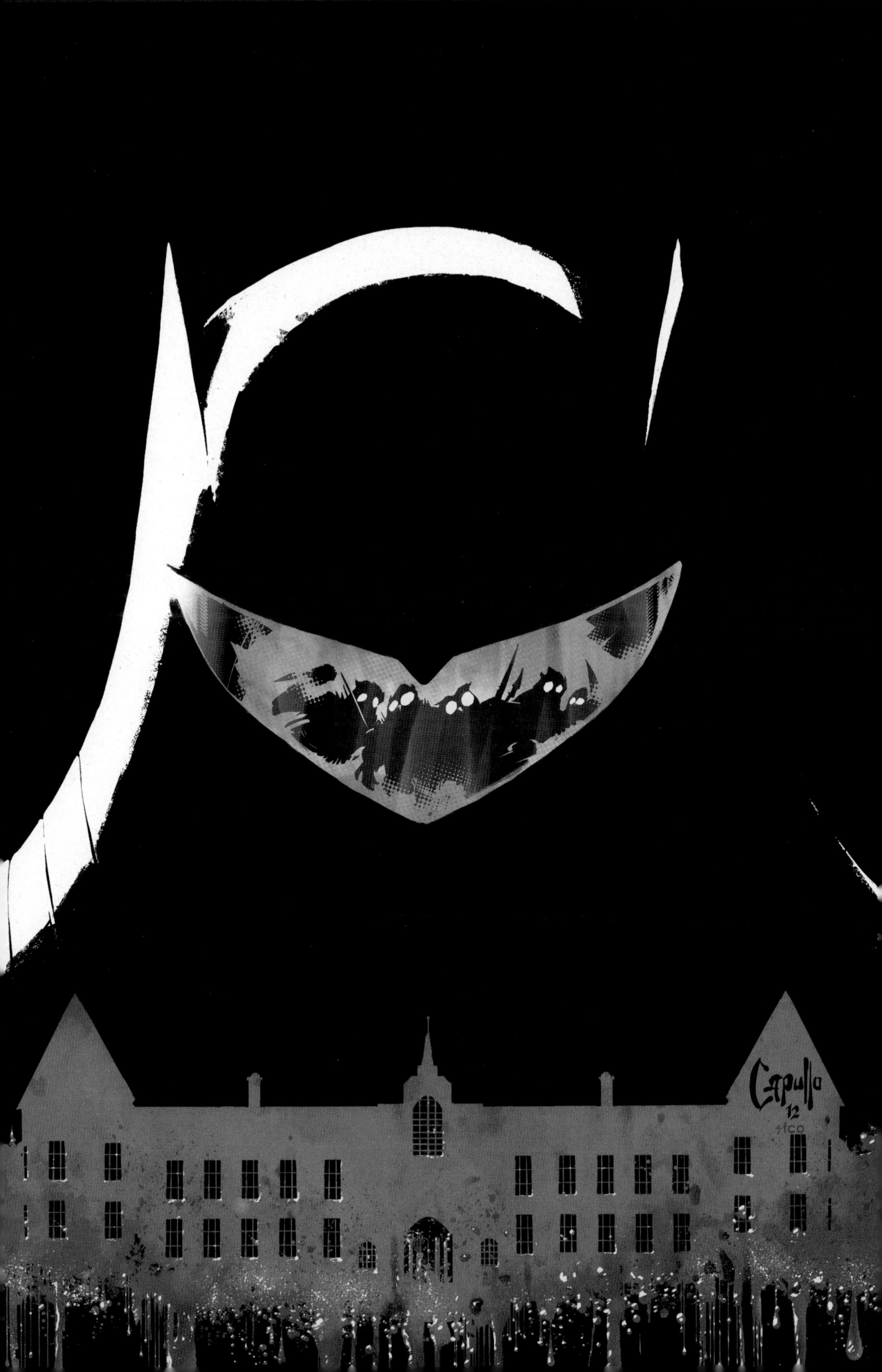
Capullo
12
+fco

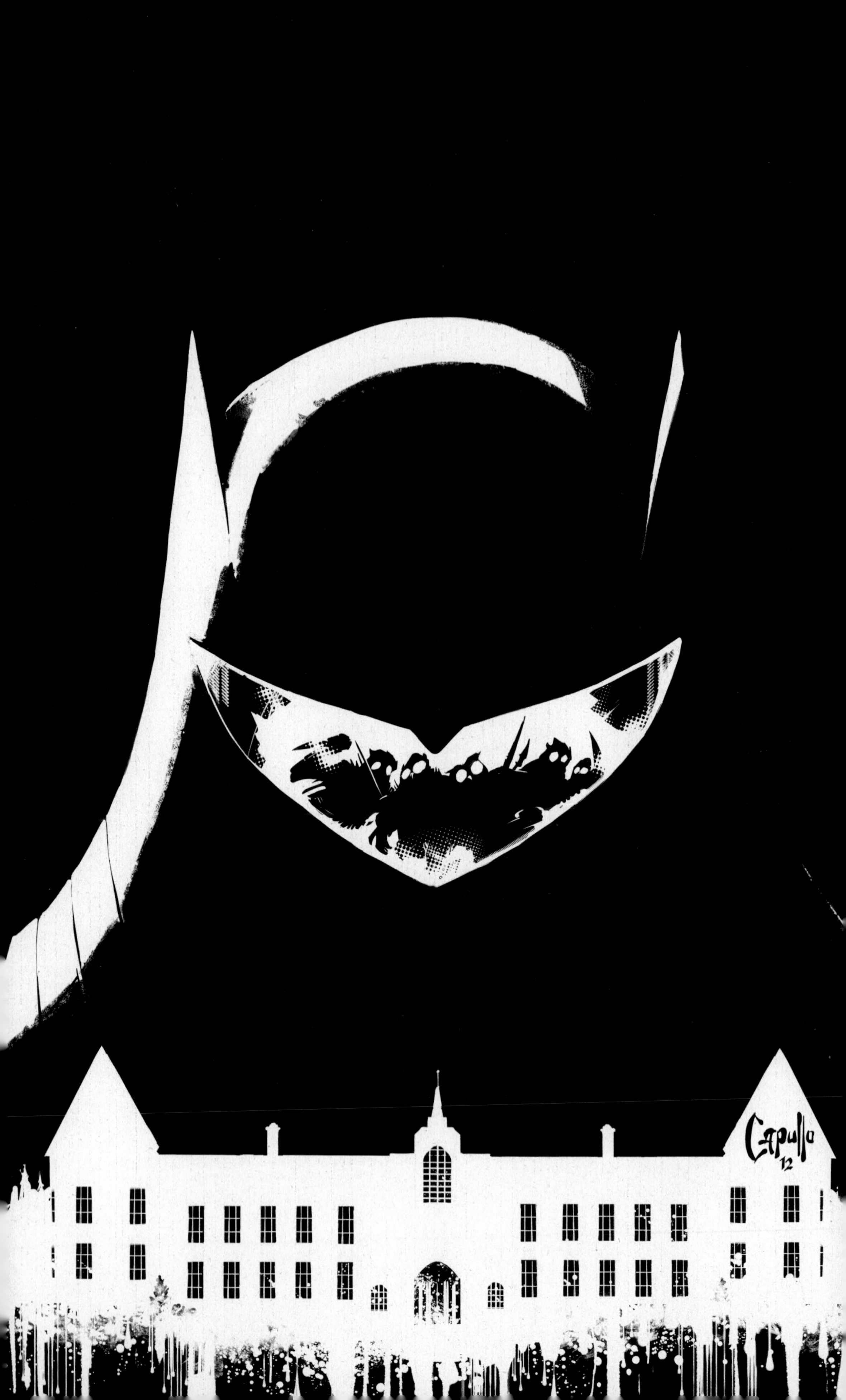

The first members of my family to live in the manor were Solomon and Joshua Wayne--brothers. They bought the house in 1855.

But they didn't move in until two years later.

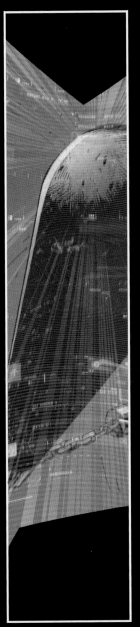

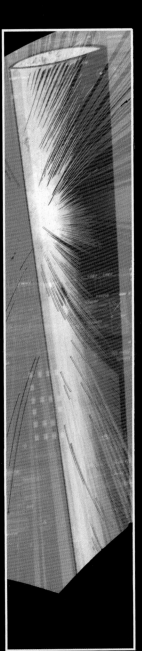

The reason was **bats**.

A massive infestation of bats in the cave system beneath the land.

They brought in a chiroptologist from Gotham University, and according to him, to get rid of the bats, they'd have to introduce a **predator** into the cave.

So the Wayne brothers did.

They carted in all sorts of birds, from Peregrine Falcons to kestrels, and unleashed them in differrent sections of the cave.

The most effective killers of bats, though, were the **tiger owls**.

My ancestors let owls loose in the cave...

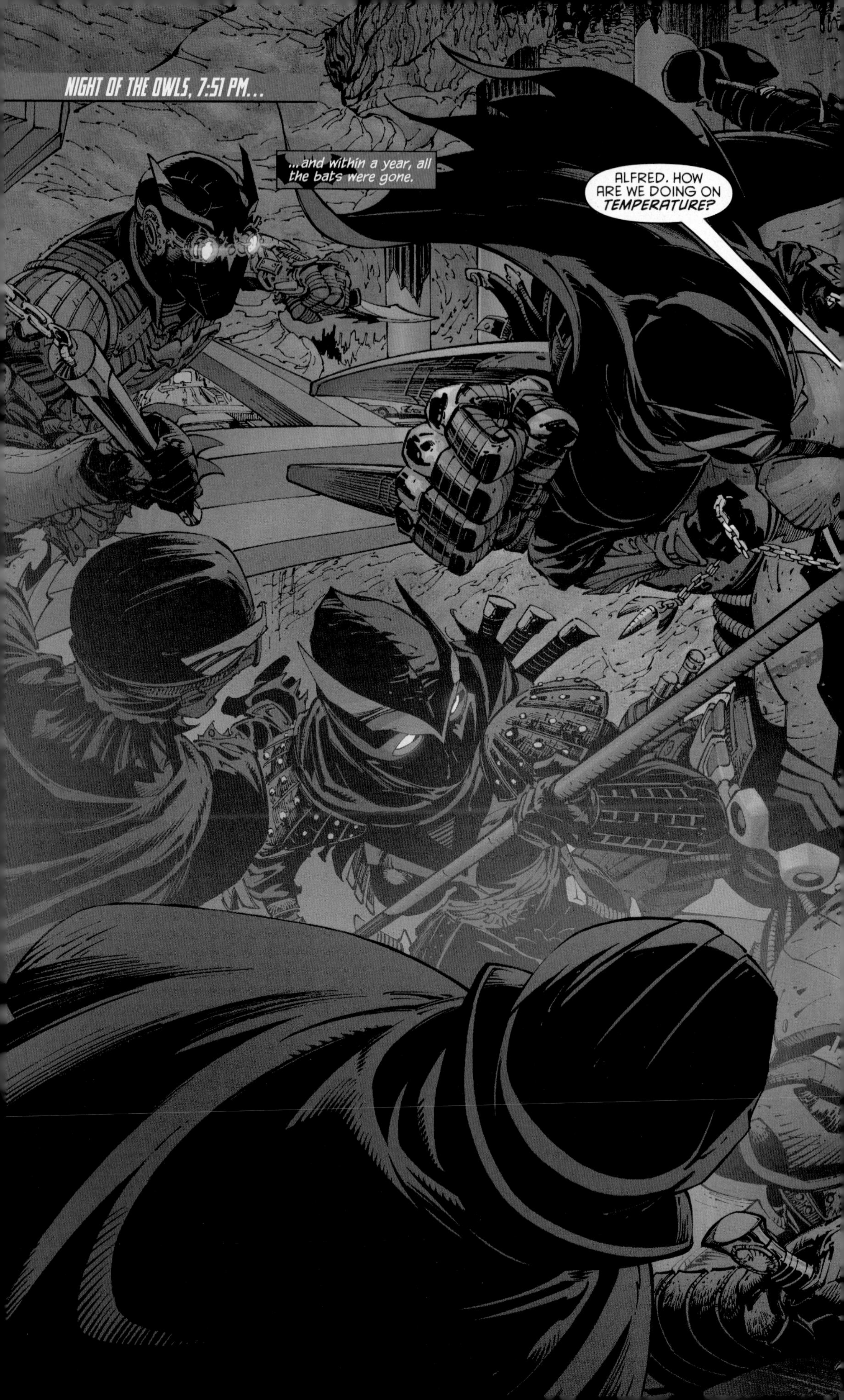
NIGHT OF THE OWLS, 7:51 PM...
...and within a year, all the bats were gone.
ALFRED. HOW ARE WE DOING ON TEMPERATURE?

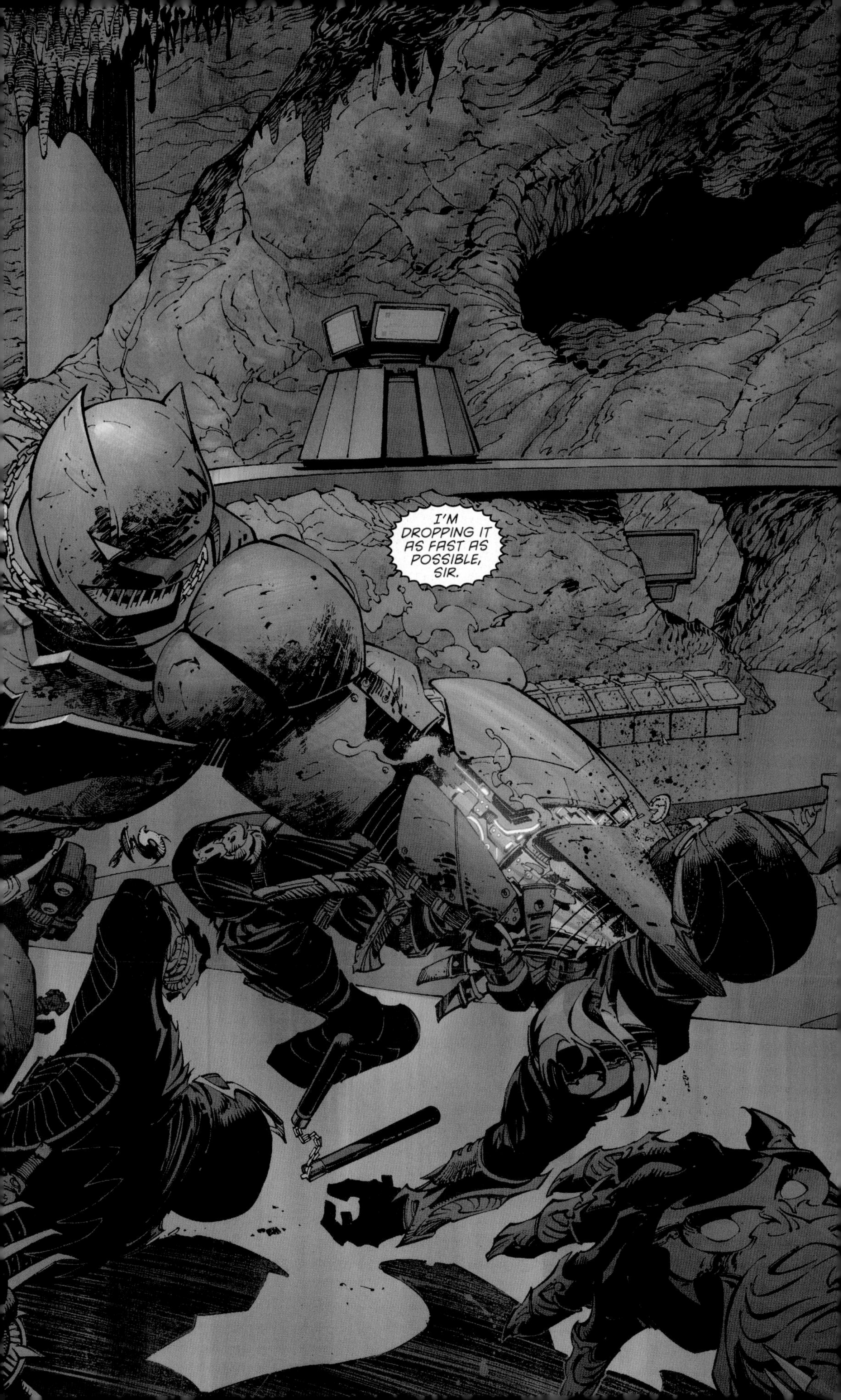
I'M DROPPING IT AS FAST AS POSSIBLE, SIR.

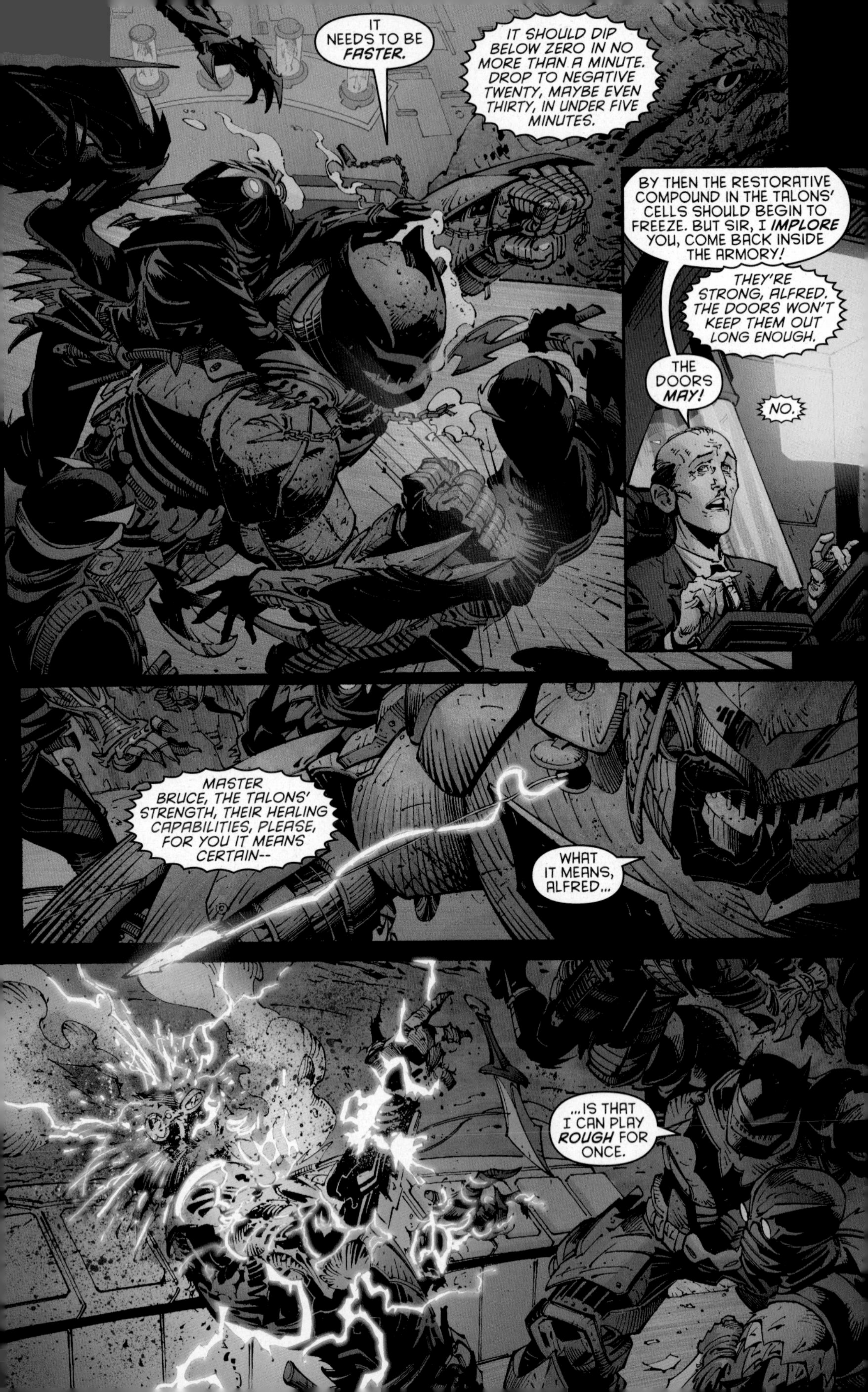
IT NEEDS TO BE FASTER.
IT SHOULD DIP BELOW ZERO IN NO MORE THAN A MINUTE. DROP TO NEGATIVE TWENTY, MAYBE EVEN THIRTY, IN UNDER FIVE MINUTES.
BY THEN THE RESTORATIVE COMPOUND IN THE TALONS' CELLS SHOULD BEGIN TO FREEZE. BUT SIR, I IMPLORE YOU, COME BACK INSIDE THE ARMORY!
THEY'RE STRONG, ALFRED. THE DOORS WON'T KEEP THEM OUT LONG ENOUGH.
THE DOORS MAY!
NO.
MASTER BRUCE, THE TALONS' STRENGTH, THEIR HEALING CAPABILITIES, PLEASE, FOR YOU IT MEANS CERTAIN--
WHAT IT MEANS, ALFRED...
...IS THAT I CAN PLAY ROUGH FOR ONCE.

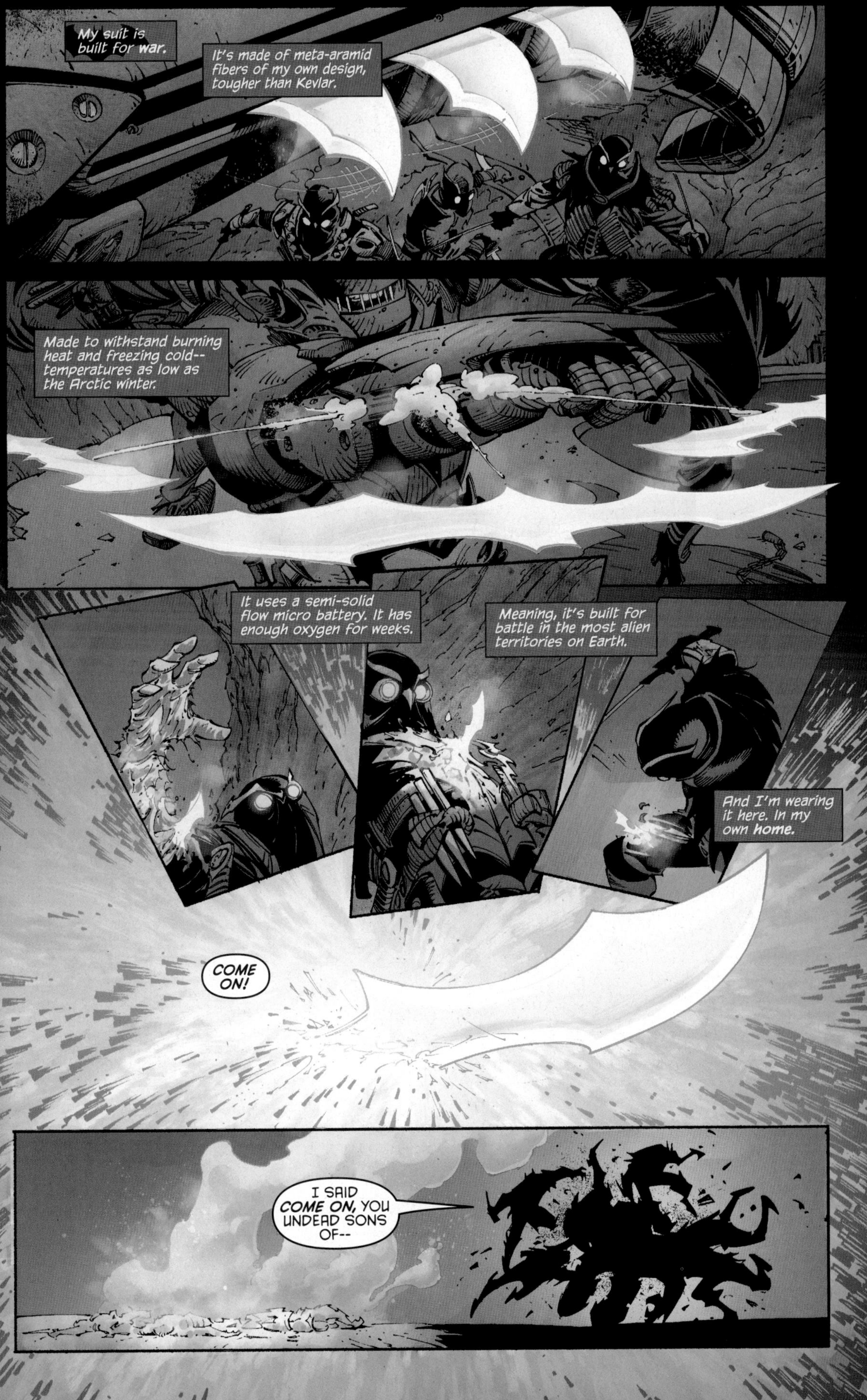
My suit is built for war.
It's made of meta-aramid fibers of my own design, tougher than Kevlar.
Made to withstand burning heat and freezing cold-- temperatures as low as the Arctic winter.
It uses a semi-solid flow micro battery. It has enough oxygen for weeks.
Meaning, it's built for battle in the most alien territories on Earth.
And I'm wearing it here. In my own home.
COME ON!
I SAID COME ON, YOU UNDEAD SONS OF--

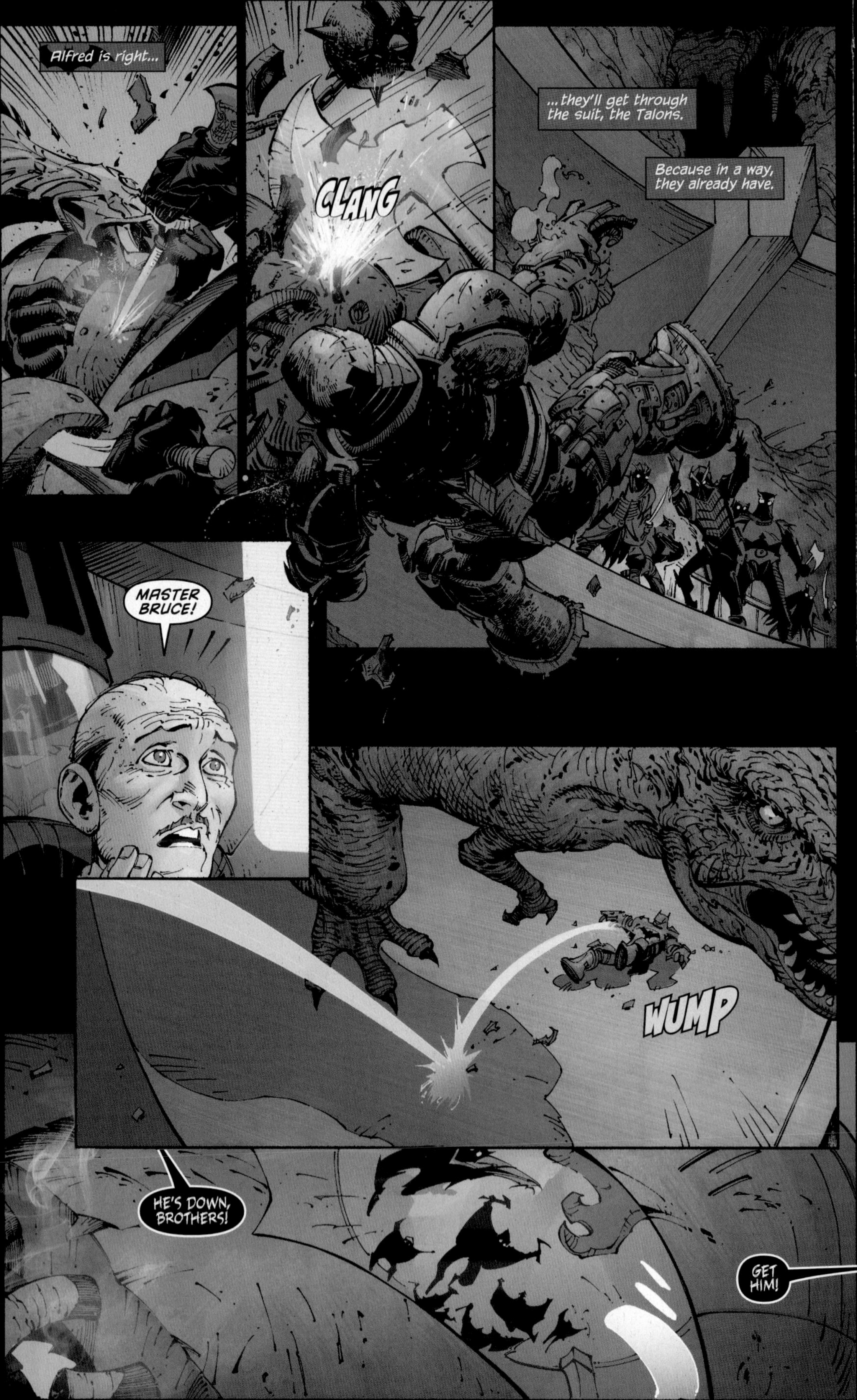
Alfred is right...
CLANG
...they'll get through the suit, the Talons.
Because in a way, they already have.
MASTER BRUCE!
WUMP
HE'S DOWN, BROTHERS!
GET HIM!

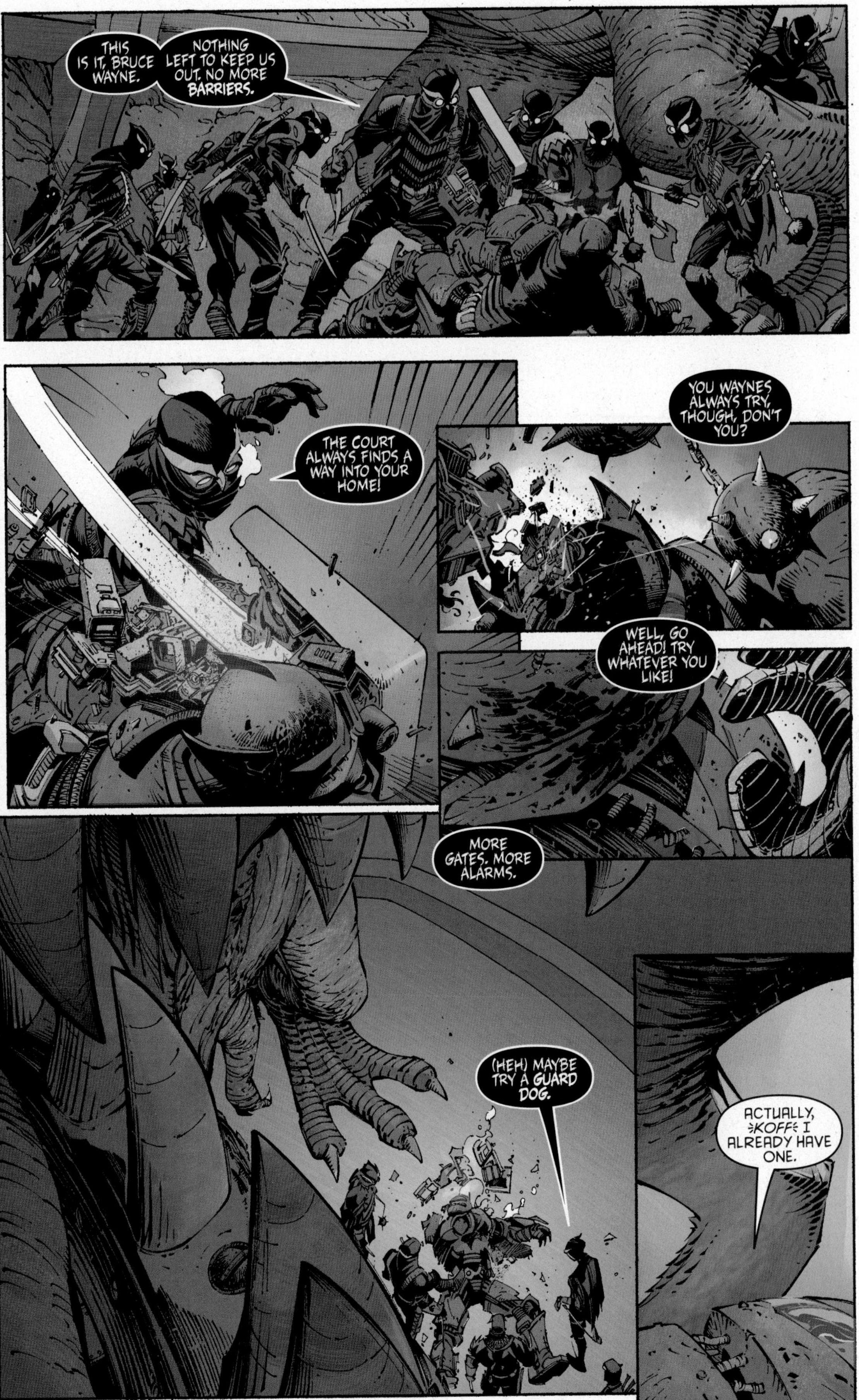
THIS IS IT, BRUCE WAYNE.
NOTHING LEFT TO KEEP US OUT. NO MORE BARRIERS.
THE COURT ALWAYS FINDS A WAY INTO YOUR HOME!
YOU WAYNES ALWAYS TRY, THOUGH, DON'T YOU?
WELL, GO AHEAD! TRY WHATEVER YOU LIKE!
MORE GATES. MORE ALARMS.
(HEH) MAYBE TRY A GUARD DOG.
ACTUALLY, *KOFF* I ALREADY HAVE ONE.

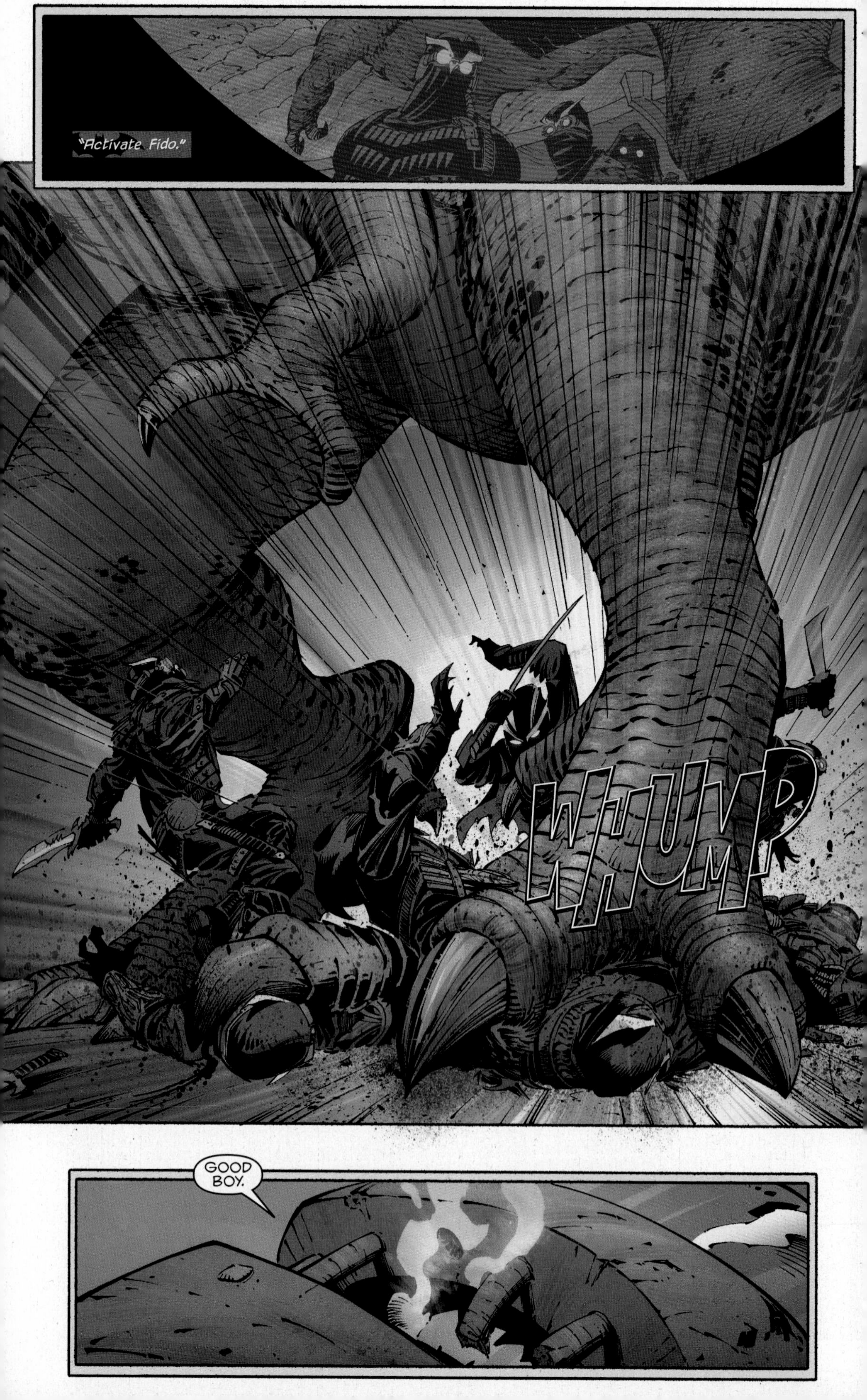
"Activate Fido."
WHUMP
GOOD BOY.

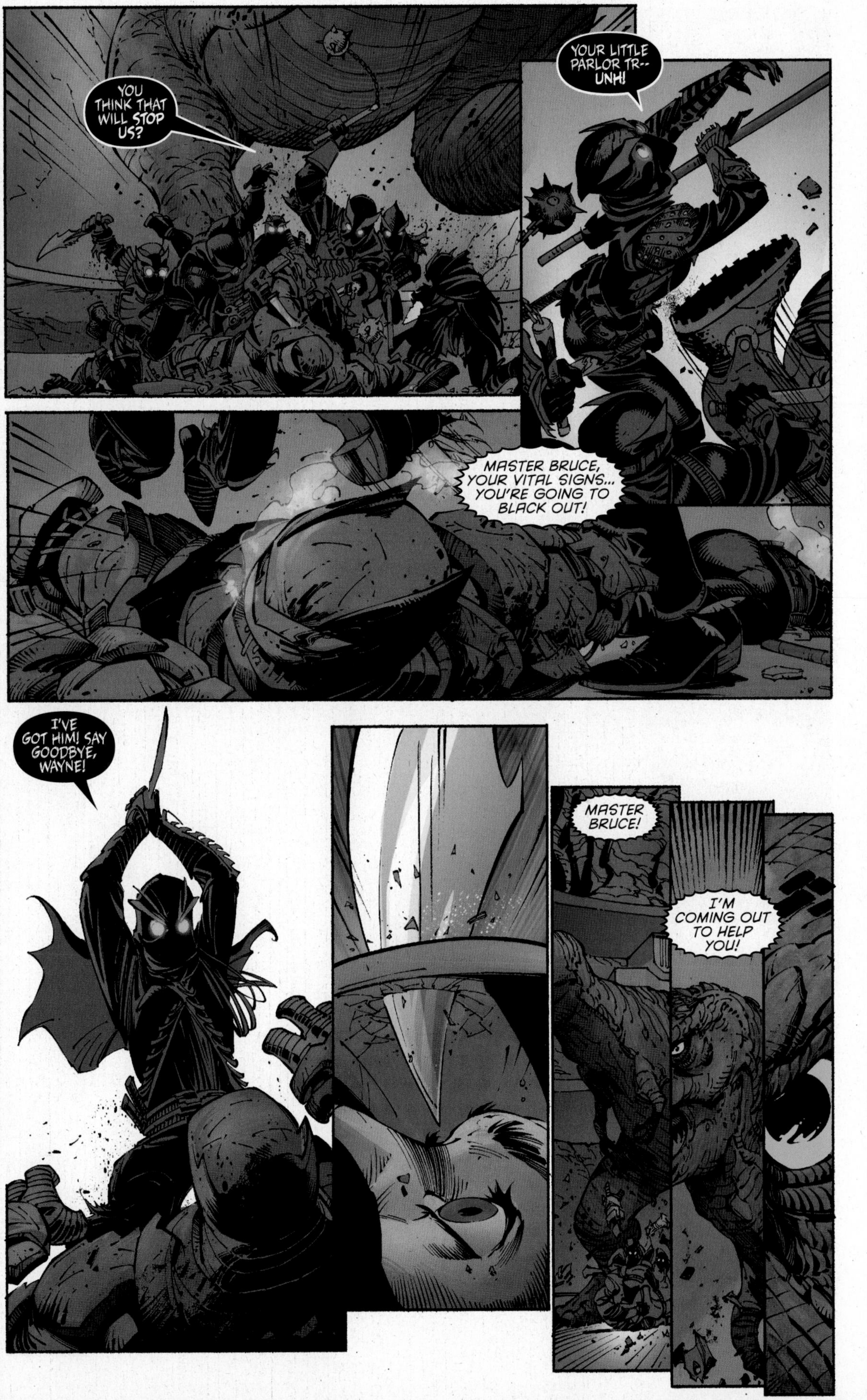
YOU THINK THAT WILL STOP US?
YOUR LITTLE PARLOR TR-- UNH!
MASTER BRUCE, YOUR VITAL SIGNS... YOU'RE GOING TO BLACK OUT!
I'VE GOT HIM! SAY GOODBYE, WAYNE!
MASTER BRUCE!
I'M COMING OUT TO HELP YOU!

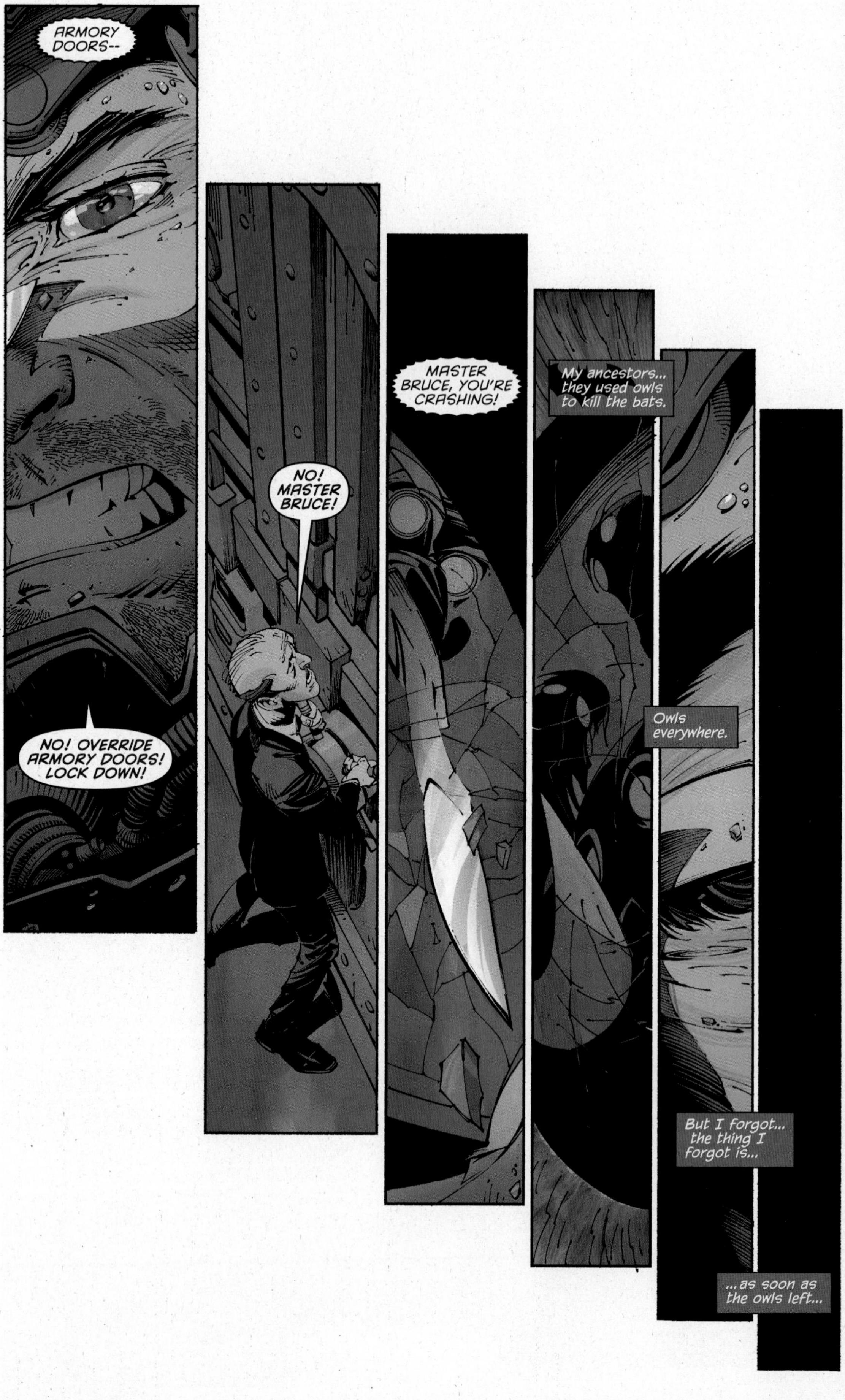
ARMORY DOORS--
NO! OVERRIDE ARMORY DOORS! LOCK DOWN!
NO! MASTER BRUCE!
MASTER BRUCE, YOU'RE CRASHING!
My ancestors... they used owls to kill the bats.
Owls everywhere.
But I forgot... the thing I forgot is...
...as soon as the owls left...

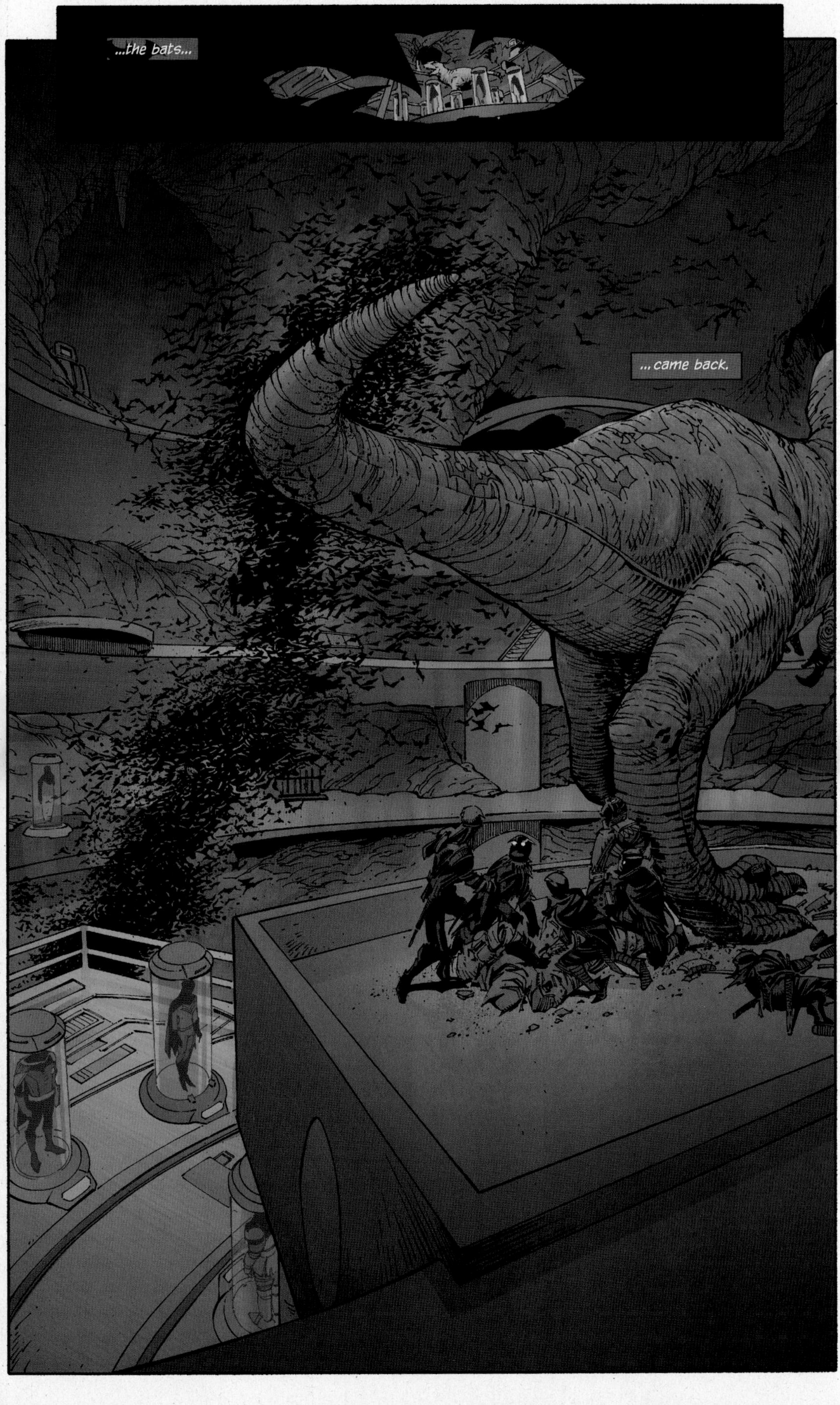
...the bats...
...came back.

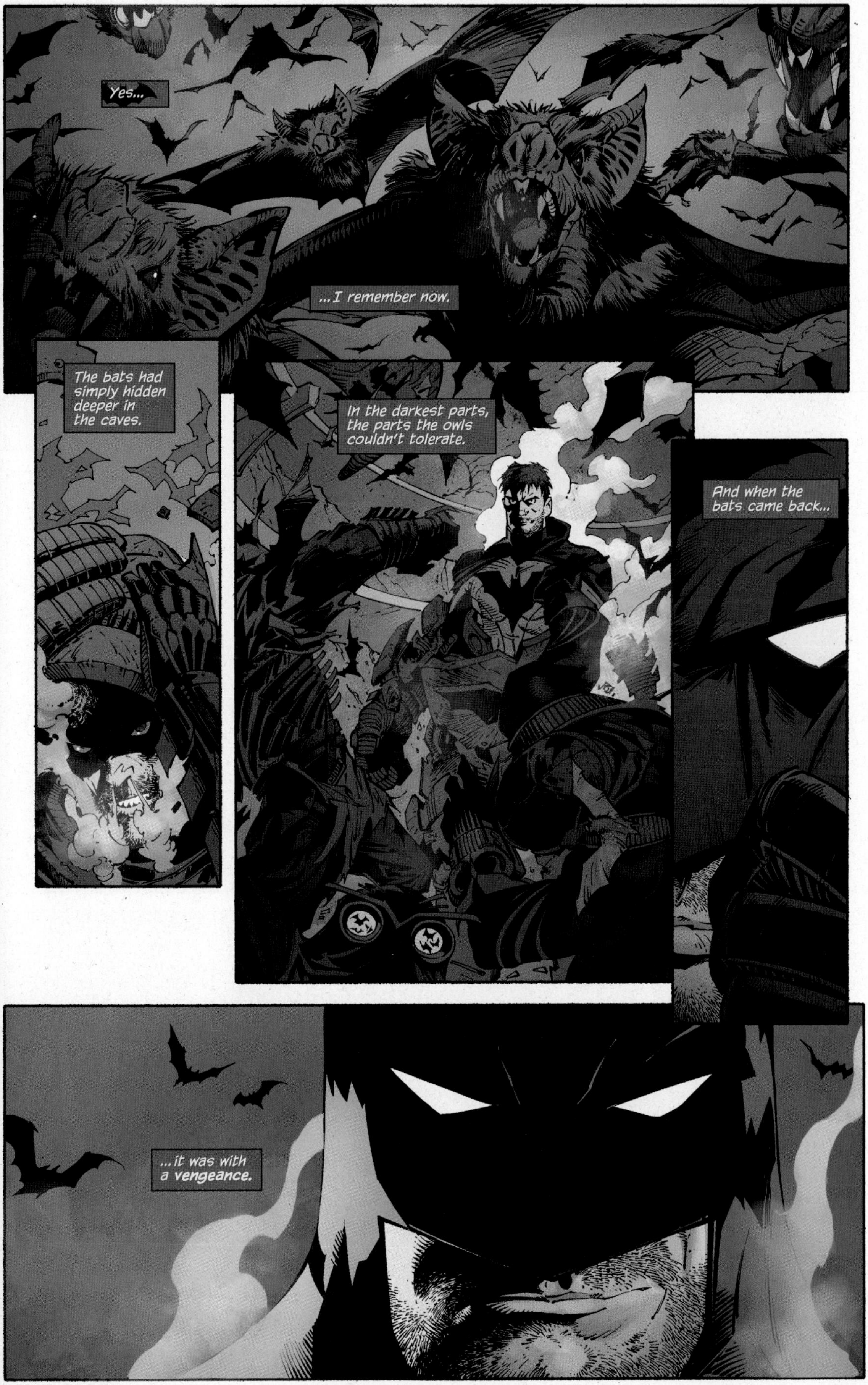
Yes...
...I remember now.
The bats had simply hidden deeper in the caves.
In the darkest parts, the parts the owls couldn't tolerate.
And when the bats came back...
...it was with a vengeance.

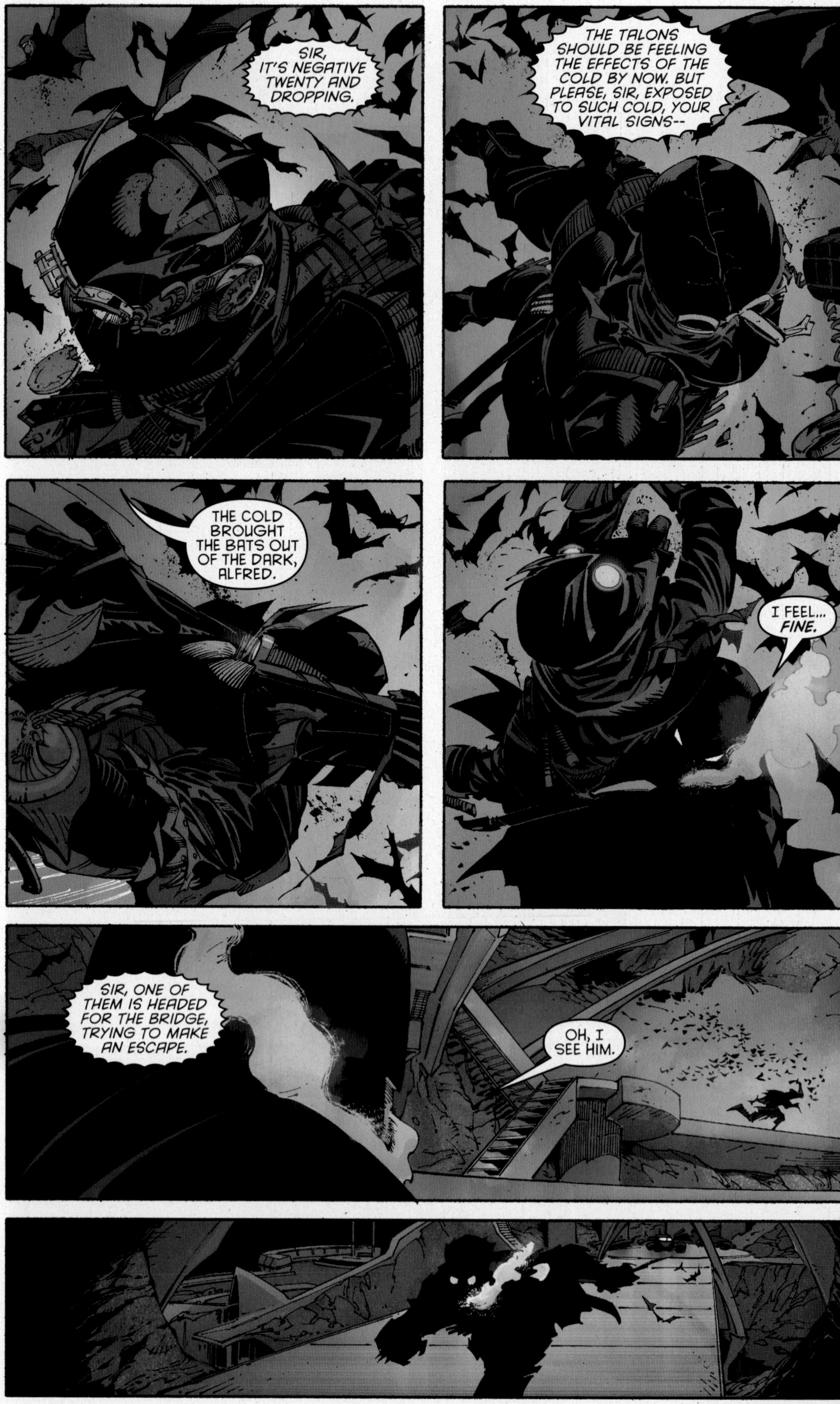
SIR, IT'S NEGATIVE TWENTY AND DROPPING.
THE TALONS SHOULD BE FEELING THE EFFECTS OF THE COLD BY NOW. BUT PLEASE, SIR, EXPOSED TO SUCH COLD, YOUR VITAL SIGNS--
THE COLD BROUGHT THE BATS OUT OF THE DARK, ALFRED.
I FEEL... FINE.
SIR, ONE OF THEM IS HEADED FOR THE BRIDGE, TRYING TO MAKE AN ESCAPE.
OH, I SEE HIM.

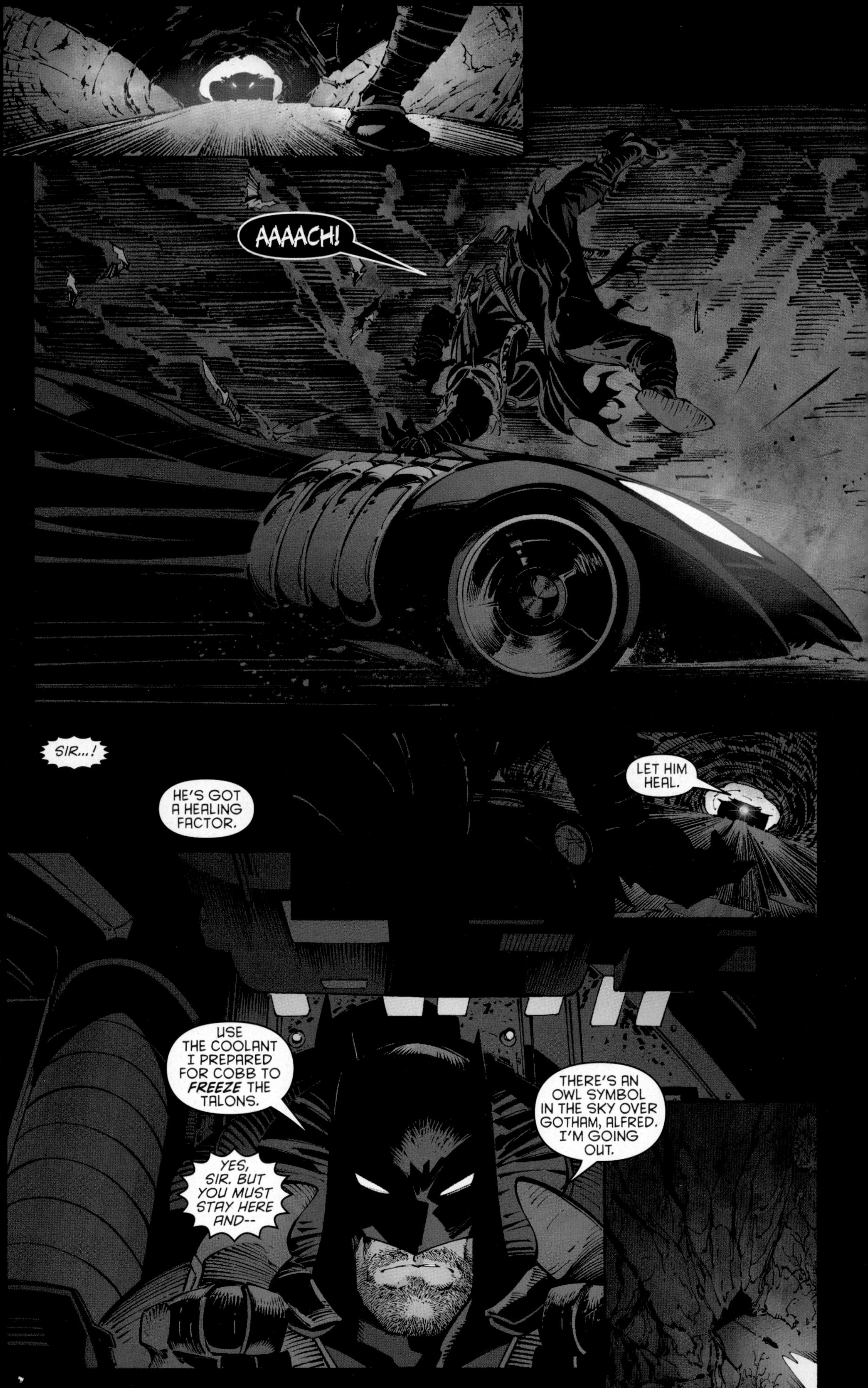
AAAACH!
SIR...!
HE'S GOT A HEALING FACTOR.
LET HIM HEAL.
USE THE COOLANT I PREPARED FOR COBB TO FREEZE THE TALONS.
YES, SIR. BUT YOU MUST STAY HERE AND--
THERE'S AN OWL SYMBOL IN THE SKY OVER GOTHAM, ALFRED. I'M GOING OUT.

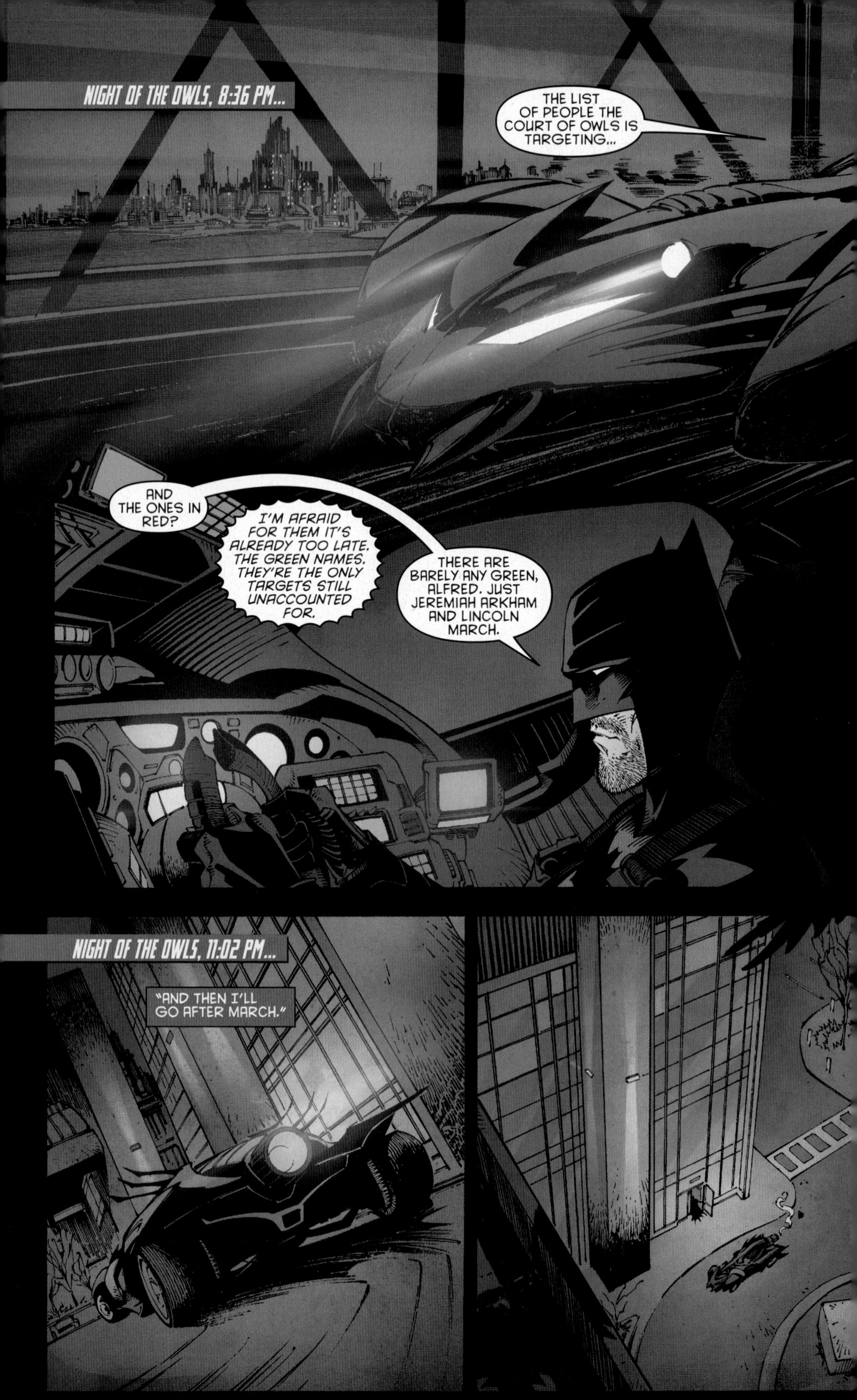
NIGHT OF THE OWLS, 8:36 PM...
THE LIST OF PEOPLE THE COURT OF OWLS IS TARGETING...
AND THE ONES IN RED?
I'M AFRAID FOR THEM IT'S ALREADY TOO LATE. THE GREEN NAMES. THEY'RE THE ONLY TARGETS STILL UNACCOUNTED FOR.
THERE ARE BARELY ANY GREEN, ALFRED. JUST JEREMIAH ARKHAM AND LINCOLN MARCH.
NIGHT OF THE OWLS, 11:02 PM...
"AND THEN I'LL GO AFTER MARCH."

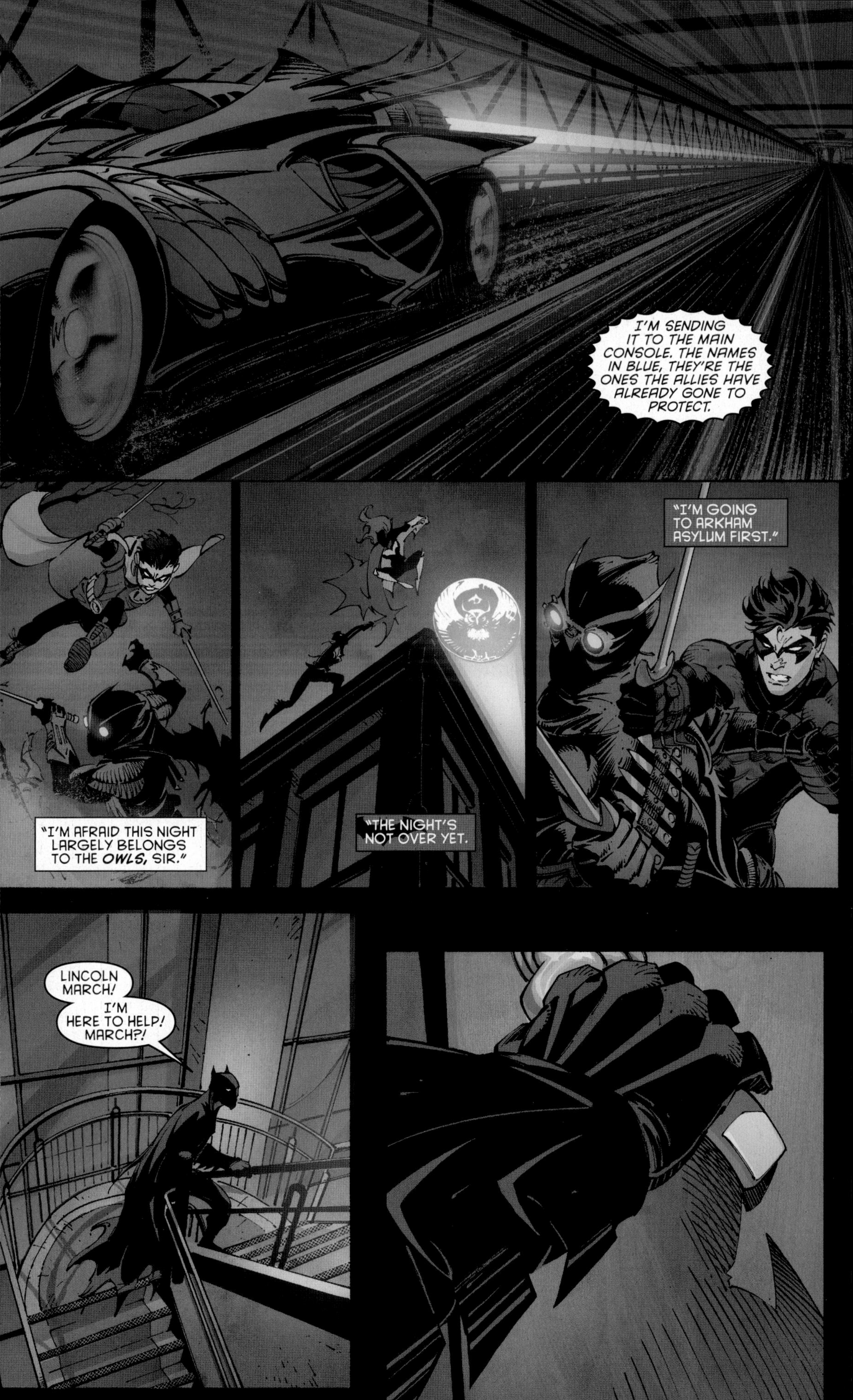
I'M SENDING IT TO THE MAIN CONSOLE. THE NAMES IN BLUE, THEY'RE THE ONES THE ALLIES HAVE ALREADY GONE TO PROTECT.
"I'M AFRAID THIS NIGHT LARGELY BELONGS TO THE OWLS, SIR."
"THE NIGHT'S NOT OVER YET.
"I'M GOING TO ARKHAM ASYLUM FIRST."
LINCOLN MARCH!
I'M HERE TO HELP! MARCH?!

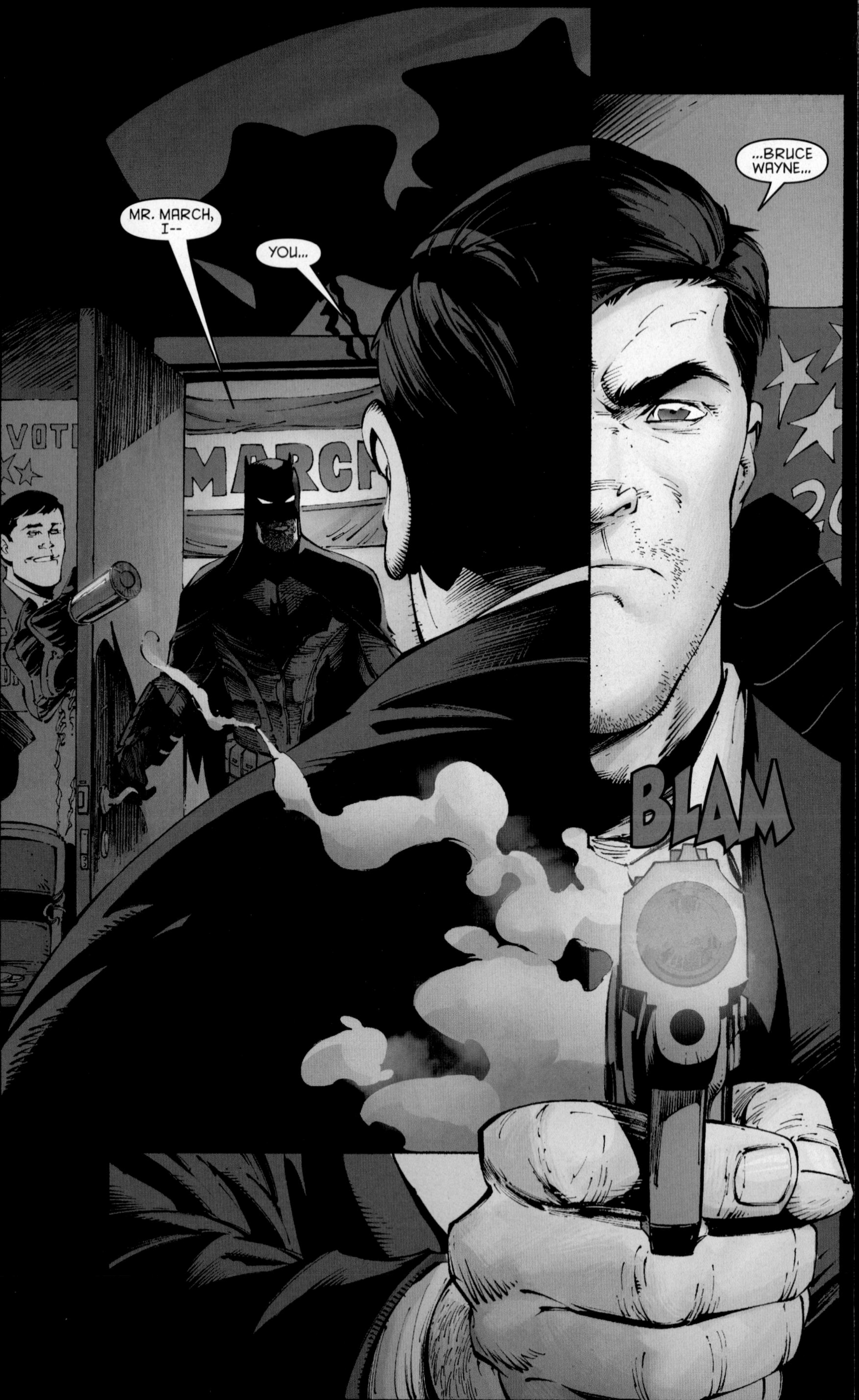
MR. MARCH, I--
YOU...
...BRUCE WAYNE...
MARCH
VOT
BLAM

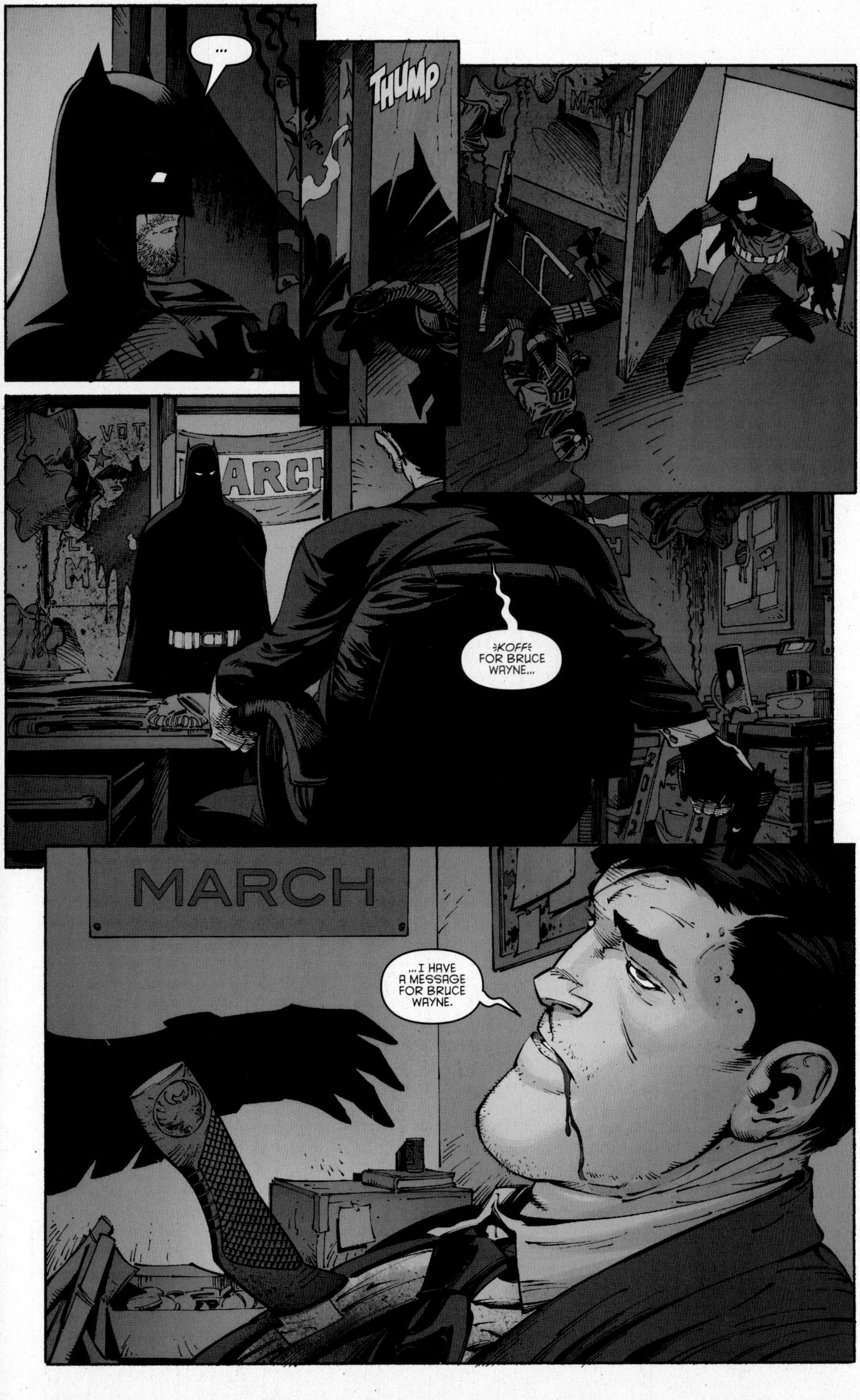
...
THUMP
MARCH
VOT
MARCH
KOFF FOR BRUCE WAYNE...
MARCH
...I HAVE A MESSAGE FOR BRUCE WAYNE.

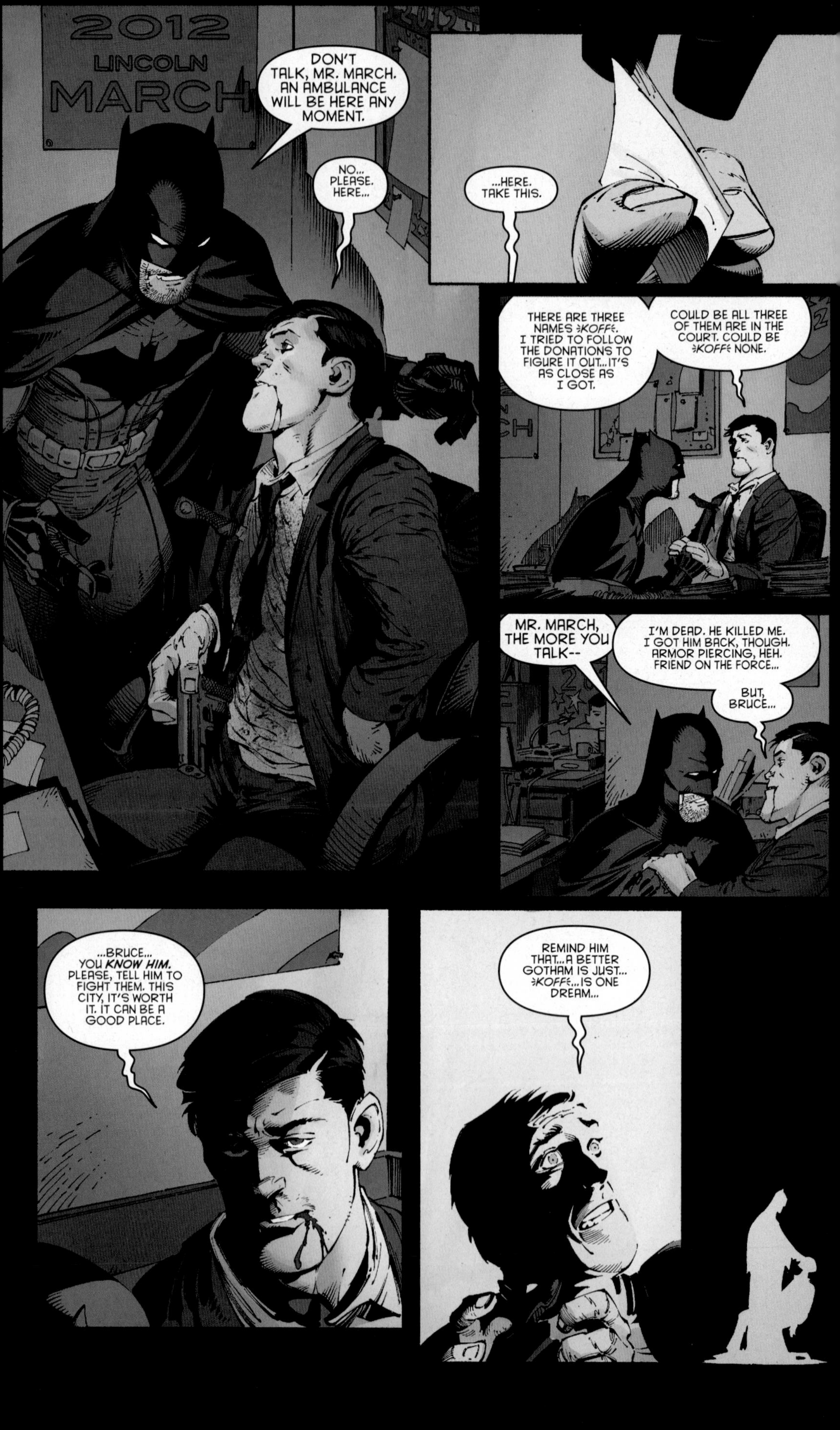

2012
LINCOLN
MARCH
DON'T TALK, MR. MARCH. AN AMBULANCE WILL BE HERE ANY MOMENT.
NO... PLEASE. HERE...
...HERE. TAKE THIS.
THERE ARE THREE NAMES *KOFF*. I TRIED TO FOLLOW THE DONATIONS TO FIGURE IT OUT...IT'S AS CLOSE AS I GOT.
COULD BE ALL THREE OF THEM ARE IN THE COURT. COULD BE *KOFF* NONE.
MR. MARCH, THE MORE YOU TALK--
I'M DEAD. HE KILLED ME. I GOT HIM BACK, THOUGH. ARMOR PIERCING, HEH. FRIEND ON THE FORCE...
BUT, BRUCE...
...BRUCE... YOU ***KNOW HIM.*** PLEASE, TELL HIM TO FIGHT THEM. THIS CITY, IT'S WORTH IT. IT CAN BE A GOOD PLACE.
REMIND HIM THAT...A BETTER GOTHAM IS JUST... *KOFF*...IS ONE DREAM...

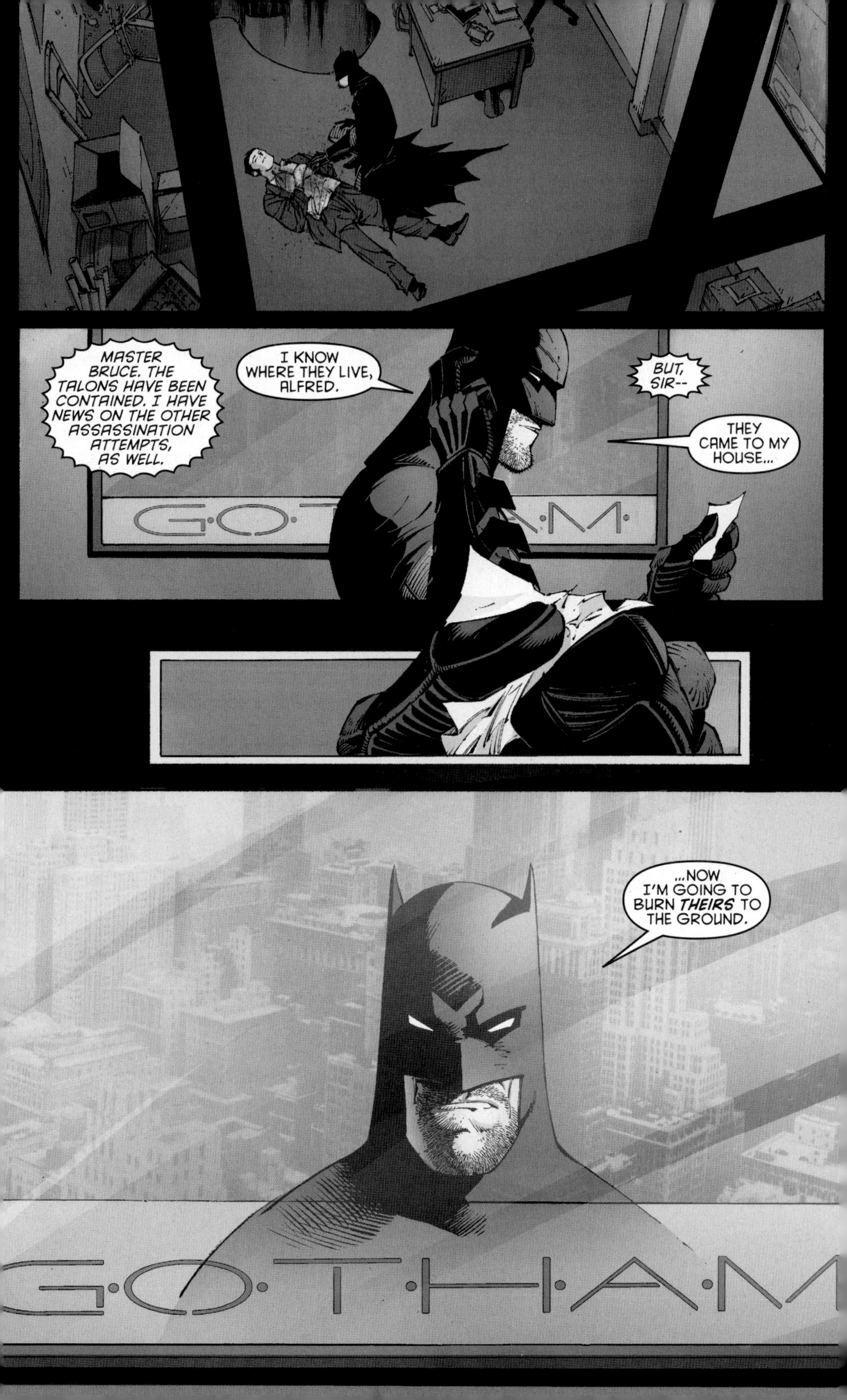
MASTER BRUCE. THE TALONS HAVE BEEN CONTAINED. I HAVE NEWS ON THE OTHER ASSASSINATION ATTEMPTS, AS WELL.
I KNOW WHERE THEY LIVE, ALFRED.
BUT, SIR--
THEY CAME TO MY HOUSE...
G·O·T·H·A·M
...NOW I'M GOING TO BURN *THEIRS* TO THE GROUND.
G·O·T·H·A·M

ASSAULT ON THE COURT

SCOTT SNYDER writer **GREG CAPULLO** penciller **JONATHAN GLAPION** inker
cover by **GREG CAPULLO** and **FCO PLASCENCIA**

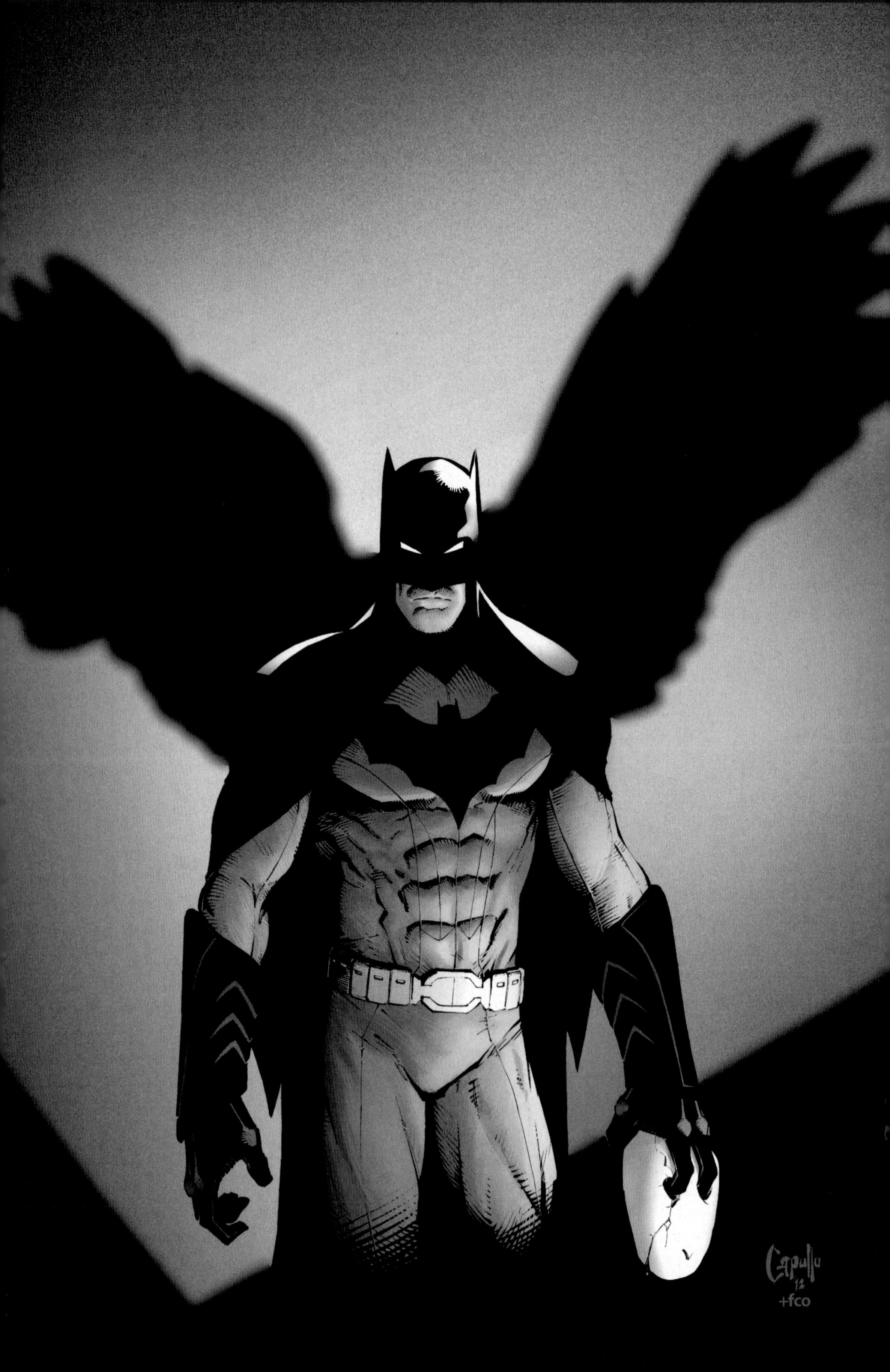
Capullo
12
+fco

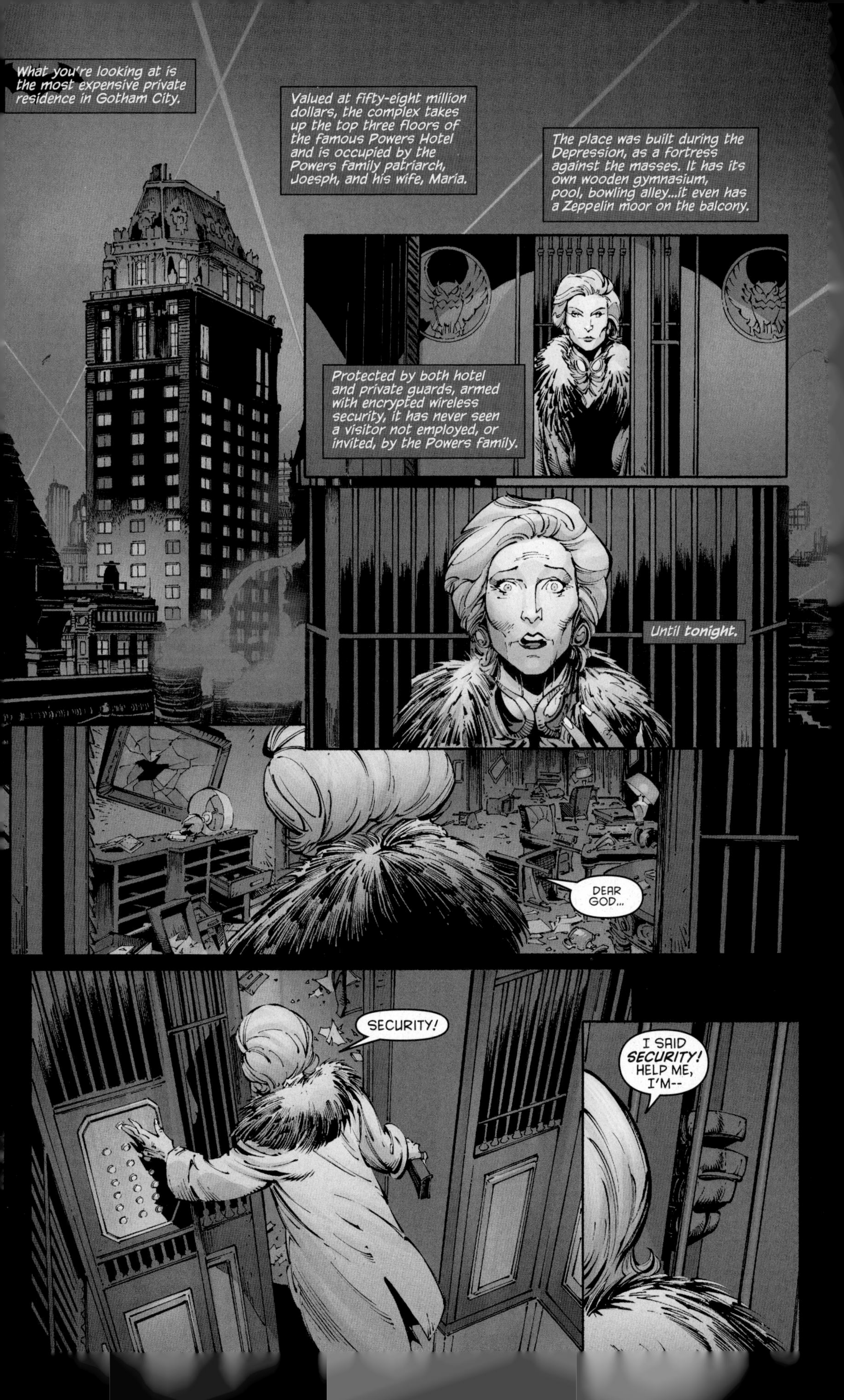
What you're looking at is the most expensive private residence in Gotham City.
Valued at fifty-eight million dollars, the complex takes up the top three floors of the famous Powers Hotel and is occupied by the Powers family patriarch, Joesph, and his wife, Maria.
The place was built during the Depression, as a fortress against the masses. It has its own wooden gymnasium, pool, bowling alley...it even has a Zeppelin moor on the balcony.
Protected by both hotel and private guards, armed with encrypted wireless security, it has never seen a visitor not employed, or invited, by the Powers family.
Until tonight.
DEAR GOD...
SECURITY!
I SAID SECURITY! HELP ME, I'M--

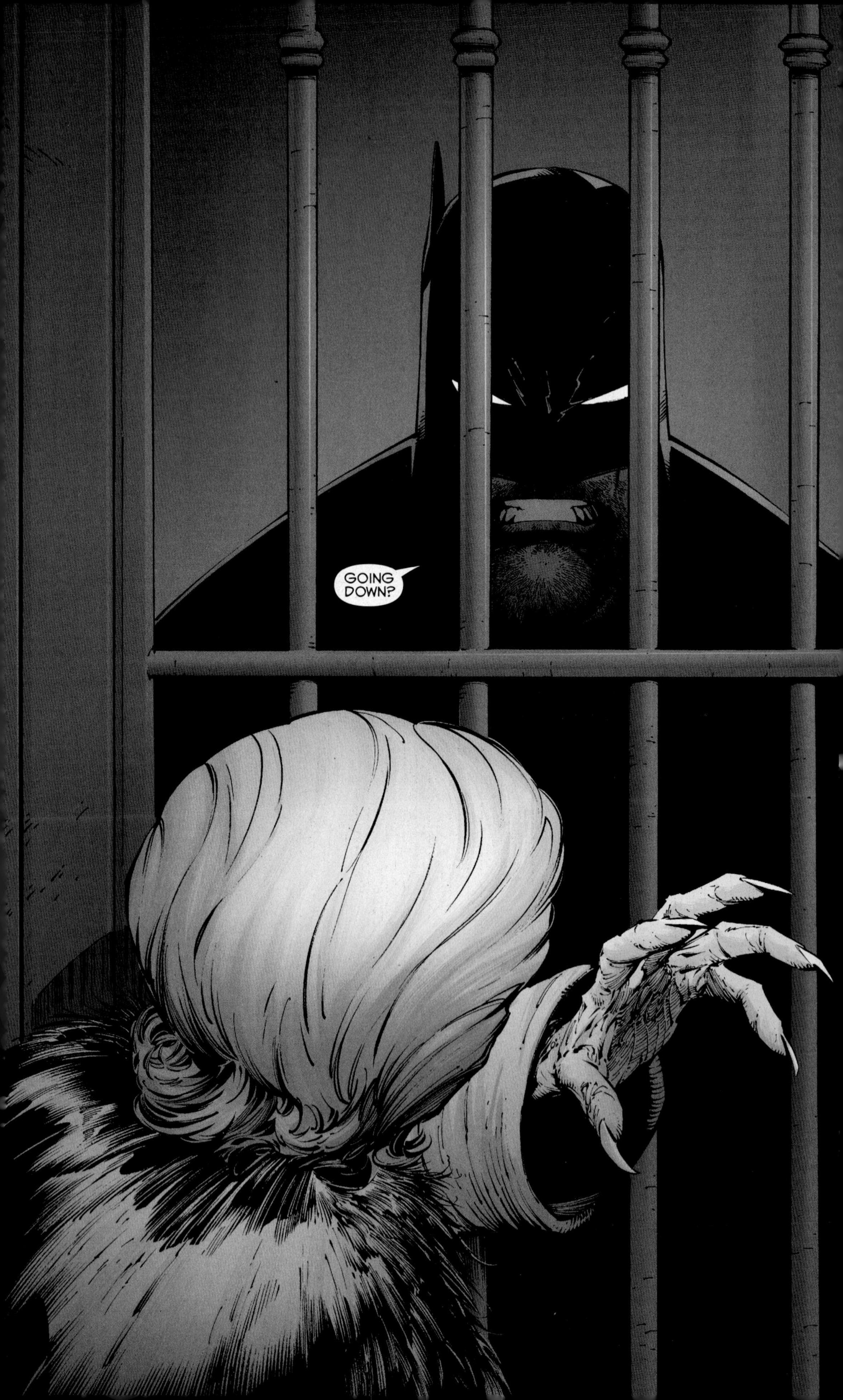
GOING DOWN?

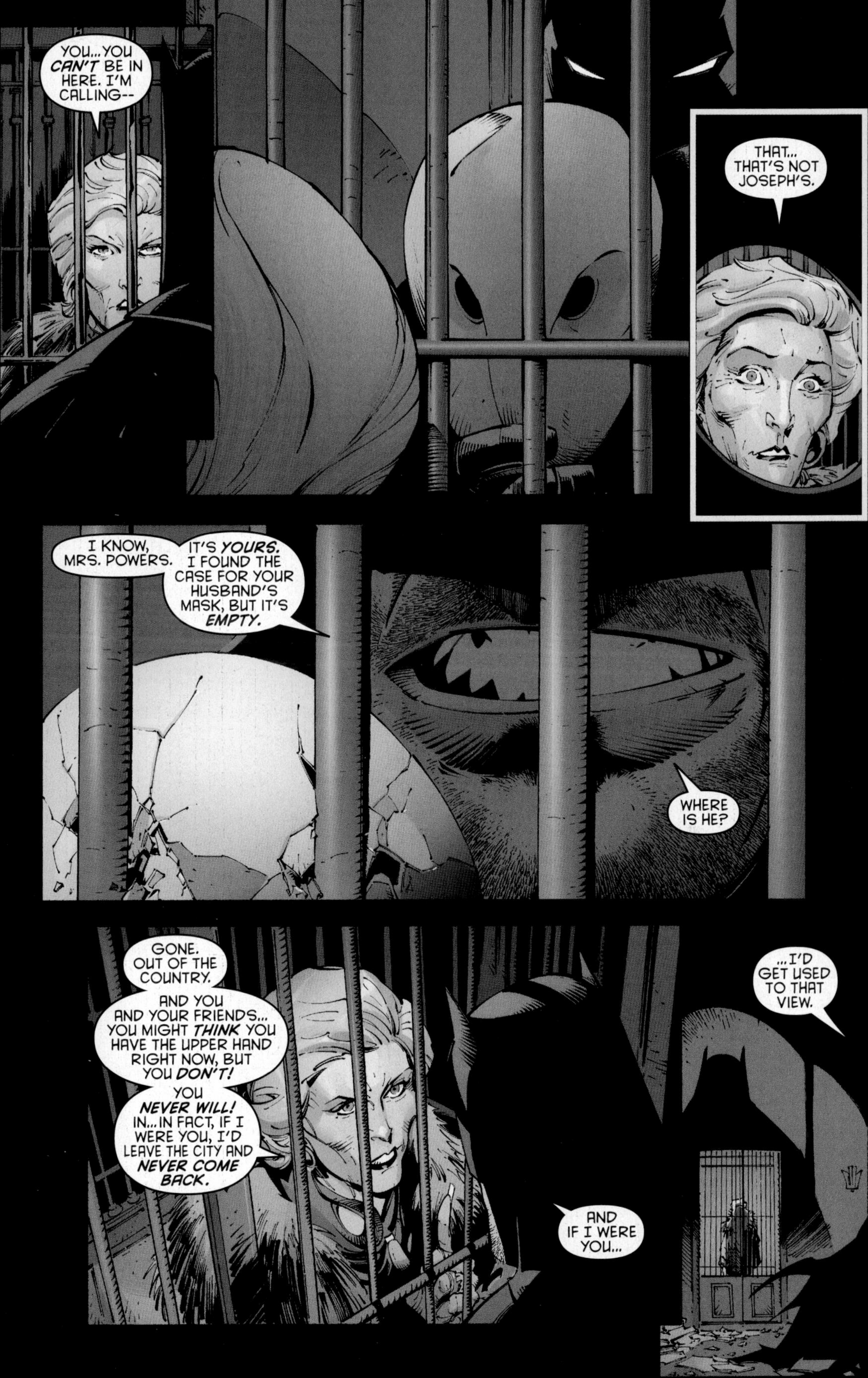
YOU...YOU CAN'T BE IN HERE. I'M CALLING--
THAT... THAT'S NOT JOSEPH'S.
I KNOW, MRS. POWERS.
IT'S YOURS. I FOUND THE CASE FOR YOUR HUSBAND'S MASK, BUT IT'S EMPTY.
WHERE IS HE?
GONE. OUT OF THE COUNTRY.
AND YOU AND YOUR FRIENDS... YOU MIGHT THINK YOU HAVE THE UPPER HAND RIGHT NOW, BUT YOU DON'T!
YOU NEVER WILL! IN...IN FACT, IF I WERE YOU, I'D LEAVE THE CITY AND NEVER COME BACK.
AND IF I WERE YOU...
...I'D GET USED TO THAT VIEW.

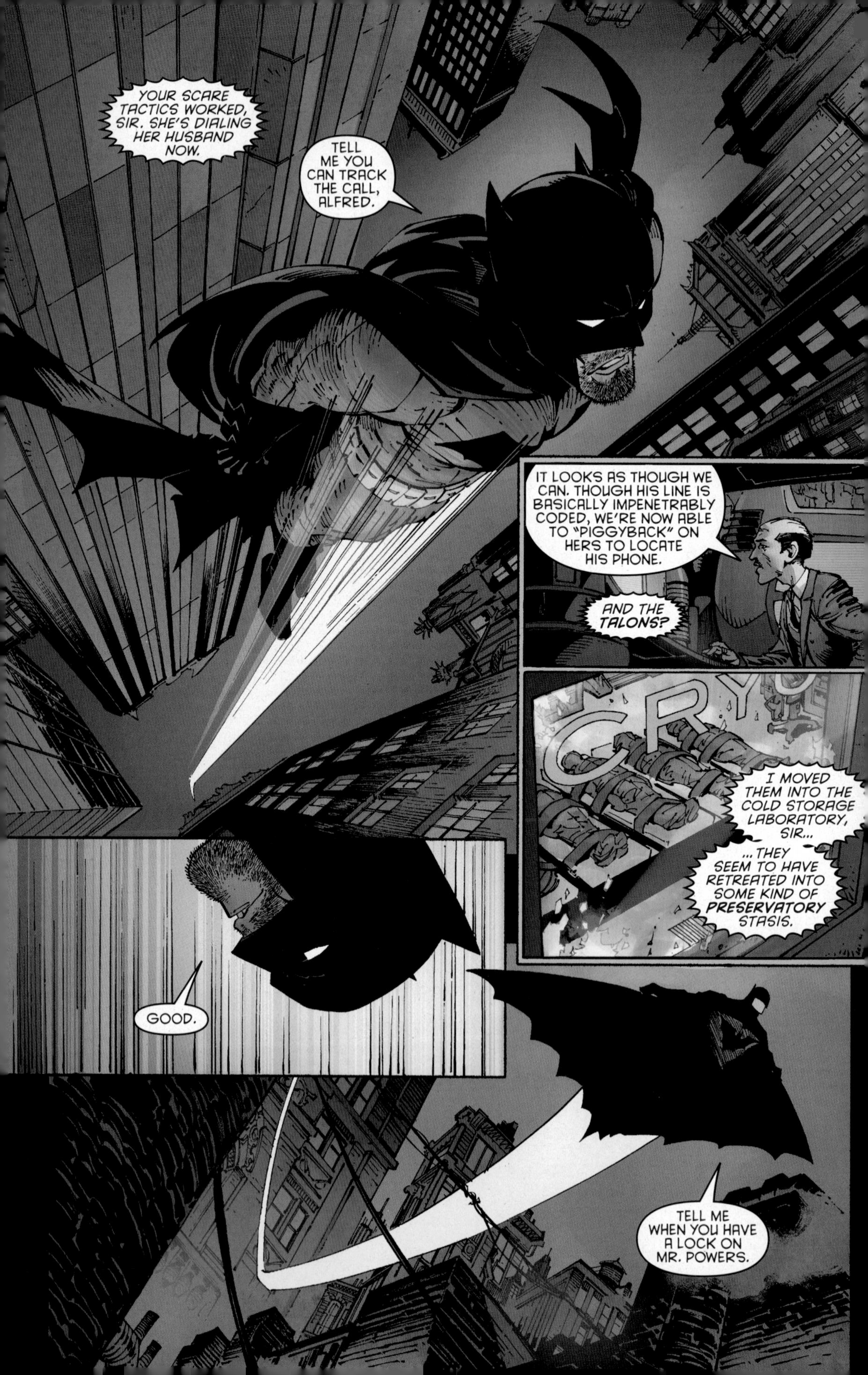
YOUR SCARE TACTICS WORKED, SIR. SHE'S DIALING HER HUSBAND NOW.
TELL ME YOU CAN TRACK THE CALL, ALFRED.
IT LOOKS AS THOUGH WE CAN. THOUGH HIS LINE IS BASICALLY IMPENETRABLY CODED, WE'RE NOW ABLE TO "PIGGYBACK" ON HERS TO LOCATE HIS PHONE.
AND THE TALONS?
CRY
I MOVED THEM INTO THE COLD STORAGE LABORATORY, SIR...
...THEY SEEM TO HAVE RETREATED INTO SOME KIND OF PRESERVATORY STASIS.
GOOD.
TELL ME WHEN YOU HAVE A LOCK ON MR. POWERS.

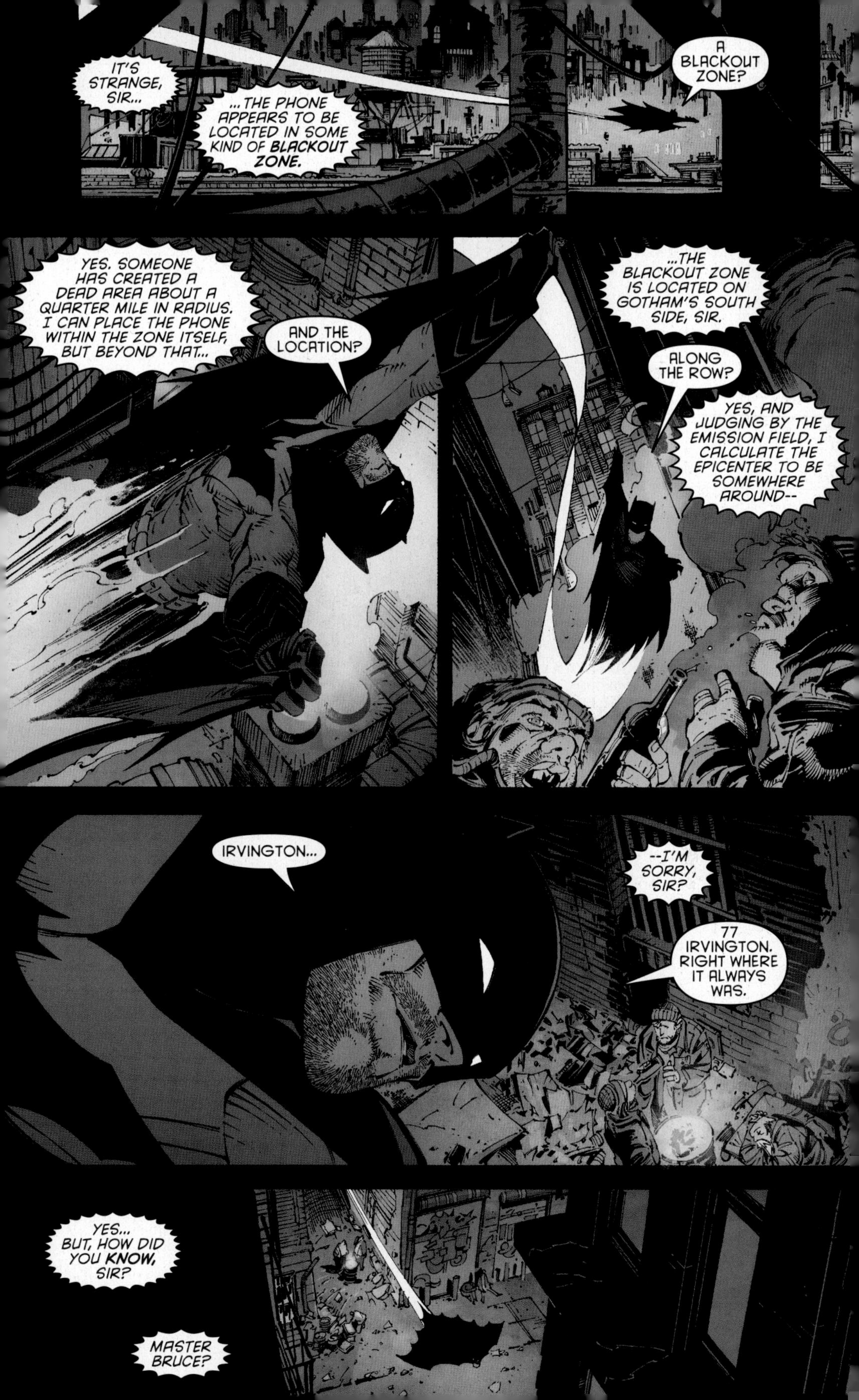
IT'S STRANGE, SIR...
...THE PHONE APPEARS TO BE LOCATED IN SOME KIND OF BLACKOUT ZONE.
A BLACKOUT ZONE?
YES. SOMEONE HAS CREATED A DEAD AREA ABOUT A QUARTER MILE IN RADIUS. I CAN PLACE THE PHONE WITHIN THE ZONE ITSELF, BUT BEYOND THAT...
AND THE LOCATION?
...THE BLACKOUT ZONE IS LOCATED ON GOTHAM'S SOUTH SIDE, SIR.
ALONG THE ROW?
YES, AND JUDGING BY THE EMISSION FIELD, I CALCULATE THE EPICENTER TO BE SOMEWHERE AROUND--
IRVINGTON...
--I'M SORRY, SIR?
77 IRVINGTON. RIGHT WHERE IT ALWAYS WAS.
YES... BUT, HOW DID YOU KNOW, SIR?
MASTER BRUCE?

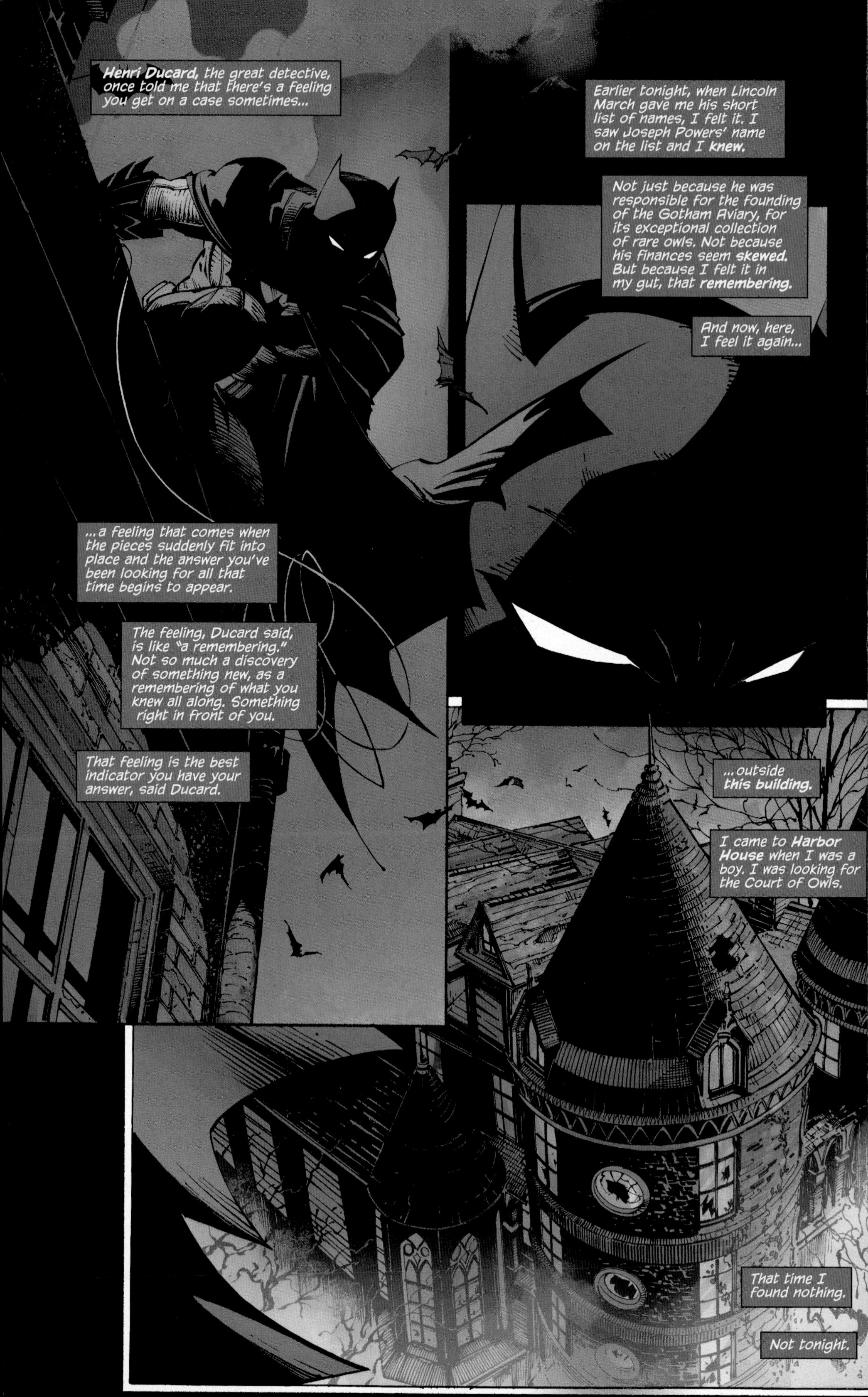
Henri Ducard, the great detective, once told me that there's a feeling you get on a case sometimes...
Earlier tonight, when Lincoln March gave me his short list of names, I felt it. I saw Joseph Powers' name on the list and I knew.
Not just because he was responsible for the founding of the Gotham Aviary, for its exceptional collection of rare owls. Not because his finances seem skewed. But because I felt it in my gut, that remembering.
And now, here, I feel it again...
...a feeling that comes when the pieces suddenly fit into place and the answer you've been looking for all that time begins to appear.
The feeling, Ducard said, is like "a remembering." Not so much a discovery of something new, as a remembering of what you knew all along. Something right in front of you.
That feeling is the best indicator you have your answer, said Ducard.
...outside this building.
I came to Harbor House when I was a boy. I was looking for the Court of Owls.
That time I found nothing.
Not tonight.

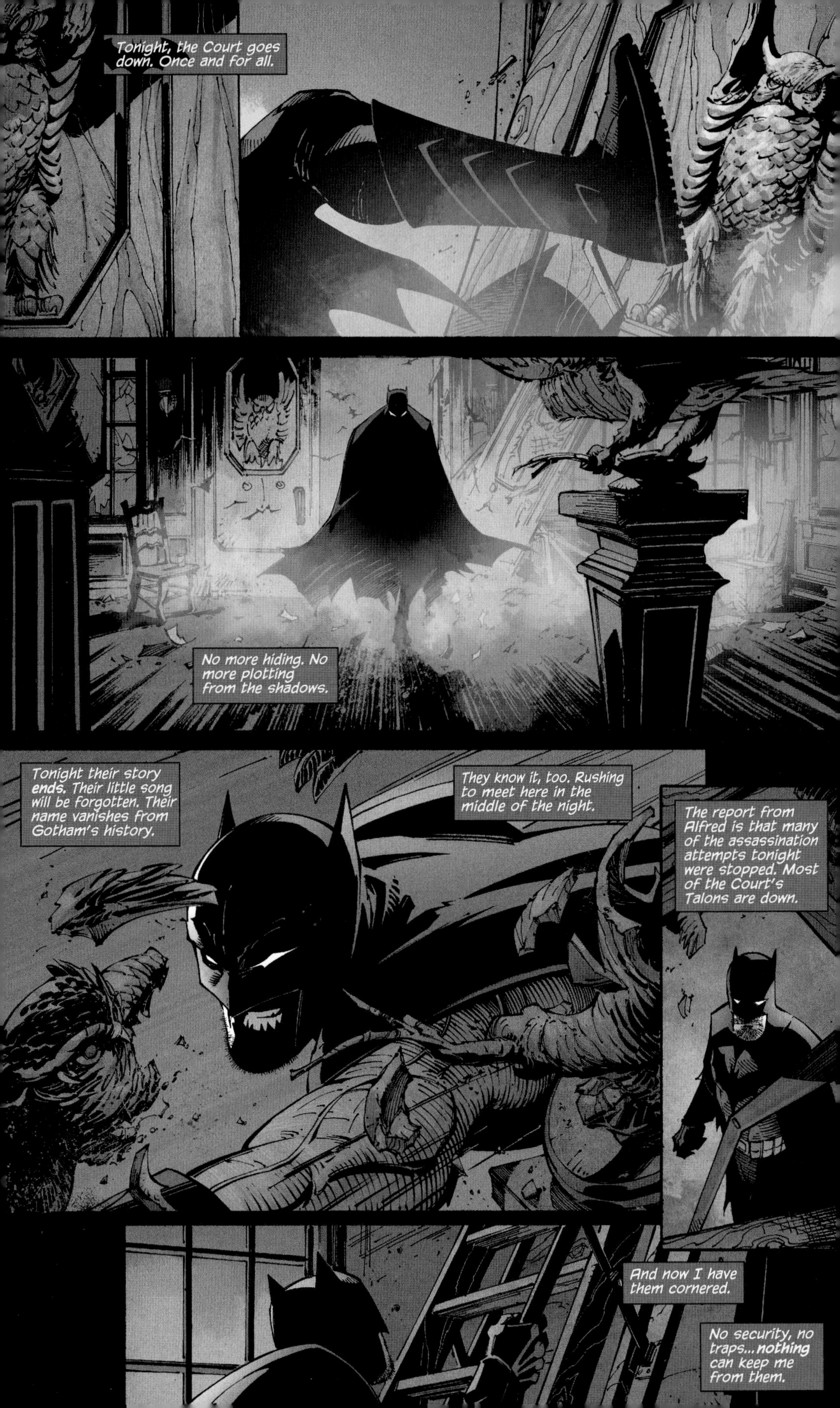

Tonight, the Court goes down. Once and for all.
No more hiding. No more plotting from the shadows.
Tonight their story **ends.** Their little song will be forgotten. Their name vanishes from Gotham's history.
They know it, too. Rushing to meet here in the middle of the night.
The report from Alfred is that many of the assassination attempts tonight were stopped. Most of the Court's Talons are down.
And now I have them cornered.
No security, no traps... **nothing** can keep me from them.

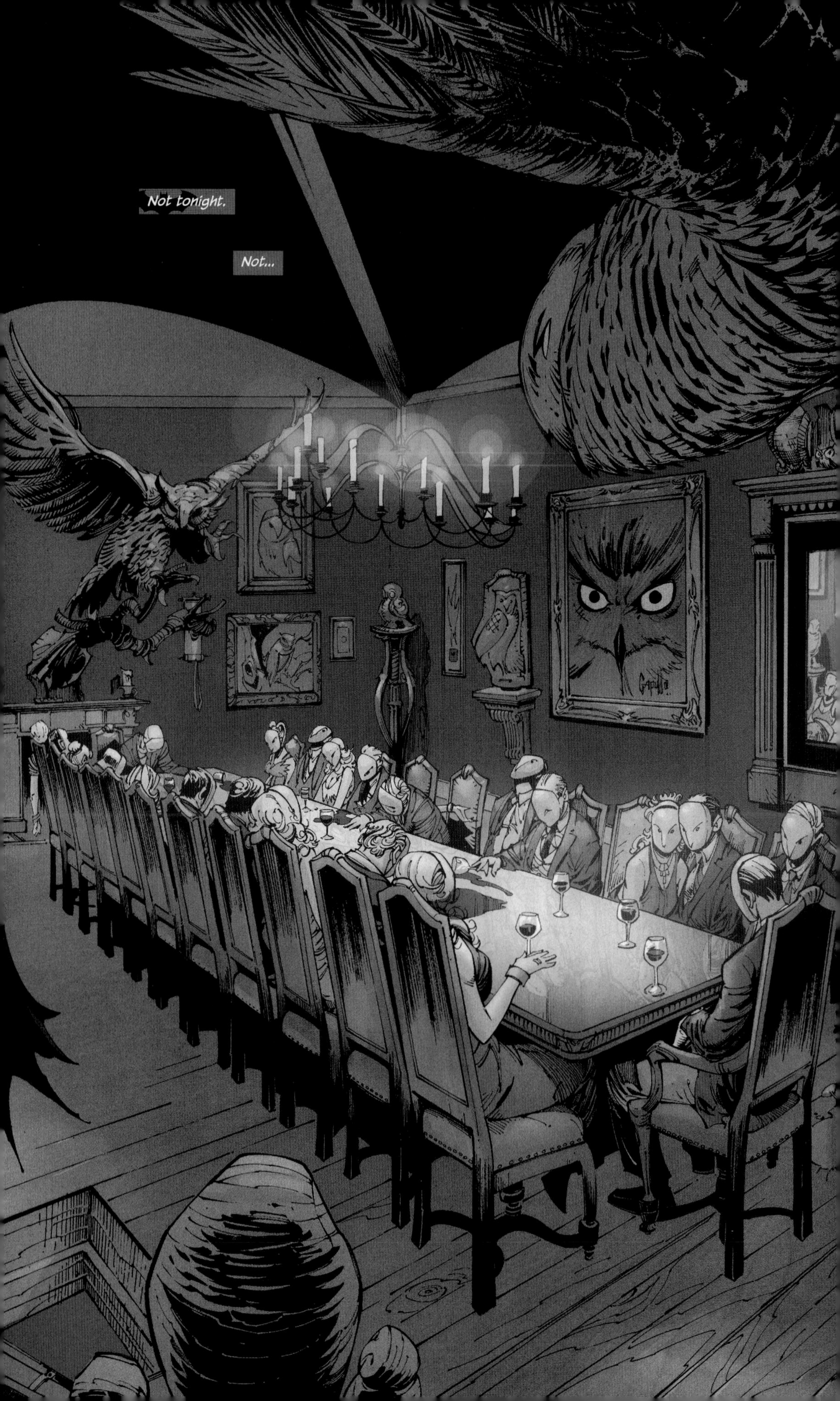
Not tonight.
Not...

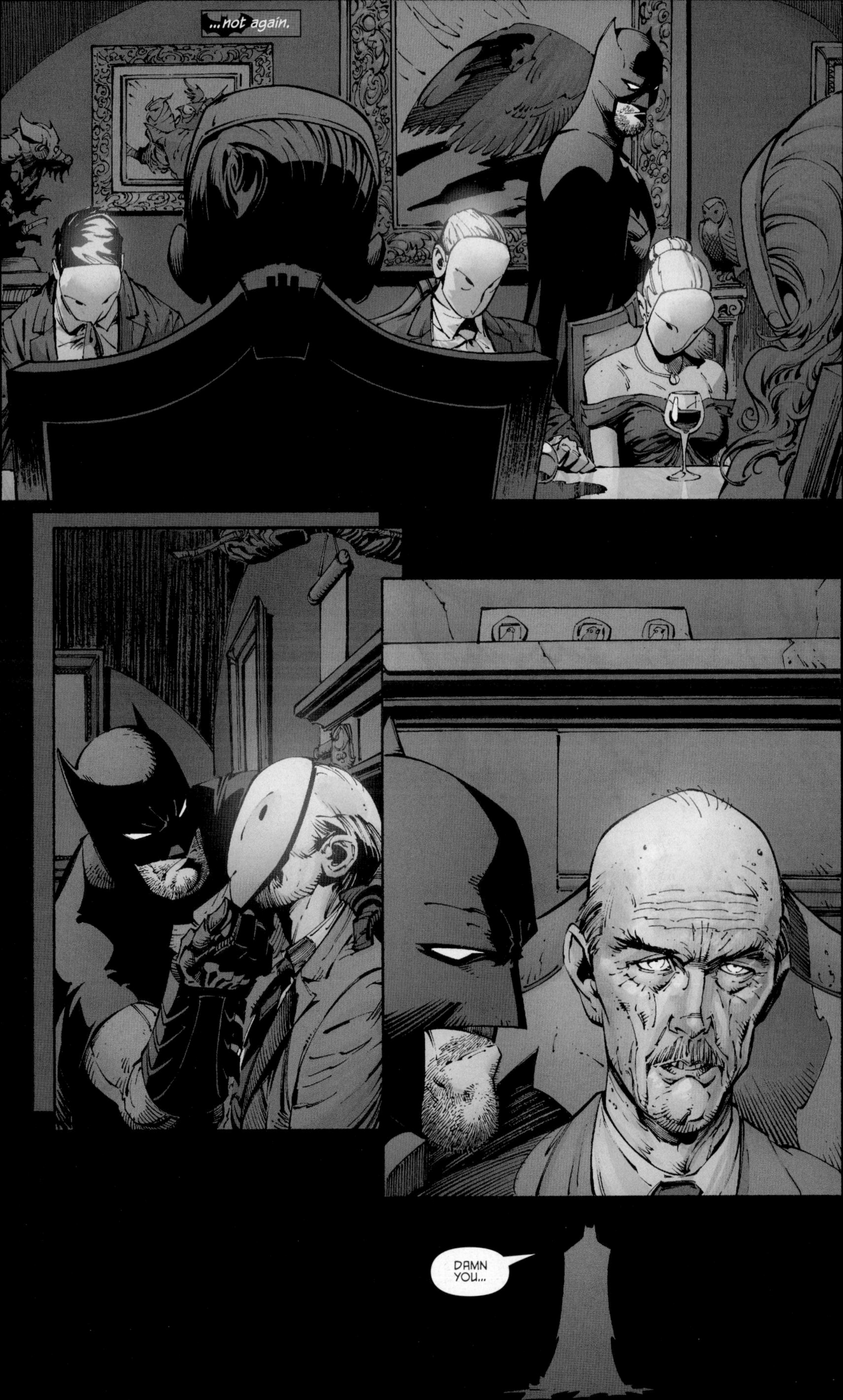
...not again.
DAMN YOU...

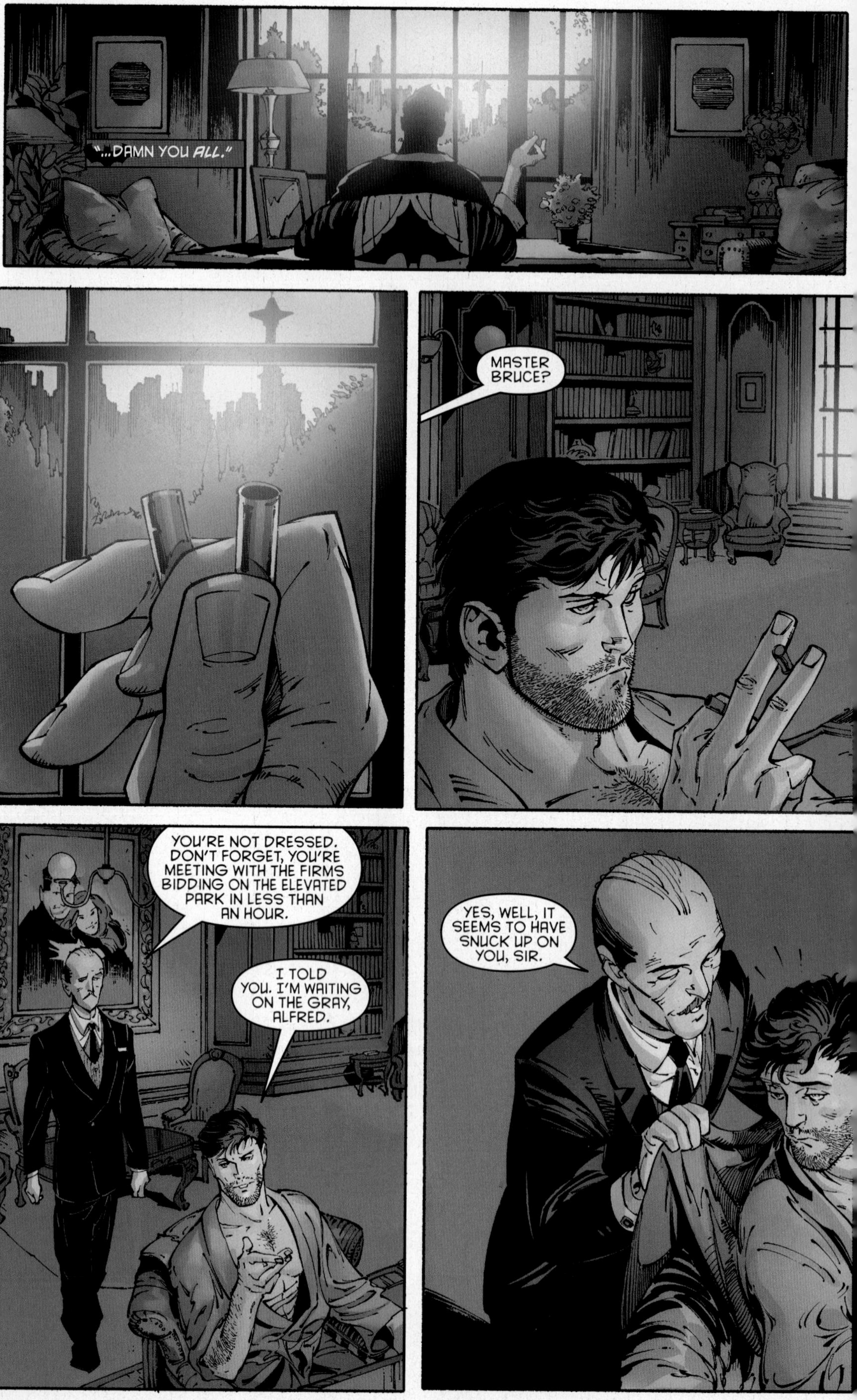
"...DAMN YOU *ALL*."
MASTER BRUCE?
YOU'RE NOT DRESSED. DON'T FORGET, YOU'RE MEETING WITH THE FIRMS BIDDING ON THE ELEVATED PARK IN LESS THAN AN HOUR.
I TOLD YOU. I'M WAITING ON THE GRAY, ALFRED.
YES, WELL, IT SEEMS TO HAVE SNUCK UP ON YOU, SIR.

SO WHY DON'T YOU GIVE ME THOSE MORBID THINGS SO I MAY RETURN THEM TO THEIR CASE, AND YOU CAN START THINKING ABOUT TREES AND PONDS AND A GREENER CITY.

IT DOESN'T *MAKE SENSE*, ALFRED. MEMBERS OF THE COURT, TAKING THEIR OWN LIVES, JUST LIKE THAT.

I RATHER THINK IT *DOES*, SIR. YOU'VE TAKEN THE CITY BACK FROM THEM.

THEN THERE'S THE MONEY. MONEY SIPHONED FROM THE DEAD MEMBERS' ACCOUNTS IN JUST THE LAST FEW WEEKS...IT FEELS MORE LIKE A SETUP. LIKE SUBTERFUGE.

YOU SAW THE AUTOPSIES, MASTER BRUCE. THE COURT MEMBERS ARE *QUITE DEAD.*

SOMETHING DOESN'T FIT ABOUT IT, ALFRED. THERE'S SOMETHING BEHIND IT. I CAN *FEEL* IT. SOMEONE CLOSE. CLOSE ALL ALONG.

THAT MAY BE, SIR. BUT THE ANSWERS WILL COME. YOU NOW KNOW THE IDENTITIES OF AT LEAST *SEVERAL* OF THE COURT OF OWLS' MAJOR FIGUREHEADS.

AND WHILE THEIR ORGANIZATION, AS YOU'VE DISCOVERED, IS CLEARLY MUCH *LARGER* THAN THIS ONE GROUPING, I'M CERTAIN YOU'LL EVENTUALLY BRING THEM ALL TO JUSTICE.

IF I MAY SPEAK FREELY, SIR, PERHAPS THE THING THAT DOESN'T FIT ABOUT THIS ENDING IS THAT IT *IS* AN ENDING.

I KNOW WHEN YOU WERE A BOY YOU THOUGHT YOU MIGHT FIND ANSWERS TO YOUR PARENTS' MURDER IN THE COURT OF OWLS, AND MY SUSPICION IS THAT PERHAPS YOU WERE HOPING YOU MIGHT FIND MORE ANSWERS *NOW.*

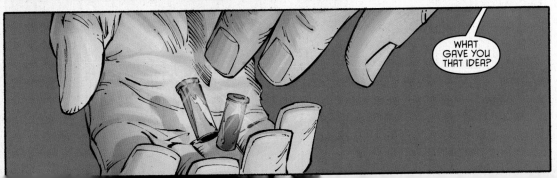

WHAT GAVE YOU THAT IDEA?

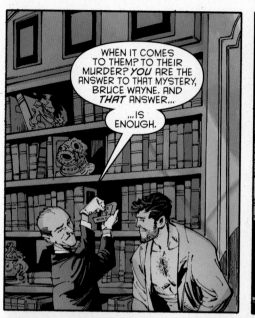

WHEN IT COMES TO THEM? TO THEIR MURDER? *YOU* ARE THE ANSWER TO THAT MYSTERY, BRUCE WAYNE. AND *THAT* ANSWER...

...IS ENOUGH.

NOW PUT ON THAT BLOODY SUIT AND GET OUT OF HERE!

ALL RIGHT, ALL RIGHT. I'M GOING.

JUST CALL ROBERTS AND TELL...

...TELL HIM...

TELL HIM *WHAT,* SIR?

TELL HIM...

...I WON'T BE ABLE TO MAKE IT.

BUT, SIR. WHERE ARE YOU--

I'M GOING AFTER HIM, ALFRED.

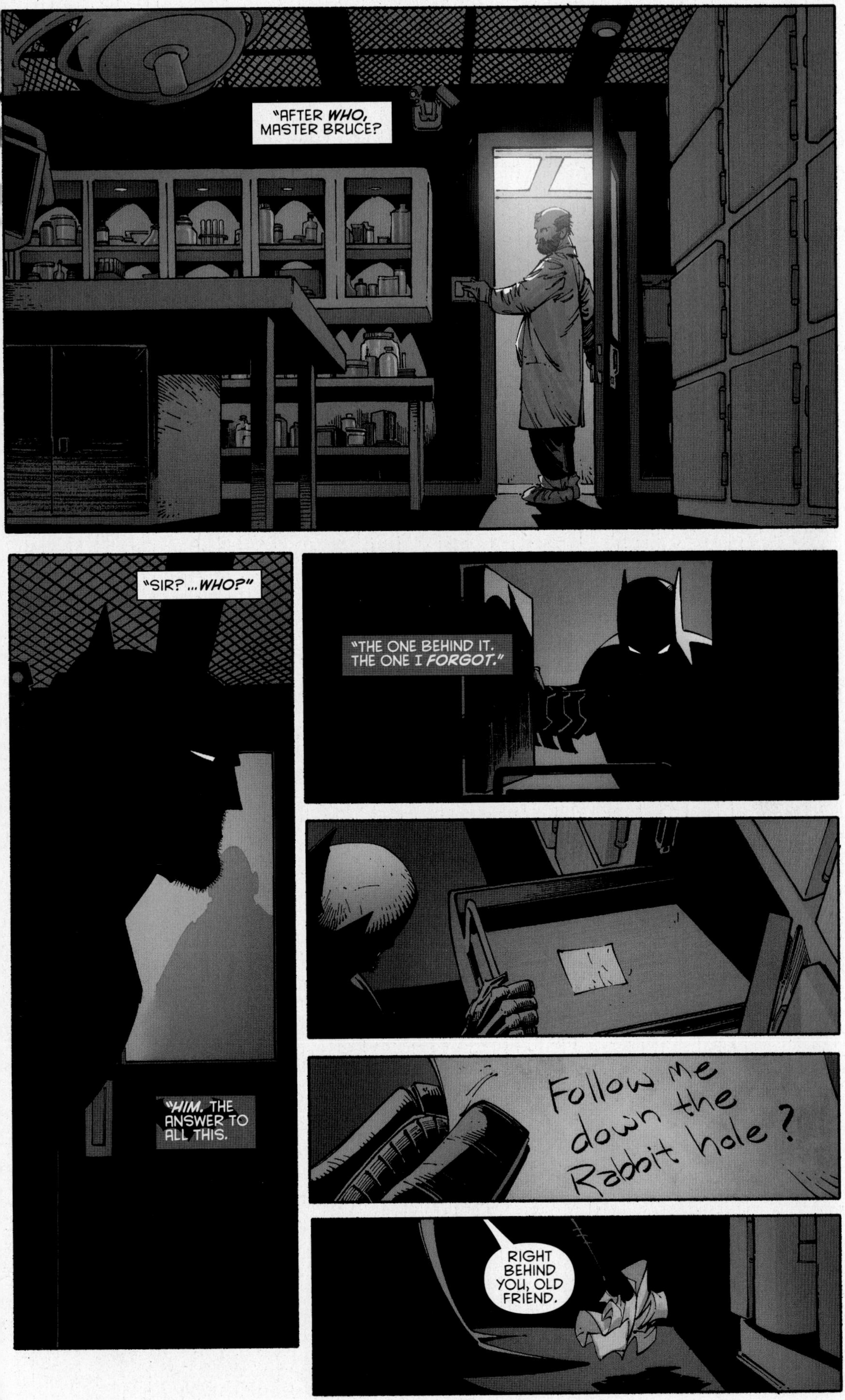
"AFTER WHO, MASTER BRUCE?
"SIR? ...WHO?"
"THE ONE BEHIND IT. THE ONE I FORGOT."
"HIM. THE ANSWER TO ALL THIS.
Follow me down the Rabbit hole?
RIGHT BEHIND YOU, OLD FRIEND.

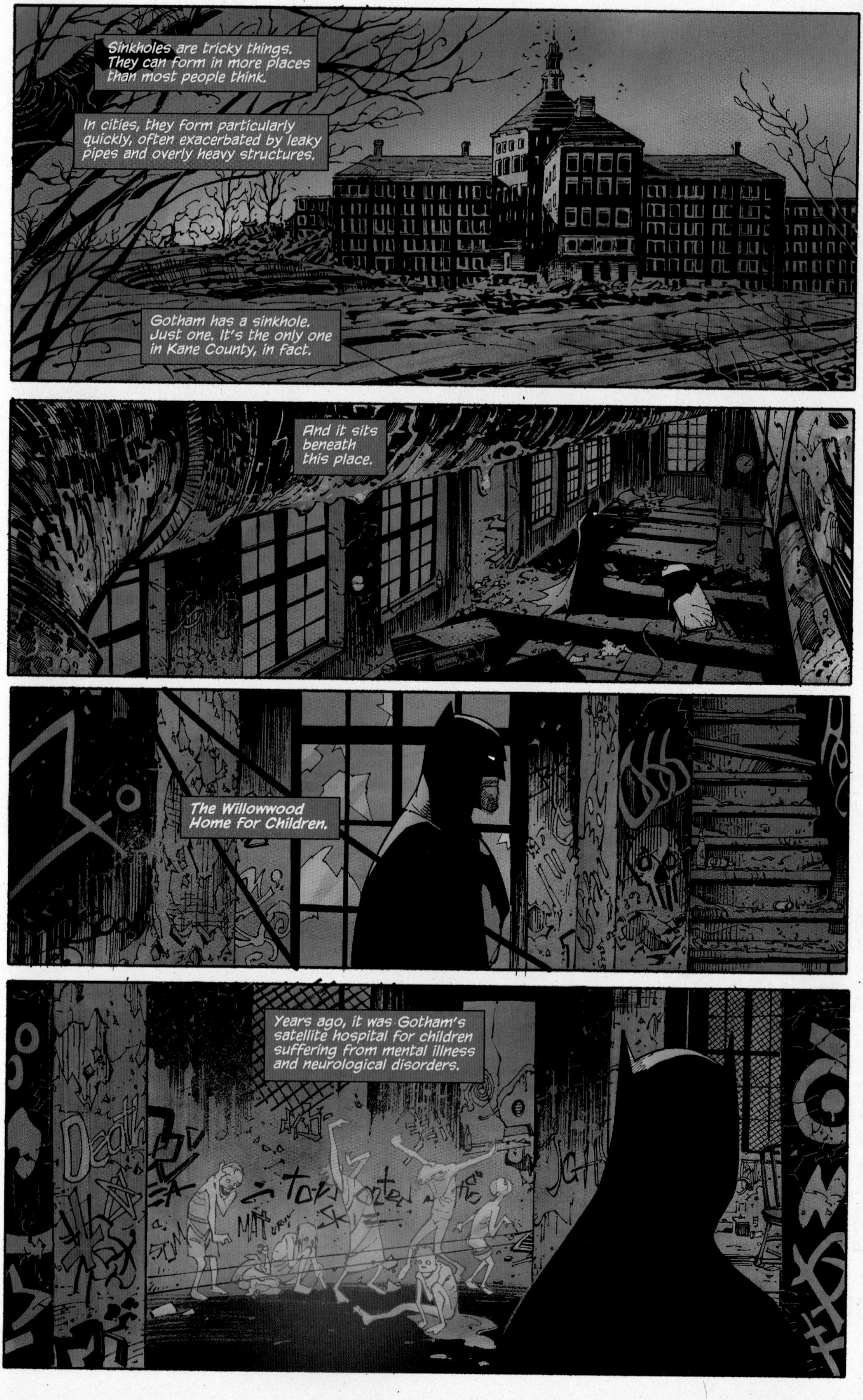
Sinkholes are tricky things. They can form in more places than most people think.
In cities, they form particularly quickly, often exacerbated by leaky pipes and overly heavy structures.
Gotham has a sinkhole. Just one. It's the only one in Kane County, in fact.
And it sits beneath this place.
The Willowwood Home for Children.
Years ago, it was Gotham's satellite hospital for children suffering from mental illness and neurological disorders.
Death

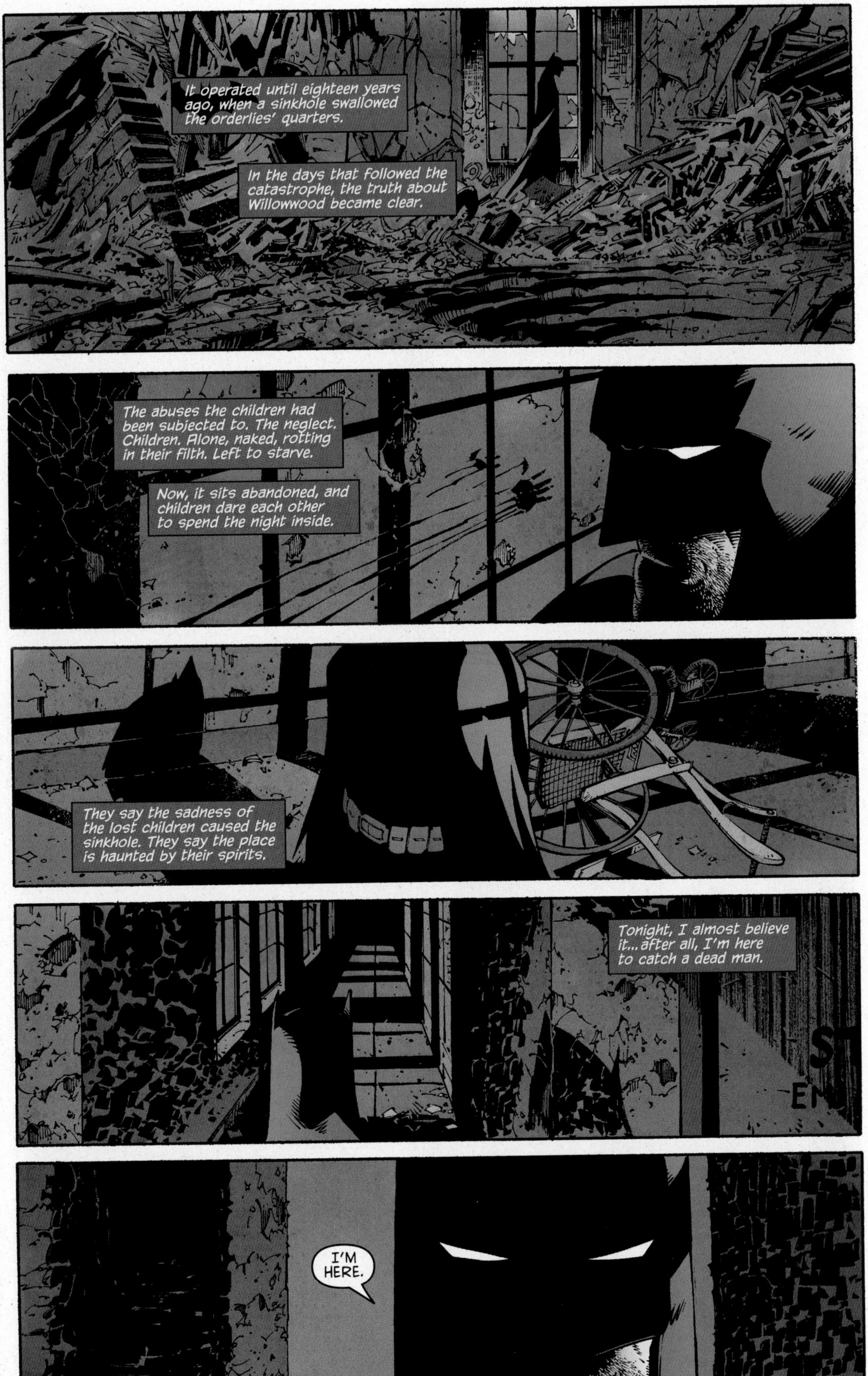
It operated until eighteen years ago, when a sinkhole swallowed the orderlies' quarters.
In the days that followed the catastrophe, the truth about Willowwood became clear.
The abuses the children had been subjected to. The neglect. Children. Alone, naked, rotting in their filth. Left to starve.
Now, it sits abandoned, and children dare each other to spend the night inside.
They say the sadness of the lost children caused the sinkhole. They say the place is haunted by their spirits.
Tonight, I almost believe it...after all, I'm here to catch a dead man.
I'M HERE.

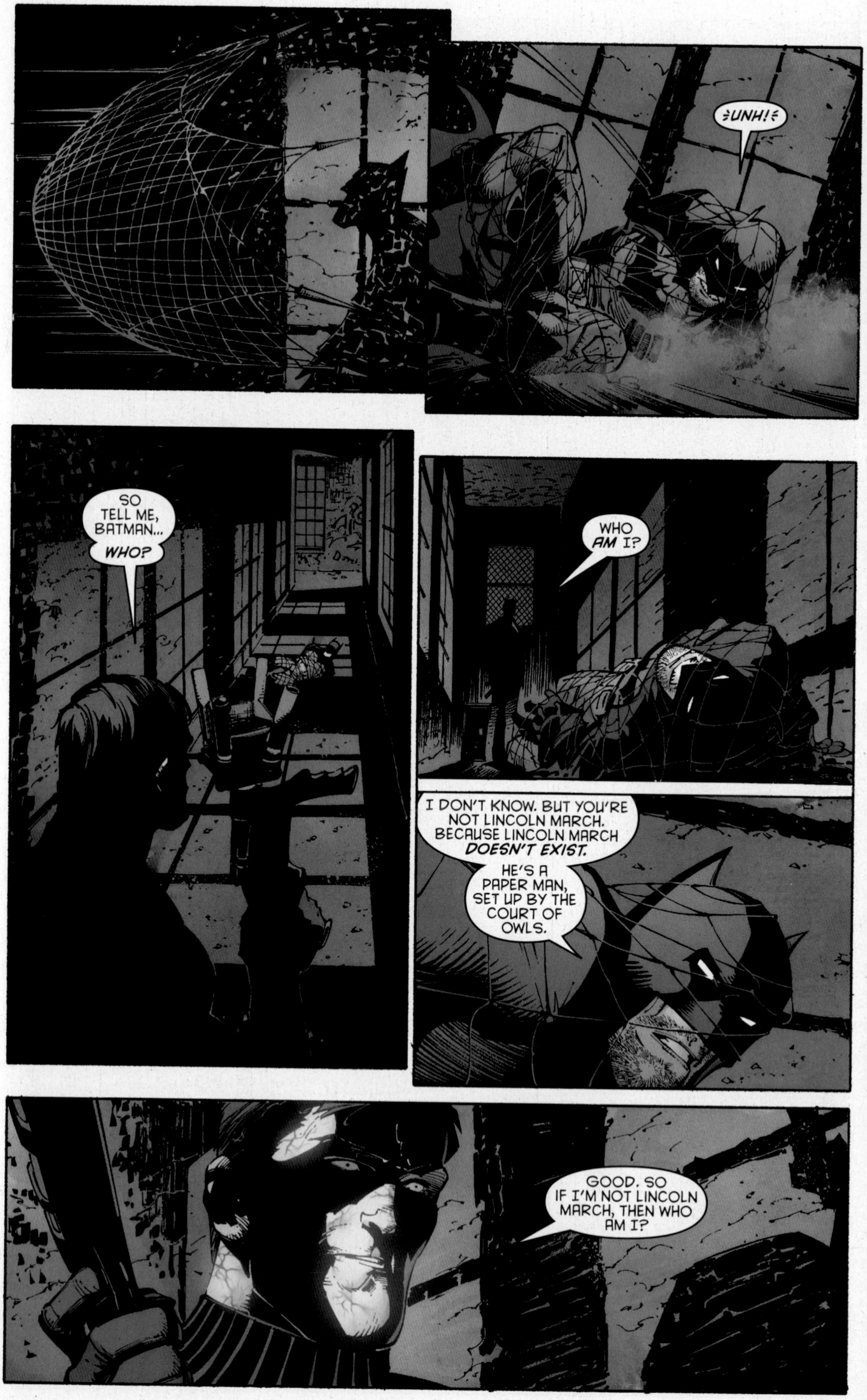
UNH!
SO TELL ME, BATMAN... WHO?
WHO AM I?
I DON'T KNOW. BUT YOU'RE NOT LINCOLN MARCH. BECAUSE LINCOLN MARCH DOESN'T EXIST.
HE'S A PAPER MAN, SET UP BY THE COURT OF OWLS.
GOOD. SO IF I'M NOT LINCOLN MARCH, THEN WHO AM I?

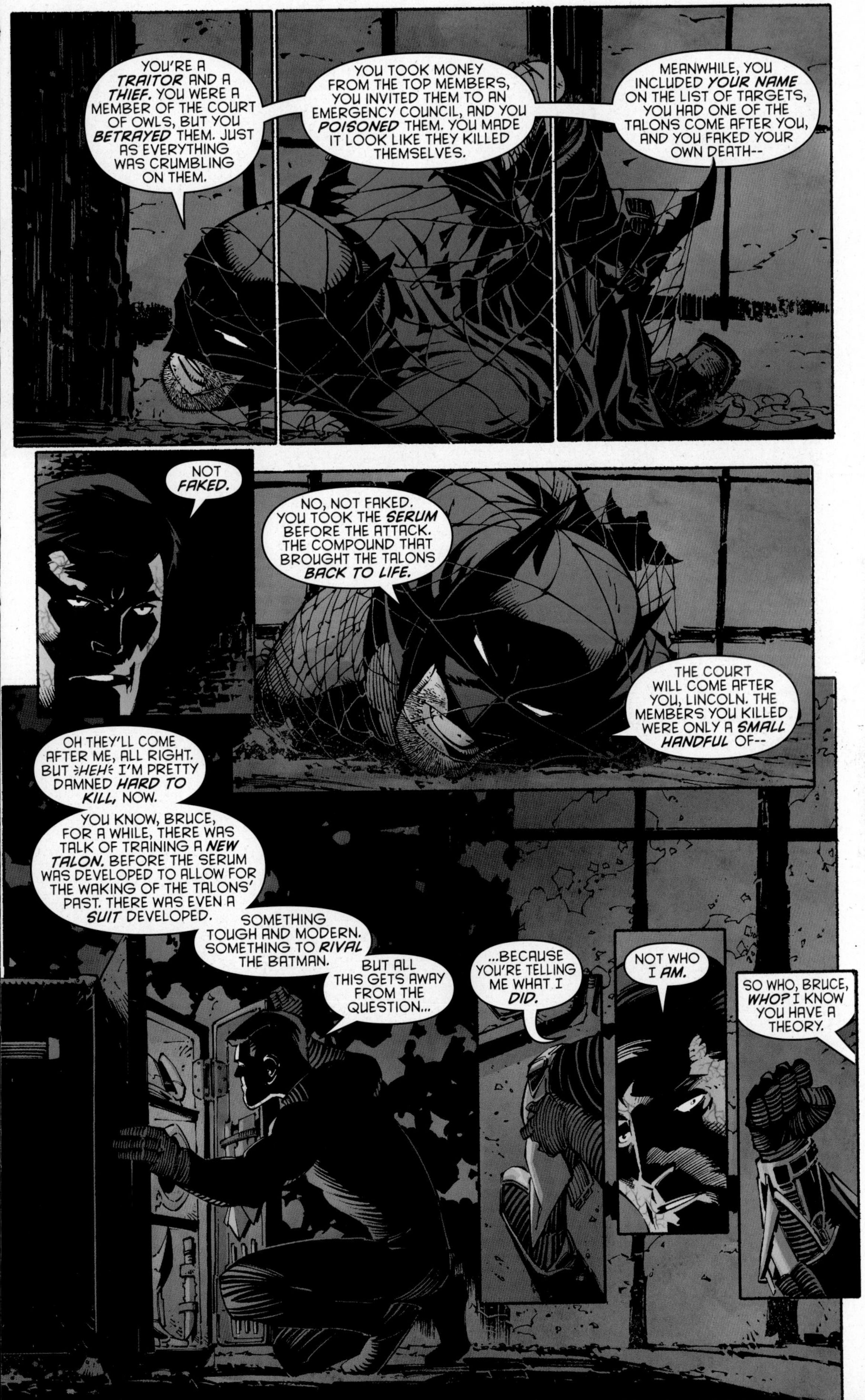
YOU'RE A TRAITOR AND A THIEF. YOU WERE A MEMBER OF THE COURT OF OWLS, BUT YOU BETRAYED THEM. JUST AS EVERYTHING WAS CRUMBLING ON THEM.
YOU TOOK MONEY FROM THE TOP MEMBERS, YOU INVITED THEM TO AN EMERGENCY COUNCIL, AND YOU POISONED THEM. YOU MADE IT LOOK LIKE THEY KILLED THEMSELVES.
MEANWHILE, YOU INCLUDED YOUR NAME ON THE LIST OF TARGETS, YOU HAD ONE OF THE TALONS COME AFTER YOU, AND YOU FAKED YOUR OWN DEATH--
NOT FAKED.
NO, NOT FAKED. YOU TOOK THE SERUM BEFORE THE ATTACK. THE COMPOUND THAT BROUGHT THE TALONS BACK TO LIFE.
THE COURT WILL COME AFTER YOU, LINCOLN. THE MEMBERS YOU KILLED WERE ONLY A SMALL HANDFUL OF--
OH THEY'LL COME AFTER ME, ALL RIGHT. BUT *HEH* I'M PRETTY DAMNED HARD TO KILL, NOW.
YOU KNOW, BRUCE, FOR A WHILE, THERE WAS TALK OF TRAINING A NEW TALON. BEFORE THE SERUM WAS DEVELOPED TO ALLOW FOR THE WAKING OF THE TALONS' PAST. THERE WAS EVEN A SUIT DEVELOPED.
SOMETHING TOUGH AND MODERN. SOMETHING TO RIVAL THE BATMAN.
BUT ALL THIS GETS AWAY FROM THE QUESTION...
...BECAUSE YOU'RE TELLING ME WHAT I DID.
NOT WHO I AM.
SO WHO, BRUCE, WHO? I KNOW YOU HAVE A THEORY.

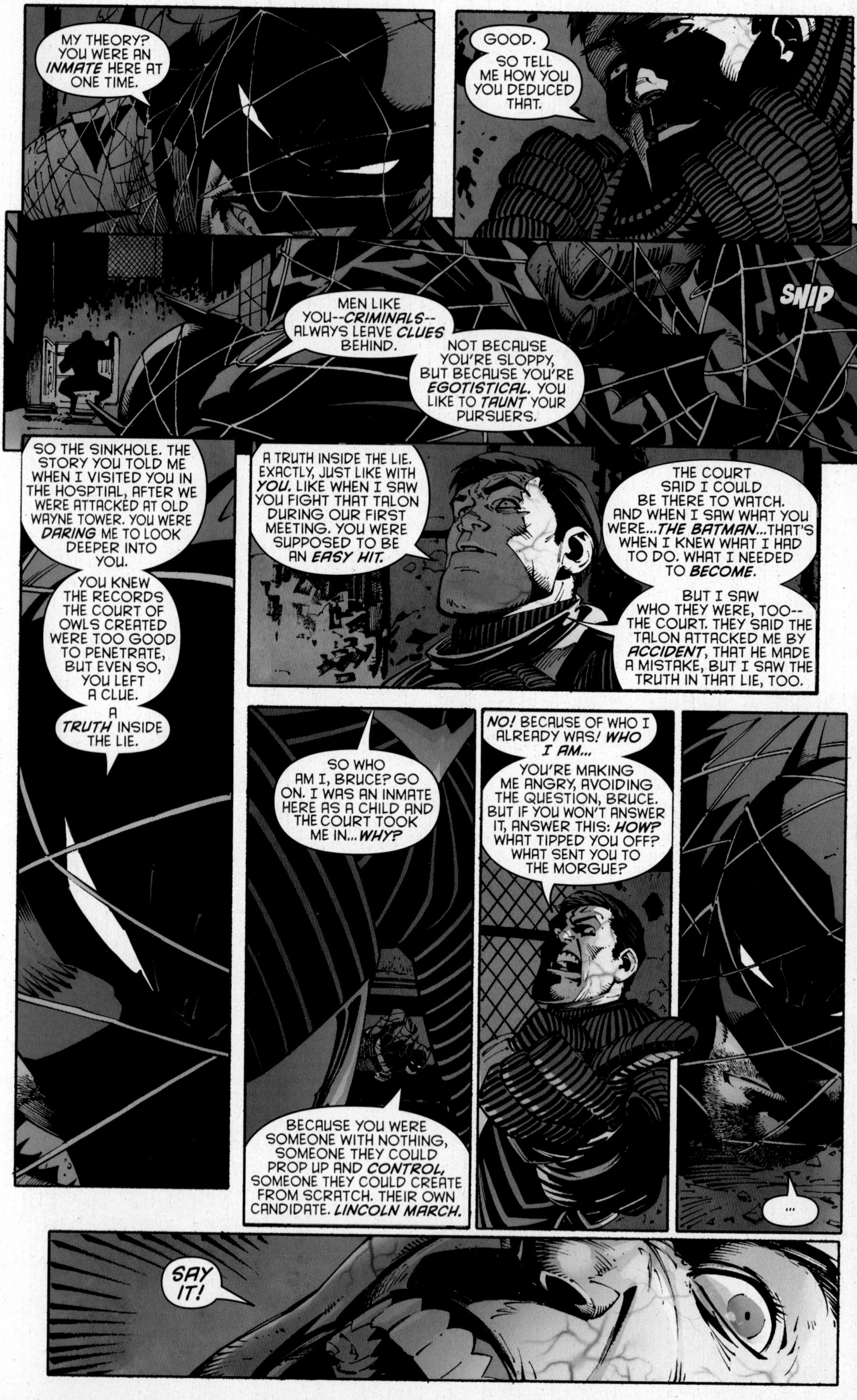
MY THEORY? YOU WERE AN INMATE HERE AT ONE TIME.
GOOD. SO TELL ME HOW YOU YOU DEDUCED THAT.
MEN LIKE YOU--CRIMINALS--ALWAYS LEAVE CLUES BEHIND.
NOT BECAUSE YOU'RE SLOPPY, BUT BECAUSE YOU'RE EGOTISTICAL. YOU LIKE TO TAUNT YOUR PURSUERS.
SNIP
SO THE SINKHOLE. THE STORY YOU TOLD ME WHEN I VISITED YOU IN THE HOSPTIAL, AFTER WE WERE ATTACKED AT OLD WAYNE TOWER. YOU WERE DARING ME TO LOOK DEEPER INTO YOU.
YOU KNEW THE RECORDS THE COURT OF OWLS CREATED WERE TOO GOOD TO PENETRATE, BUT EVEN SO, YOU LEFT A CLUE.
A TRUTH INSIDE THE LIE.
A TRUTH INSIDE THE LIE. EXACTLY, JUST LIKE WITH YOU. LIKE WHEN I SAW YOU FIGHT THAT TALON DURING OUR FIRST MEETING. YOU WERE SUPPOSED TO BE AN EASY HIT.
THE COURT SAID I COULD BE THERE TO WATCH. AND WHEN I SAW WHAT YOU WERE...THE BATMAN...THAT'S WHEN I KNEW WHAT I HAD TO DO. WHAT I NEEDED TO BECOME.
BUT I SAW WHO THEY WERE, TOO--THE COURT. THEY SAID THE TALON ATTACKED ME BY ACCIDENT, THAT HE MADE A MISTAKE, BUT I SAW THE TRUTH IN THAT LIE, TOO.
SO WHO AM I, BRUCE? GO ON. I WAS AN INMATE HERE AS A CHILD AND THE COURT TOOK ME IN...WHY?
BECAUSE YOU WERE SOMEONE WITH NOTHING, SOMEONE THEY COULD PROP UP AND CONTROL, SOMEONE THEY COULD CREATE FROM SCRATCH. THEIR OWN CANDIDATE. LINCOLN MARCH.
NO! BECAUSE OF WHO I ALREADY WAS! WHO I AM...
YOU'RE MAKING ME ANGRY, AVOIDING THE QUESTION, BRUCE. BUT IF YOU WON'T ANSWER IT, ANSWER THIS: HOW? WHAT TIPPED YOU OFF? WHAT SENT YOU TO THE MORGUE?
...
SAY IT!

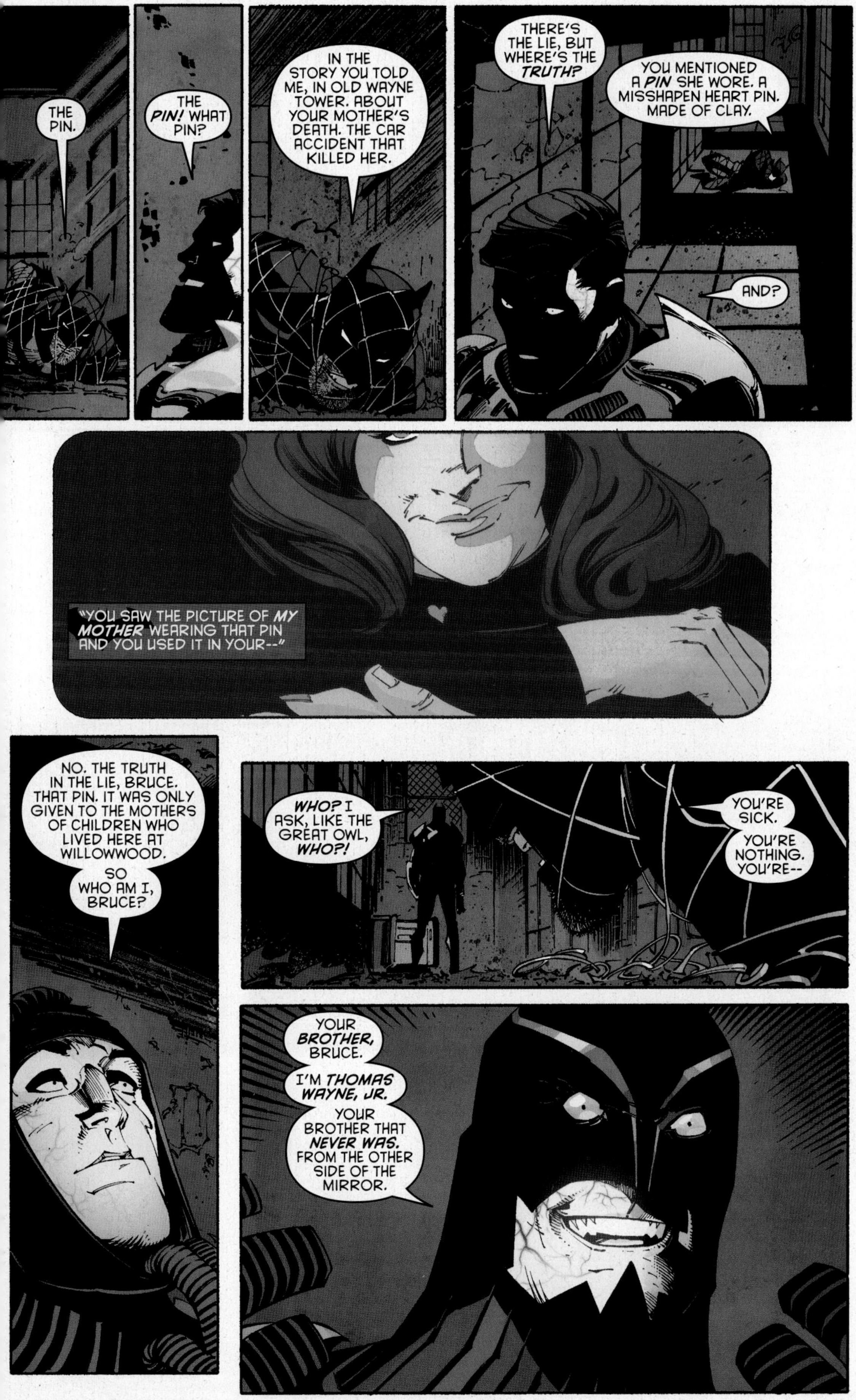
THE PIN.
THE PIN! WHAT PIN?
IN THE STORY YOU TOLD ME, IN OLD WAYNE TOWER. ABOUT YOUR MOTHER'S DEATH. THE CAR ACCIDENT THAT KILLED HER.
THERE'S THE LIE, BUT WHERE'S THE TRUTH?
YOU MENTIONED A PIN SHE WORE. A MISSHAPEN HEART PIN. MADE OF CLAY.
AND?
"YOU SAW THE PICTURE OF MY MOTHER WEARING THAT PIN AND YOU USED IT IN YOUR--"
NO. THE TRUTH IN THE LIE, BRUCE. THAT PIN. IT WAS ONLY GIVEN TO THE MOTHERS OF CHILDREN WHO LIVED HERE AT WILLOWWOOD.
SO WHO AM I, BRUCE?
WHO? I ASK, LIKE THE GREAT OWL, WHO?!
YOU'RE SICK.
YOU'RE NOTHING. YOU'RE--
YOUR BROTHER, BRUCE.
I'M THOMAS WAYNE, JR.
YOUR BROTHER THAT NEVER WAS. FROM THE OTHER SIDE OF THE MIRROR.

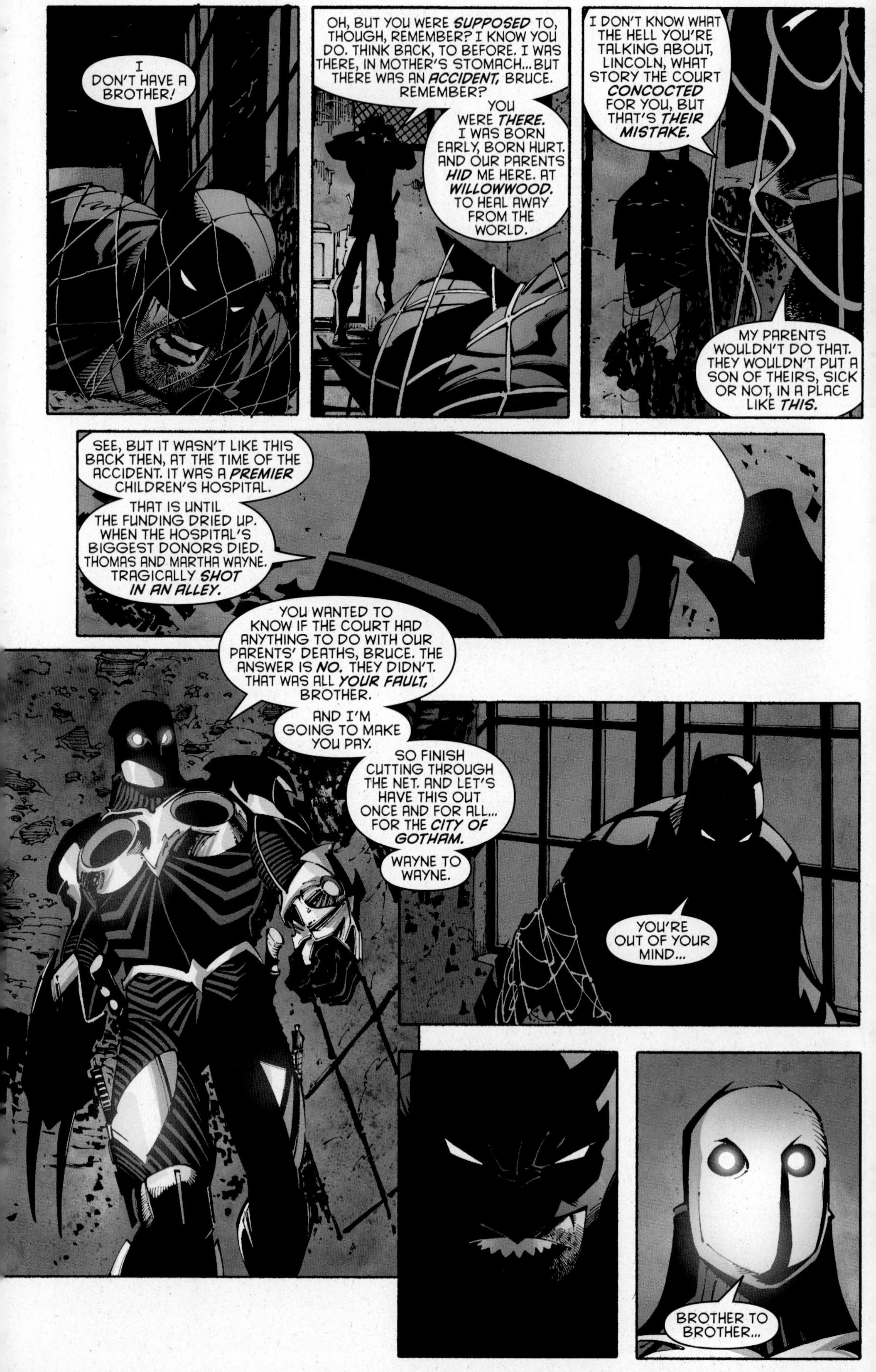
I DON'T HAVE A BROTHER!
OH, BUT YOU WERE SUPPOSED TO, THOUGH, REMEMBER? I KNOW YOU DO. THINK BACK, TO BEFORE. I WAS THERE, IN MOTHER'S STOMACH... BUT THERE WAS AN ACCIDENT, BRUCE. REMEMBER?
YOU WERE THERE. I WAS BORN EARLY, BORN HURT. AND OUR PARENTS HID ME HERE. AT WILLOWWOOD. TO HEAL AWAY FROM THE WORLD.
I DON'T KNOW WHAT THE HELL YOU'RE TALKING ABOUT, LINCOLN, WHAT STORY THE COURT CONCOCTED FOR YOU, BUT THAT'S THEIR MISTAKE.
MY PARENTS WOULDN'T DO THAT. THEY WOULDN'T PUT A SON OF THEIRS, SICK OR NOT, IN A PLACE LIKE THIS.
SEE, BUT IT WASN'T LIKE THIS BACK THEN, AT THE TIME OF THE ACCIDENT. IT WAS A PREMIER CHILDREN'S HOSPITAL.
THAT IS UNTIL THE FUNDING DRIED UP. WHEN THE HOSPITAL'S BIGGEST DONORS DIED. THOMAS AND MARTHA WAYNE. TRAGICALLY SHOT IN AN ALLEY.
YOU WANTED TO KNOW IF THE COURT HAD ANYTHING TO DO WITH OUR PARENTS' DEATHS, BRUCE. THE ANSWER IS NO. THEY DIDN'T. THAT WAS ALL YOUR FAULT, BROTHER.
AND I'M GOING TO MAKE YOU PAY.
SO FINISH CUTTING THROUGH THE NET. AND LET'S HAVE THIS OUT ONCE AND FOR ALL... FOR THE CITY OF GOTHAM.
WAYNE TO WAYNE.
YOU'RE OUT OF YOUR MIND...
BROTHER TO BROTHER...

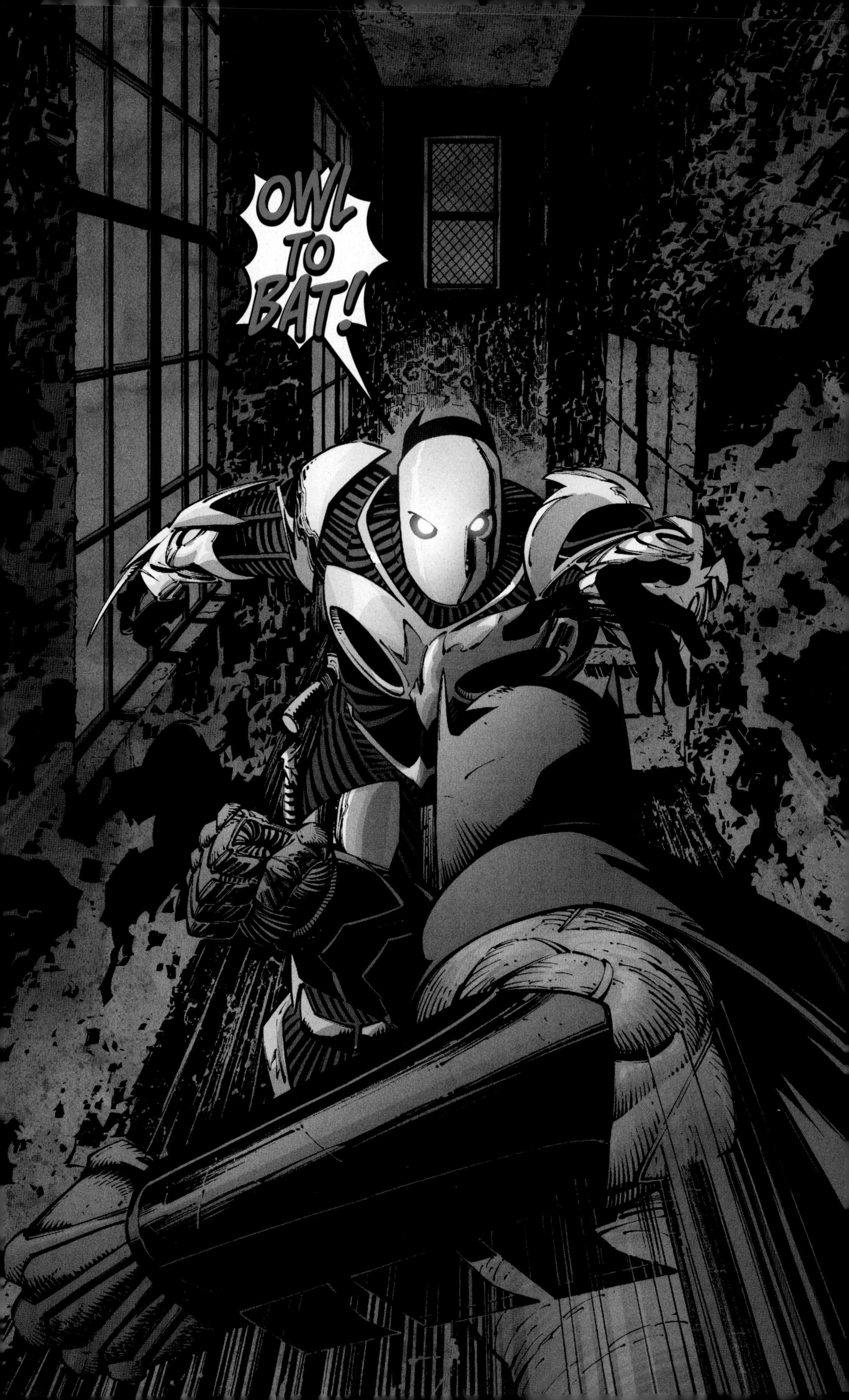
OWL TO BAT!

MY BROTHER'S KEEPER SCOTT SNYDER writer GREG CAPULLO penciller JONATHAN GLAPION inker

THE FALL OF THE HOUSE OF WAYNE SCOTT SNYDER & JAMES TYNION IV writers RAFAEL ALBUQUERQUE artist

cover by GREG CAPULLO and FCO PLASCENCIA

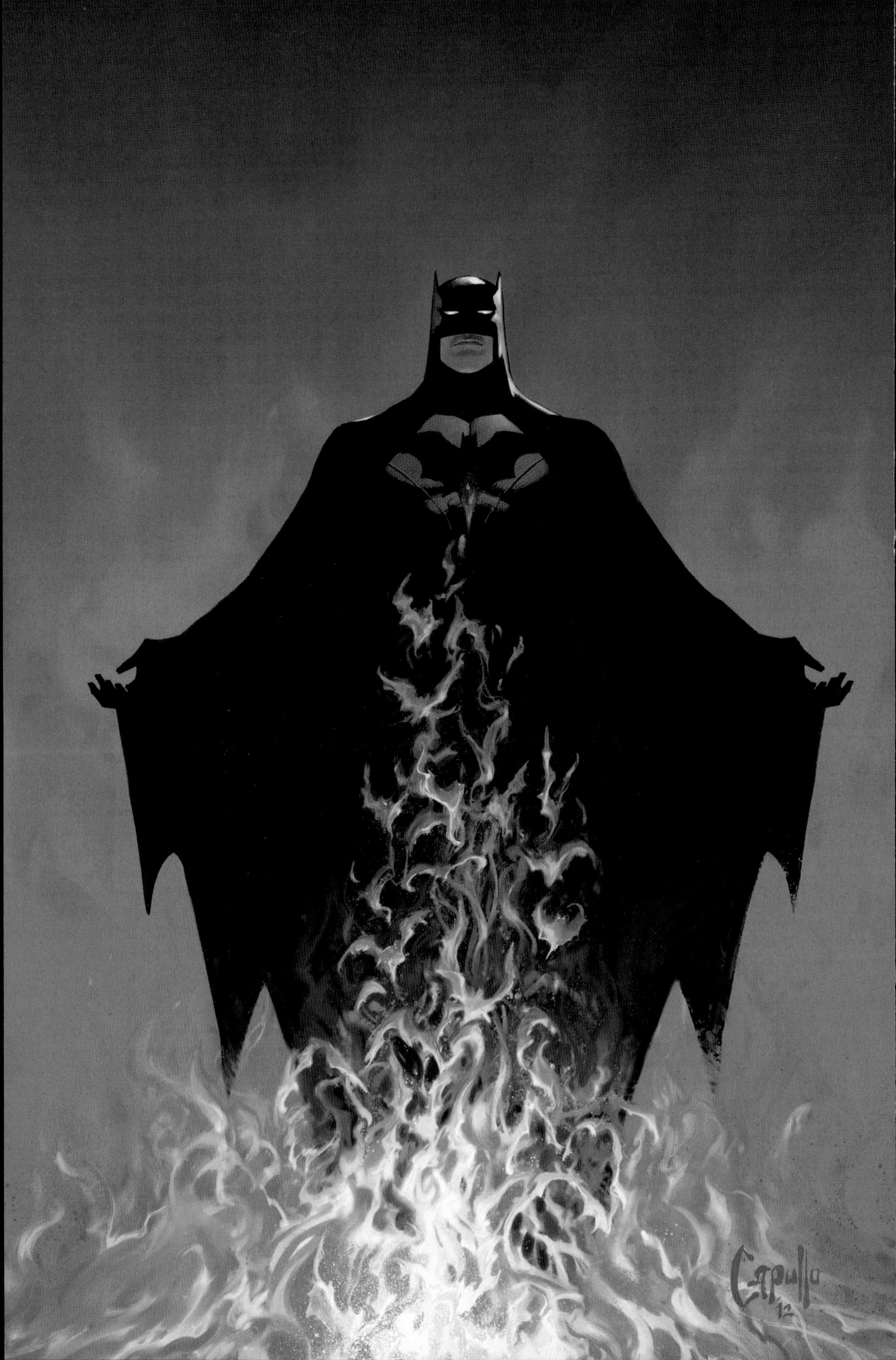

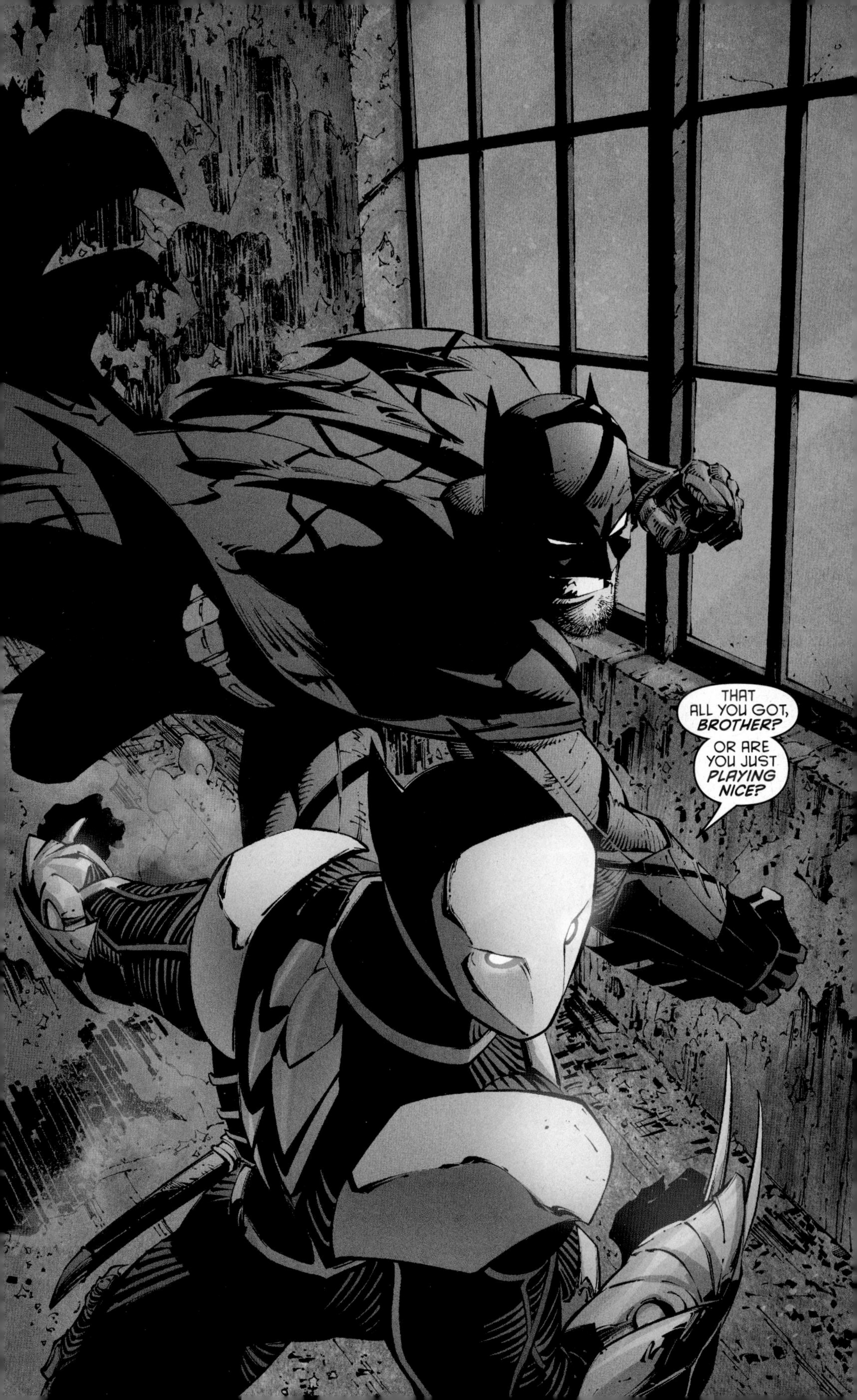
THAT ALL YOU GOT, *BROTHER?* OR ARE YOU JUST *PLAYING NICE?*

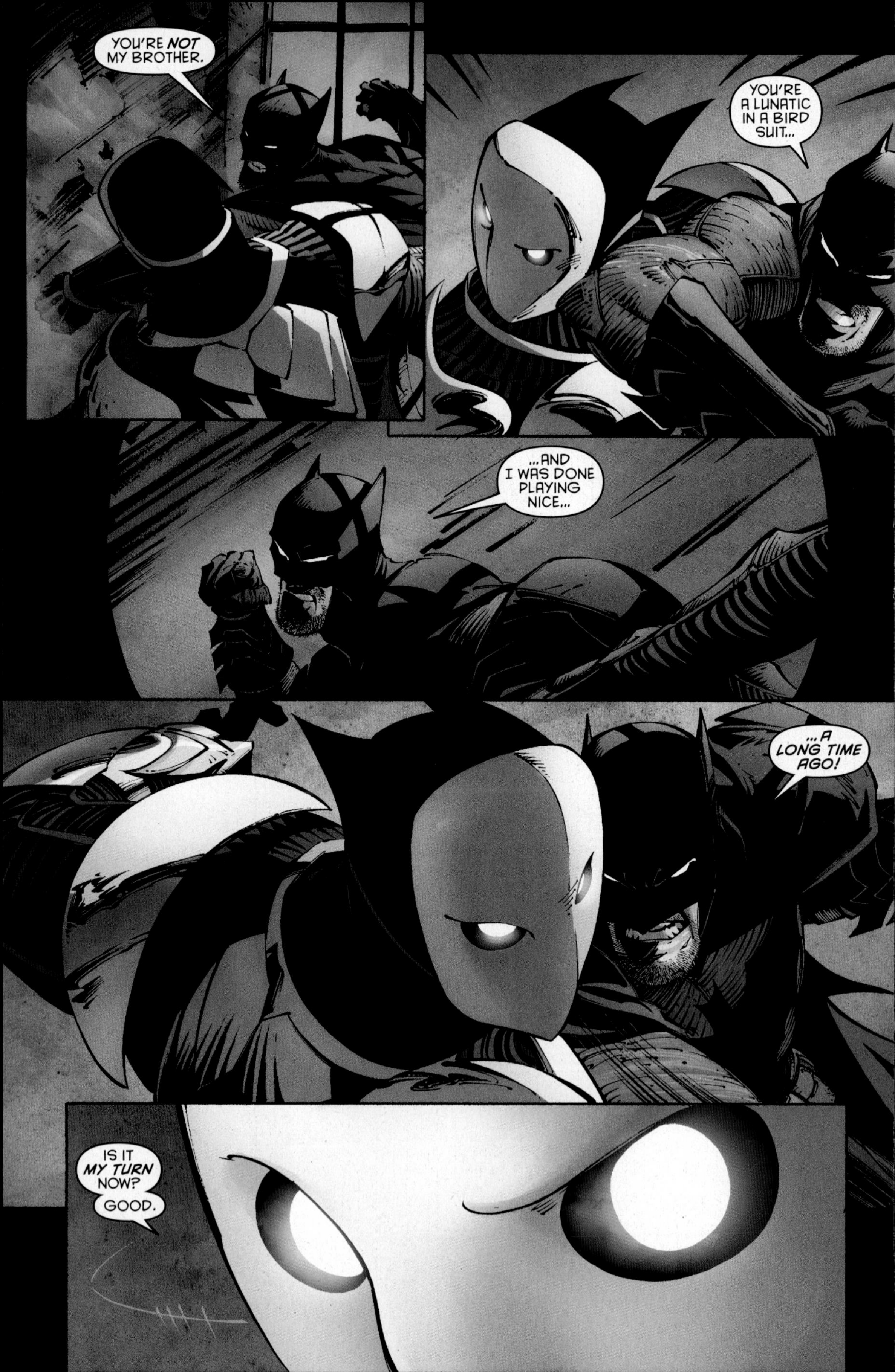
YOU'RE *NOT* MY BROTHER.
YOU'RE A LUNATIC IN A BIRD SUIT...
...AND I WAS DONE PLAYING NICE...
...A *LONG TIME AGO!*
IS IT *MY TURN* NOW?
GOOD.

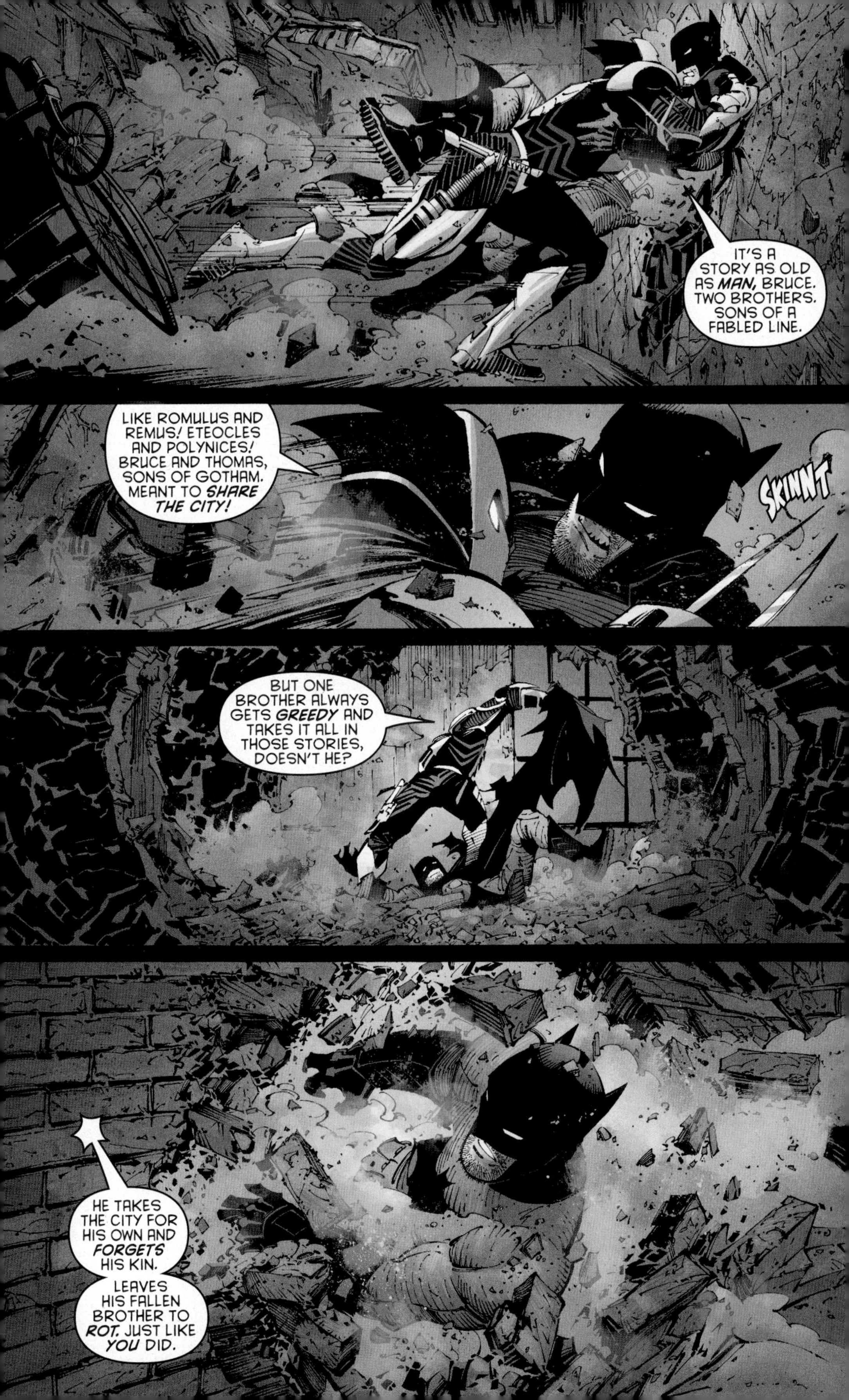
IT'S A STORY AS OLD AS MAN, BRUCE. TWO BROTHERS. SONS OF A FABLED LINE.
LIKE ROMULUS AND REMUS! ETEOCLES AND POLYNICES! BRUCE AND THOMAS, SONS OF GOTHAM. MEANT TO SHARE THE CITY!
SKINNT
BUT ONE BROTHER ALWAYS GETS GREEDY AND TAKES IT ALL IN THOSE STORIES, DOESN'T HE?
HE TAKES THE CITY FOR HIS OWN AND FORGETS HIS KIN.
LEAVES HIS FALLEN BROTHER TO ROT. JUST LIKE YOU DID.

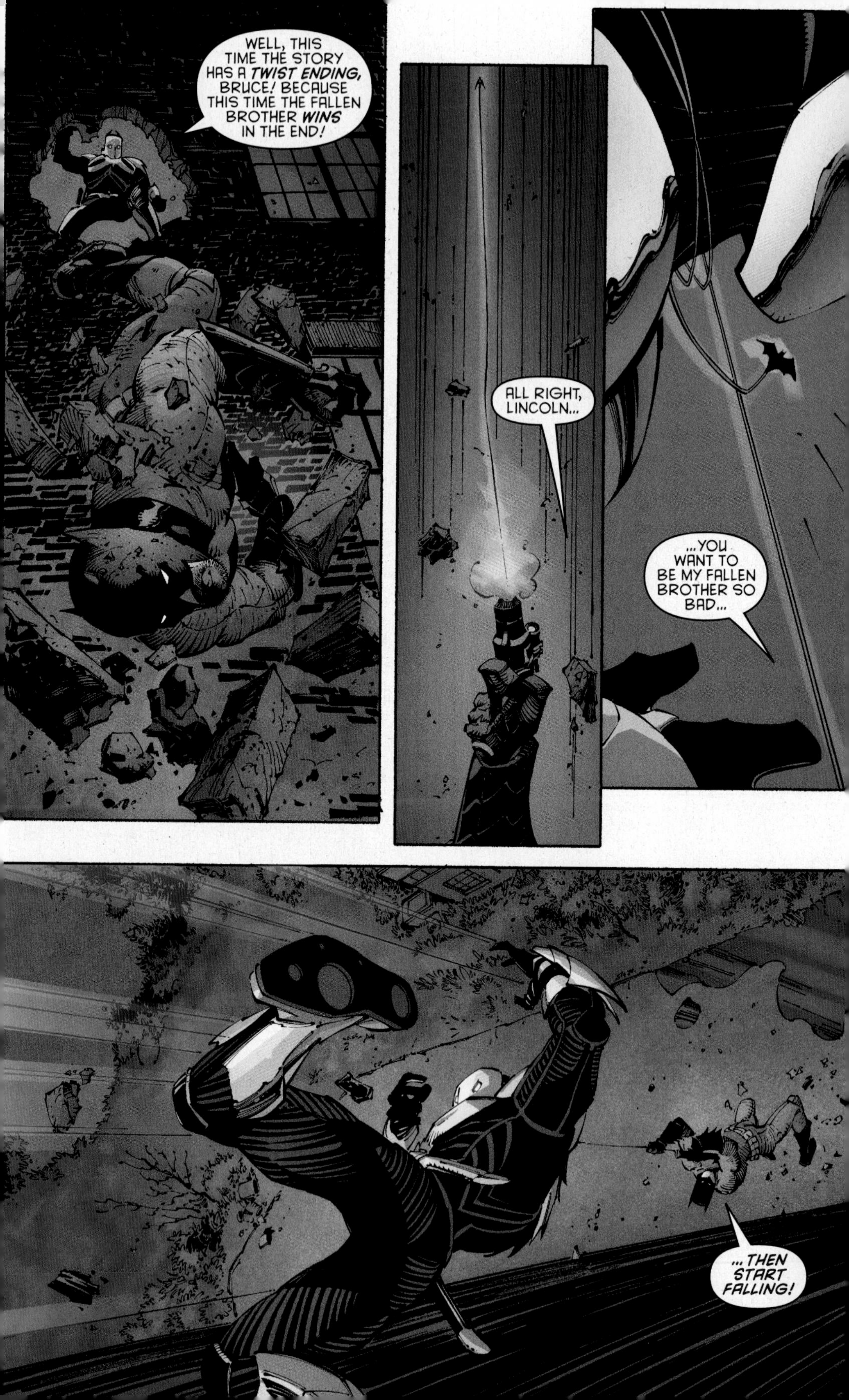
WELL, THIS TIME THE STORY HAS A TWIST ENDING, BRUCE! BECAUSE THIS TIME THE FALLEN BROTHER WINS IN THE END!
ALL RIGHT, LINCOLN...
...YOU WANT TO BE MY FALLEN BROTHER SO BAD...
...THEN START FALLING!

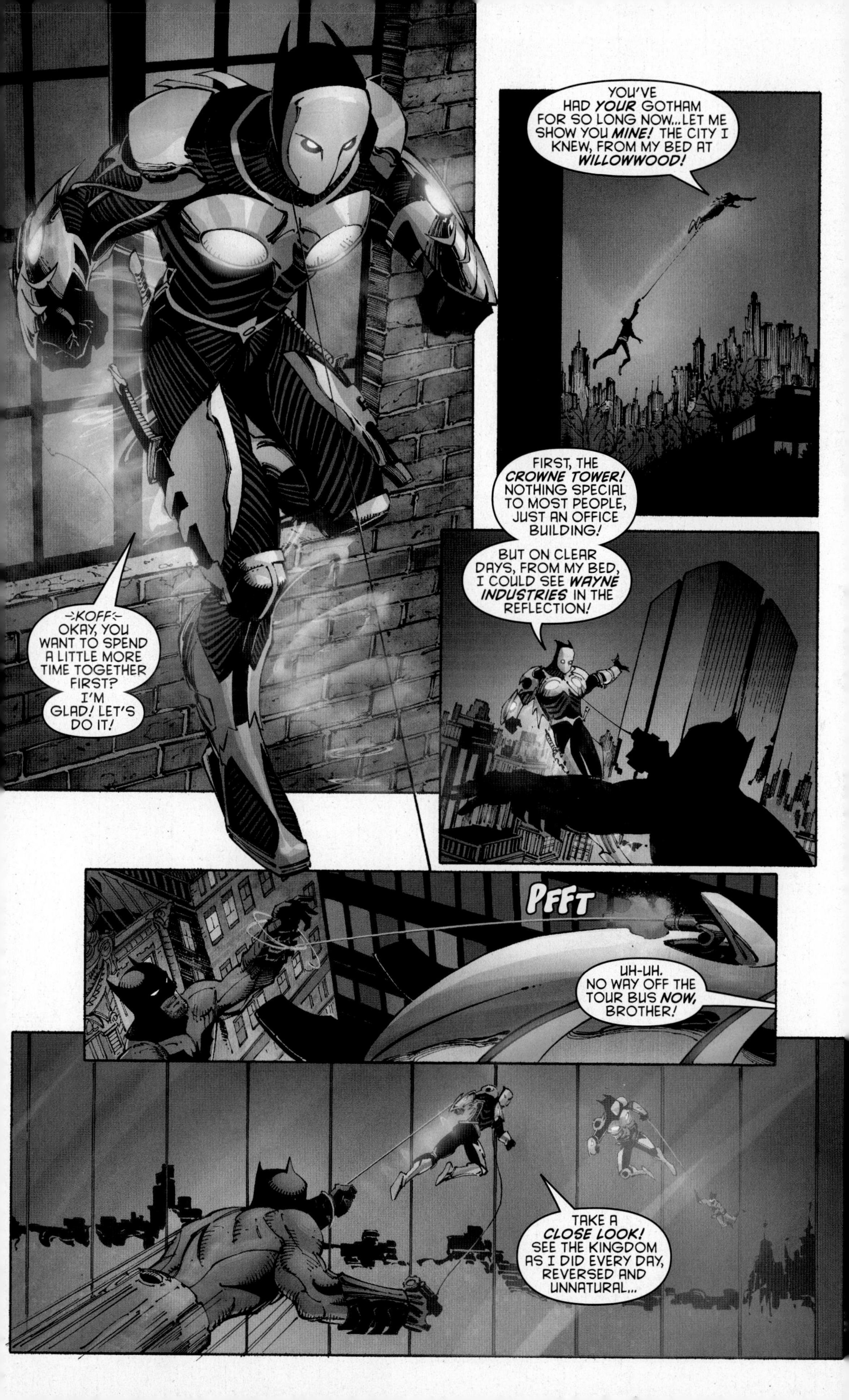
YOU'VE HAD YOUR GOTHAM FOR SO LONG NOW...LET ME SHOW YOU MINE! THE CITY I KNEW, FROM MY BED AT WILLOWWOOD!
FIRST, THE CROWNE TOWER! NOTHING SPECIAL TO MOST PEOPLE, JUST AN OFFICE BUILDING!
BUT ON CLEAR DAYS, FROM MY BED, I COULD SEE WAYNE INDUSTRIES IN THE REFLECTION!
-KOFF- OKAY, YOU WANT TO SPEND A LITTLE MORE TIME TOGETHER FIRST? I'M GLAD! LET'S DO IT!
PFFT
UH-UH. NO WAY OFF THE TOUR BUS NOW, BROTHER!
TAKE A CLOSE LOOK! SEE THE KINGDOM AS I DID EVERY DAY, REVERSED AND UNNATURAL...

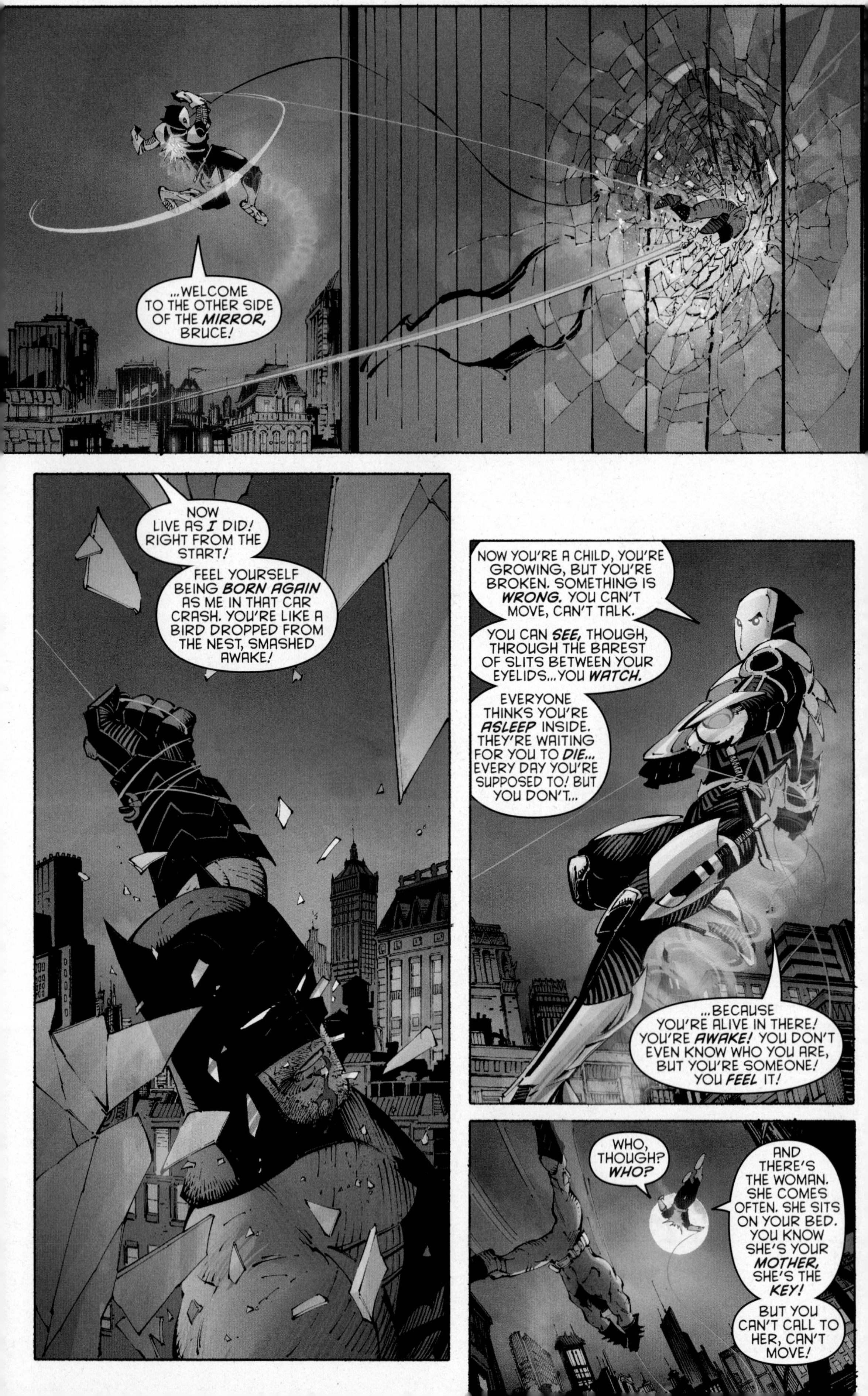

...WELCOME TO THE OTHER SIDE OF THE MIRROR, BRUCE!
NOW LIVE AS I DID! RIGHT FROM THE START!
FEEL YOURSELF BEING BORN AGAIN AS ME IN THAT CAR CRASH. YOU'RE LIKE A BIRD DROPPED FROM THE NEST, SMASHED AWAKE!
NOW YOU'RE A CHILD, YOU'RE GROWING, BUT YOU'RE BROKEN. SOMETHING IS WRONG. YOU CAN'T MOVE, CAN'T TALK.
YOU CAN SEE, THOUGH, THROUGH THE BAREST OF SLITS BETWEEN YOUR EYELIDS...YOU WATCH.
EVERYONE THINKS YOU'RE ASLEEP INSIDE. THEY'RE WAITING FOR YOU TO DIE... EVERY DAY YOU'RE SUPPOSED TO! BUT YOU DON'T...
...BECAUSE YOU'RE ALIVE IN THERE! YOU'RE AWAKE! YOU DON'T EVEN KNOW WHO YOU ARE, BUT YOU'RE SOMEONE! YOU FEEL IT!
WHO, THOUGH? WHO?
AND THERE'S THE WOMAN. SHE COMES OFTEN. SHE SITS ON YOUR BED. YOU KNOW SHE'S YOUR MOTHER, SHE'S THE KEY!
BUT YOU CAN'T CALL TO HER, CAN'T MOVE!

AND THEN ONE DAY, SHE'S ON THE TELEVISION IN YOUR ROOM. AND YOU *KNOW!*

A *REVELATION!* SUDDENLY YOU KNOW WHO YOU *ARE,* BECAUSE THE OWLS ARE THERE NOW, TOO. *WHISPERING* TO YOU AT NIGHT.

TELLING YOU WHAT YOU *ALREADY KNEW* ALL ALONG-- THAT YOU'RE *THOMAS WAYNE, JR.* A SON OF THE CITY!

YOUR PARENTS ARE GONE, BUT YOUR *BROTHER!* YOUR *BROTHER* IS STILL OUT THERE!

AND YOU THINK TO YOURSELF, *HE'LL* COME FOR ME, WON'T HE? HE'LL COME FOR ME...

YOU WAIT EVERY DAY, ALL DAY, THE OWLS WHISPERING AS THE HOUSE AROUND YOU GOES TO HELL.

BUT HE DOESN'T COME. ONLY THE *OWLS* COME, AND SOON ENOUGH, THEY SAVE YOU FROM THAT PLACE, THEY START TO HELP YOU HEAL, FIX YOUR MIND.

STILL YOU WAIT FOR YOUR BROTHER... HE *MUST* REMEMBER YOU! YOU KNOW HE DOES! BUT ALL YOU HEAR IS THE TIME PASSING. THE BIG CHURCH BELL RINGING... *BONG! BONG! BONG!*

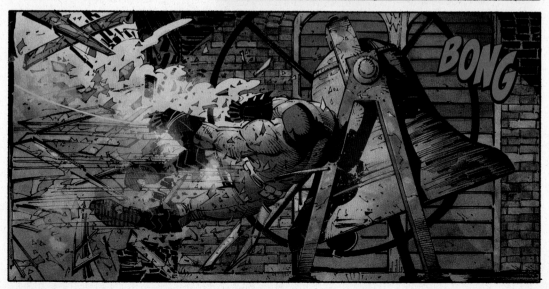

BONG

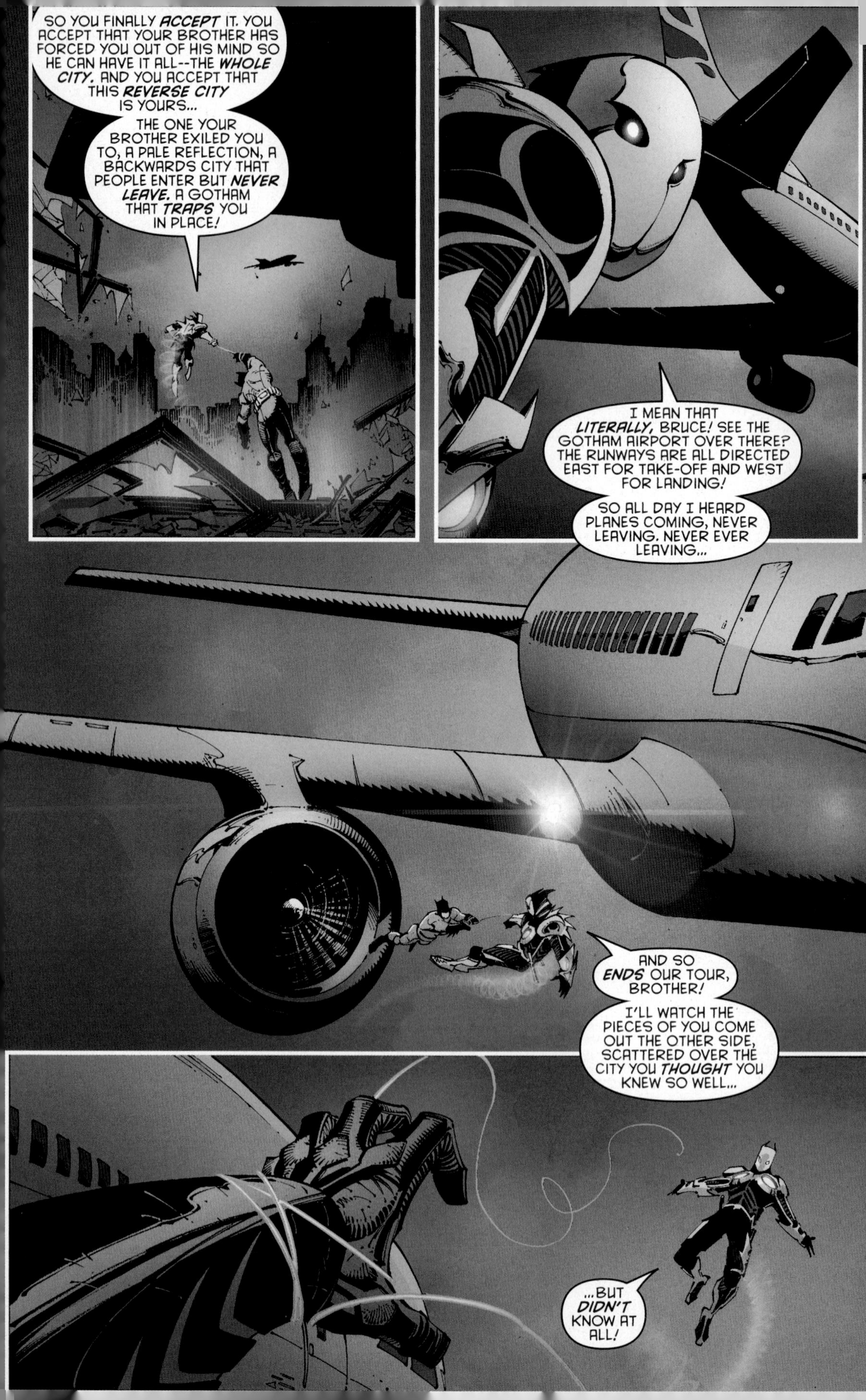
SO YOU FINALLY ACCEPT IT. YOU ACCEPT THAT YOUR BROTHER HAS FORCED YOU OUT OF HIS MIND SO HE CAN HAVE IT ALL--THE WHOLE CITY. AND YOU ACCEPT THAT THIS REVERSE CITY IS YOURS...
THE ONE YOUR BROTHER EXILED YOU TO, A PALE REFLECTION, A BACKWARDS CITY THAT PEOPLE ENTER BUT NEVER LEAVE. A GOTHAM THAT TRAPS YOU IN PLACE!
I MEAN THAT LITERALLY, BRUCE! SEE THE GOTHAM AIRPORT OVER THERE? THE RUNWAYS ARE ALL DIRECTED EAST FOR TAKE-OFF AND WEST FOR LANDING!
SO ALL DAY I HEARD PLANES COMING, NEVER LEAVING. NEVER EVER LEAVING...
AND SO ENDS OUR TOUR, BROTHER!
I'LL WATCH THE PIECES OF YOU COME OUT THE OTHER SIDE, SCATTERED OVER THE CITY YOU THOUGHT YOU KNEW SO WELL...
...BUT DIDN'T KNOW AT ALL!

IT'S OKAY, BRUCE! YOU CAN *LET GO* NOW!

YOUR BROTHER IS WATCHING OVER YOU. JUST AS HE *ALWAYS* HAS.

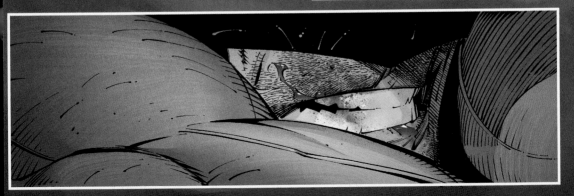

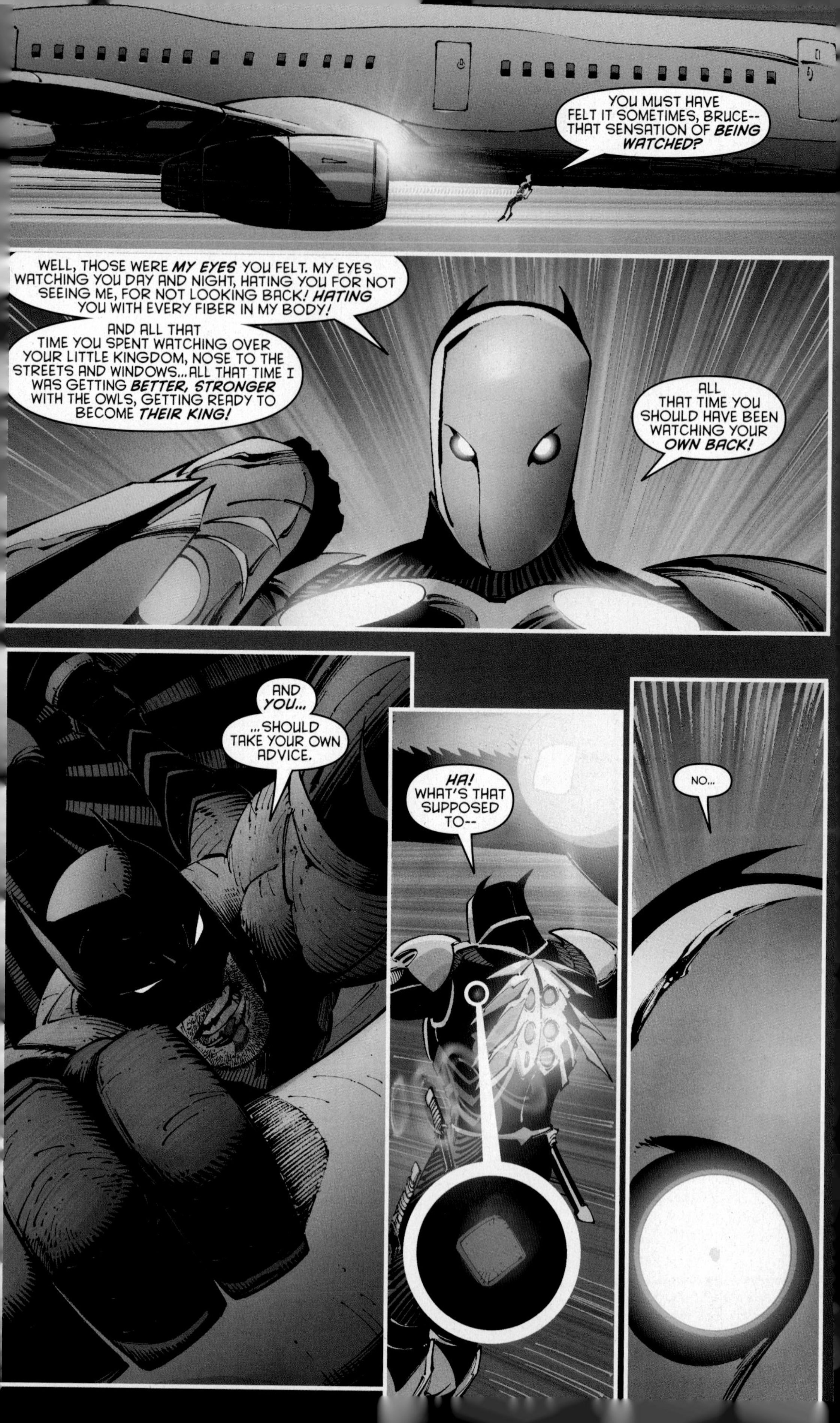
YOU MUST HAVE FELT IT SOMETIMES, BRUCE--THAT SENSATION OF *BEING WATCHED?*
WELL, THOSE WERE *MY EYES* YOU FELT. MY EYES WATCHING YOU DAY AND NIGHT, HATING YOU FOR NOT SEEING ME, FOR NOT LOOKING BACK! *HATING* YOU WITH EVERY FIBER IN MY BODY!
AND ALL THAT TIME YOU SPENT WATCHING OVER YOUR LITTLE KINGDOM, NOSE TO THE STREETS AND WINDOWS...ALL THAT TIME I WAS GETTING *BETTER, STRONGER* WITH THE OWLS, GETTING READY TO BECOME *THEIR KING!*
ALL THAT TIME YOU SHOULD HAVE BEEN WATCHING YOUR *OWN BACK!*
AND *YOU...*
...SHOULD TAKE YOUR OWN ADVICE.
HA! WHAT'S THAT SUPPOSED TO--
NO...

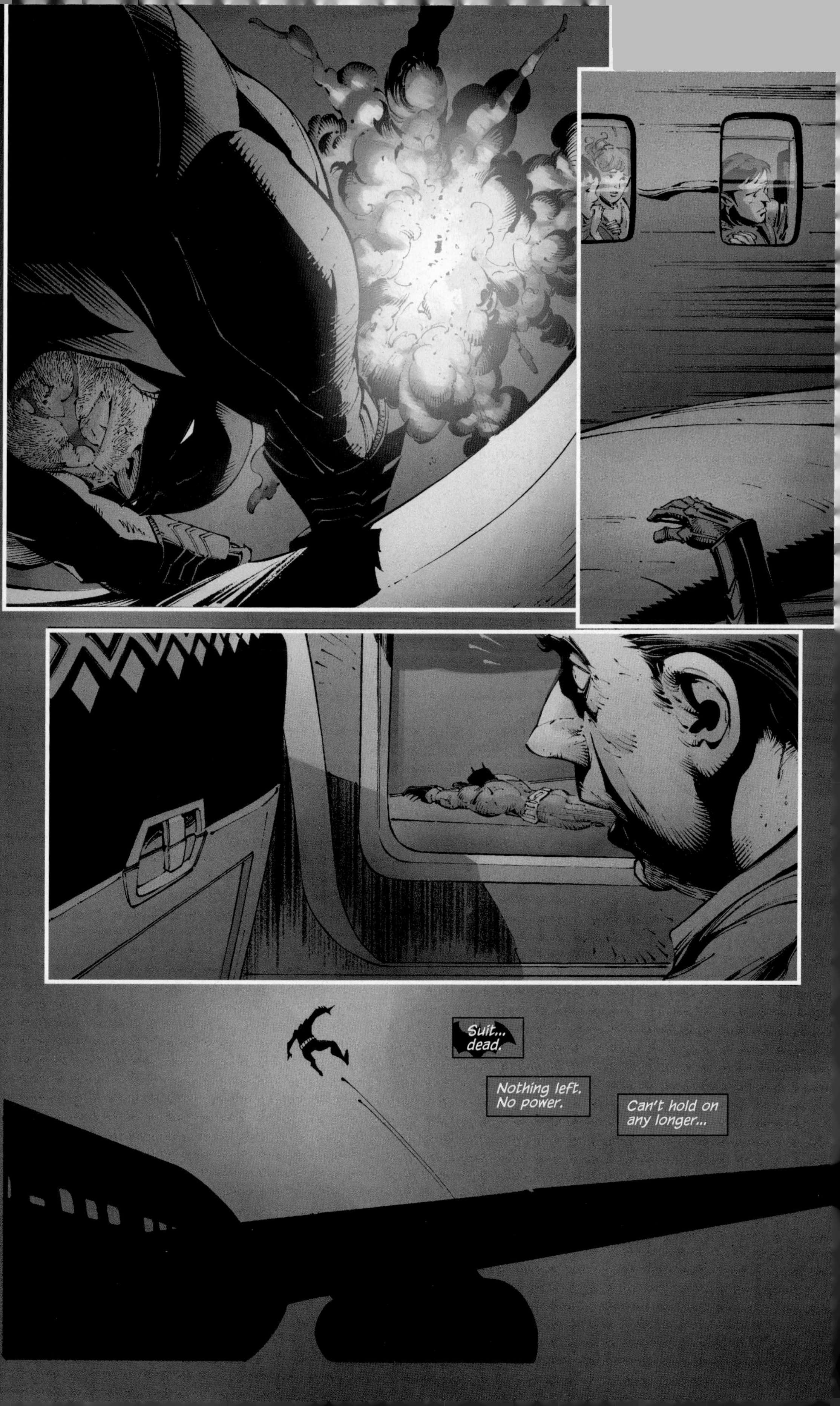
Suit... dead.
Nothing left. No power.
Can't hold on any longer...

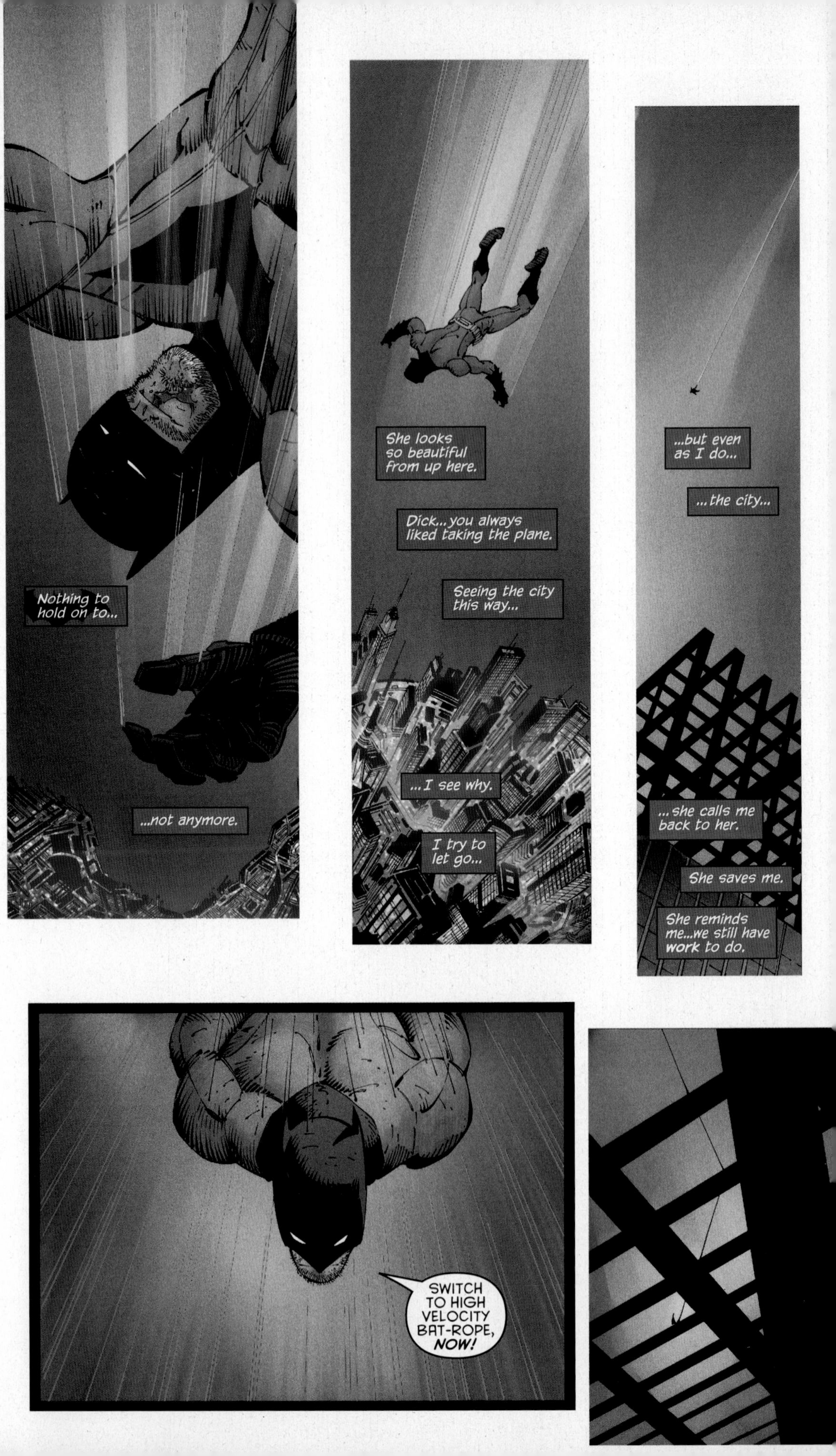
Nothing to hold on to...
...not anymore.
She looks so beautiful from up here.
Dick... you always liked taking the plane.
Seeing the city this way...
...I see why.
I try to let go...
...but even as I do...
...the city...
...she calls me back to her.
She saves me.
She reminds me...we still have work to do.
SWITCH TO HIGH VELOCITY BAT-ROPE, NOW!

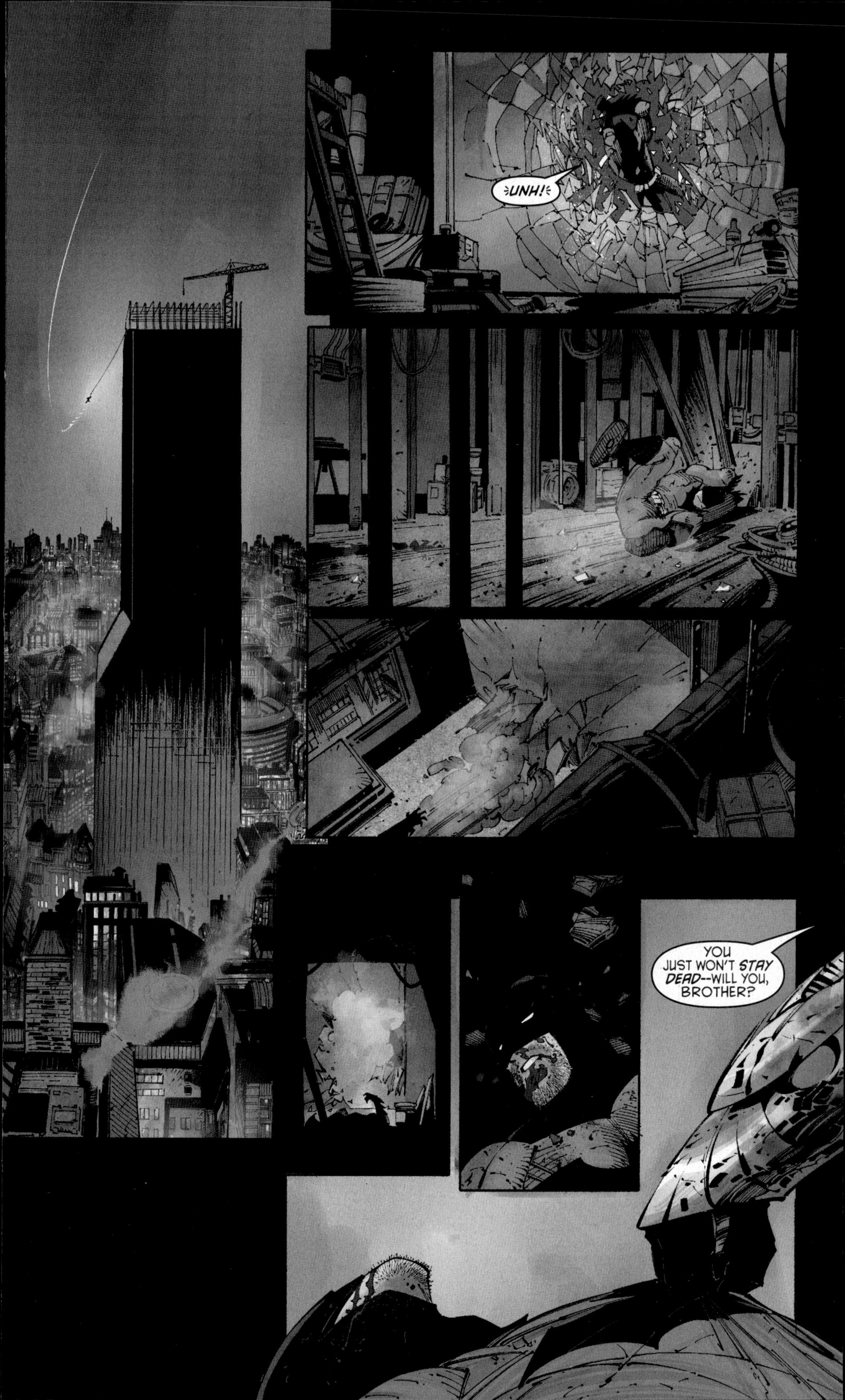
UNH!
YOU JUST WON'T STAY DEAD--WILL YOU, BROTHER?

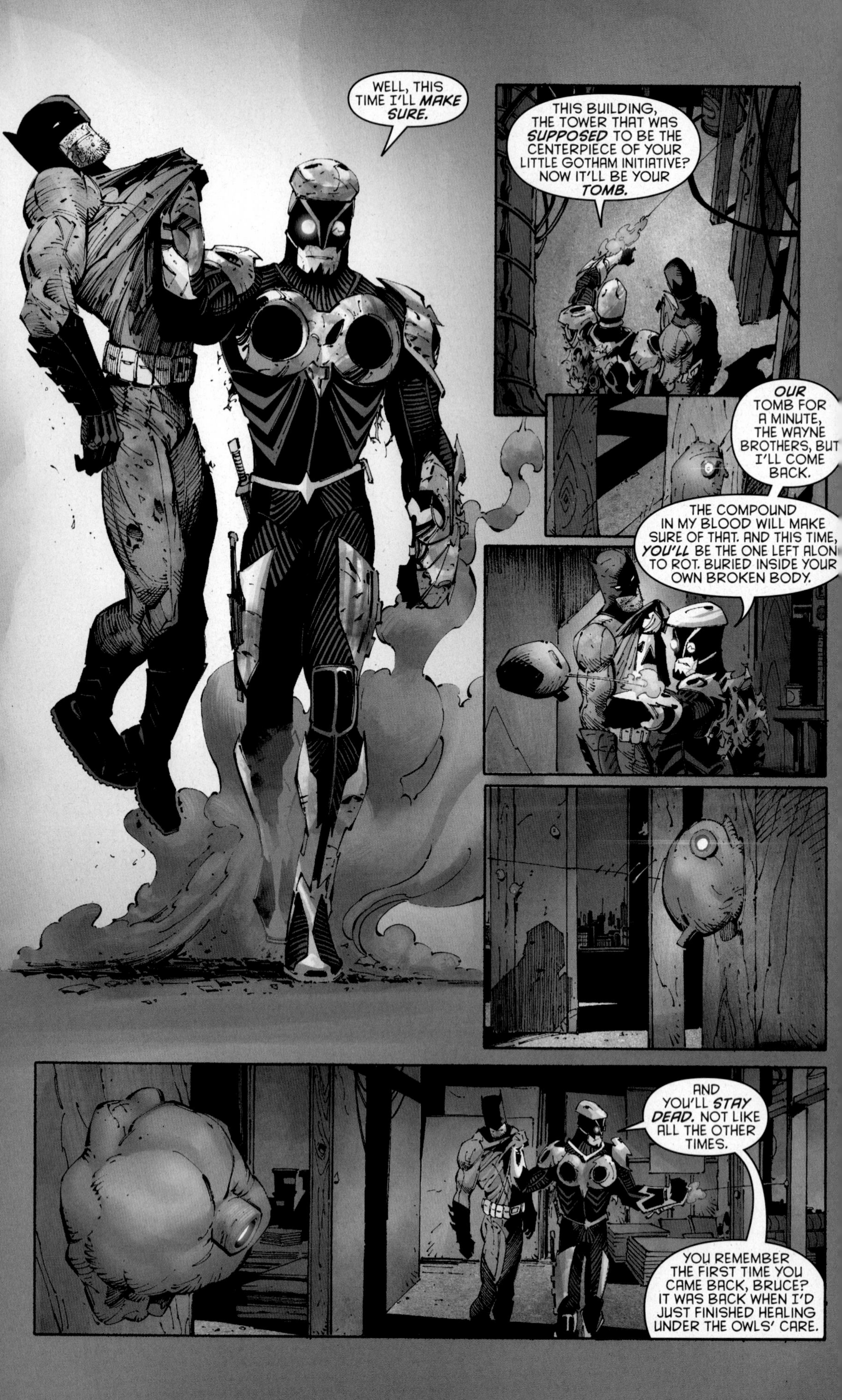
WELL, THIS TIME I'LL *MAKE SURE.*
THIS BUILDING, THE TOWER THAT WAS *SUPPOSED* TO BE THE CENTERPIECE OF YOUR LITTLE GOTHAM INITIATIVE? NOW IT'LL BE YOUR *TOMB.*
OUR TOMB FOR A MINUTE, THE WAYNE BROTHERS, BUT I'LL COME BACK.
THE COMPOUND IN MY BLOOD WILL MAKE SURE OF THAT. AND THIS TIME, *YOU'LL* BE THE ONE LEFT ALON TO ROT. BURIED INSIDE YOUR OWN BROKEN BODY.
AND YOU'LL *STAY DEAD.* NOT LIKE ALL THE OTHER TIMES.
YOU REMEMBER THE FIRST TIME YOU CAME BACK, BRUCE? IT WAS BACK WHEN I'D JUST FINISHED HEALING UNDER THE OWLS' CARE.

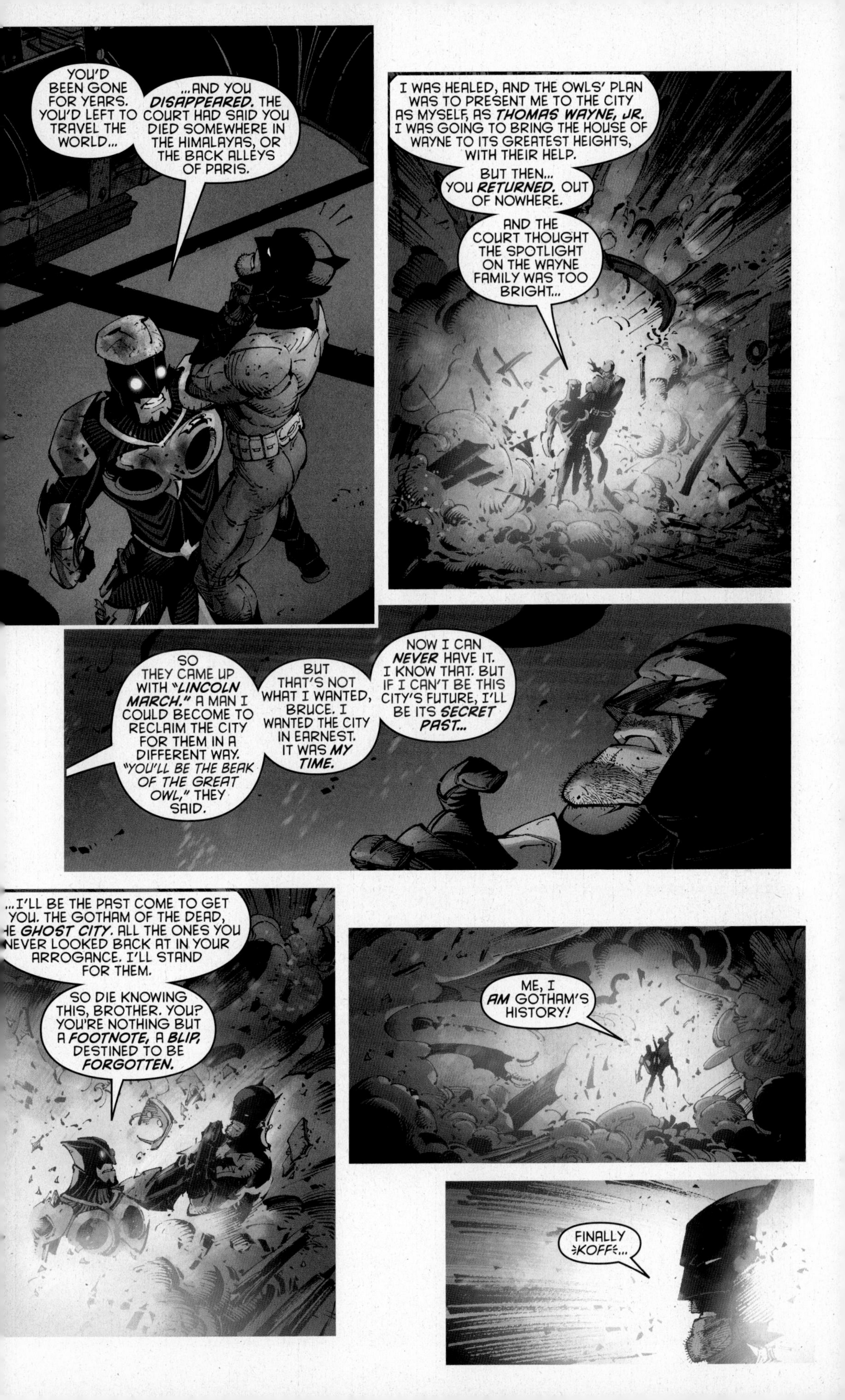
YOU'D BEEN GONE FOR YEARS. YOU'D LEFT TO TRAVEL THE WORLD...
...AND YOU DISAPPEARED. THE COURT HAD SAID YOU DIED SOMEWHERE IN THE HIMALAYAS, OR THE BACK ALLEYS OF PARIS.
I WAS HEALED, AND THE OWLS' PLAN WAS TO PRESENT ME TO THE CITY AS MYSELF, AS THOMAS WAYNE, JR. I WAS GOING TO BRING THE HOUSE OF WAYNE TO ITS GREATEST HEIGHTS, WITH THEIR HELP.
BUT THEN... YOU RETURNED. OUT OF NOWHERE.
AND THE COURT THOUGHT THE SPOTLIGHT ON THE WAYNE FAMILY WAS TOO BRIGHT...
SO THEY CAME UP WITH "LINCOLN MARCH." A MAN I COULD BECOME TO RECLAIM THE CITY FOR THEM IN A DIFFERENT WAY. "YOU'LL BE THE BEAK OF THE GREAT OWL," THEY SAID.
BUT THAT'S NOT WHAT I WANTED, BRUCE. I WANTED THE CITY IN EARNEST. IT WAS MY TIME.
NOW I CAN NEVER HAVE IT. I KNOW THAT. BUT IF I CAN'T BE THIS CITY'S FUTURE, I'LL BE ITS SECRET PAST...
...I'LL BE THE PAST COME TO GET YOU. THE GOTHAM OF THE DEAD, HE GHOST CITY. ALL THE ONES YOU NEVER LOOKED BACK AT IN YOUR ARROGANCE. I'LL STAND FOR THEM.
SO DIE KNOWING THIS, BROTHER. YOU? YOU'RE NOTHING BUT A FOOTNOTE, A BLIP, DESTINED TO BE FORGOTTEN.
ME, I AM GOTHAM'S HISTORY!
FINALLY KOFF...

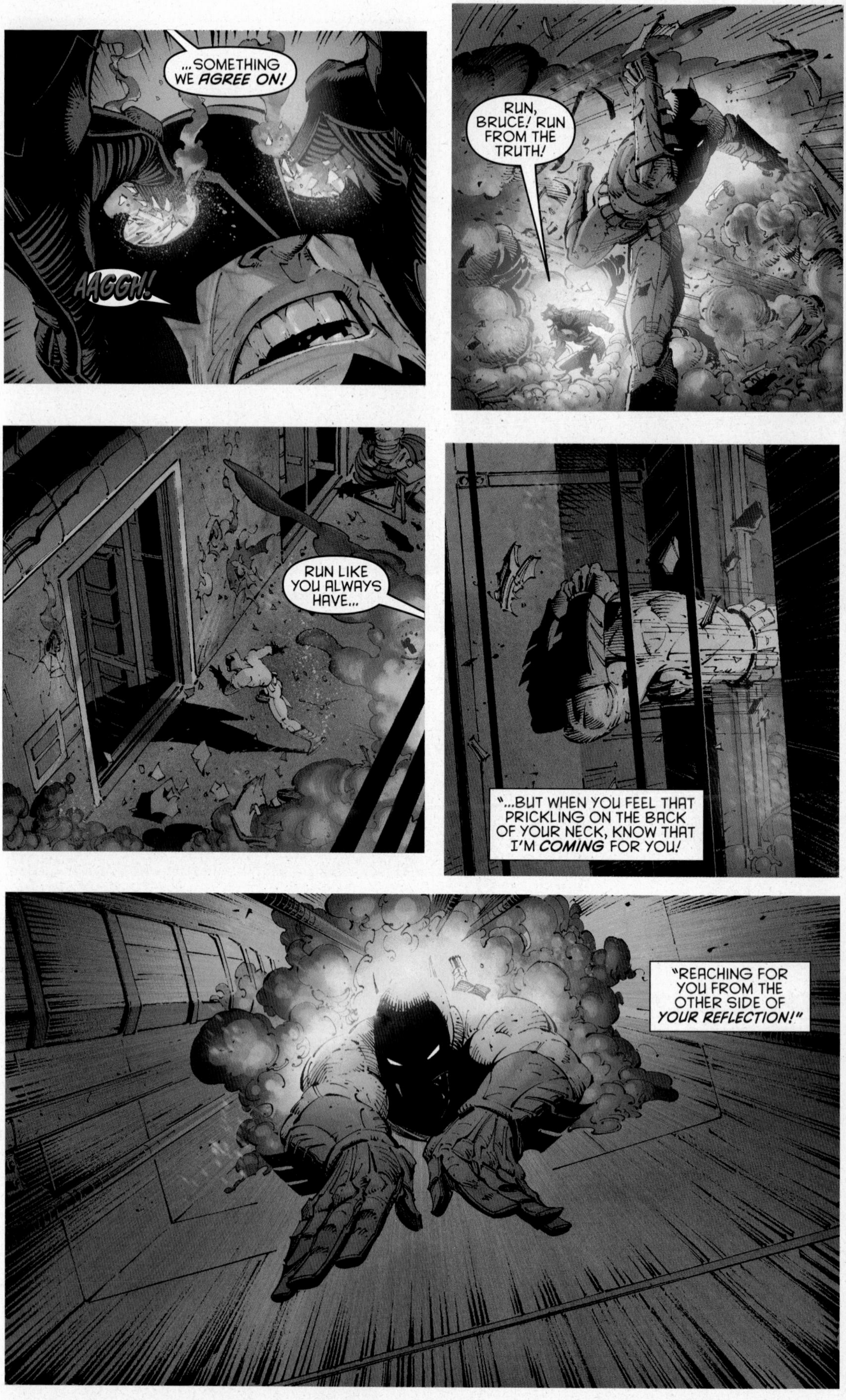
...SOMETHING WE AGREE ON!
AAGGH!
RUN, BRUCE! RUN FROM THE TRUTH!
RUN LIKE YOU ALWAYS HAVE...
"...BUT WHEN YOU FEEL THAT PRICKLING ON THE BACK OF YOUR NECK, KNOW THAT I'M COMING FOR YOU!
"REACHING FOR YOU FROM THE OTHER SIDE OF YOUR REFLECTION!"

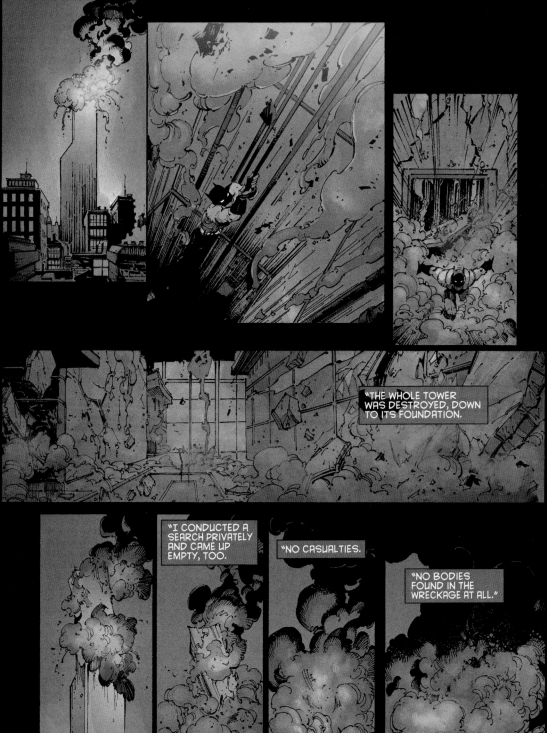

"THE WHOLE TOWER WAS DESTROYED, DOWN TO ITS FOUNDATION.

"I CONDUCTED A SEARCH PRIVATELY AND CAME UP EMPTY, TOO.

"NO CASUALTIES.

"NO BODIES FOUND IN THE WRECKAGE AT ALL."

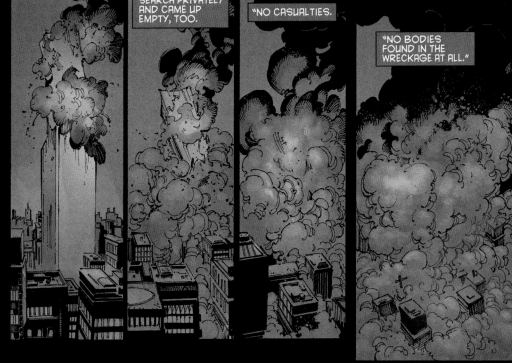

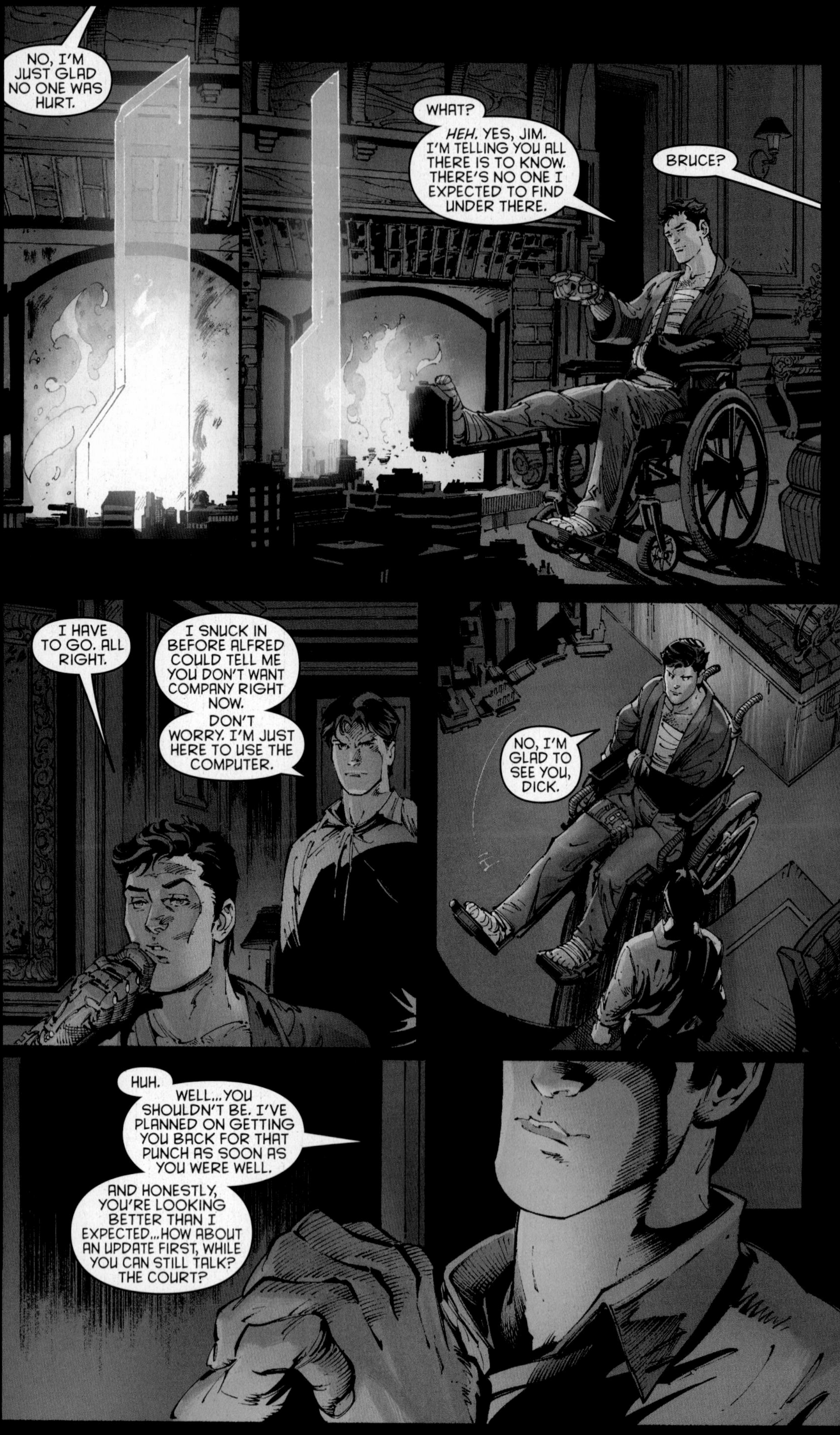
NO, I'M JUST GLAD NO ONE WAS HURT.
WHAT?
HEH. YES, JIM. I'M TELLING YOU ALL THERE IS TO KNOW. THERE'S NO ONE I EXPECTED TO FIND UNDER THERE.
BRUCE?
I HAVE TO GO. ALL RIGHT.
I SNUCK IN BEFORE ALFRED COULD TELL ME YOU DON'T WANT COMPANY RIGHT NOW.
DON'T WORRY. I'M JUST HERE TO USE THE COMPUTER.
NO, I'M GLAD TO SEE YOU, DICK.
HUH.
WELL...YOU SHOULDN'T BE. I'VE PLANNED ON GETTING YOU BACK FOR THAT PUNCH AS SOON AS YOU WERE WELL.
AND HONESTLY, YOU'RE LOOKING BETTER THAN I EXPECTED...HOW ABOUT AN UPDATE FIRST, WHILE YOU CAN STILL TALK? THE COURT?

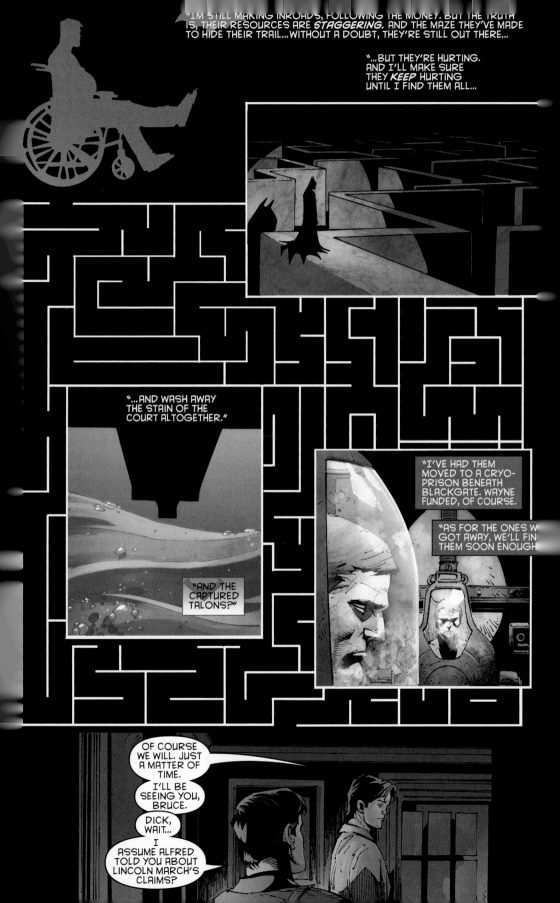

"I'M STILL MAKING INROADS, FOLLOWING THE MONEY. BUT THE TRUTH IS, THEIR RESOURCES ARE *STAGGERING.* AND THE MAZE THEY'VE MADE TO HIDE THEIR TRAIL...WITHOUT A DOUBT, THEY'RE STILL OUT THERE...

"...BUT THEY'RE HURTING. AND I'LL MAKE SURE THEY *KEEP* HURTING UNTIL I FIND THEM ALL...

"...AND WASH AWAY THE STAIN OF THE COURT ALTOGETHER."

"I'VE HAD THEM MOVED TO A CRYO-PRISON BENEATH BLACKGATE. WAYNE FUNDED, OF COURSE.

"AND THE CAPTURED TALONS?"

"AS FOR THE ONES W GOT AWAY, WE'LL FIN THEM SOON ENOUGH

OF COURSE WE WILL. JUST A MATTER OF TIME.

I'LL BE SEEING YOU, BRUCE.

DICK, WAIT...

I ASSUME ALFRED TOLD YOU ABOUT LINCOLN MARCH'S CLAIMS?

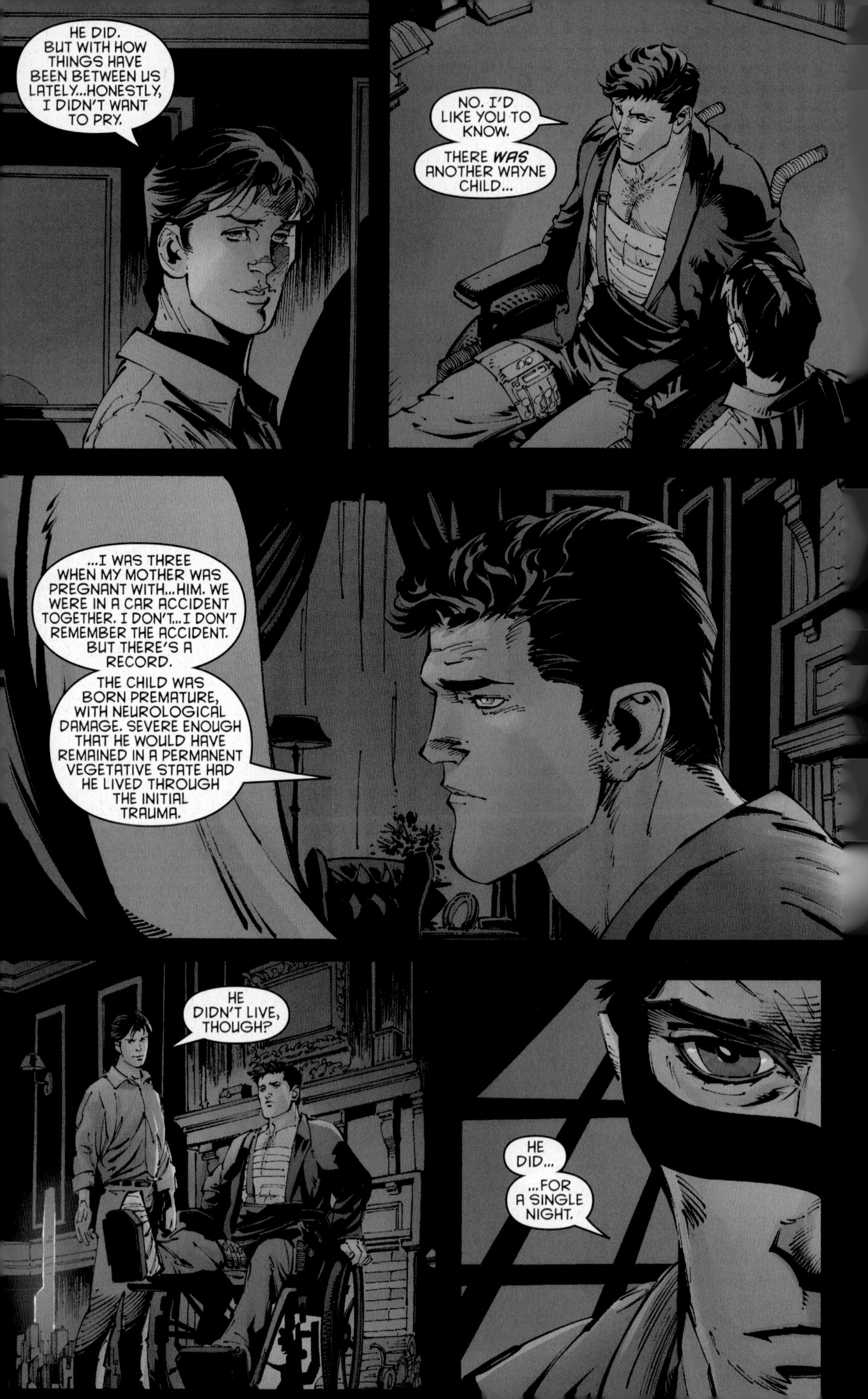
HE DID. BUT WITH HOW THINGS HAVE BEEN BETWEEN US LATELY...HONESTLY, I DIDN'T WANT TO PRY.
NO. I'D LIKE YOU TO KNOW.
THERE *WAS* ANOTHER WAYNE CHILD...
...I WAS THREE WHEN MY MOTHER WAS PREGNANT WITH...HIM. WE WERE IN A CAR ACCIDENT TOGETHER. I DON'T...I DON'T REMEMBER THE ACCIDENT. BUT THERE'S A RECORD.
THE CHILD WAS BORN PREMATURE, WITH NEUROLOGICAL DAMAGE. SEVERE ENOUGH THAT HE WOULD HAVE REMAINED IN A PERMANENT VEGETATIVE STATE HAD HE LIVED THROUGH THE INITIAL TRAUMA.
HE DIDN'T LIVE, THOUGH?
HE DID...
...FOR A SINGLE NIGHT.

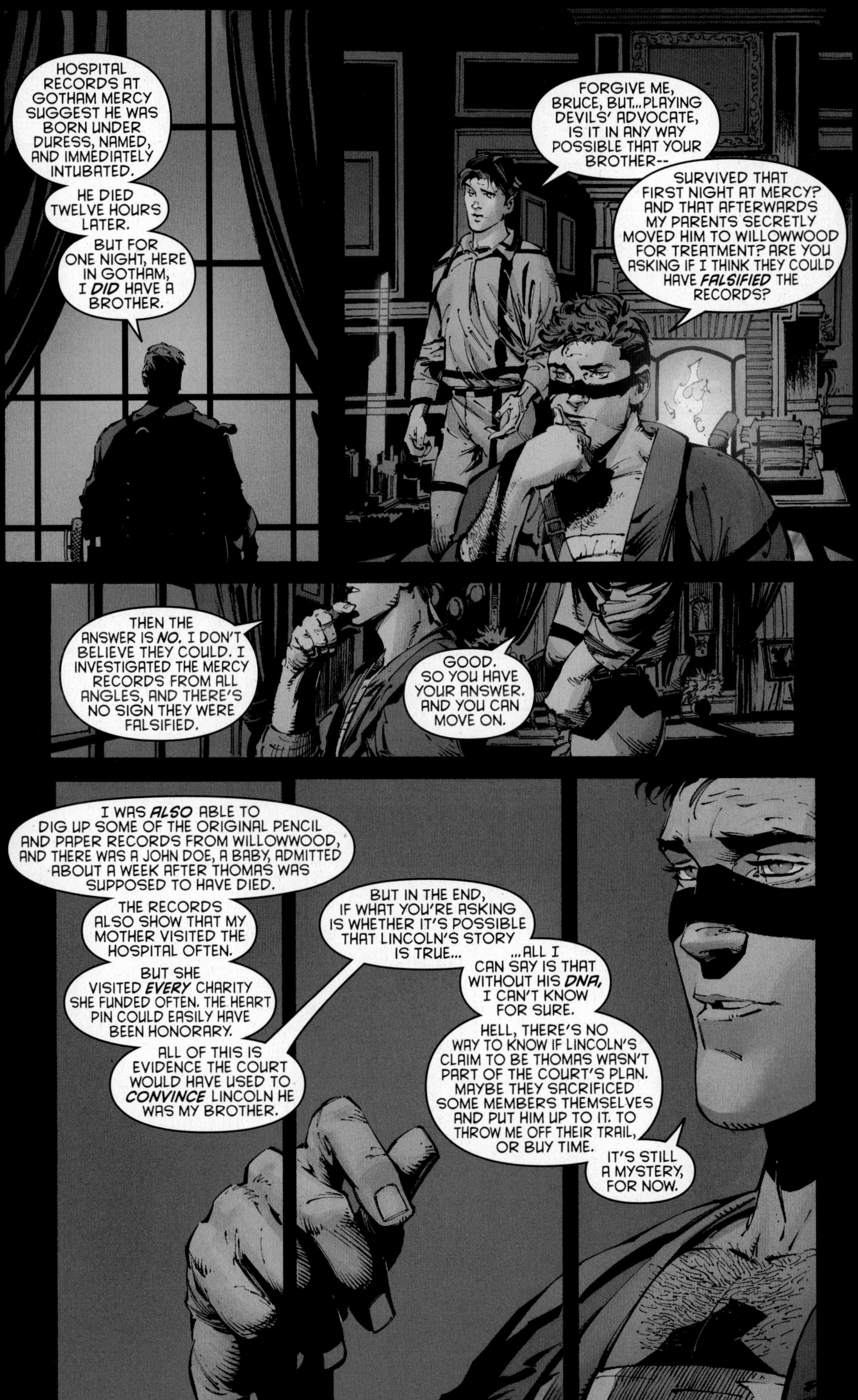
HOSPITAL RECORDS AT GOTHAM MERCY SUGGEST HE WAS BORN UNDER DURESS, NAMED, AND IMMEDIATELY INTUBATED.
HE DIED TWELVE HOURS LATER.
BUT FOR ONE NIGHT, HERE IN GOTHAM, I *DID* HAVE A BROTHER.
FORGIVE ME, BRUCE, BUT...PLAYING DEVILS' ADVOCATE, IS IT IN ANY WAY POSSIBLE THAT YOUR BROTHER--
SURVIVED THAT FIRST NIGHT AT MERCY? AND THAT AFTERWARDS MY PARENTS SECRETLY MOVED HIM TO WILLOWWOOD FOR TREATMENT? ARE YOU ASKING IF I THINK THEY COULD HAVE *FALSIFIED* THE RECORDS?
THEN THE ANSWER IS *NO.* I DON'T BELIEVE THEY COULD. I INVESTIGATED THE MERCY RECORDS FROM ALL ANGLES, AND THERE'S NO SIGN THEY WERE FALSIFIED.
GOOD. SO YOU HAVE YOUR ANSWER. AND YOU CAN MOVE ON.
I WAS *ALSO* ABLE TO DIG UP SOME OF THE ORIGINAL PENCIL AND PAPER RECORDS FROM WILLOWWOOD, AND THERE WAS A JOHN DOE, A BABY, ADMITTED ABOUT A WEEK AFTER THOMAS WAS SUPPOSED TO HAVE DIED.
THE RECORDS ALSO SHOW THAT MY MOTHER VISITED THE HOSPITAL OFTEN.
BUT SHE VISITED *EVERY* CHARITY SHE FUNDED OFTEN. THE HEART PIN COULD EASILY HAVE BEEN HONORARY.
ALL OF THIS IS EVIDENCE THE COURT WOULD HAVE USED TO *CONVINCE* LINCOLN HE WAS MY BROTHER.
BUT IN THE END, IF WHAT YOU'RE ASKING IS WHETHER IT'S POSSIBLE THAT LINCOLN'S STORY IS TRUE...
...ALL I CAN SAY IS THAT WITHOUT HIS *DNA,* I CAN'T KNOW FOR SURE.
HELL, THERE'S NO WAY TO KNOW IF LINCOLN'S CLAIM TO BE THOMAS WASN'T PART OF THE COURT'S PLAN. MAYBE THEY SACRIFICED SOME MEMBERS THEMSELVES AND PUT HIM UP TO IT. TO THROW ME OFF THEIR TRAIL, OR BUY TIME.
IT'S STILL A MYSTERY, FOR NOW.

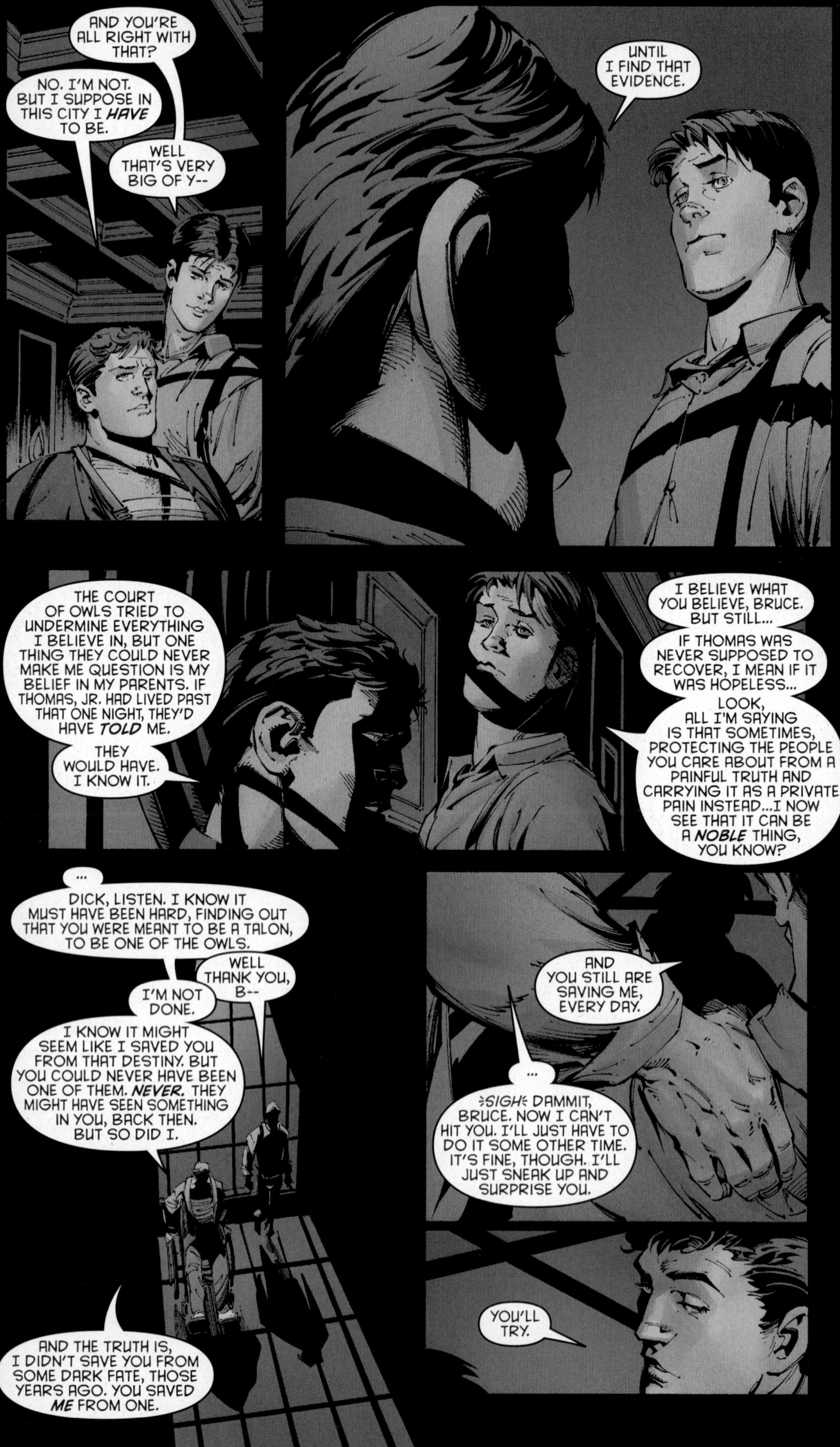
AND YOU'RE ALL RIGHT WITH THAT?
NO. I'M NOT. BUT I SUPPOSE IN THIS CITY I *HAVE* TO BE.
WELL THAT'S VERY BIG OF Y--
UNTIL I FIND THAT EVIDENCE.
THE COURT OF OWLS TRIED TO UNDERMINE EVERYTHING I BELIEVE IN, BUT ONE THING THEY COULD NEVER MAKE ME QUESTION IS MY BELIEF IN MY PARENTS. IF THOMAS, JR. HAD LIVED PAST THAT ONE NIGHT, THEY'D HAVE *TOLD* ME.
THEY WOULD HAVE. I KNOW IT.
I BELIEVE WHAT YOU BELIEVE, BRUCE. BUT STILL...
IF THOMAS WAS NEVER SUPPOSED TO RECOVER, I MEAN IF IT WAS HOPELESS...
LOOK, ALL I'M SAYING IS THAT SOMETIMES, PROTECTING THE PEOPLE YOU CARE ABOUT FROM A PAINFUL TRUTH AND CARRYING IT AS A PRIVATE PAIN INSTEAD...I NOW SEE THAT IT CAN BE A *NOBLE* THING, YOU KNOW?
...
DICK, LISTEN. I KNOW IT MUST HAVE BEEN HARD, FINDING OUT THAT YOU WERE MEANT TO BE A TALON, TO BE ONE OF THE OWLS.
WELL THANK YOU, B--
I'M NOT DONE.
I KNOW IT MIGHT SEEM LIKE I SAVED YOU FROM THAT DESTINY. BUT YOU COULD NEVER HAVE BEEN ONE OF THEM. *NEVER.* THEY MIGHT HAVE SEEN SOMETHING IN YOU, BACK THEN. BUT SO DID I.
AND THE TRUTH IS, I DIDN'T SAVE YOU FROM SOME DARK FATE, THOSE YEARS AGO. YOU SAVED *ME* FROM ONE.
AND YOU STILL ARE SAVING ME, EVERY DAY.
...
SIGH DAMMIT, BRUCE. NOW I CAN'T HIT YOU. I'LL JUST HAVE TO DO IT SOME OTHER TIME. IT'S FINE, THOUGH. I'LL JUST SNEAK UP AND SURPRISE YOU.
YOU'LL TRY.

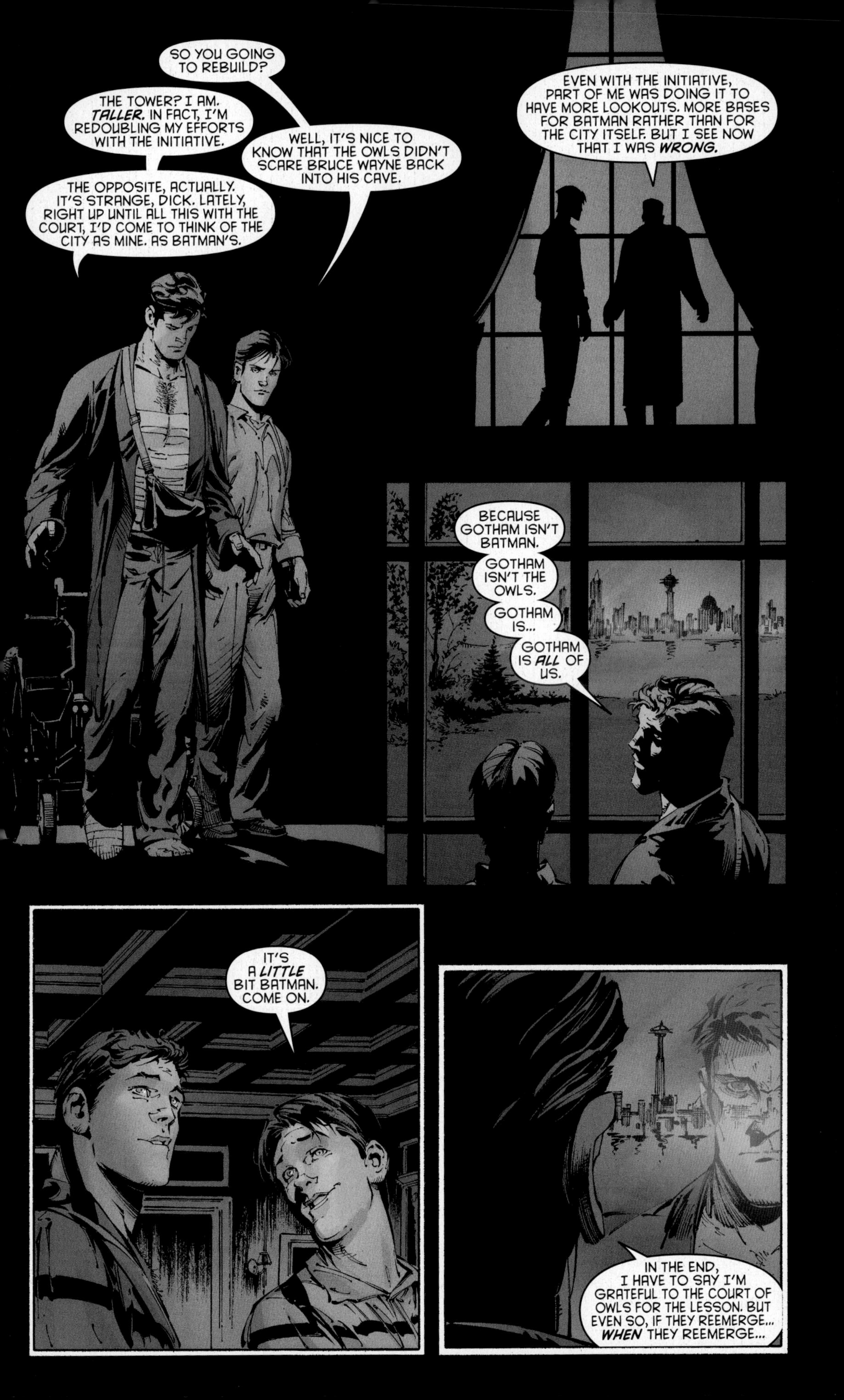
SO YOU GOING TO REBUILD?
THE TOWER? I AM. *TALLER.* IN FACT, I'M REDOUBLING MY EFFORTS WITH THE INITIATIVE.
WELL, IT'S NICE TO KNOW THAT THE OWLS DIDN'T SCARE BRUCE WAYNE BACK INTO HIS CAVE.
THE OPPOSITE, ACTUALLY. IT'S STRANGE, DICK. LATELY, RIGHT UP UNTIL ALL THIS WITH THE COURT, I'D COME TO THINK OF THE CITY AS MINE. AS BATMAN'S.
EVEN WITH THE INITIATIVE, PART OF ME WAS DOING IT TO HAVE MORE LOOKOUTS. MORE BASES FOR BATMAN RATHER THAN FOR THE CITY ITSELF. BUT I SEE NOW THAT I WAS *WRONG.*
BECAUSE GOTHAM ISN'T BATMAN.
GOTHAM ISN'T THE OWLS.
GOTHAM IS...
GOTHAM IS *ALL* OF US.
IT'S A *LITTLE* BIT BATMAN. COME ON.
IN THE END, I HAVE TO SAY I'M GRATEFUL TO THE COURT OF OWLS FOR THE LESSON. BUT EVEN SO, IF THEY REEMERGE... *WHEN* THEY REEMERGE...

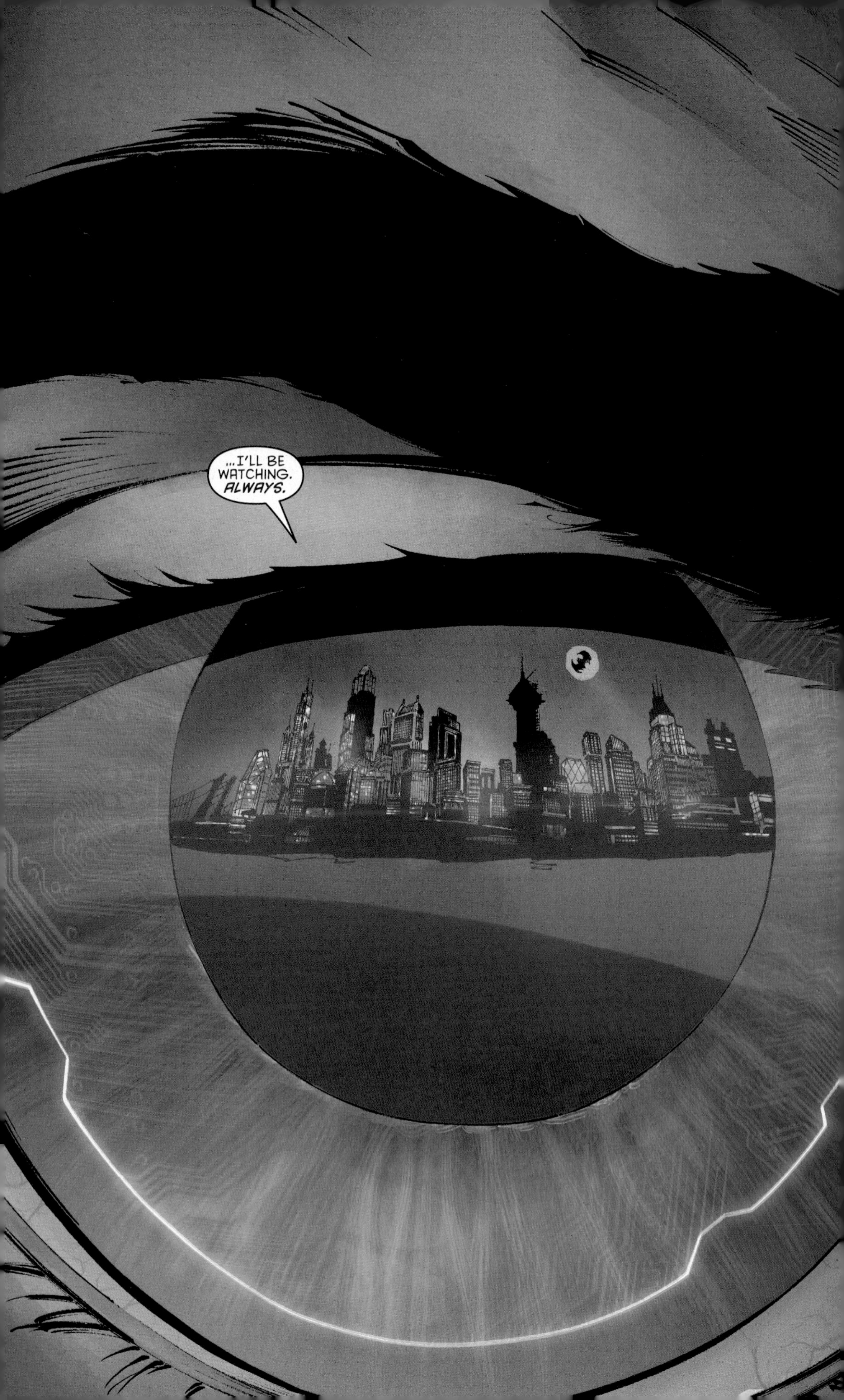
...I'LL BE WATCHING. ALWAYS.

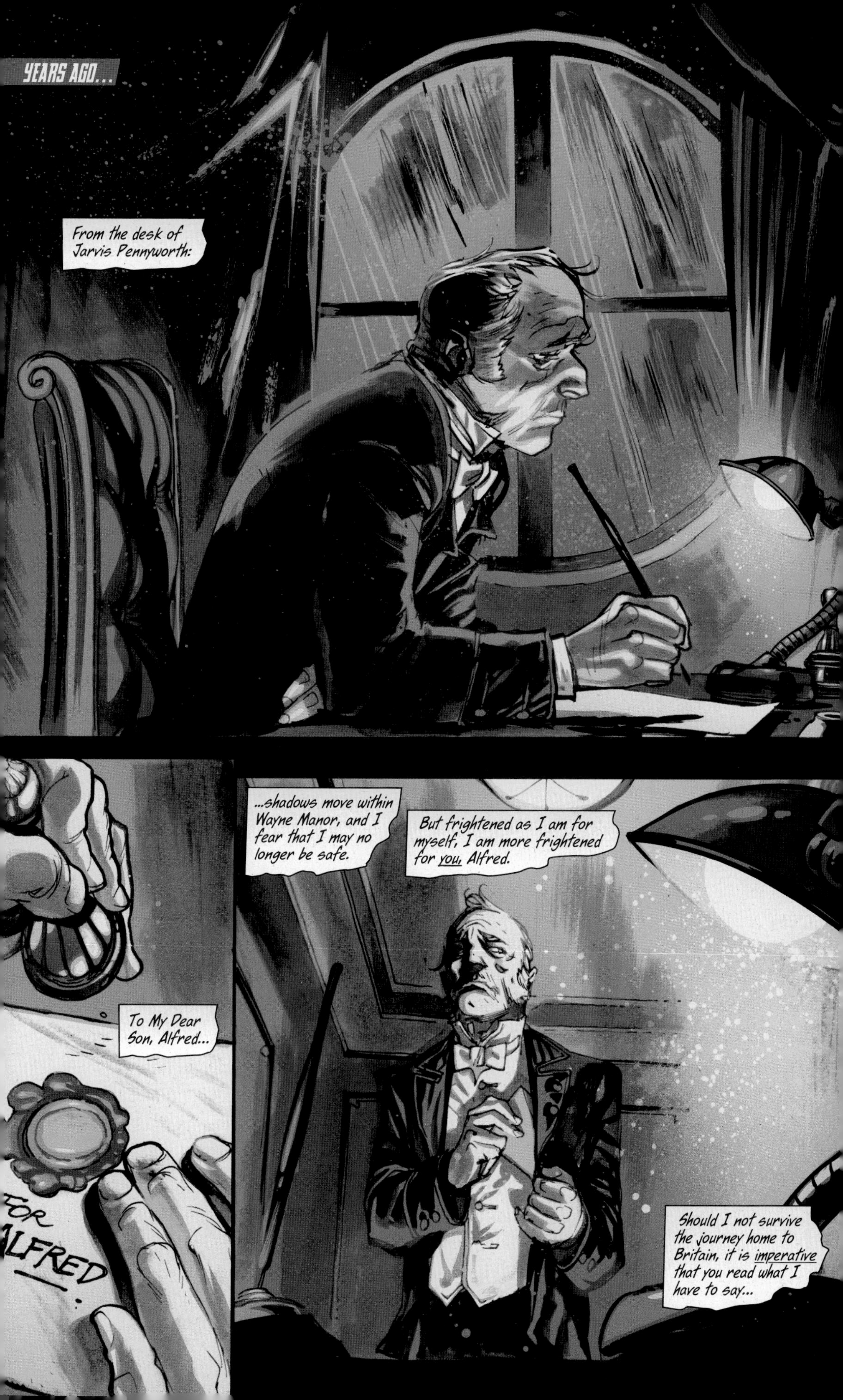
YEARS AGO...
From the desk of Jarvis Pennyworth:
To My Dear Son, Alfred...
FOR ALFRED
...shadows move within Wayne Manor, and I fear that I may no longer be safe.
But frightened as I am for myself, I am more frightened for you, Alfred.
Should I not survive the journey home to Britain, it is imperative that you read what I have to say...

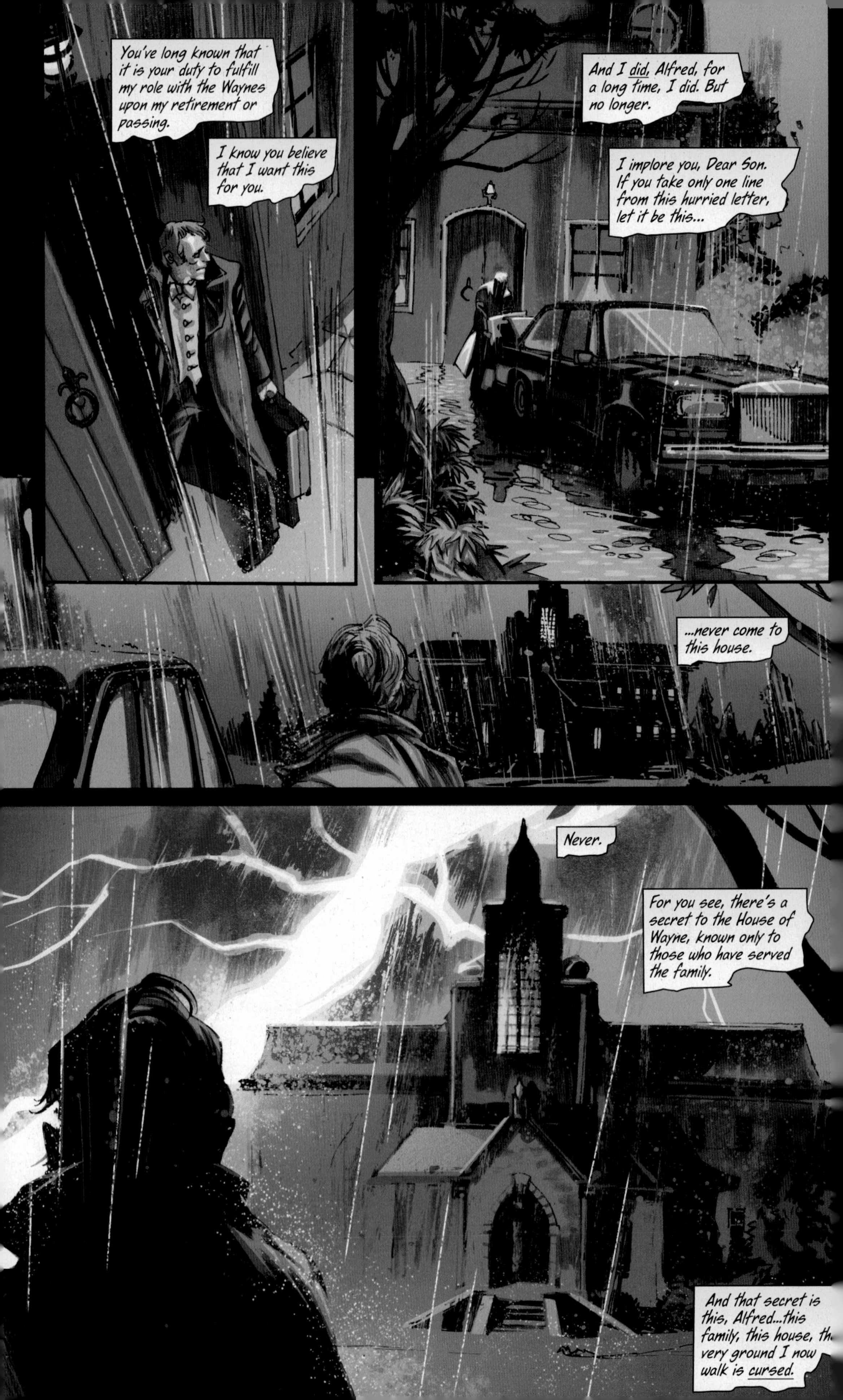

You've long known that it is your duty to fulfill my role with the Waynes upon my retirement or passing.
I know you believe that I want this for you.
And I did, Alfred, for a long time, I did. But no longer.
I implore you, Dear Son. If you take only one line from this hurried letter, let it be this...
...never come to this house.
Never.
For you see, there's a secret to the House of Wayne, known only to those who have served the family.
And that secret is this, Alfred...this family, this house, th very ground I now walk is cursed.

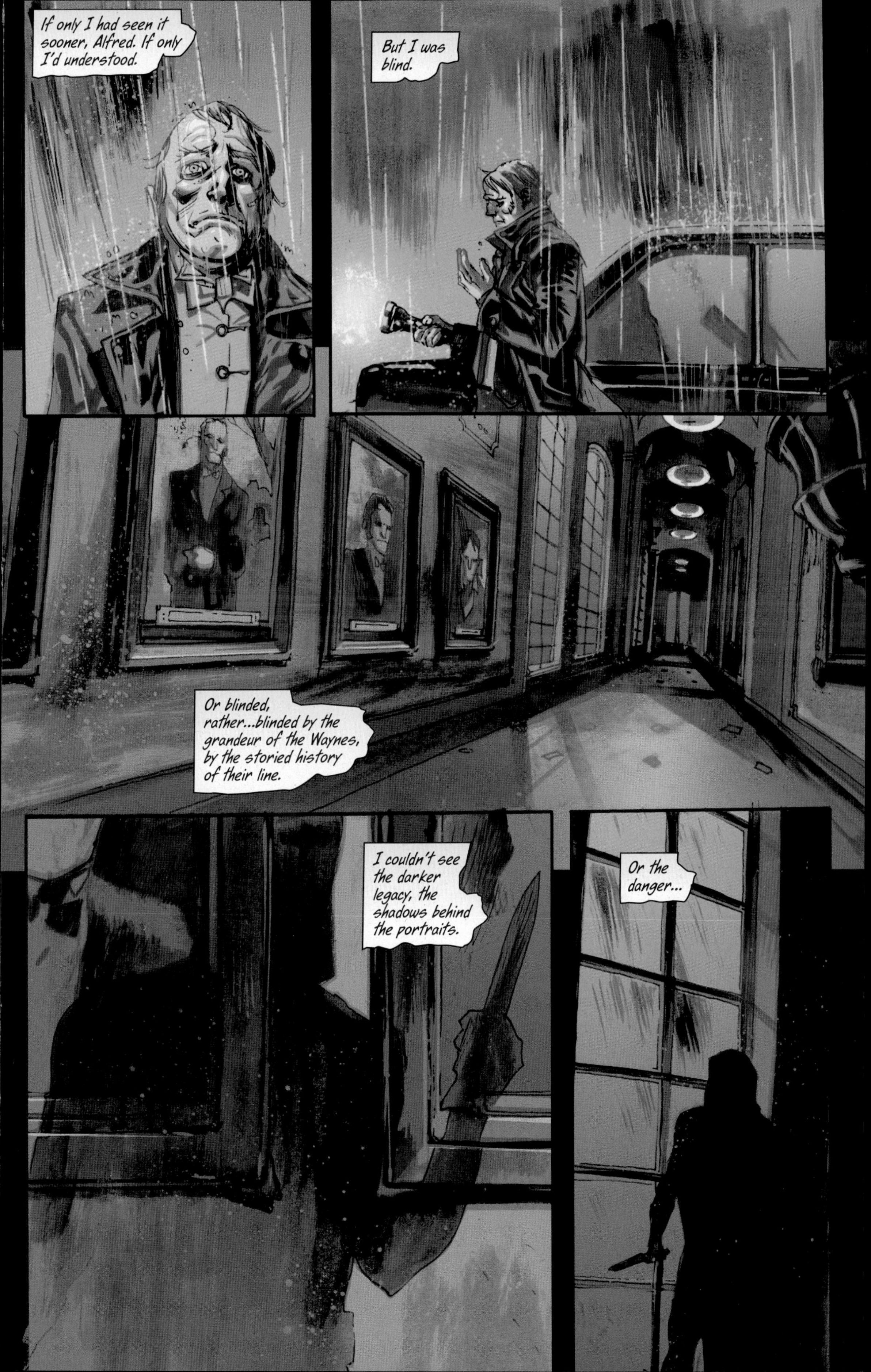
If only I had seen it sooner, Alfred. If only I'd understood.
But I was blind.
Or blinded, rather...blinded by the grandeur of the Waynes, by the storied history of their line.
I couldn't see the darker legacy, the shadows behind the portraits.
Or the danger...

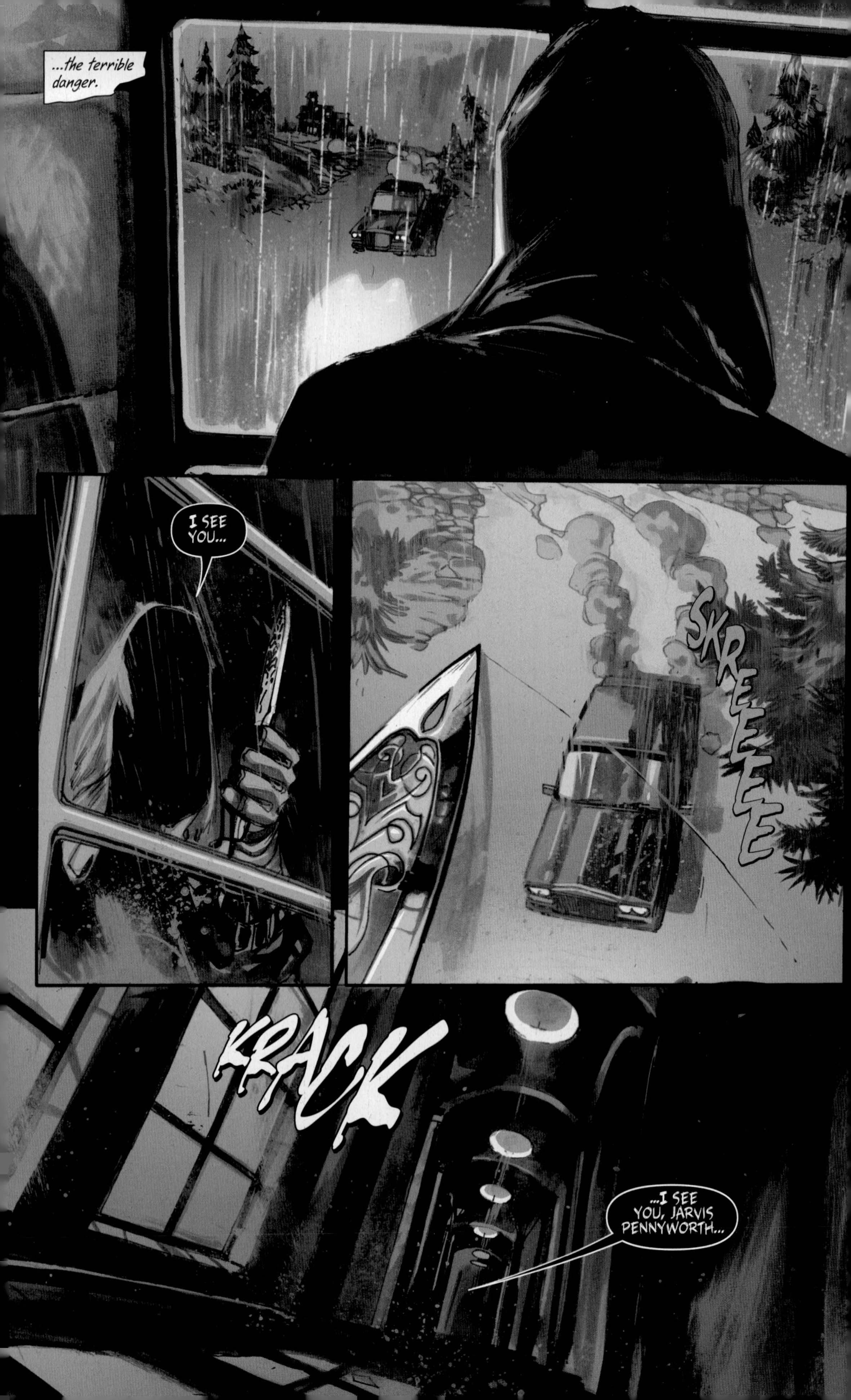
...the terrible danger.
I SEE YOU...
SKREEEEE
KRACK
...I SEE YOU, JARVIS PENNYWORTH...

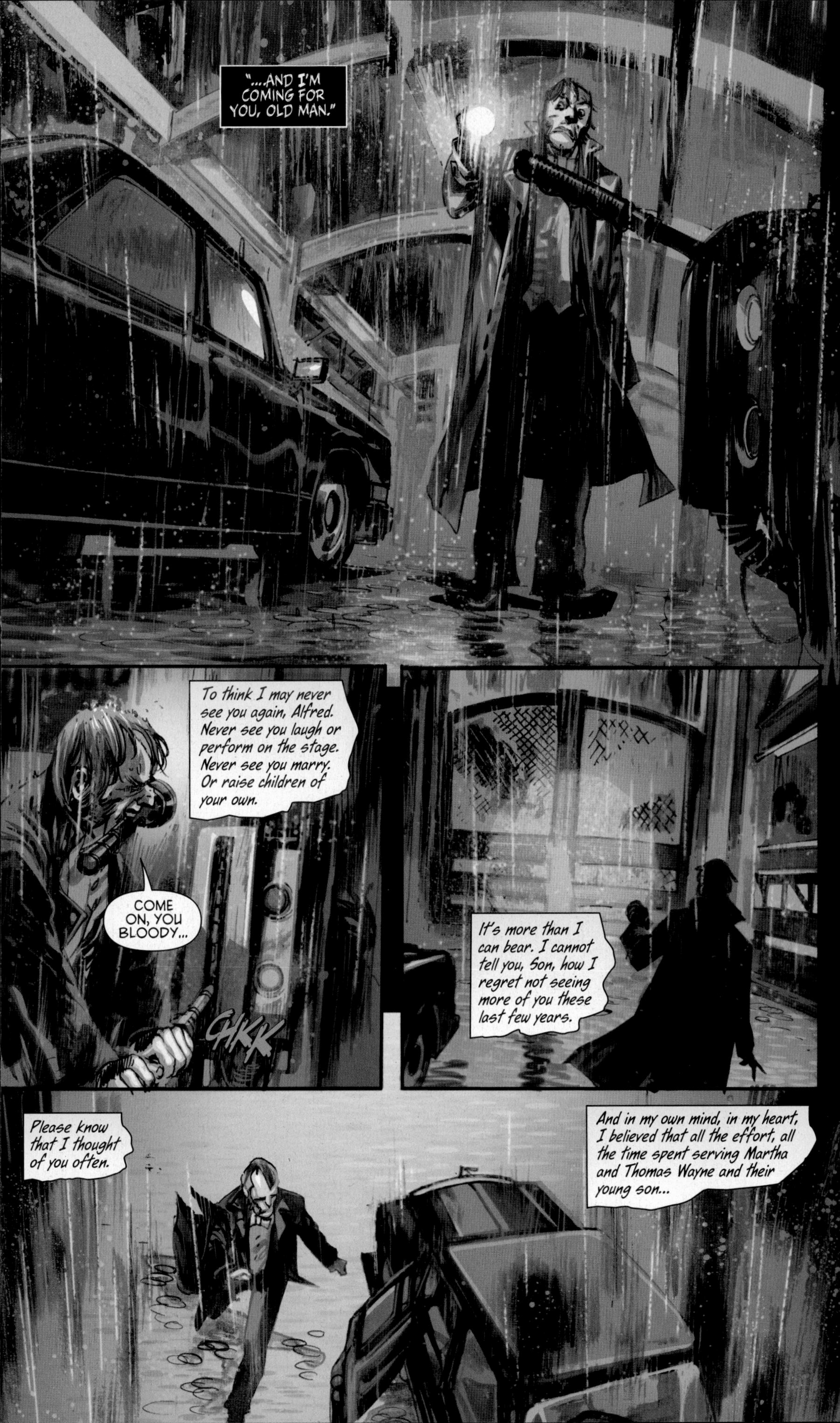
"...AND I'M COMING FOR YOU, OLD MAN."
To think I may never see you again, Alfred. Never see you laugh or perform on the stage. Never see you marry. Or raise children of your own.
COME ON, YOU BLOODY...
CHKK
It's more than I can bear. I cannot tell you, Son, how I regret not seeing more of you these last few years.
Please know that I thought of you often.
And in my own mind, in my heart, I believed that all the effort, all the time spent serving Martha and Thomas Wayne and their young son...

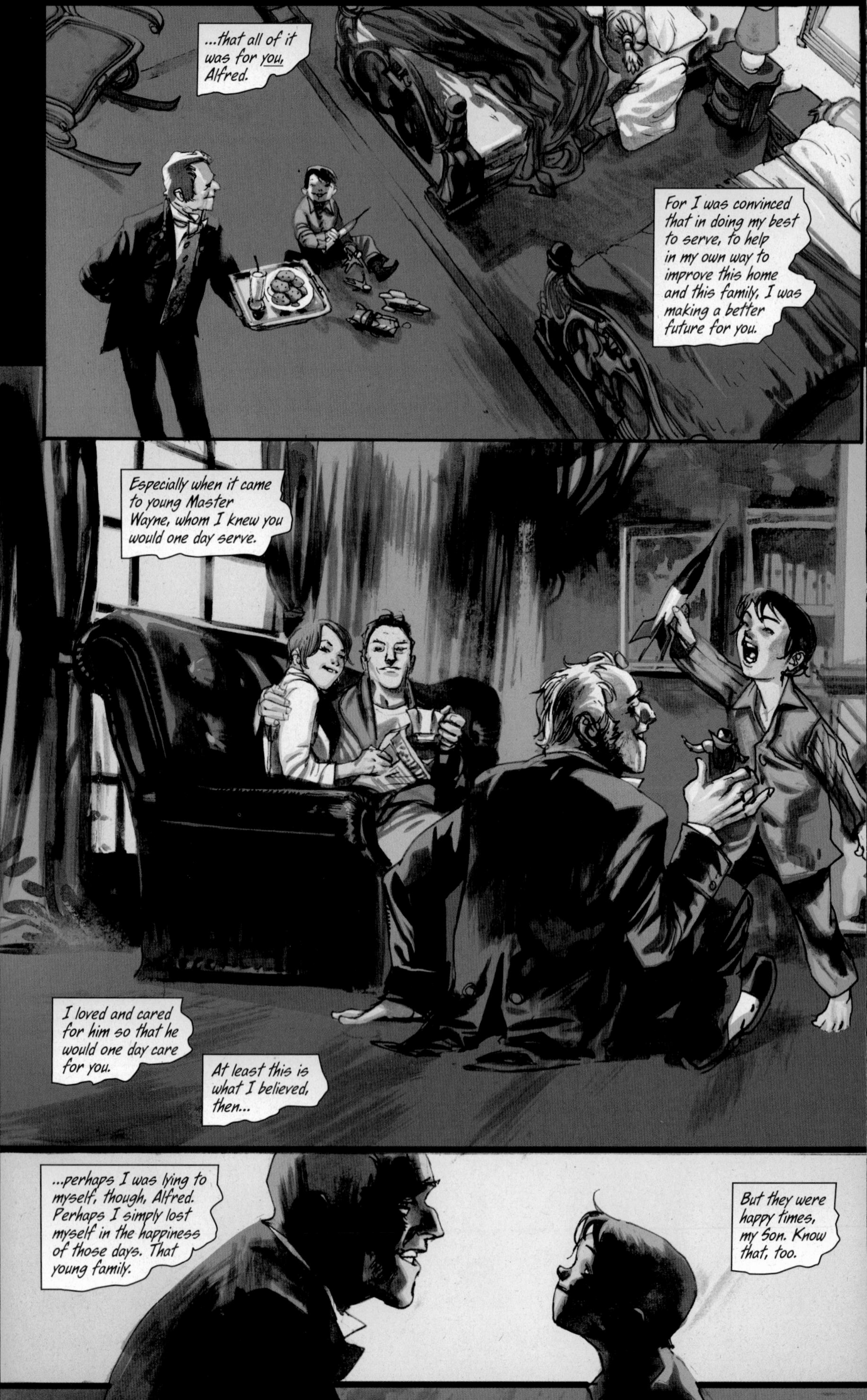

...that all of it was for you, Alfred.
For I was convinced that in doing my best to serve, to help in my own way to improve this home and this family, I was making a better future for you.
Especially when it came to young Master Wayne, whom I knew you would one day serve.
I loved and cared for him so that he would one day care for you.
At least this is what I believed, then...
...perhaps I was lying to myself, though, Alfred. Perhaps I simply lost myself in the happiness of those days. That young family.
But they were happy times, my Son. Know that, too.

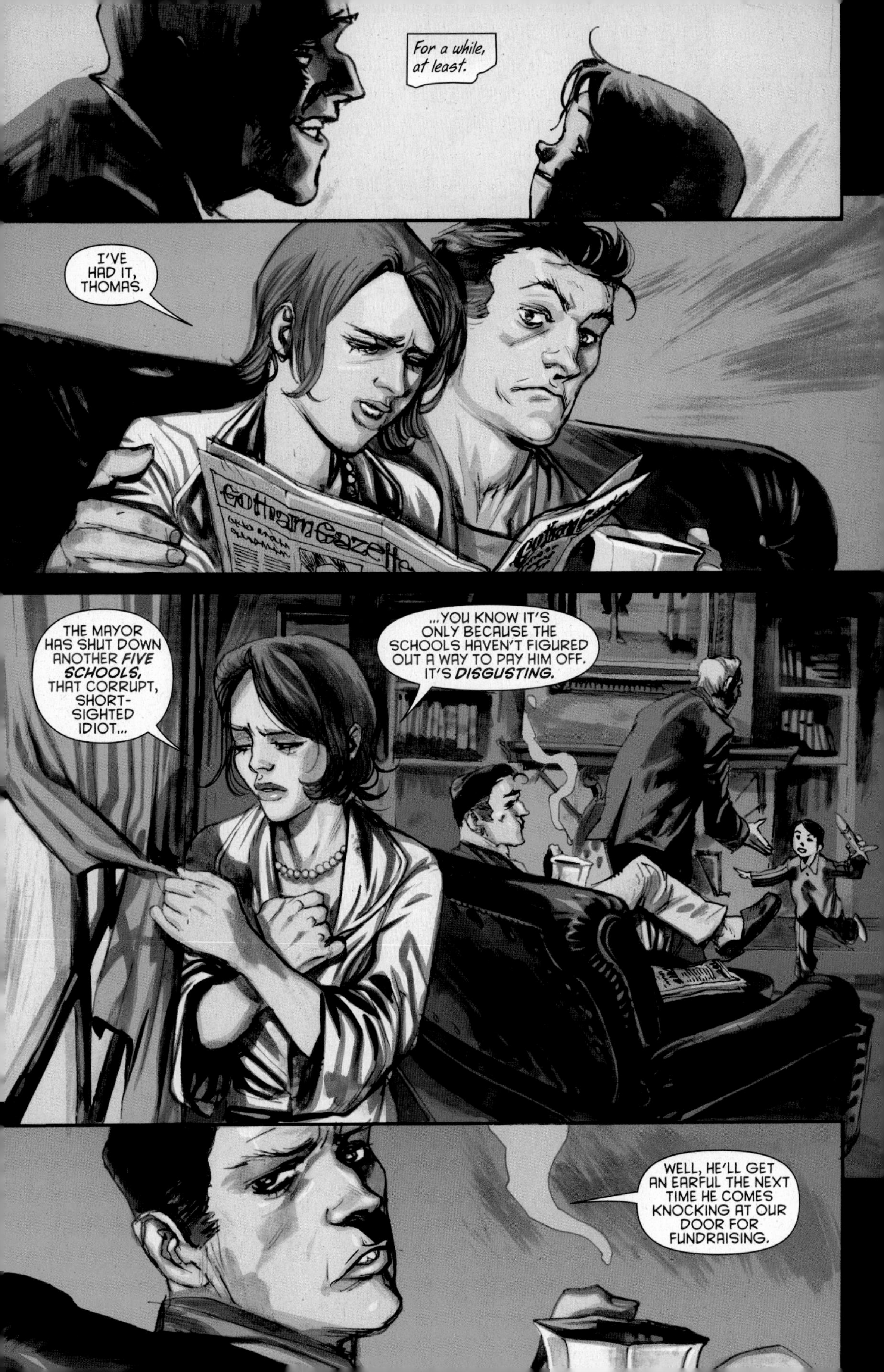
For a while, at least.
I'VE HAD IT, THOMAS.
Gotham Gazette
THE MAYOR HAS SHUT DOWN ANOTHER FIVE SCHOOLS, THAT CORRUPT, SHORT-SIGHTED IDIOT...
...YOU KNOW IT'S ONLY BECAUSE THE SCHOOLS HAVEN'T FIGURED OUT A WAY TO PAY HIM OFF. IT'S DISGUSTING.
WELL, HE'LL GET AN EARFUL THE NEXT TIME HE COMES KNOCKING AT OUR DOOR FOR FUNDRAISING.

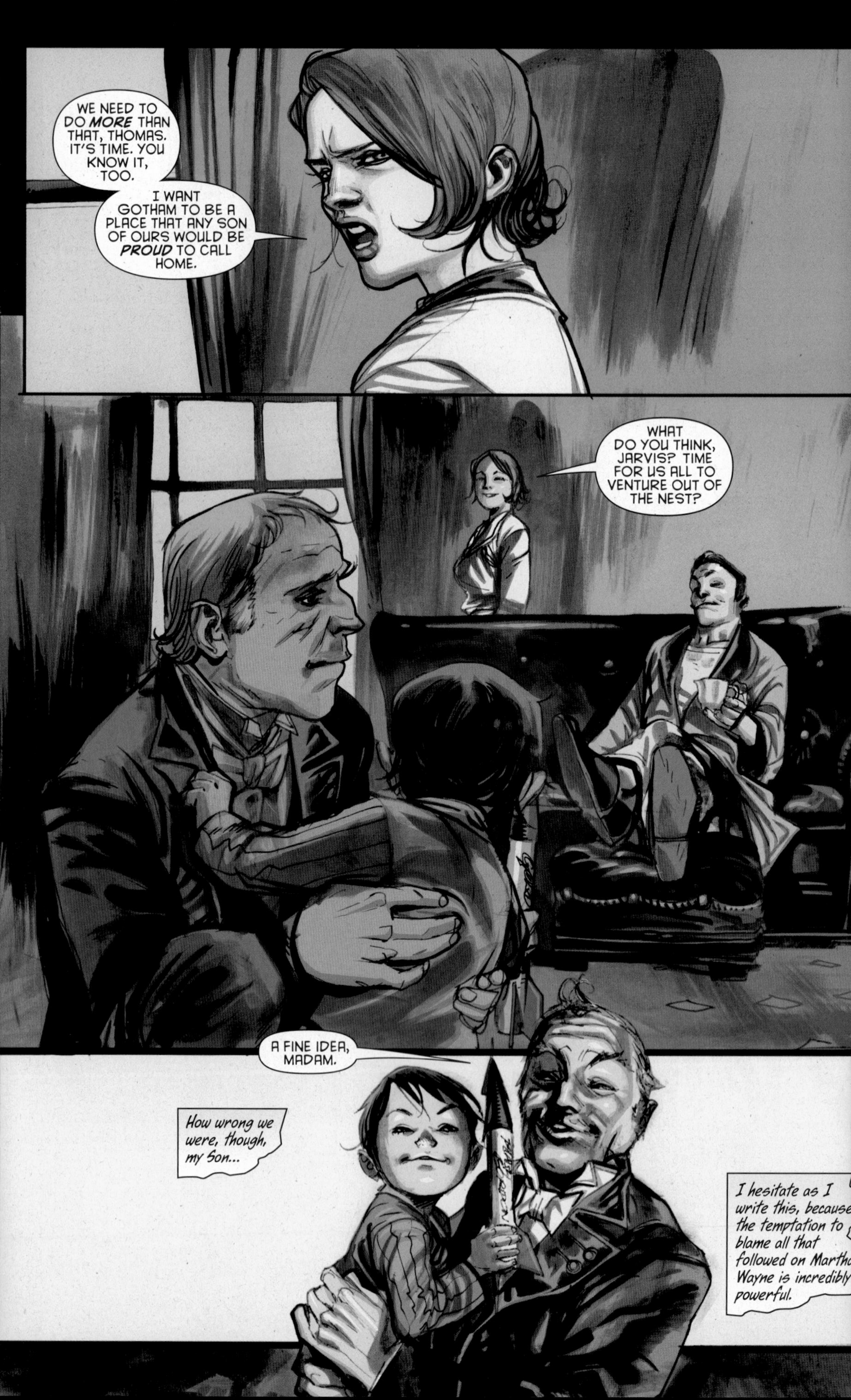
WE NEED TO DO *MORE* THAN THAT, THOMAS. IT'S TIME. YOU KNOW IT, TOO.
I WANT GOTHAM TO BE A PLACE THAT ANY SON OF OURS WOULD BE *PROUD* TO CALL HOME.
WHAT DO YOU THINK, JARVIS? TIME FOR US ALL TO VENTURE OUT OF THE NEST?
A FINE IDEA, MADAM.
How wrong we were, though, my Son...
I hesitate as I write this, because the temptation to blame all that followed on Martha Wayne is incredibly powerful.

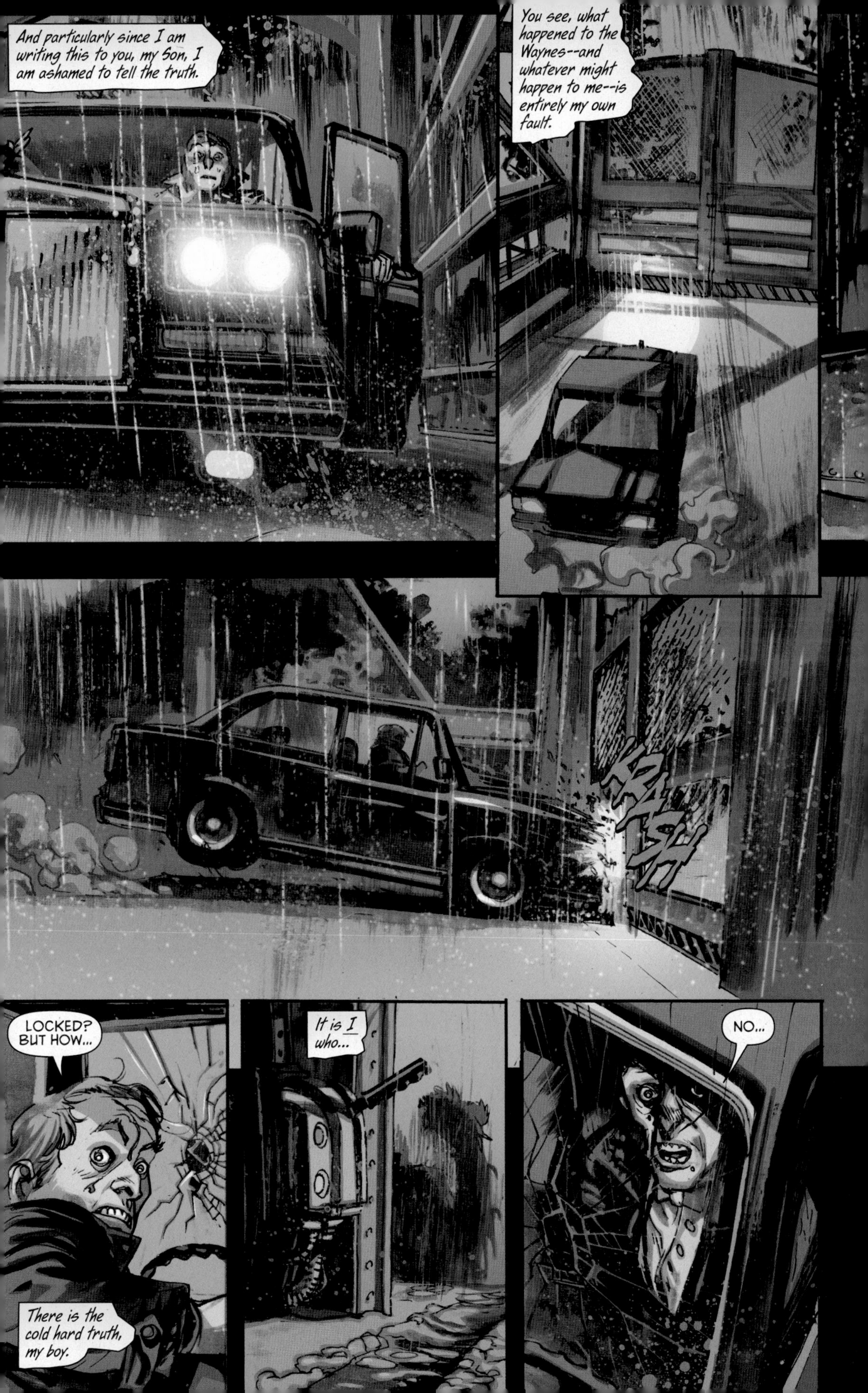

And particularly since I am writing this to you, my Son, I am ashamed to tell the truth.
You see, what happened to the Waynes--and whatever might happen to me--is entirely my own fault.
LOCKED? BUT HOW...
There is the cold hard truth, my boy.
It is I who...
NO...

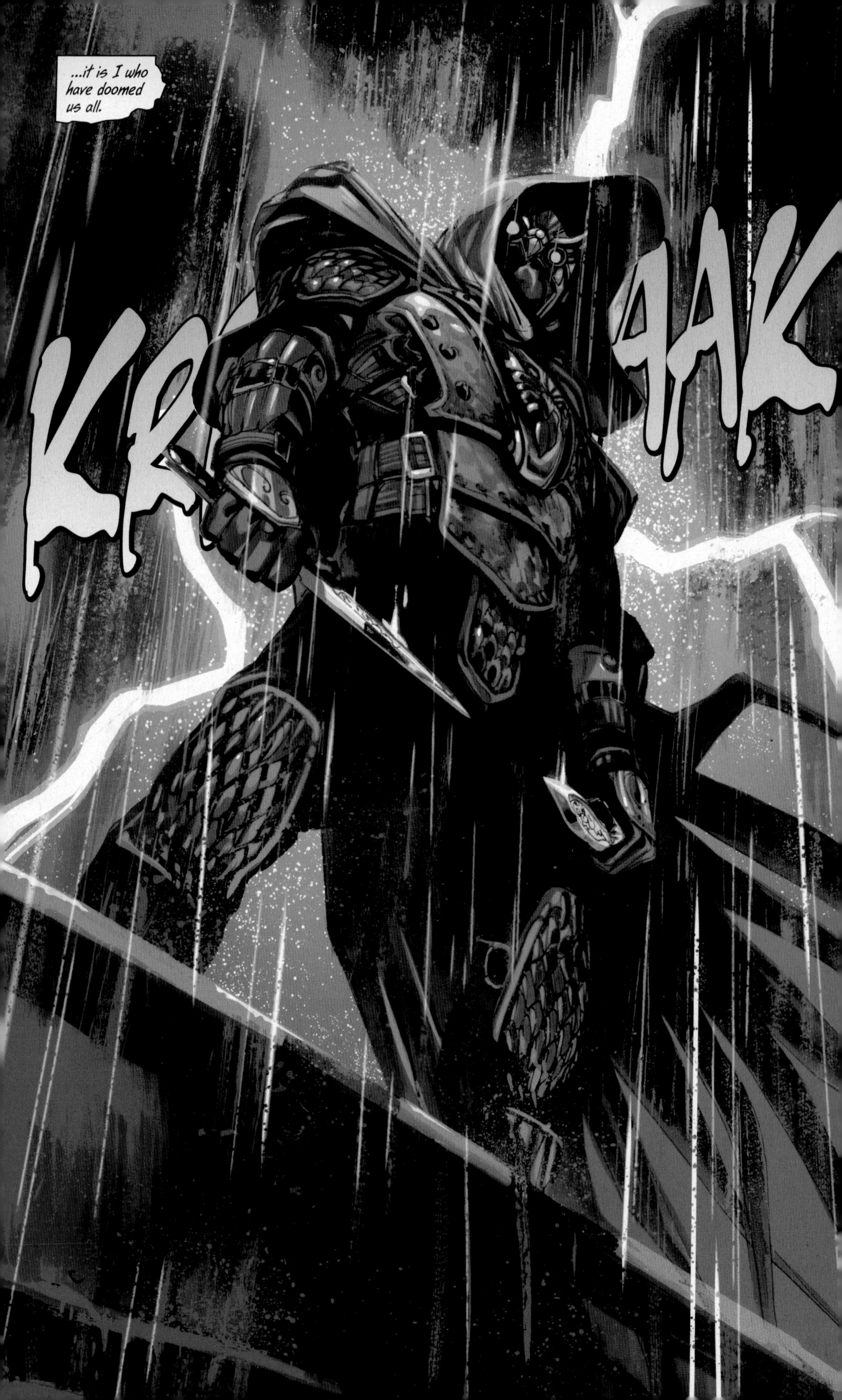
...it is I who have doomed us all.
KR
AAK

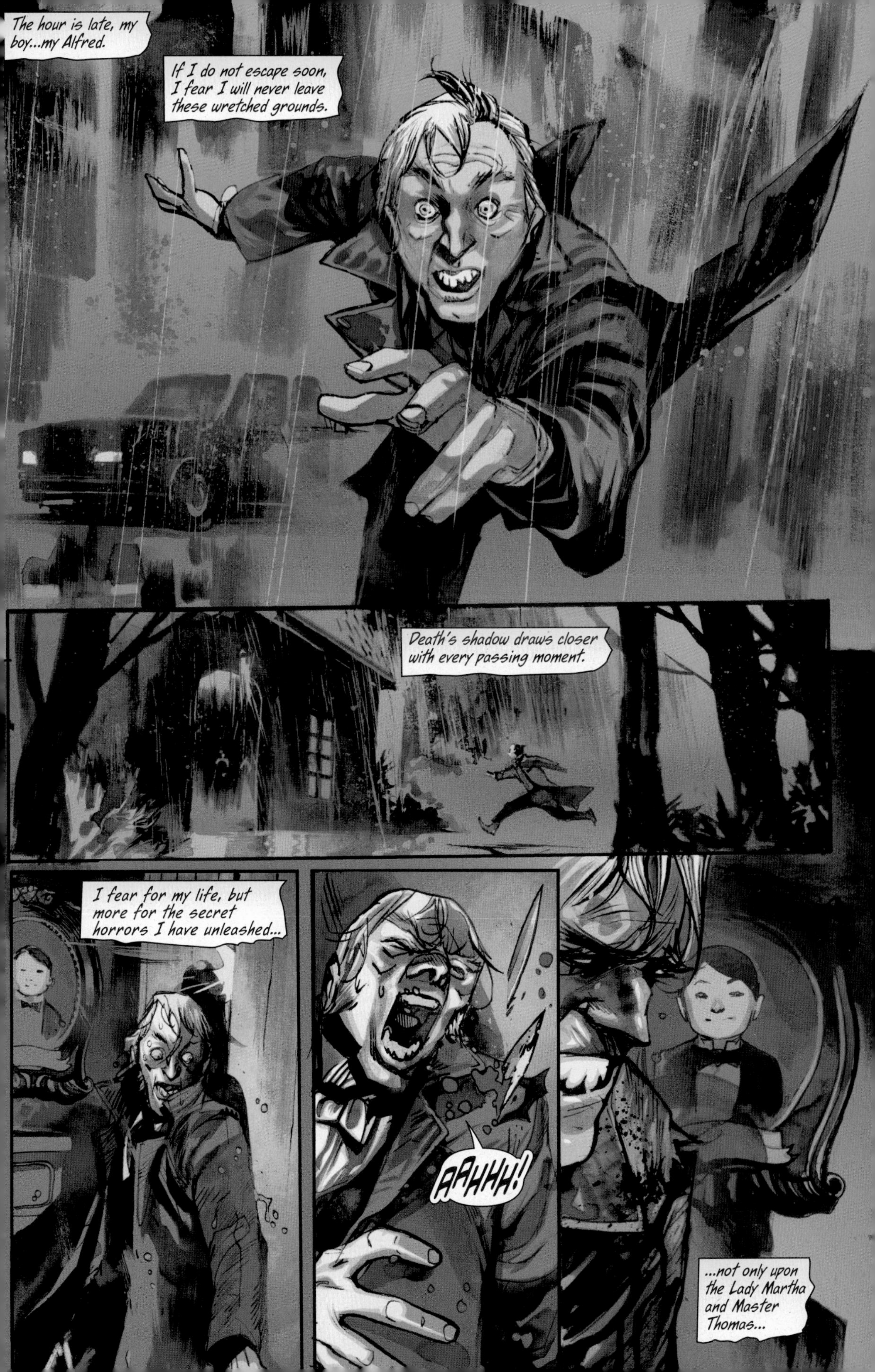
The hour is late, my boy...my Alfred.
If I do not escape soon, I fear I will never leave these wretched grounds.
Death's shadow draws closer with every passing moment.
I fear for my life, but more for the secret horrors I have unleashed...
AAHHH!
...not only upon the Lady Martha and Master Thomas...

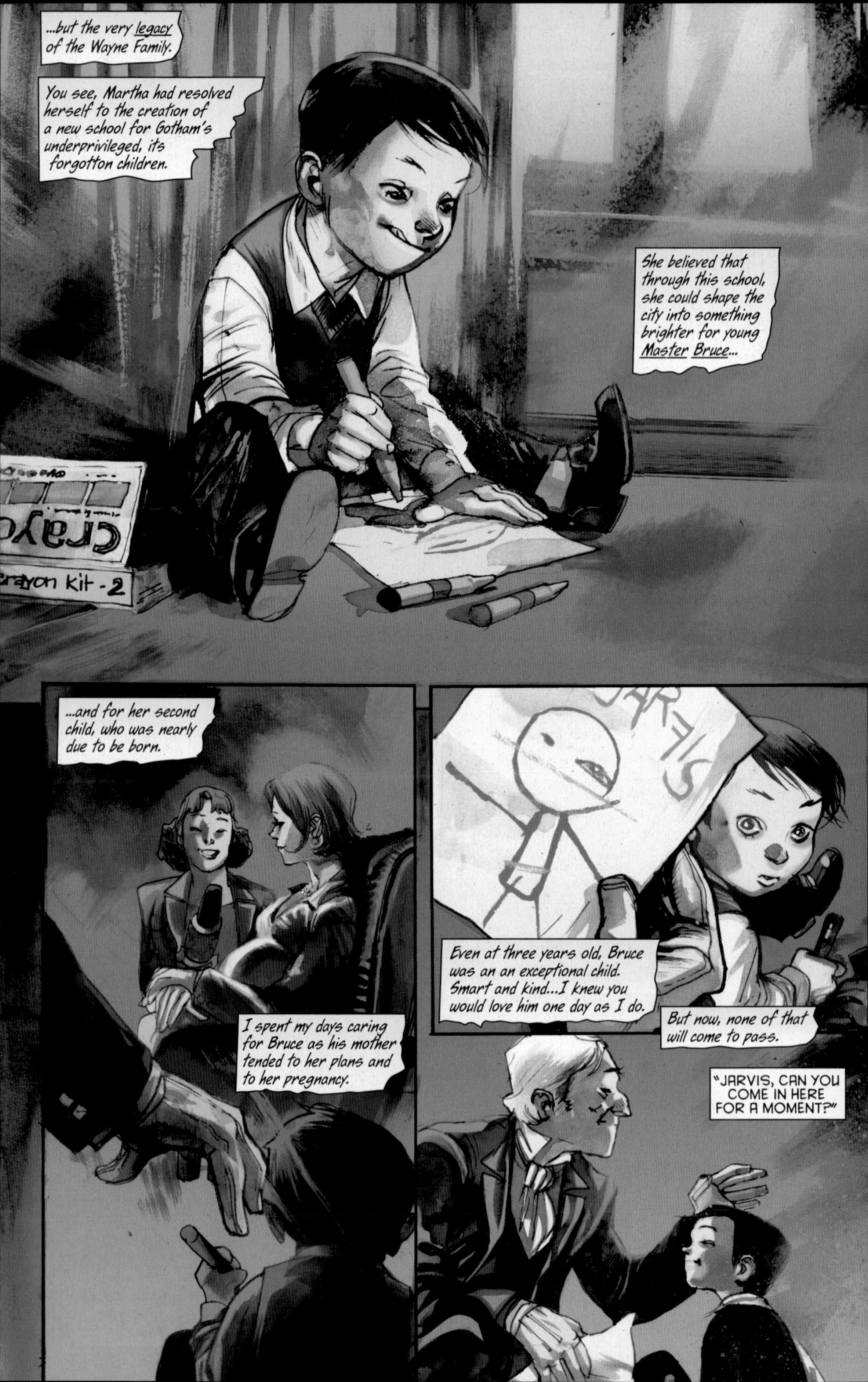
...but the very legacy of the Wayne Family.
You see, Martha had resolved herself to the creation of a new school for Gotham's underprivileged, its forgotton children.
She believed that through this school, she could shape the city into something brighter for young Master Bruce...
crayon kit - 2
...and for her second child, who was nearly due to be born.
I spent my days caring for Bruce as his mother tended to her plans and to her pregnancy.
Even at three years old, Bruce was an an exceptional child. Smart and kind...I knew you would love him one day as I do.
But now, none of that will come to pass.
"JARVIS, CAN YOU COME IN HERE FOR A MOMENT?"

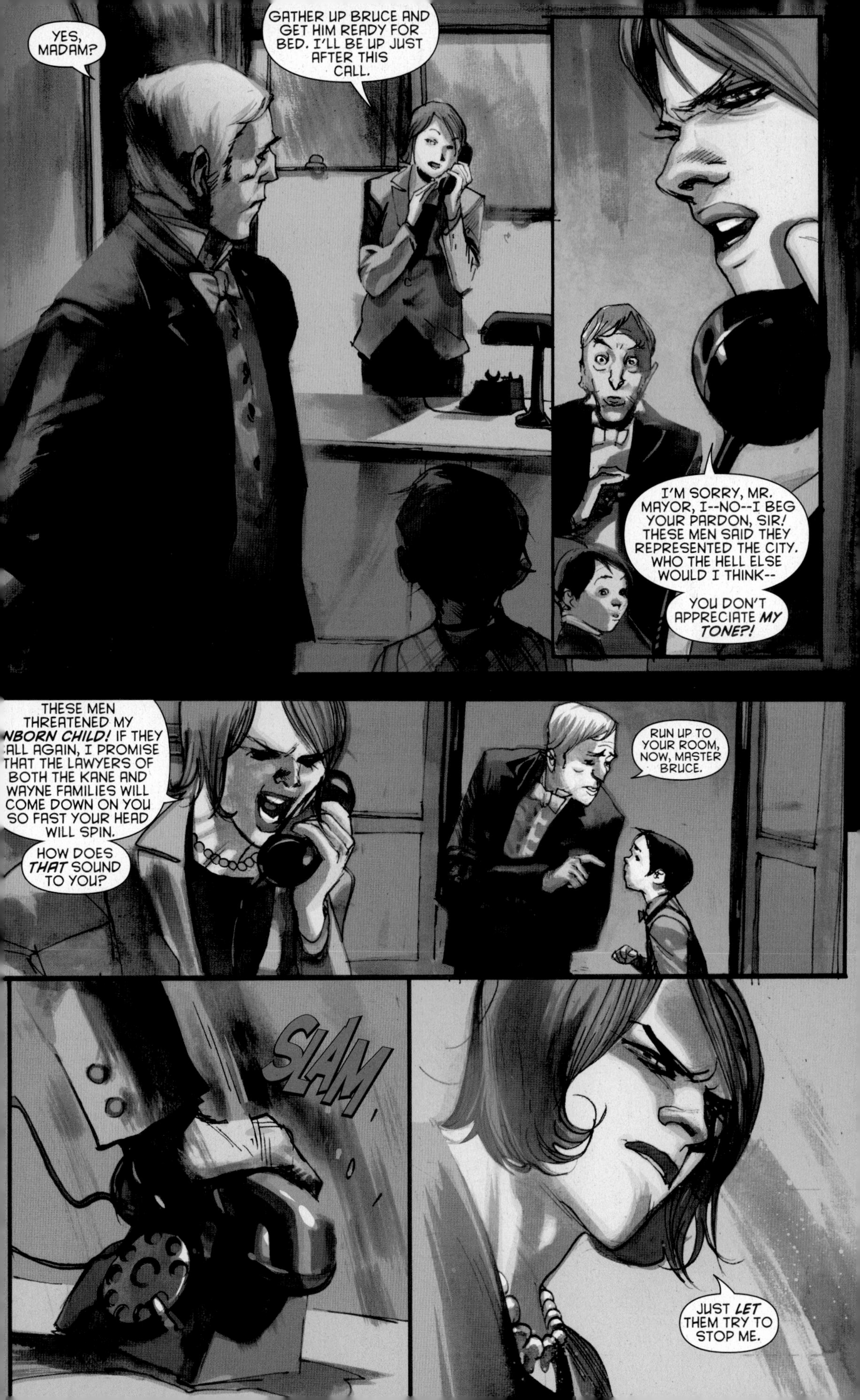
YES, MADAM?
GATHER UP BRUCE AND GET HIM READY FOR BED. I'LL BE UP JUST AFTER THIS CALL.
I'M SORRY, MR. MAYOR, I--NO--I BEG YOUR PARDON, SIR! THESE MEN SAID THEY REPRESENTED THE CITY. WHO THE HELL ELSE WOULD I THINK--
YOU DON'T APPRECIATE MY TONE?!
THESE MEN THREATENED MY NBORN CHILD! IF THEY ALL AGAIN, I PROMISE THAT THE LAWYERS OF BOTH THE KANE AND WAYNE FAMILIES WILL COME DOWN ON YOU SO FAST YOUR HEAD WILL SPIN.
HOW DOES THAT SOUND TO YOU?
RUN UP TO YOUR ROOM, NOW, MASTER BRUCE.
SLAM
JUST LET THEM TRY TO STOP ME.

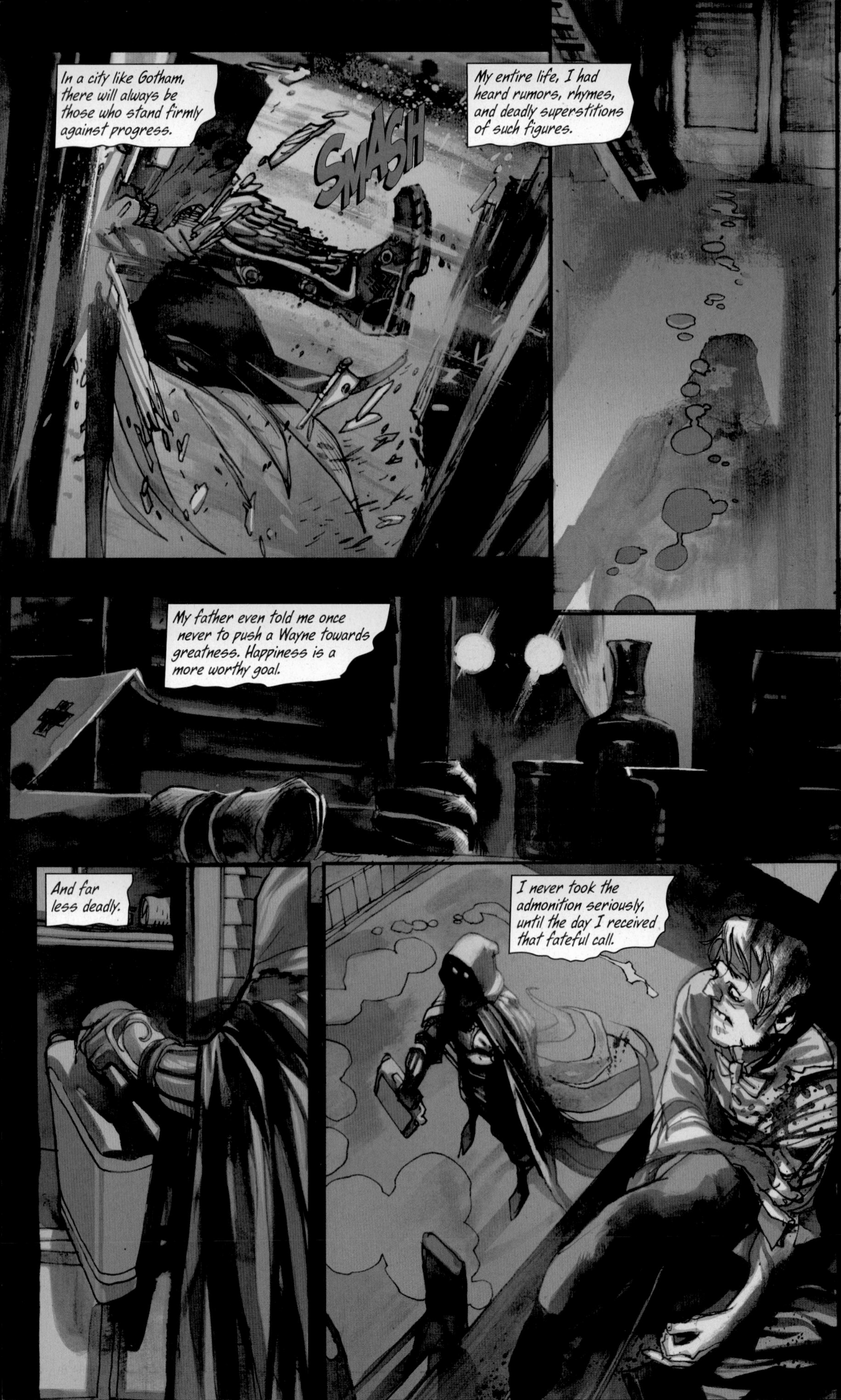
In a city like Gotham, there will always be those who stand firmly against progress.
SMASH
My entire life, I had heard rumors, rhymes, and deadly superstitions of such figures.
My father even told me once never to push a Wayne towards greatness. Happiness is a more worthy goal.
And far less deadly.
I never took the admonition seriously, until the day I received that fateful call.

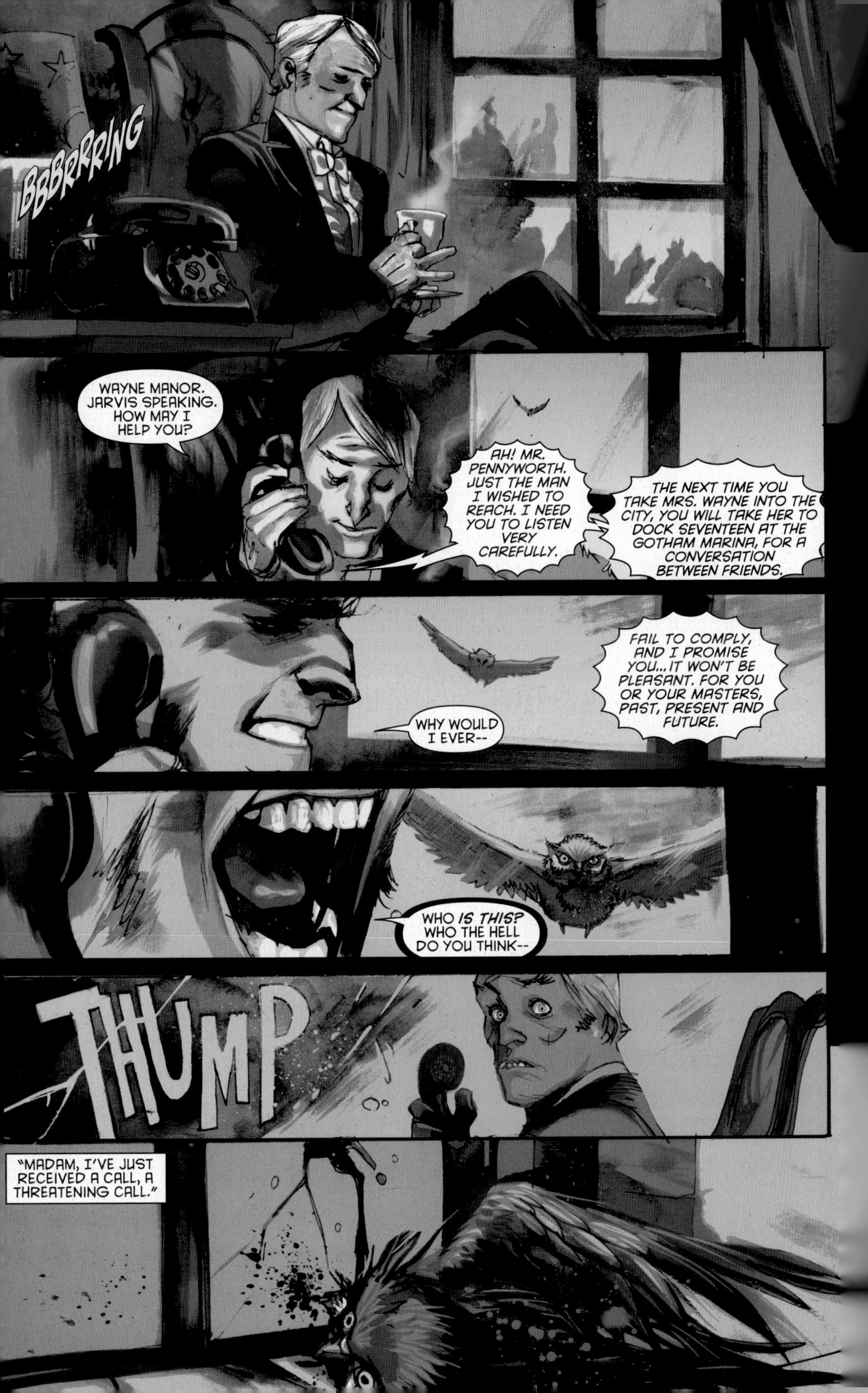
BBBRRRING
WAYNE MANOR. JARVIS SPEAKING. HOW MAY I HELP YOU?
AH! MR. PENNYWORTH. JUST THE MAN I WISHED TO REACH. I NEED YOU TO LISTEN VERY CAREFULLY.
THE NEXT TIME YOU TAKE MRS. WAYNE INTO THE CITY, YOU WILL TAKE HER TO DOCK SEVENTEEN AT THE GOTHAM MARINA, FOR A CONVERSATION BETWEEN FRIENDS.
WHY WOULD I EVER--
FAIL TO COMPLY, AND I PROMISE YOU...IT WON'T BE PLEASANT. FOR YOU OR YOUR MASTERS, PAST, PRESENT AND FUTURE.
WHO IS THIS? WHO THE HELL DO YOU THINK--
THUMP
"MADAM, I'VE JUST RECEIVED A CALL, A THREATENING CALL."

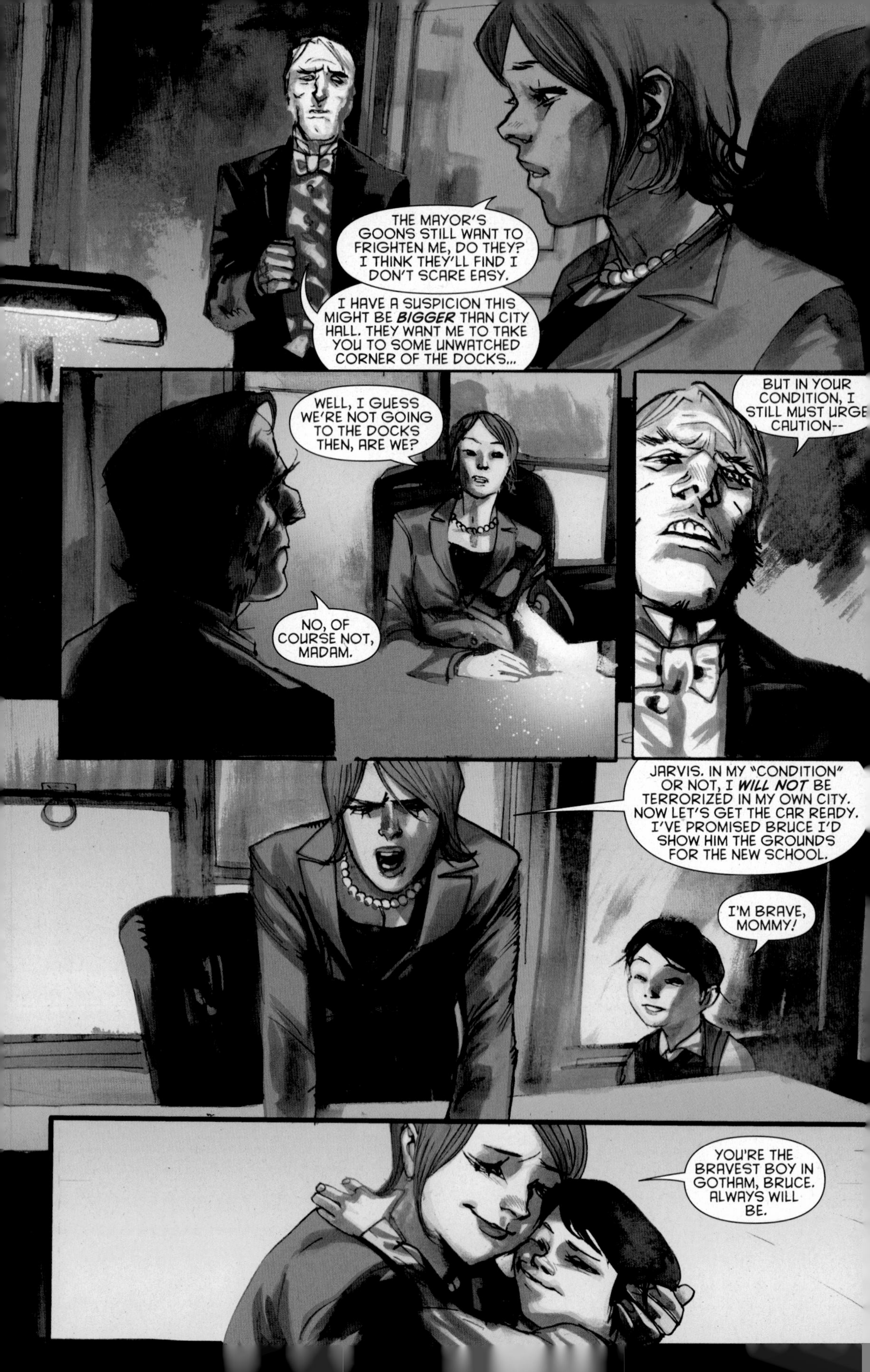
THE MAYOR'S GOONS STILL WANT TO FRIGHTEN ME, DO THEY? I THINK THEY'LL FIND I DON'T SCARE EASY.
I HAVE A SUSPICION THIS MIGHT BE **BIGGER** THAN CITY HALL. THEY WANT ME TO TAKE YOU TO SOME UNWATCHED CORNER OF THE DOCKS...
WELL, I GUESS WE'RE NOT GOING TO THE DOCKS THEN, ARE WE?
NO, OF COURSE NOT, MADAM.
BUT IN YOUR CONDITION, I STILL MUST URGE CAUTION--
JARVIS. IN MY "CONDITION" OR NOT, I **WILL NOT** BE TERRORIZED IN MY OWN CITY. NOW LET'S GET THE CAR READY. I'VE PROMISED BRUCE I'D SHOW HIM THE GROUNDS FOR THE NEW SCHOOL.
I'M BRAVE, MOMMY!
YOU'RE THE BRAVEST BOY IN GOTHAM, BRUCE. ALWAYS WILL BE.

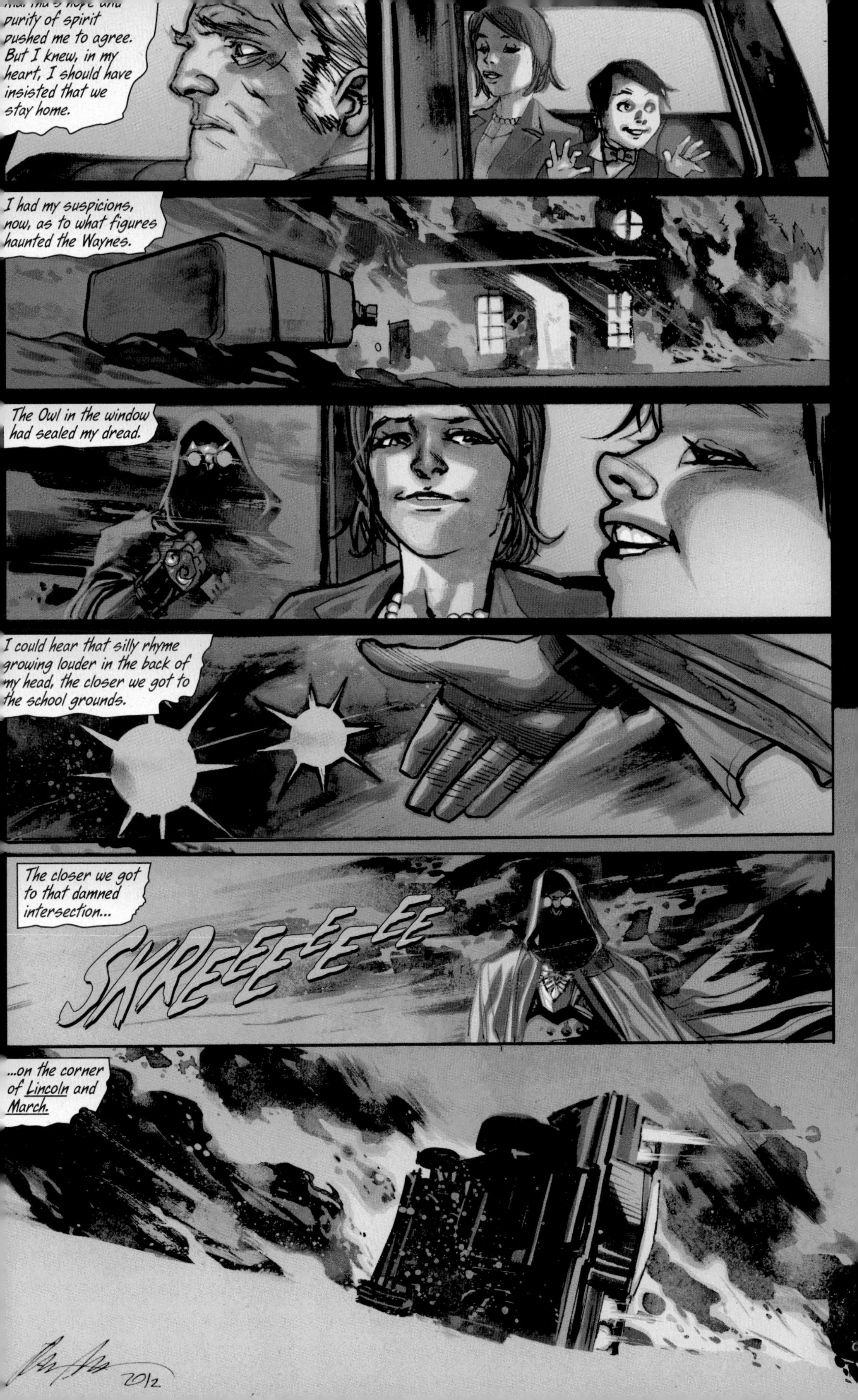
purity of spirit pushed me to agree. But I knew, in my heart, I should have insisted that we stay home.
I had my suspicions, now, as to what figures haunted the Waynes.
The Owl in the window had sealed my dread.
I could hear that silly rhyme growing louder in the back of my head, the closer we got to the school grounds.
The closer we got to that damned intersection...
SKREEEEEEE
...on the corner of Lincoln and March.
2012

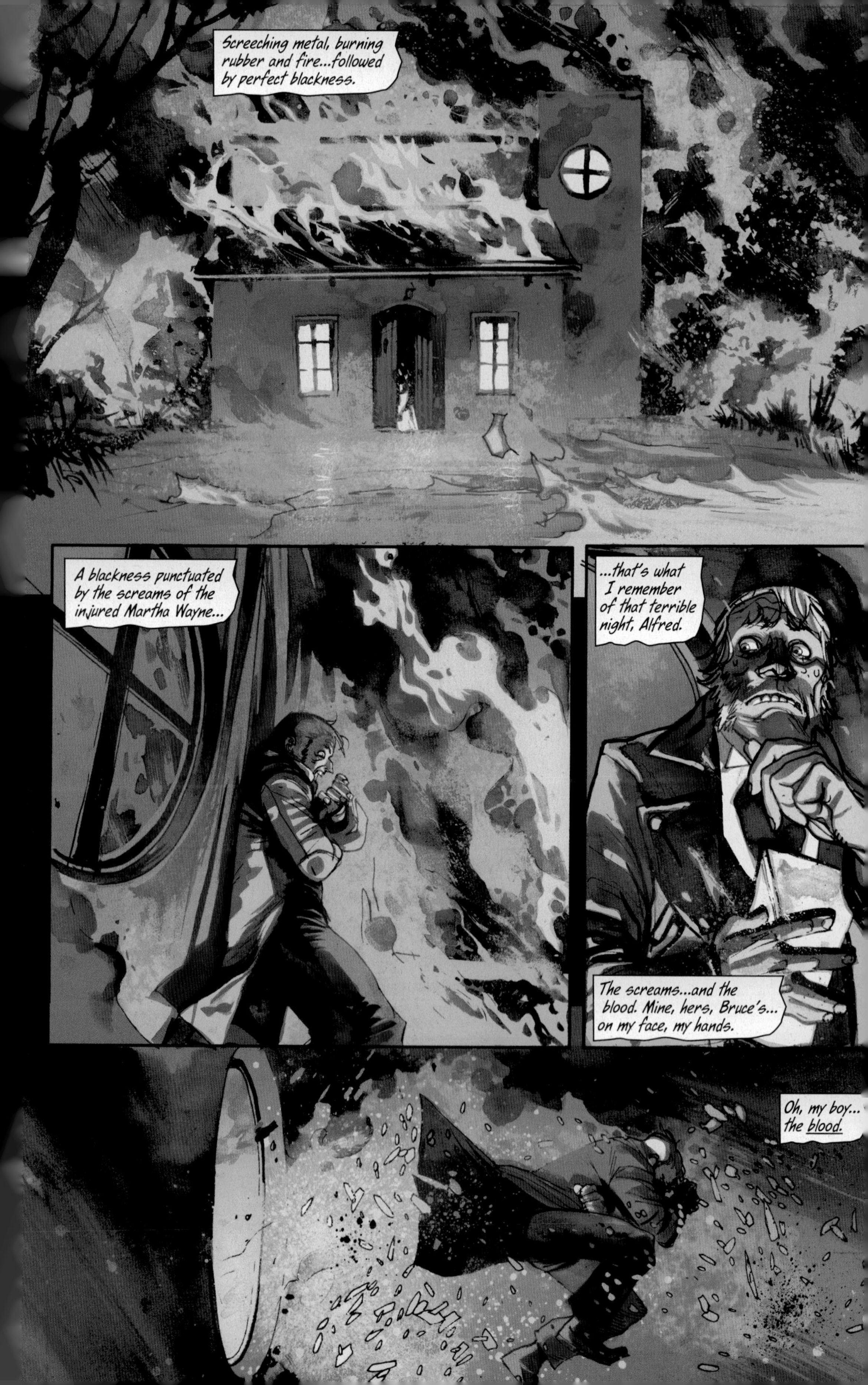
Screeching metal, burning rubber and fire...followed by perfect blackness.
A blackness punctuated by the screams of the injured Martha Wayne...
...that's what I remember of that terrible night, Alfred.
The screams...and the blood. Mine, hers, Bruce's... on my face, my hands.
Oh, my boy... the blood.

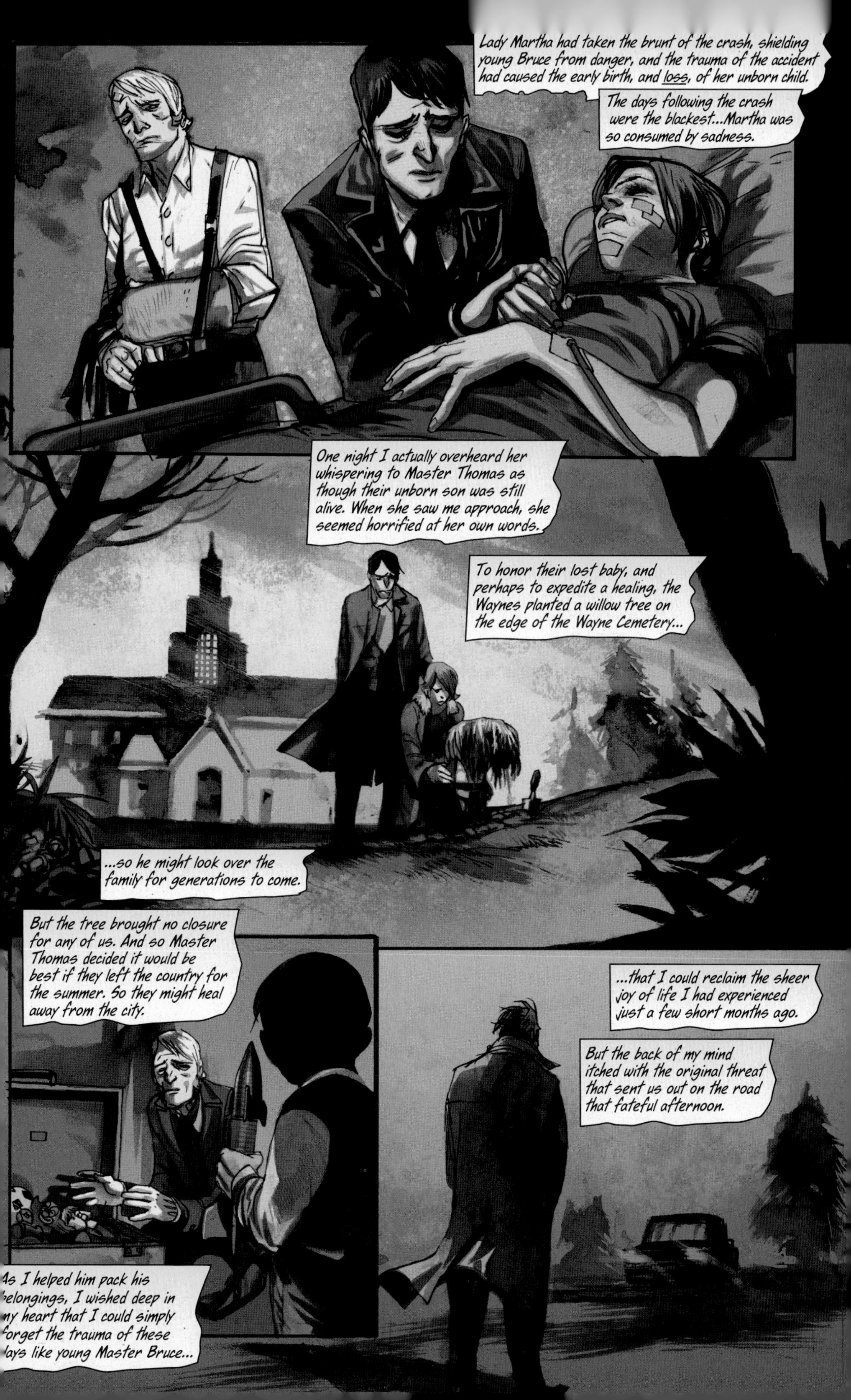

Lady Martha had taken the brunt of the crash, shielding young Bruce from danger, and the trauma of the accident had caused the early birth, and loss, of her unborn child.
The days following the crash were the blackest...Martha was so consumed by sadness.
One night I actually overheard her whispering to Master Thomas as though their unborn son was still alive. When she saw me approach, she seemed horrified at her own words.
To honor their lost baby, and perhaps to expedite a healing, the Waynes planted a willow tree on the edge of the Wayne Cemetery...
...so he might look over the family for generations to come.
But the tree brought no closure for any of us. And so Master Thomas decided it would be best if they left the country for the summer. So they might heal away from the city.
As I helped him pack his elongings, I wished deep in ny heart that I could simply orget the trauma of these lays like young Master Bruce...
...that I could reclaim the sheer joy of life I had experienced just a few short months ago.
But the back of my mind itched with the original threat that sent us out on the road that fateful afternoon.

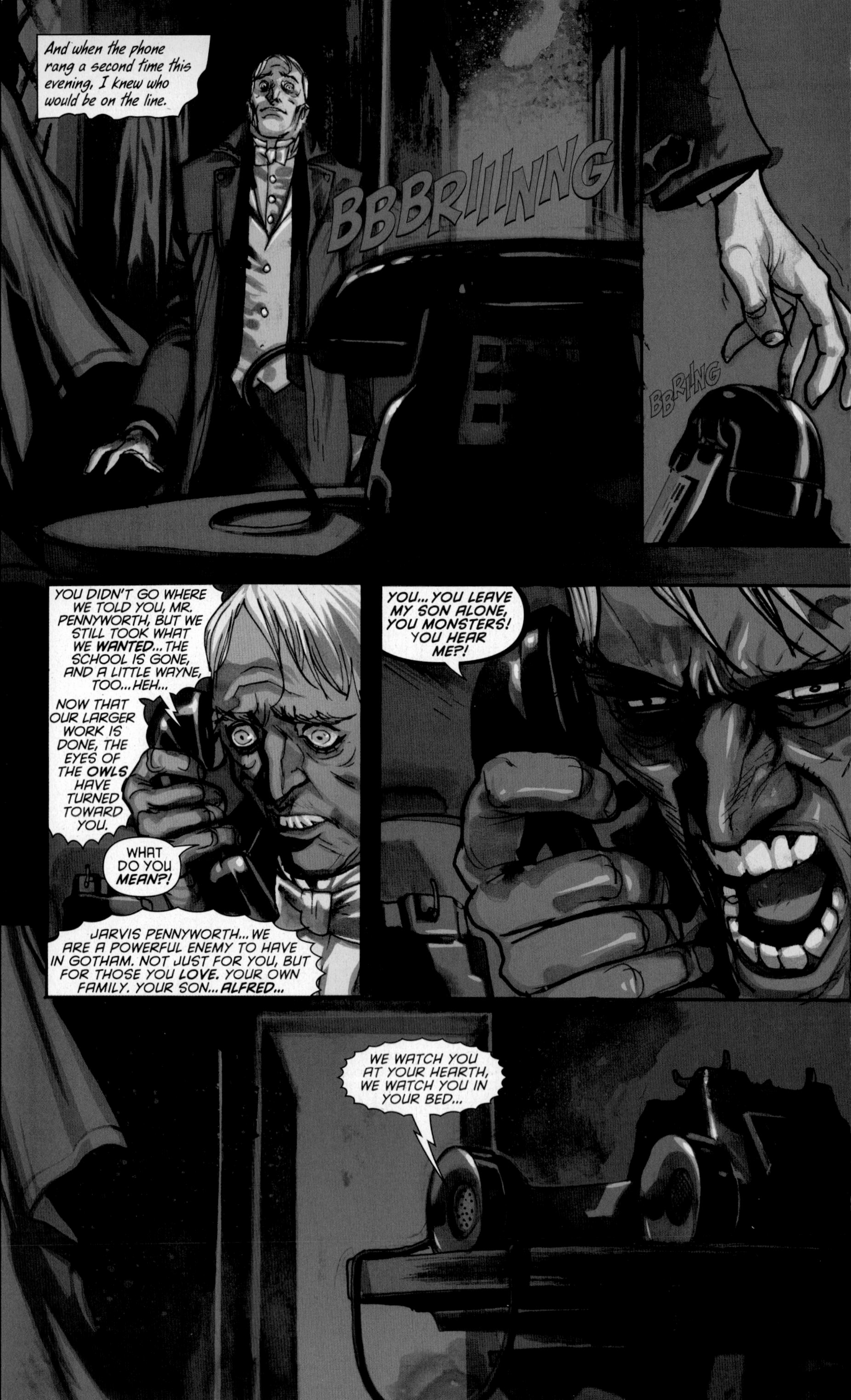
And when the phone rang a second time this evening, I knew who would be on the line.
BBBRIIINNG
BBRIING
YOU DIDN'T GO WHERE WE TOLD YOU, MR. PENNYWORTH, BUT WE STILL TOOK WHAT WE WANTED... THE SCHOOL IS GONE, AND A LITTLE WAYNE, TOO... HEH...
NOW THAT OUR LARGER WORK IS DONE, THE EYES OF THE OWLS HAVE TURNED TOWARD YOU.
WHAT DO YOU MEAN?!
JARVIS PENNYWORTH... WE ARE A POWERFUL ENEMY TO HAVE IN GOTHAM. NOT JUST FOR YOU, BUT FOR THOSE YOU LOVE. YOUR OWN FAMILY. YOUR SON... ALFRED...
YOU... YOU LEAVE MY SON ALONE, YOU MONSTERS! YOU HEAR ME?!
WE WATCH YOU AT YOUR HEARTH, WE WATCH YOU IN YOUR BED...

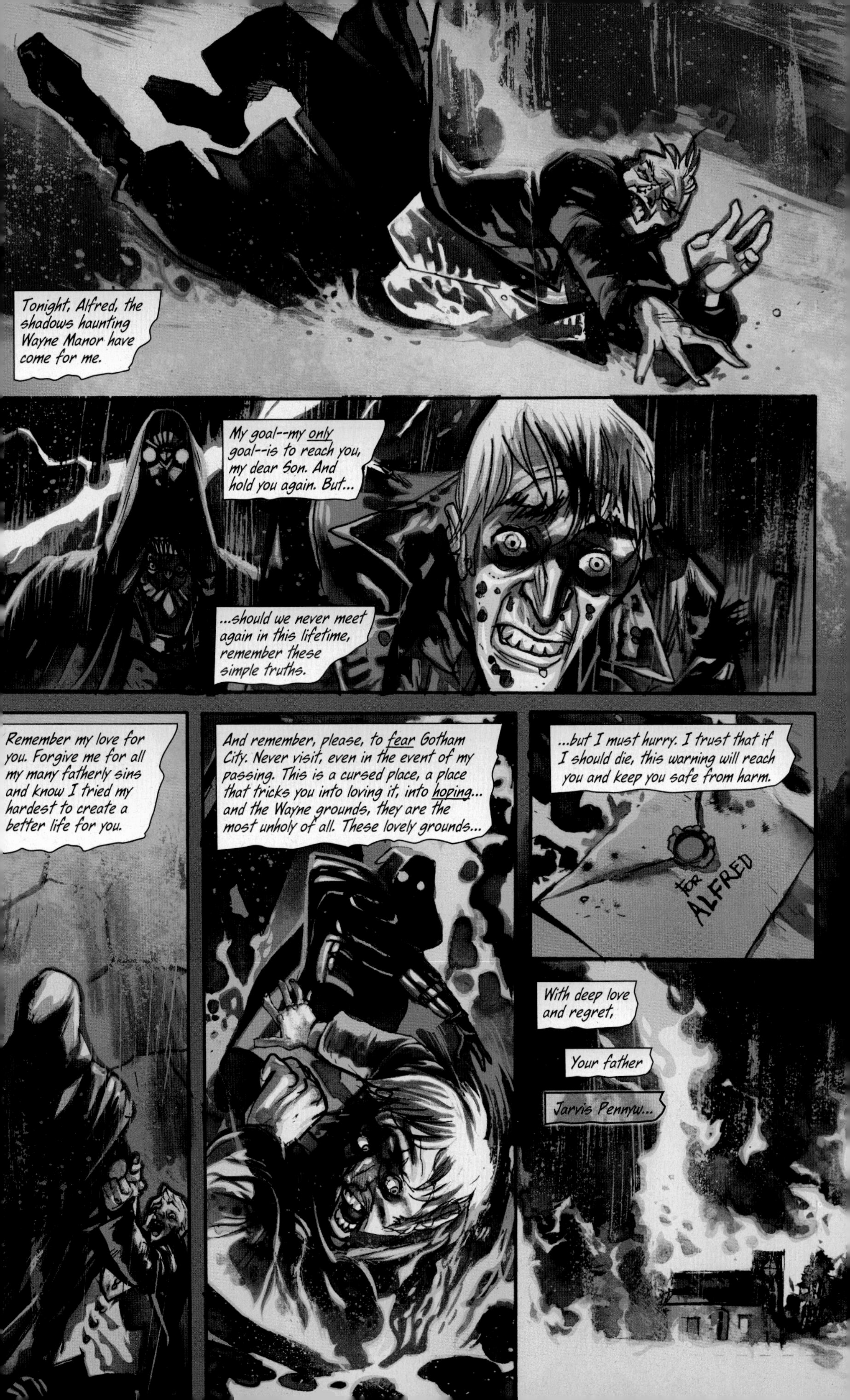
Tonight, Alfred, the shadows haunting Wayne Manor have come for me.
My goal--my only goal--is to reach you, my dear Son. And hold you again. But...
...should we never meet again in this lifetime, remember these simple truths.
Remember my love for you. Forgive me for all my many fatherly sins and know I tried my hardest to create a better life for you.
And remember, please, to fear Gotham City. Never visit, even in the event of my passing. This is a cursed place, a place that tricks you into loving it, into hoping... and the Wayne grounds, they are the most unholy of all. These lovely grounds...
...but I must hurry. I trust that if I should die, this warning will reach you and keep you safe from harm.
FOR ALFRED
With deep love and regret,
Your father
Jarvis Pennyw...

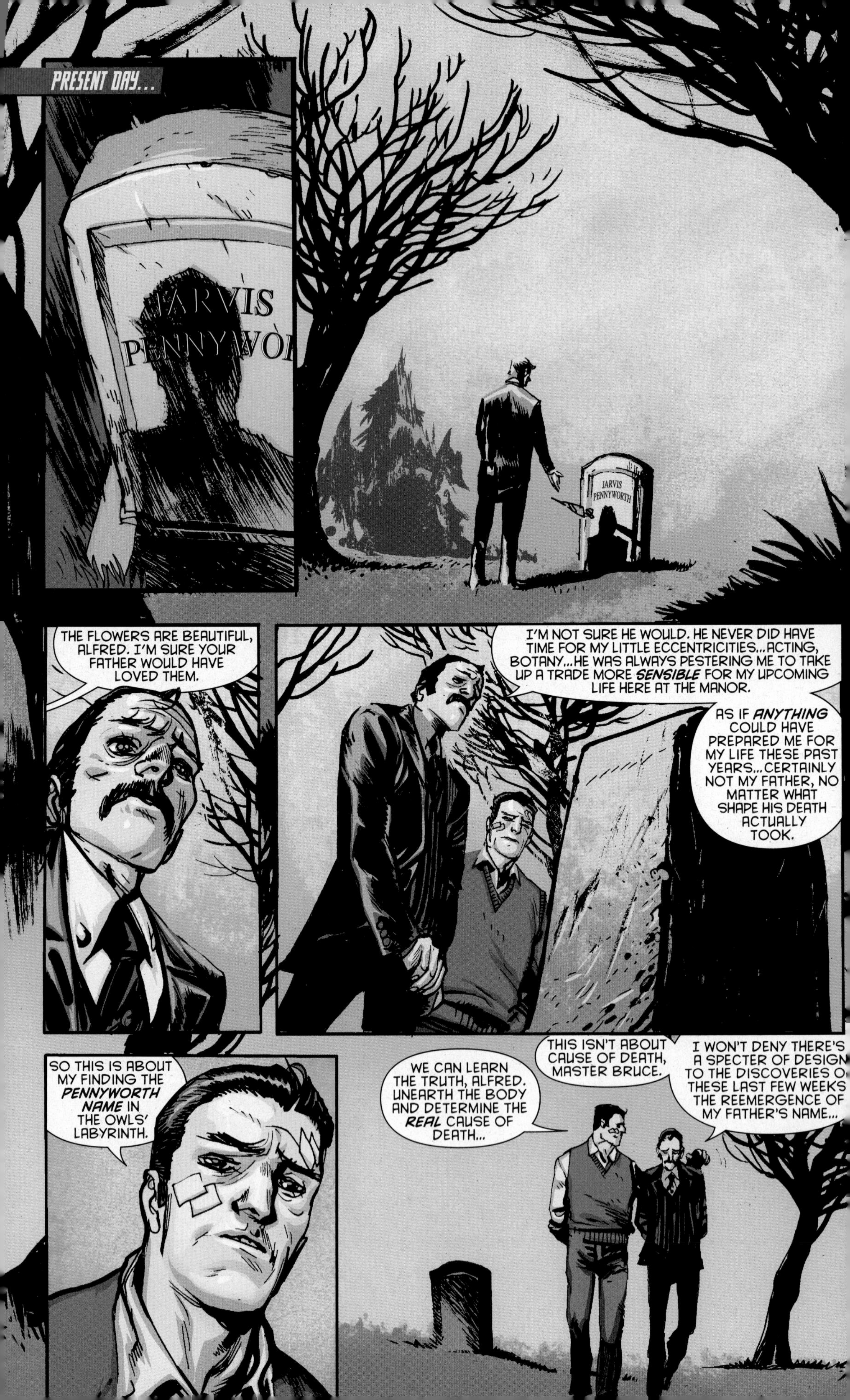
PRESENT DAY...
JARVIS PENNYWOR
JARVIS PENNYWORTH
THE FLOWERS ARE BEAUTIFUL, ALFRED. I'M SURE YOUR FATHER WOULD HAVE LOVED THEM.
I'M NOT SURE HE WOULD. HE NEVER DID HAVE TIME FOR MY LITTLE ECCENTRICITIES...ACTING, BOTANY...HE WAS ALWAYS PESTERING ME TO TAKE UP A TRADE MORE SENSIBLE FOR MY UPCOMING LIFE HERE AT THE MANOR.
AS IF ANYTHING COULD HAVE PREPARED ME FOR MY LIFE THESE PAST YEARS...CERTAINLY NOT MY FATHER, NO MATTER WHAT SHAPE HIS DEATH ACTUALLY TOOK.
SO THIS IS ABOUT MY FINDING THE PENNYWORTH NAME IN THE OWLS' LABYRINTH.
WE CAN LEARN THE TRUTH, ALFRED. UNEARTH THE BODY AND DETERMINE THE REAL CAUSE OF DEATH...
THIS ISN'T ABOUT CAUSE OF DEATH, MASTER BRUCE.
I WON'T DENY THERE'S A SPECTER OF DESIGN TO THE DISCOVERIES O THESE LAST FEW WEEKS THE REEMERGENCE OF MY FATHER'S NAME...

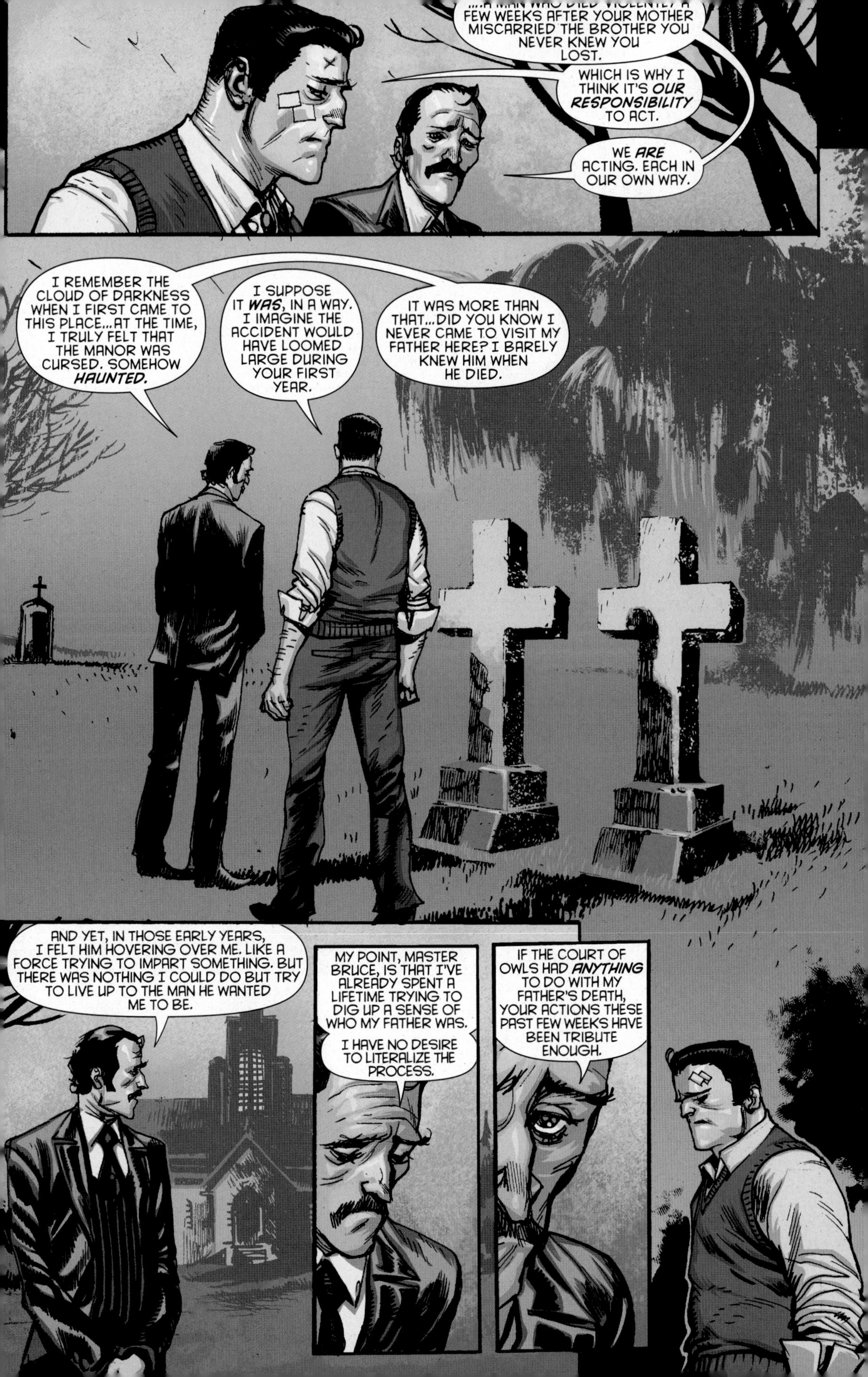

FEW WEEKS AFTER YOUR MOTHER MISCARRIED THE BROTHER YOU NEVER KNEW YOU LOST.
WHICH IS WHY I THINK IT'S *OUR RESPONSIBILITY* TO ACT.
WE *ARE* ACTING. EACH IN OUR OWN WAY.
I REMEMBER THE CLOUD OF DARKNESS WHEN I FIRST CAME TO THIS PLACE...AT THE TIME, I TRULY FELT THAT THE MANOR WAS CURSED. SOMEHOW *HAUNTED.*
I SUPPOSE IT *WAS*, IN A WAY. I IMAGINE THE ACCIDENT WOULD HAVE LOOMED LARGE DURING YOUR FIRST YEAR.
IT WAS MORE THAN THAT...DID YOU KNOW I NEVER CAME TO VISIT MY FATHER HERE? I BARELY KNEW HIM WHEN HE DIED.
AND YET, IN THOSE EARLY YEARS, I FELT HIM HOVERING OVER ME. LIKE A FORCE TRYING TO IMPART SOMETHING. BUT THERE WAS NOTHING I COULD DO BUT TRY TO LIVE UP TO THE MAN HE WANTED ME TO BE.
MY POINT, MASTER BRUCE, IS THAT I'VE ALREADY SPENT A LIFETIME TRYING TO DIG UP A SENSE OF WHO MY FATHER WAS.
I HAVE NO DESIRE TO LITERALIZE THE PROCESS.
IF THE COURT OF OWLS HAD *ANYTHING* TO DO WITH MY FATHER'S DEATH, YOUR ACTIONS THESE PAST FEW WEEKS HAVE BEEN TRIBUTE ENOUGH.

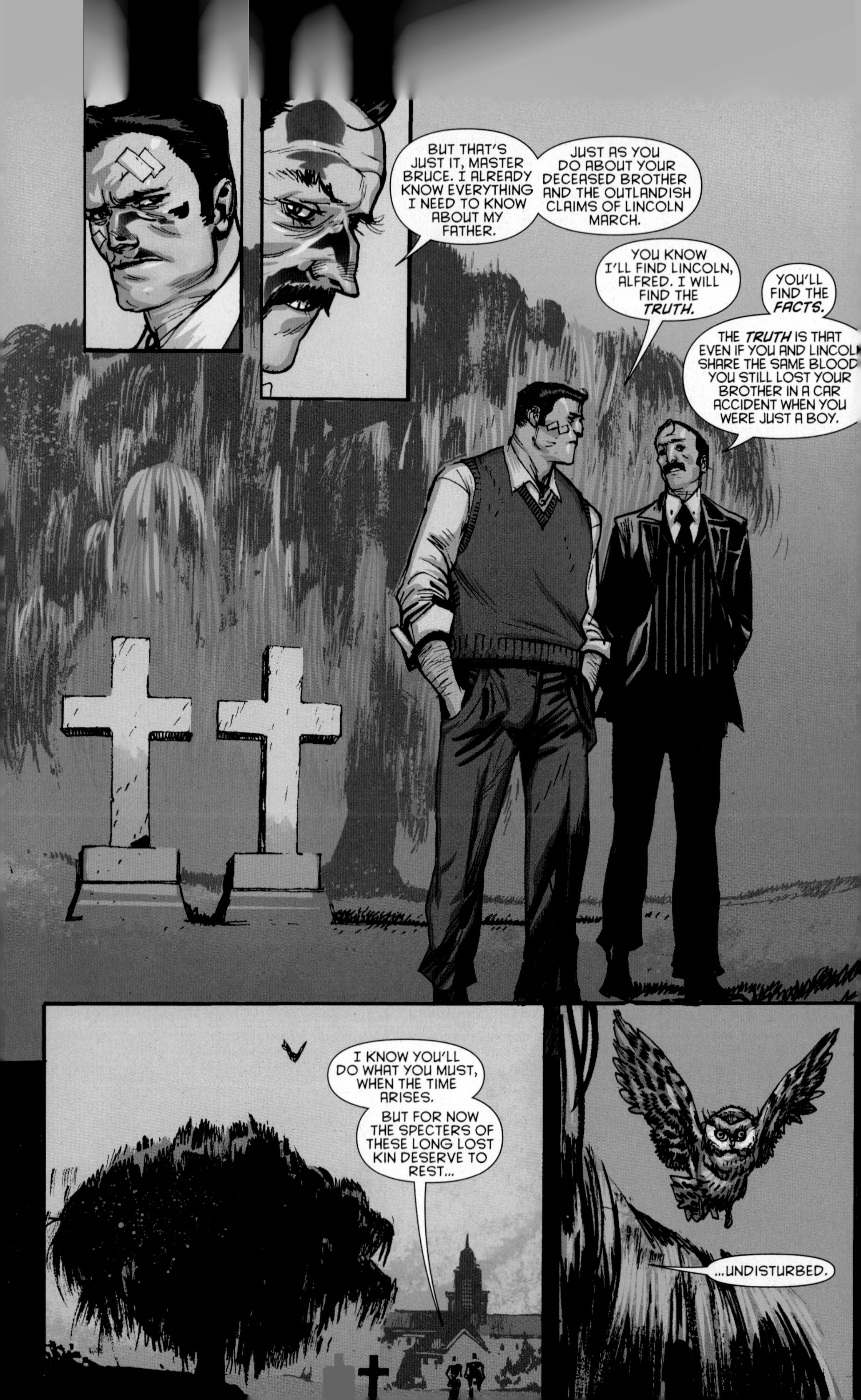
BUT THAT'S JUST IT, MASTER BRUCE. I ALREADY KNOW EVERYTHING I NEED TO KNOW ABOUT MY FATHER.
JUST AS YOU DO ABOUT YOUR DECEASED BROTHER AND THE OUTLANDISH CLAIMS OF LINCOLN MARCH.
YOU KNOW I'LL FIND LINCOLN, ALFRED. I WILL FIND THE TRUTH.
YOU'LL FIND THE FACTS.
THE TRUTH IS THAT EVEN IF YOU AND LINCOL SHARE THE SAME BLOOD YOU STILL LOST YOUR BROTHER IN A CAR ACCIDENT WHEN YOU WERE JUST A BOY.
I KNOW YOU'LL DO WHAT YOU MUST, WHEN THE TIME ARISES.
BUT FOR NOW THE SPECTERS OF THESE LONG LOST KIN DESERVE TO REST...
...UNDISTURBED.

GHOST IN THE MACHINE

SCOTT SNYDER & JAMES TYNION IV writers BECKY CLOONAN artist ANDY CLARKE additional art SANDU FLOREA additional inks
cover by GREG CAPULLO and FCO PLASCENCIA

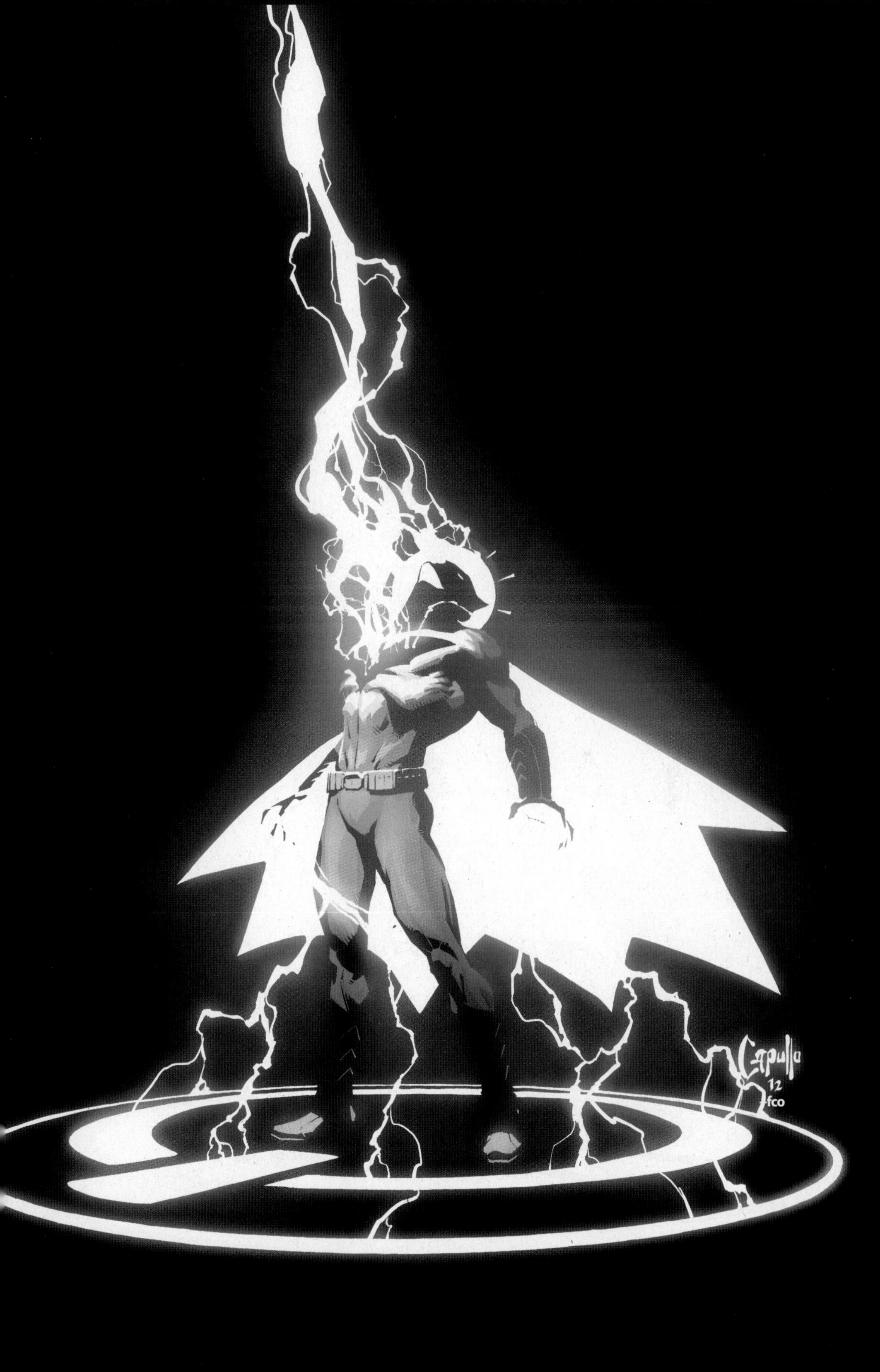
Capullo
'12
fco

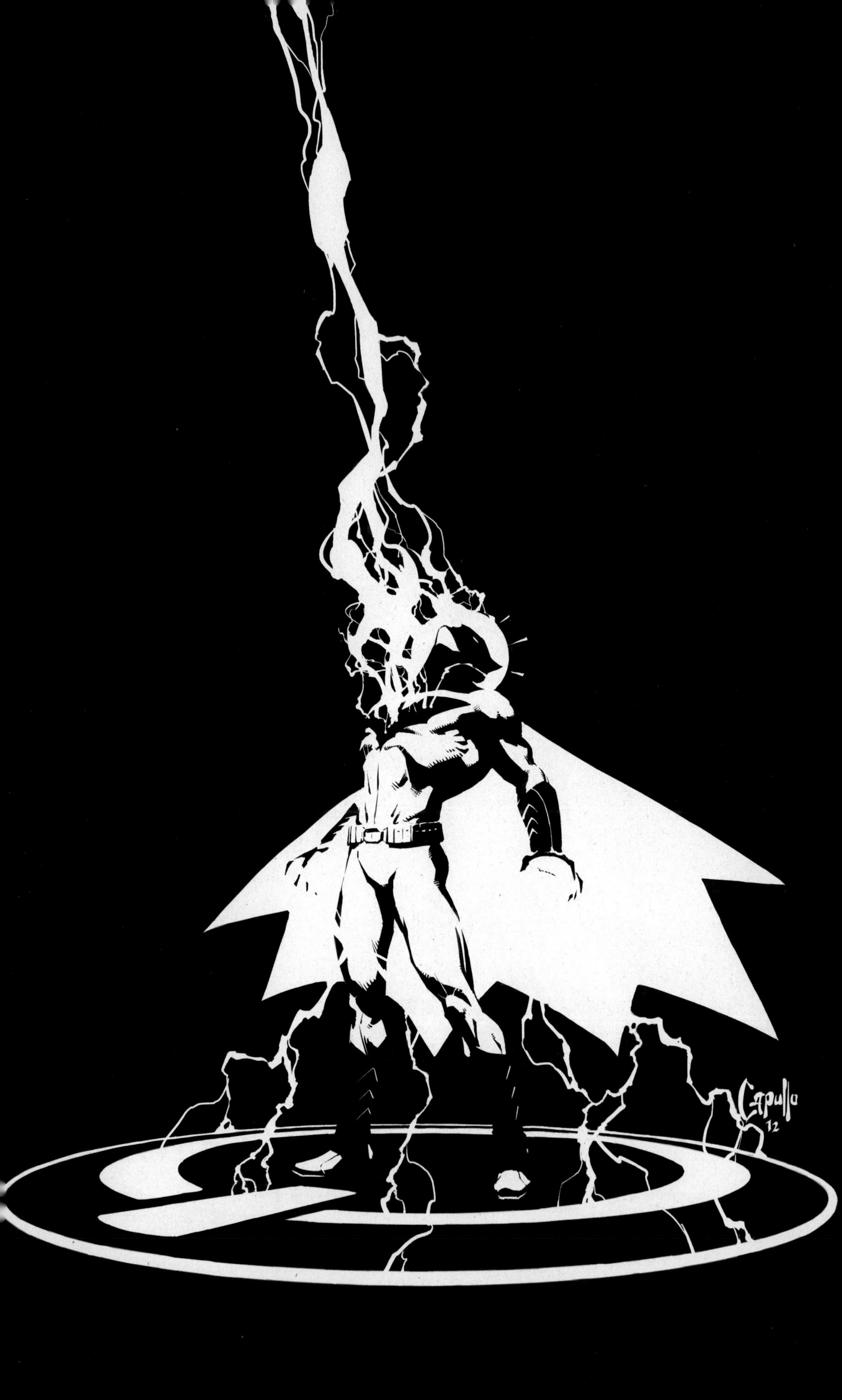
Capullo
'12

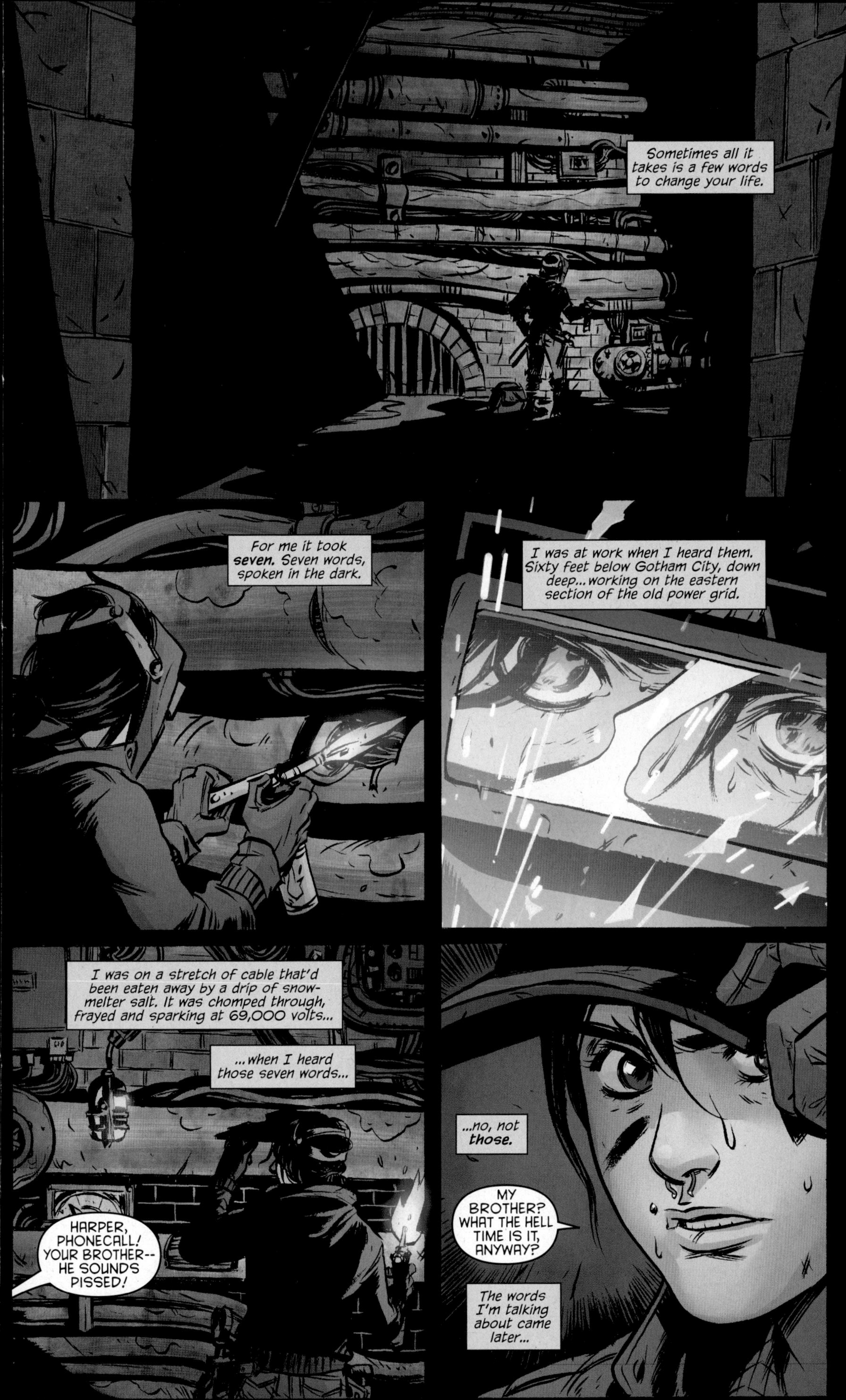
Sometimes all it takes is a few words to change your life.
For me it took **seven.** Seven words, spoken in the dark.
I was at work when I heard them. Sixty feet below Gotham City, down deep...working on the eastern section of the old power grid.
I was on a stretch of cable that'd been eaten away by a drip of snow-melter salt. It was chomped through, frayed and sparking at 69,000 volts...
...when I heard those seven words...
HARPER, PHONECALL! YOUR BROTHER-- HE SOUNDS PISSED!
...no, not **those.**
MY BROTHER? WHAT THE HELL TIME IS IT, ANYWAY?
The words I'm talking about came later...

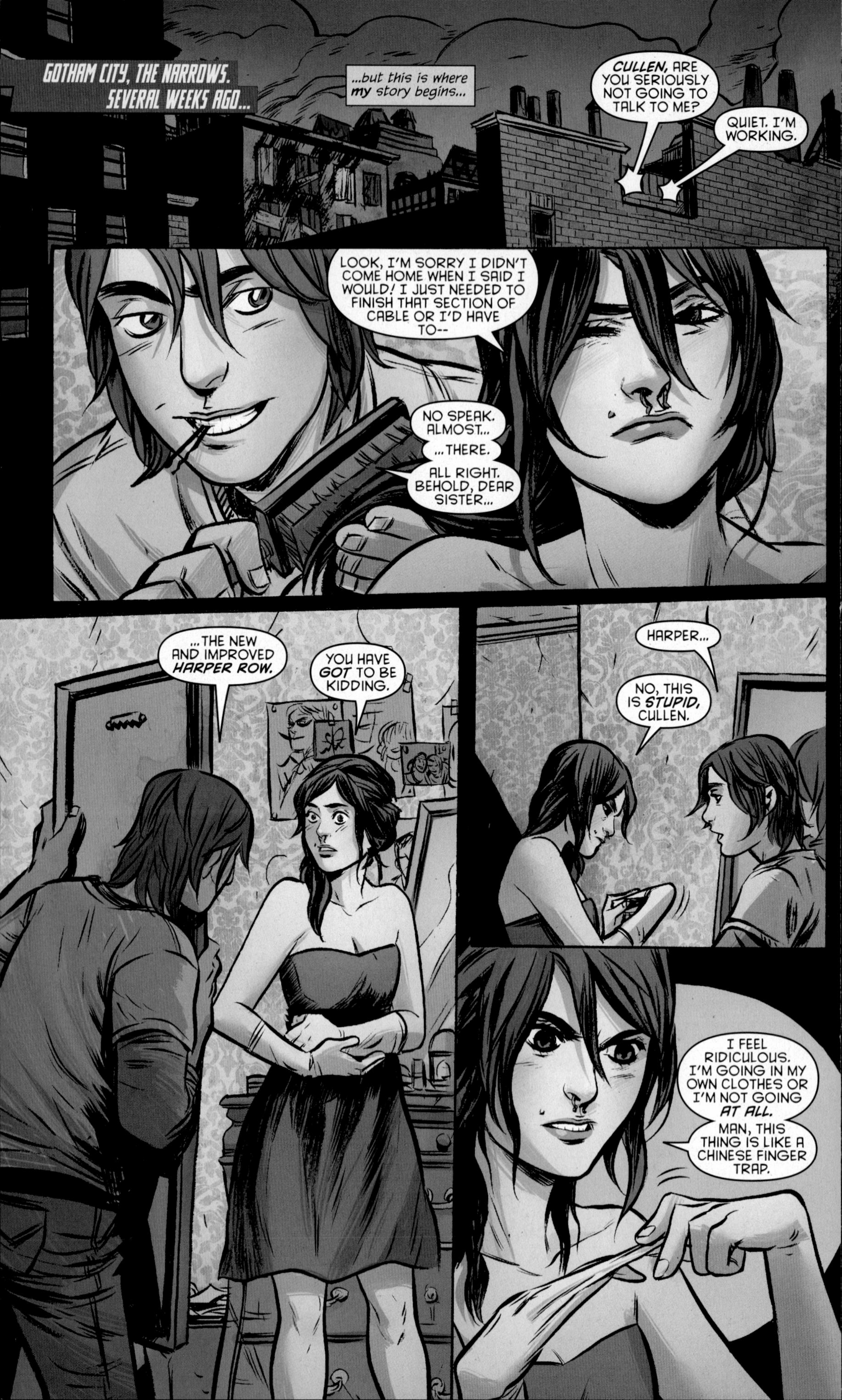

GOTHAM CITY, THE NARROWS. SEVERAL WEEKS AGO...
...but this is where my story begins...
CULLEN, ARE YOU SERIOUSLY NOT GOING TO TALK TO ME?
QUIET. I'M WORKING.
LOOK, I'M SORRY I DIDN'T COME HOME WHEN I SAID I WOULD! I JUST NEEDED TO FINISH THAT SECTION OF CABLE OR I'D HAVE TO--
NO SPEAK. ALMOST...
...THERE.
ALL RIGHT. BEHOLD, DEAR SISTER...
...THE NEW AND IMPROVED HARPER ROW.
YOU HAVE GOT TO BE KIDDING.
HARPER...
NO, THIS IS STUPID, CULLEN.
I FEEL RIDICULOUS. I'M GOING IN MY OWN CLOTHES OR I'M NOT GOING AT ALL.
MAN, THIS THING IS LIKE A CHINESE FINGER TRAP.

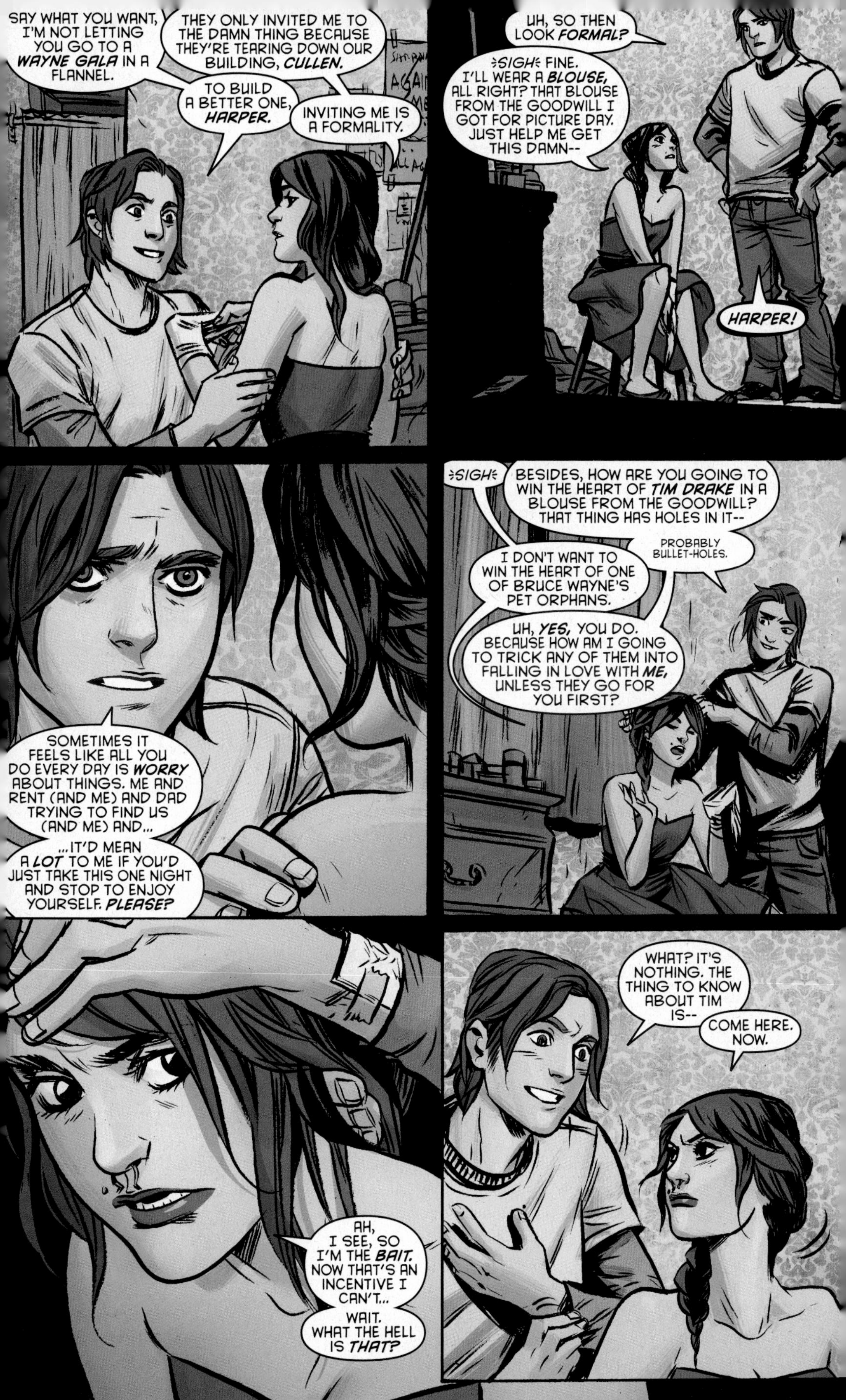
SAY WHAT YOU WANT, I'M NOT LETTING YOU GO TO A *WAYNE GALA* IN A FLANNEL.
THEY ONLY INVITED ME TO THE DAMN THING BECAUSE THEY'RE TEARING DOWN OUR BUILDING, *CULLEN.*
TO BUILD A BETTER ONE, *HARPER.*
INVITING ME IS A FORMALITY.
UH, SO THEN LOOK *FORMAL?*
SIGH FINE. I'LL WEAR A *BLOUSE,* ALL RIGHT? THAT BLOUSE FROM THE GOODWILL I GOT FOR PICTURE DAY. JUST HELP ME GET THIS DAMN--
HARPER!
SOMETIMES IT FEELS LIKE ALL YOU DO EVERY DAY IS *WORRY* ABOUT THINGS. ME AND RENT (AND ME) AND DAD TRYING TO FIND US (AND ME) AND...
...IT'D MEAN A *LOT* TO ME IF YOU'D JUST TAKE THIS ONE NIGHT AND STOP TO ENJOY YOURSELF. *PLEASE?*
SIGH
BESIDES, HOW ARE YOU GOING TO WIN THE HEART OF *TIM DRAKE* IN A BLOUSE FROM THE GOODWILL? THAT THING HAS HOLES IN IT--
PROBABLY BULLET-HOLES.
I DON'T WANT TO WIN THE HEART OF ONE OF BRUCE WAYNE'S PET ORPHANS.
UH, *YES,* YOU DO. BECAUSE HOW AM I GOING TO TRICK ANY OF THEM INTO FALLING IN LOVE WITH *ME,* UNLESS THEY GO FOR YOU FIRST?
AH, I SEE, SO I'M THE *BAIT.* NOW THAT'S AN INCENTIVE I CAN'T...
WAIT. WHAT THE HELL IS *THAT?*
WHAT? IT'S NOTHING. THE THING TO KNOW ABOUT TIM IS--
COME HERE. NOW.

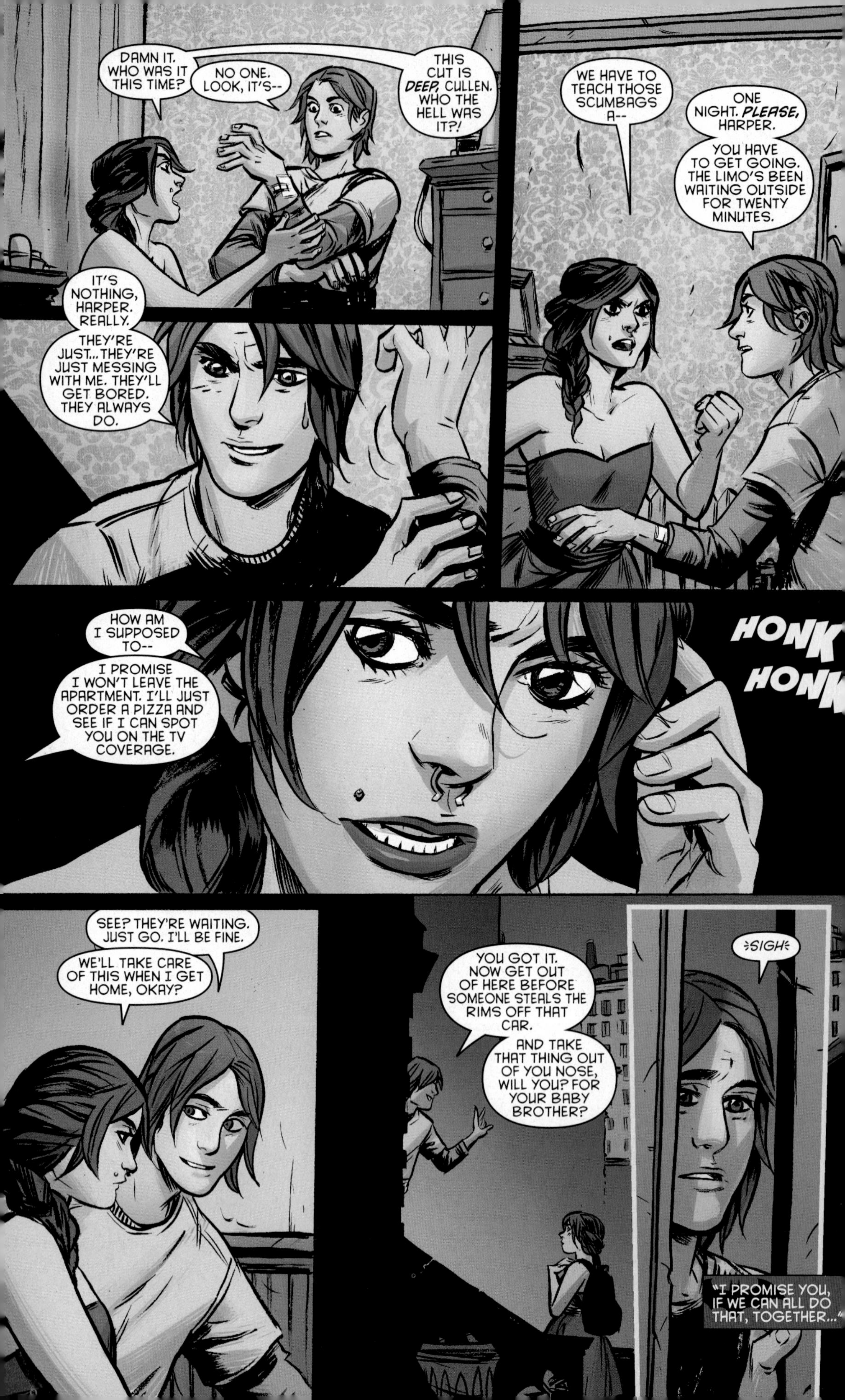
DAMN IT. WHO WAS IT THIS TIME?
NO ONE. LOOK, IT'S--
THIS CUT IS *DEEP,* CULLEN. WHO THE HELL WAS IT?!
IT'S NOTHING, HARPER. REALLY.
THEY'RE JUST... THEY'RE JUST MESSING WITH ME. THEY'LL GET BORED. THEY ALWAYS DO.
WE HAVE TO TEACH THOSE SCUMBAGS A--
ONE NIGHT. *PLEASE,* HARPER.
YOU HAVE TO GET GOING. THE LIMO'S BEEN WAITING OUTSIDE FOR TWENTY MINUTES.
HOW AM I SUPPOSED TO--
I PROMISE I WON'T LEAVE THE APARTMENT. I'LL JUST ORDER A PIZZA AND SEE IF I CAN SPOT YOU ON THE TV COVERAGE.
HONK
HONK
SEE? THEY'RE WAITING. JUST GO. I'LL BE FINE.
WE'LL TAKE CARE OF THIS WHEN I GET HOME, OKAY?
YOU GOT IT. NOW GET OUT OF HERE BEFORE SOMEONE STEALS THE RIMS OFF THAT CAR.
AND TAKE THAT THING OUT OF YOU NOSE, WILL YOU? FOR YOUR BABY BROTHER?
SIGH
"I PROMISE YOU, IF WE CAN ALL DO THAT, TOGETHER..."

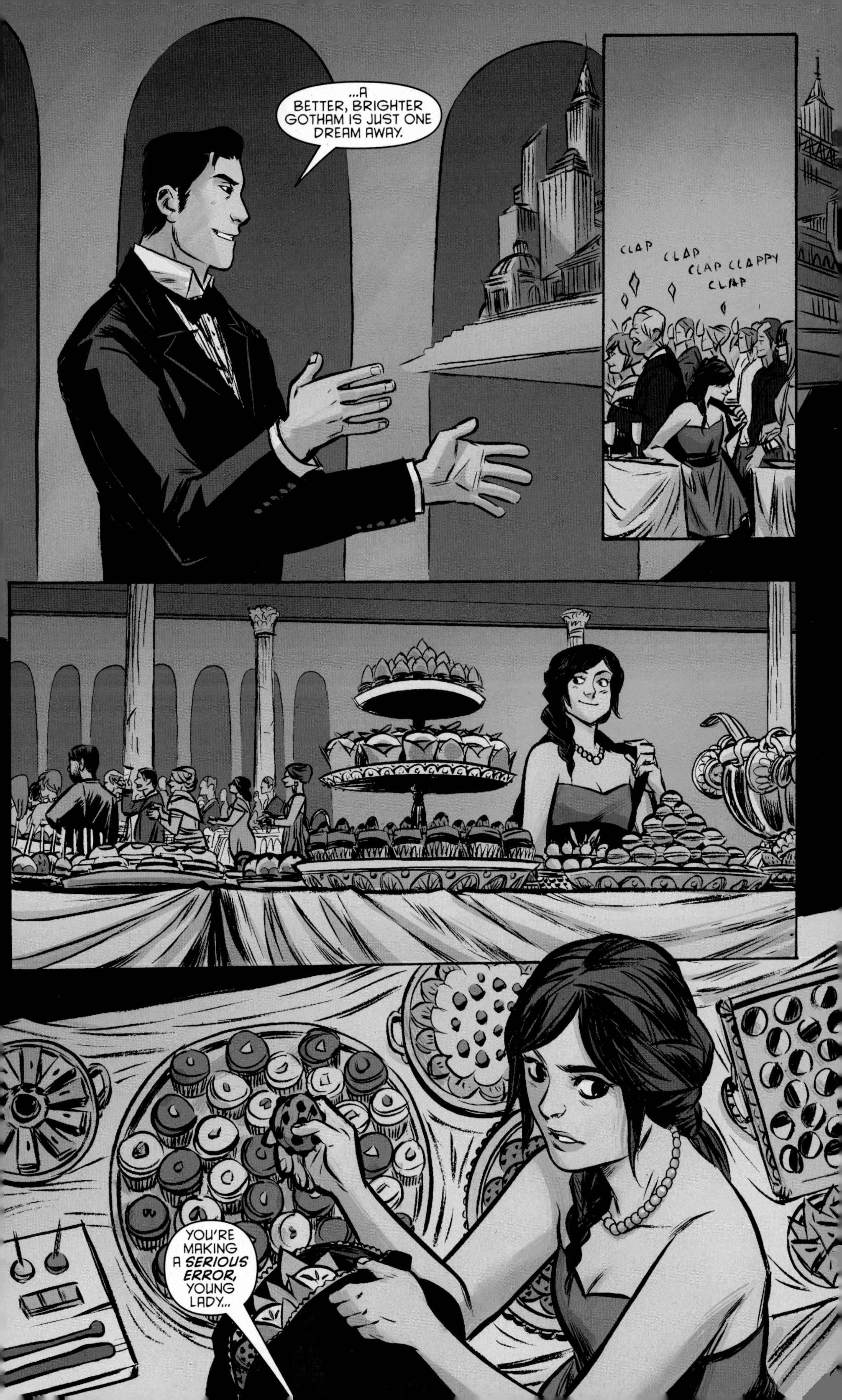
...A BETTER, BRIGHTER GOTHAM IS JUST ONE DREAM AWAY.
CLAP
CLAP
CLAP CLAPPY
CLAP
YOU'RE MAKING A *SERIOUS ERROR,* YOUNG LADY...

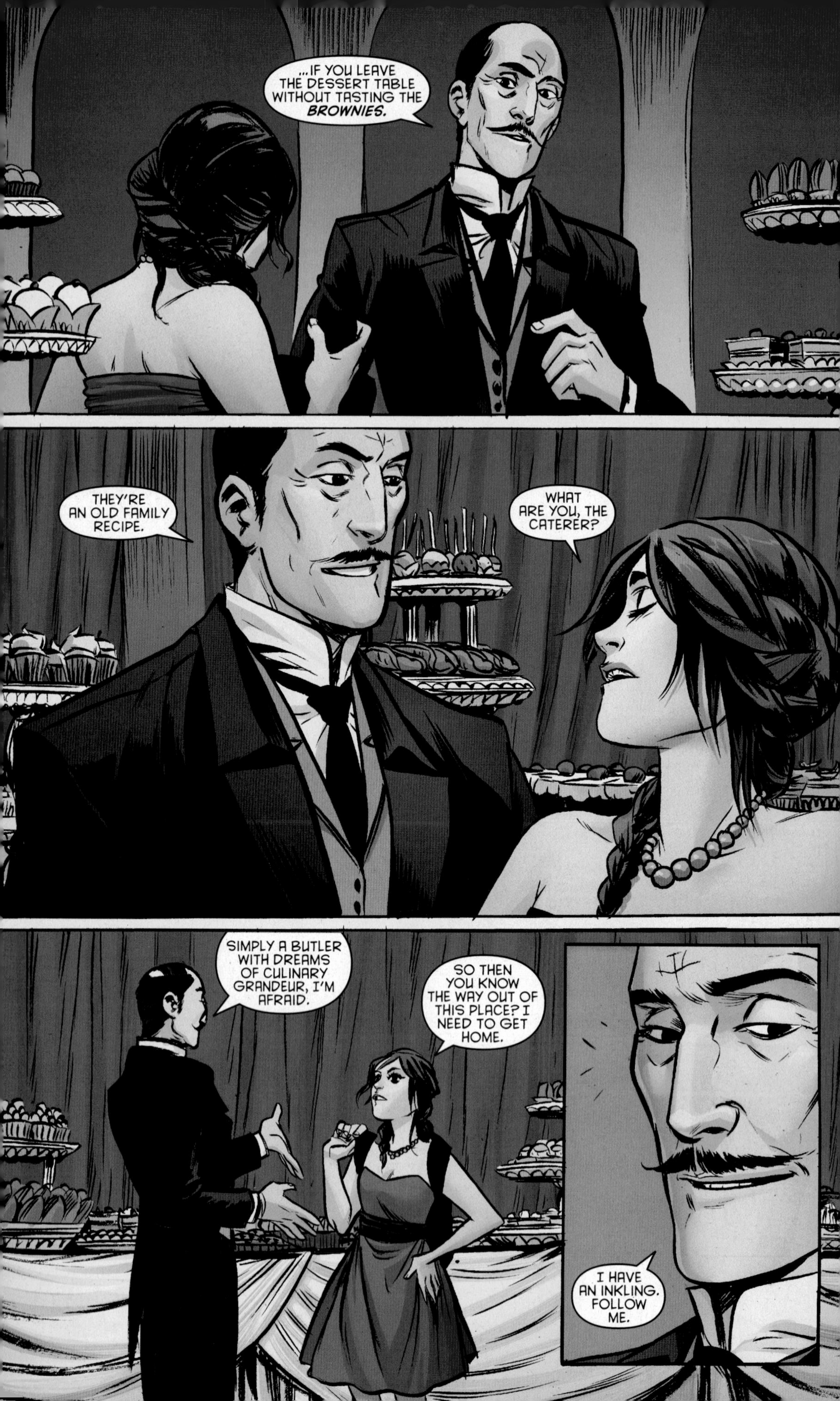
...IF YOU LEAVE THE DESSERT TABLE WITHOUT TASTING THE *BROWNIES.*
THEY'RE AN OLD FAMILY RECIPE.
WHAT ARE YOU, THE CATERER?
SIMPLY A BUTLER WITH DREAMS OF CULINARY GRANDEUR, I'M AFRAID.
SO THEN YOU KNOW THE WAY OUT OF THIS PLACE? I NEED TO GET HOME.
I HAVE AN INKLING. FOLLOW ME.

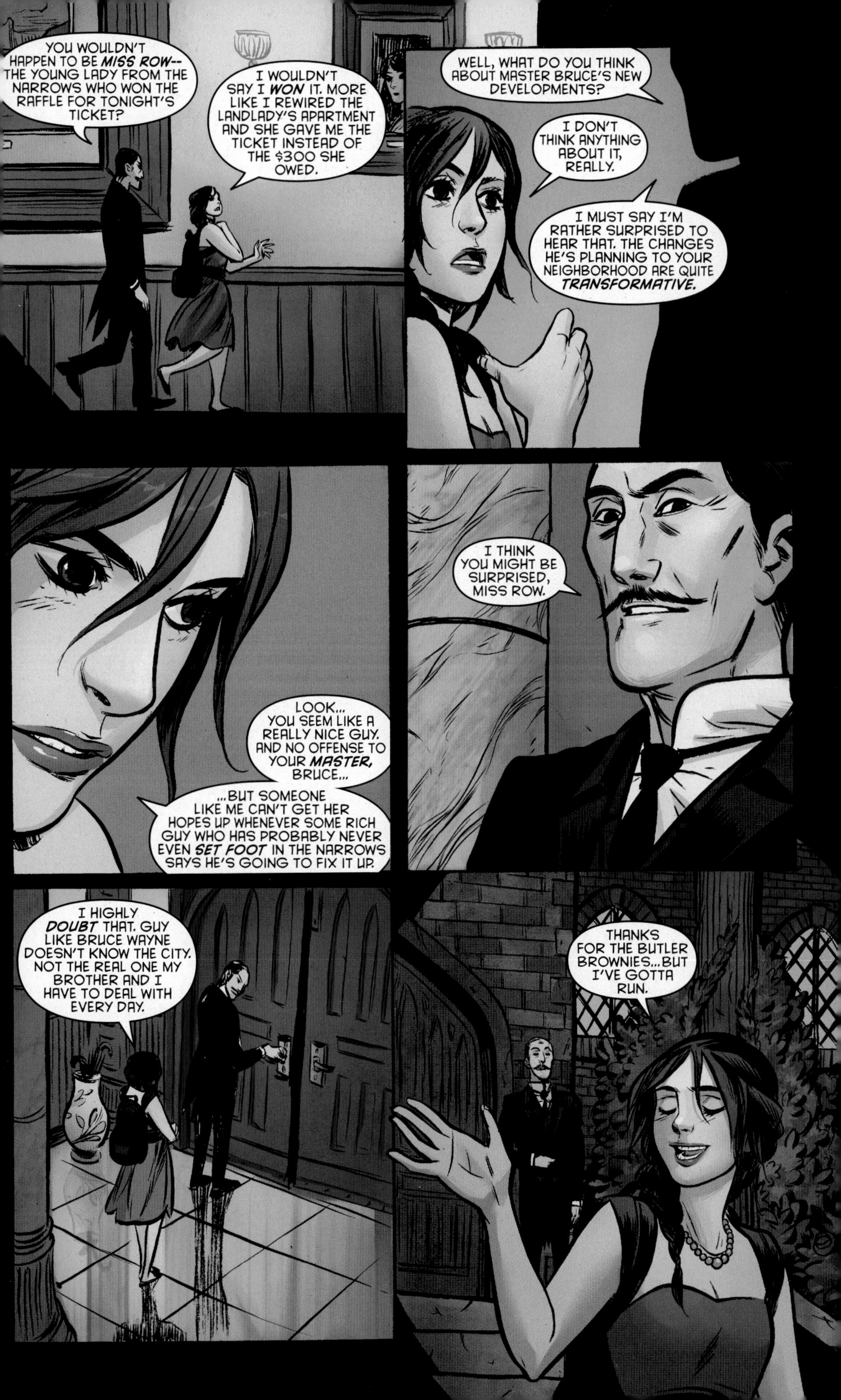

YOU WOULDN'T HAPPEN TO BE MISS ROW-- THE YOUNG LADY FROM THE NARROWS WHO WON THE RAFFLE FOR TONIGHT'S TICKET?
I WOULDN'T SAY I WON IT. MORE LIKE I REWIRED THE LANDLADY'S APARTMENT AND SHE GAVE ME THE TICKET INSTEAD OF THE $300 SHE OWED.
WELL, WHAT DO YOU THINK ABOUT MASTER BRUCE'S NEW DEVELOPMENTS?
I DON'T THINK ANYTHING ABOUT IT, REALLY.
I MUST SAY I'M RATHER SURPRISED TO HEAR THAT. THE CHANGES HE'S PLANNING TO YOUR NEIGHBORHOOD ARE QUITE TRANSFORMATIVE.
LOOK... YOU SEEM LIKE A REALLY NICE GUY. AND NO OFFENSE TO YOUR MASTER, BRUCE...
...BUT SOMEONE LIKE ME CAN'T GET HER HOPES UP WHENEVER SOME RICH GUY WHO HAS PROBABLY NEVER EVEN SET FOOT IN THE NARROWS SAYS HE'S GOING TO FIX IT UP.
I THINK YOU MIGHT BE SURPRISED, MISS ROW.
I HIGHLY DOUBT THAT. GUY LIKE BRUCE WAYNE DOESN'T KNOW THE CITY. NOT THE REAL ONE MY BROTHER AND I HAVE TO DEAL WITH EVERY DAY.
THANKS FOR THE BUTLER BROWNIES...BUT I'VE GOTTA RUN.

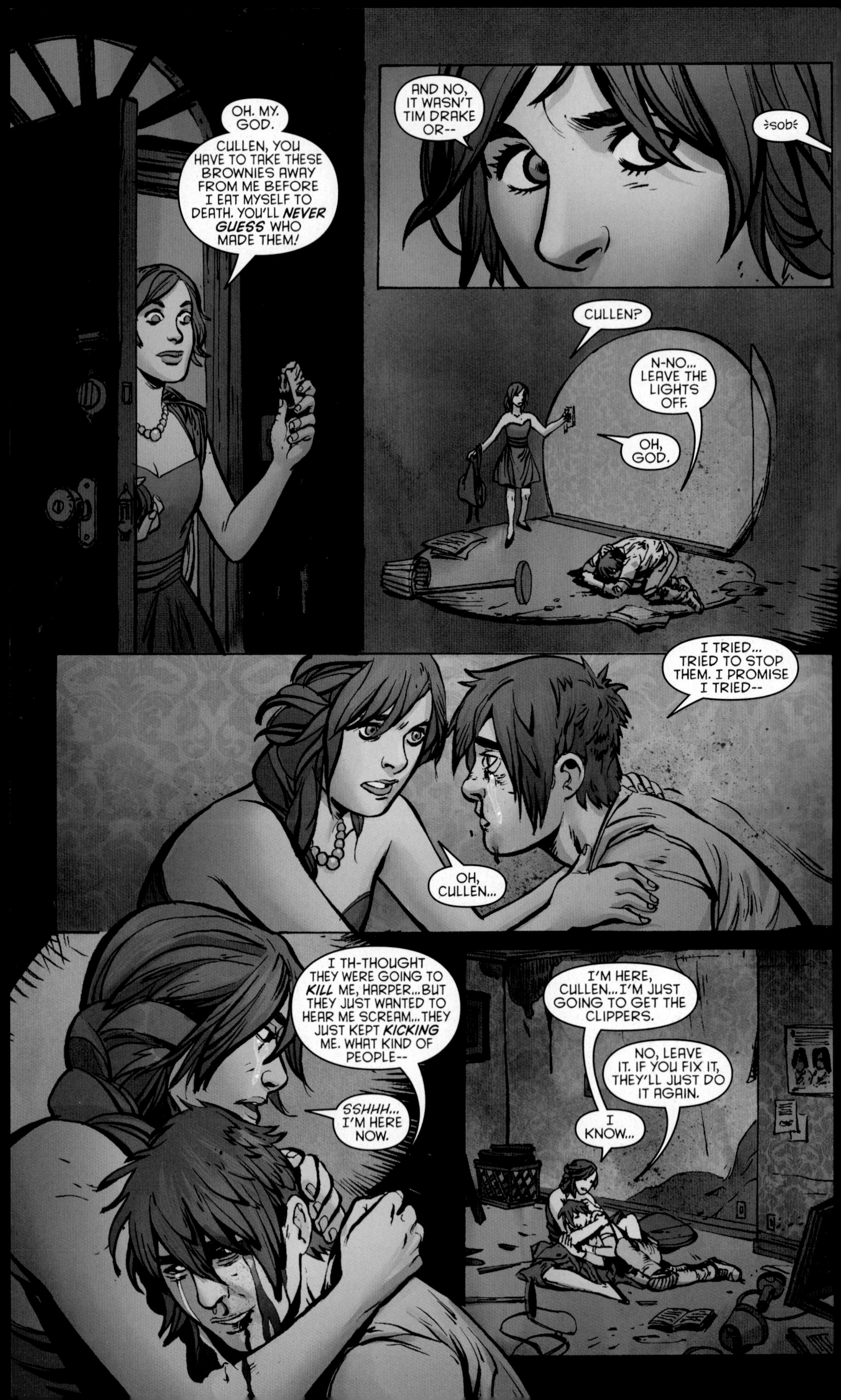
OH. MY. GOD.
CULLEN, YOU HAVE TO TAKE THESE BROWNIES AWAY FROM ME BEFORE I EAT MYSELF TO DEATH. YOU'LL *NEVER GUESS* WHO MADE THEM!
AND NO, IT WASN'T TIM DRAKE OR--
sob
CULLEN?
N-NO... LEAVE THE LIGHTS OFF.
OH, GOD.
I TRIED... TRIED TO STOP THEM. I PROMISE I TRIED--
OH, CULLEN...
I TH-THOUGHT THEY WERE GOING TO *KILL* ME, HARPER...BUT THEY JUST WANTED TO HEAR ME SCREAM...THEY JUST KEPT *KICKING* ME. WHAT KIND OF PEOPLE--
SSHHH... I'M HERE NOW.
I'M HERE, CULLEN...I'M JUST GOING TO GET THE CLIPPERS.
NO, LEAVE IT. IF YOU FIX IT, THEY'LL JUST DO IT AGAIN.
I KNOW...

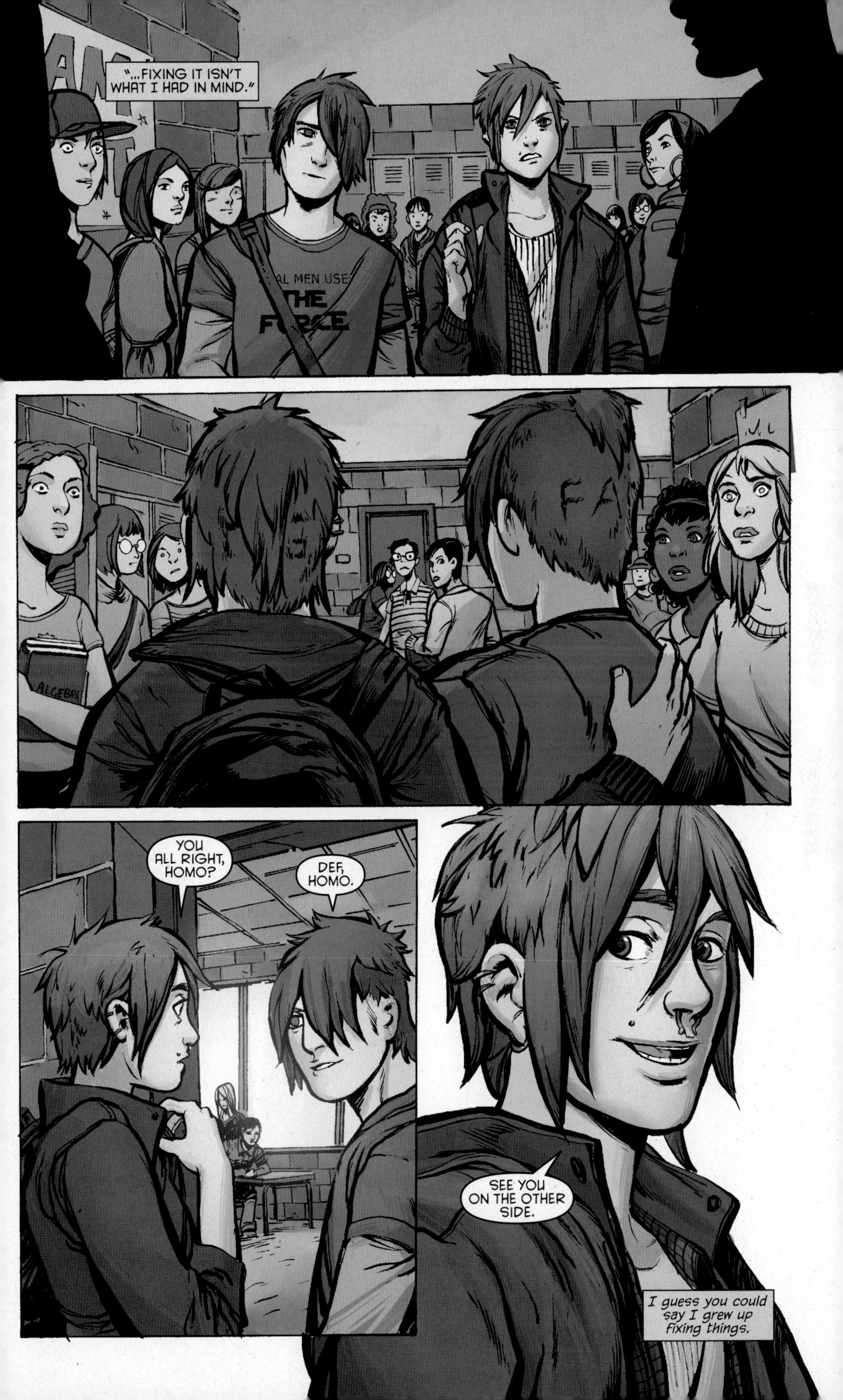
"...FIXING IT ISN'T WHAT I HAD IN MIND."
REAL MEN USE THE FORCE
ALGEBRA
YOU ALL RIGHT, HOMO?
DEF, HOMO.
SEE YOU ON THE OTHER SIDE.
I guess you could say I grew up fixing things.

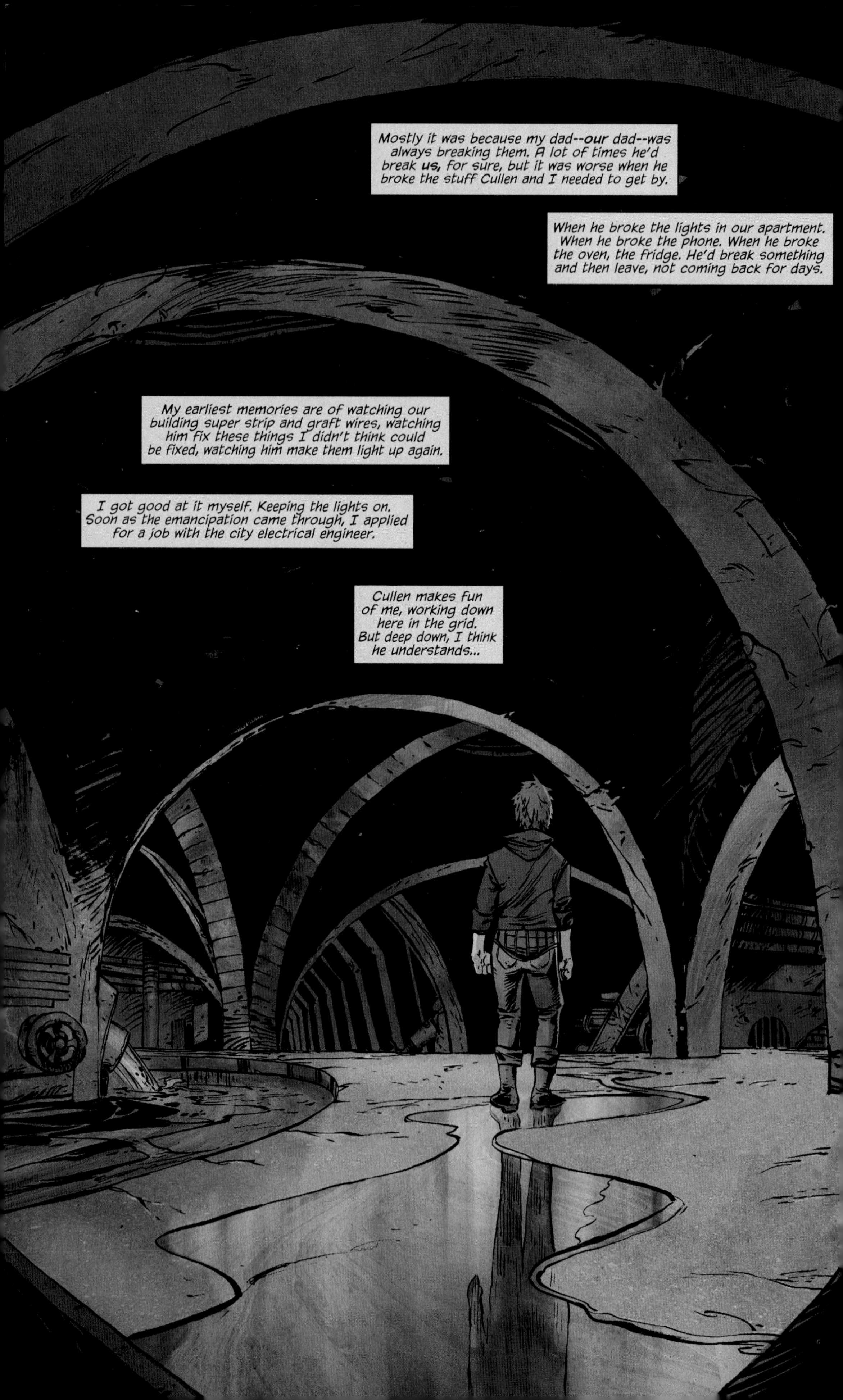
Mostly it was because my dad--**our** dad--was always breaking them. A lot of times he'd break **us,** for sure, but it was worse when he broke the stuff Cullen and I needed to get by.
When he broke the lights in our apartment. When he broke the phone. When he broke the oven, the fridge. He'd break something and then leave, not coming back for days.
My earliest memories are of watching our building super strip and graft wires, watching him fix these things I didn't think could be fixed, watching him make them light up again.
I got good at it myself. Keeping the lights on. Soon as the emancipation came through, I applied for a job with the city electrical engineer.
Cullen makes fun of me, working down here in the grid. But deep down, I think he understands...

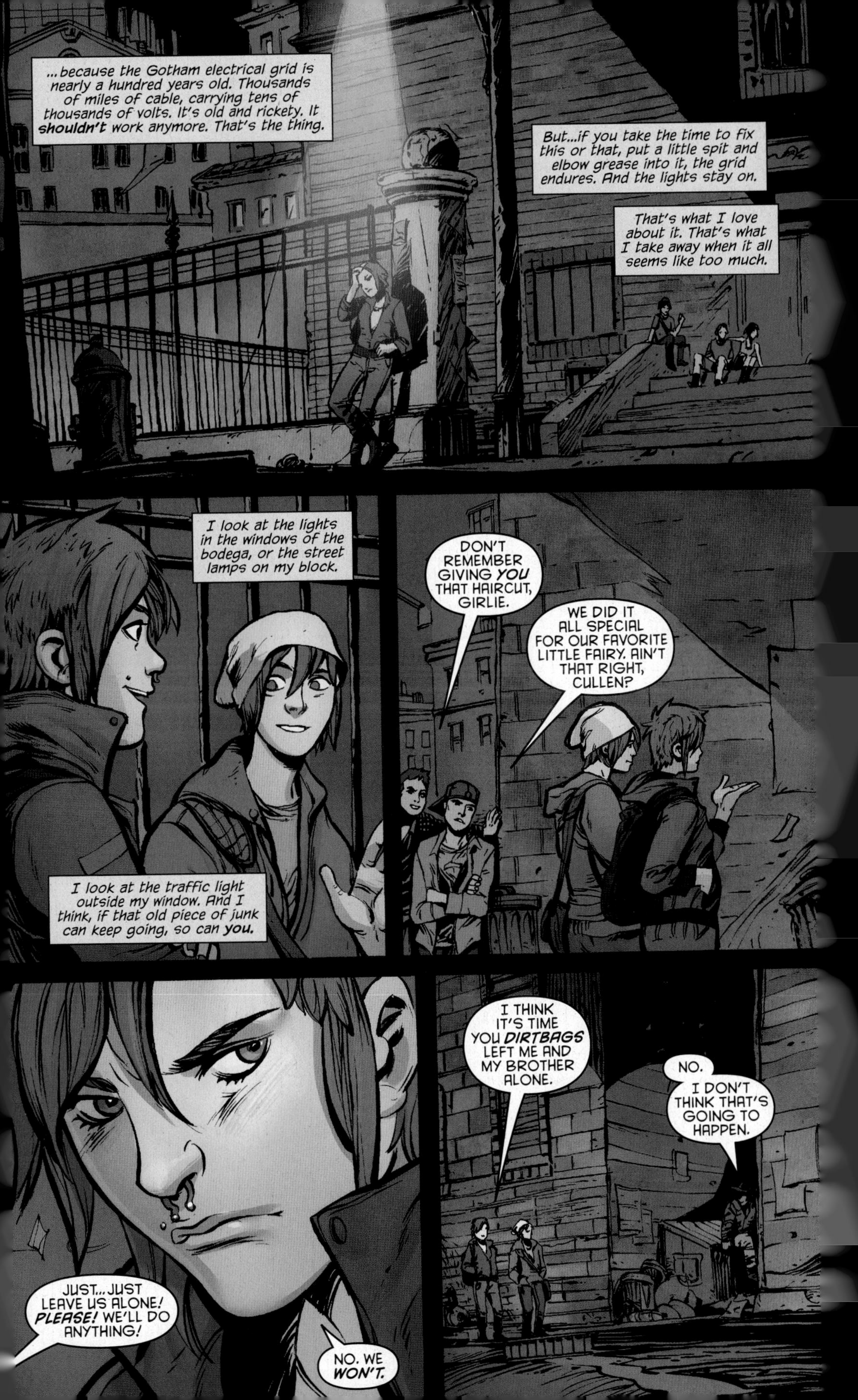

...because the Gotham electrical grid is nearly a hundred years old. Thousands of miles of cable, carrying tens of thousands of volts. It's old and rickety. It **shouldn't** work anymore. That's the thing.
But...if you take the time to fix this or that, put a little spit and elbow grease into it, the grid endures. And the lights stay on.
That's what I love about it. That's what I take away when it all seems like too much.
I look at the lights in the windows of the bodega, or the street lamps on my block.
I look at the traffic light outside my window. And I think, if that old piece of junk can keep going, so can **you.**
DON'T REMEMBER GIVING ***YOU*** THAT HAIRCUT, GIRLIE.
WE DID IT ALL SPECIAL FOR OUR FAVORITE LITTLE FAIRY. AIN'T THAT RIGHT, CULLEN?
JUST... JUST LEAVE US ALONE! ***PLEASE!*** WE'LL DO ANYTHING!
NO. WE ***WON'T.***
I THINK IT'S TIME YOU ***DIRTBAGS*** LEFT ME AND MY BROTHER ALONE.
NO.
I DON'T THINK THAT'S GOING TO HAPPEN.

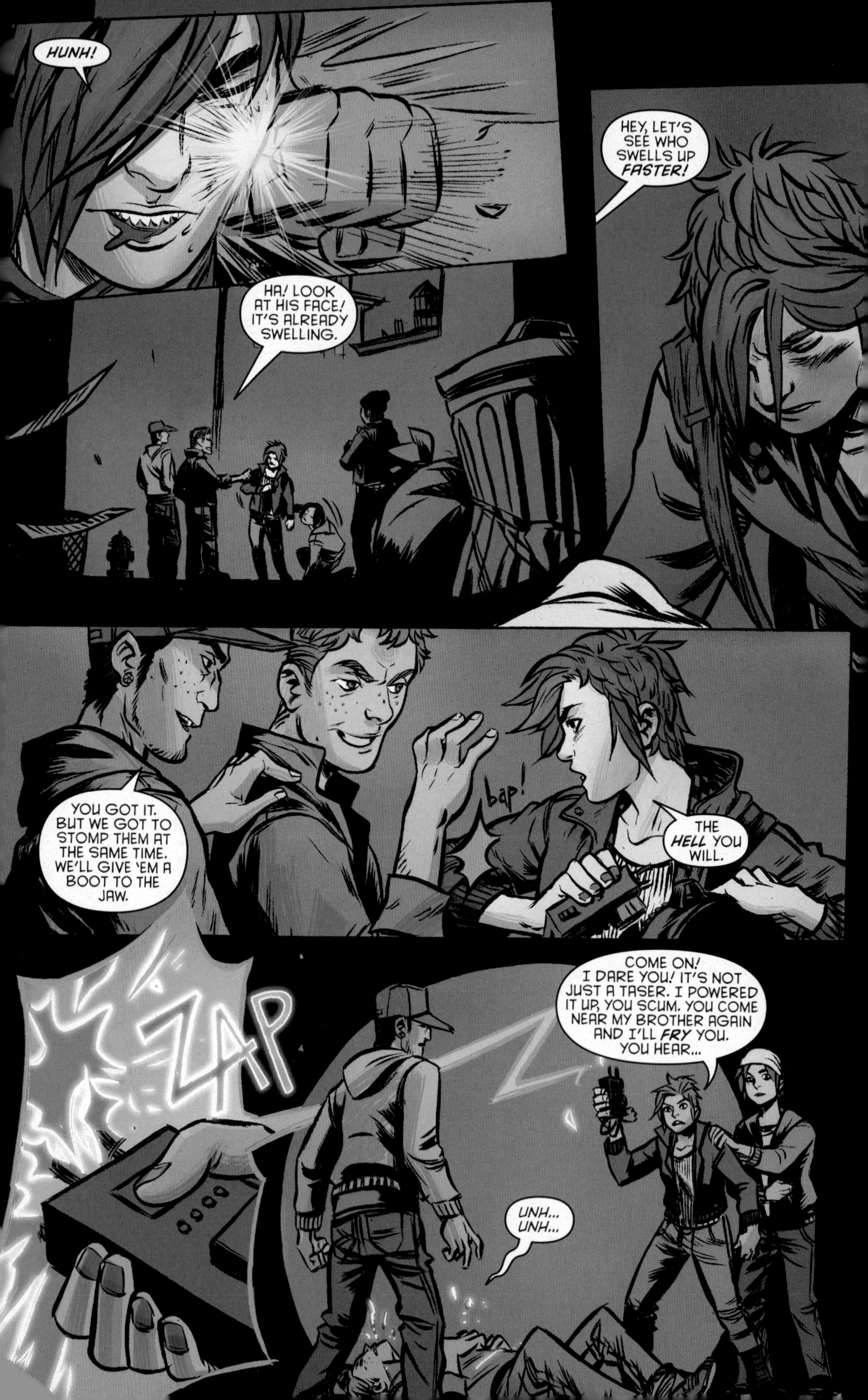
HUNH!
HEY, LET'S SEE WHO SWELLS UP FASTER!
HA! LOOK AT HIS FACE! IT'S ALREADY SWELLING.
YOU GOT IT. BUT WE GOT TO STOMP THEM AT THE SAME TIME. WE'LL GIVE 'EM A BOOT TO THE JAW.
bap!
THE HELL YOU WILL.
ZAP
COME ON! I DARE YOU! IT'S NOT JUST A TASER. I POWERED IT UP, YOU SCUM. YOU COME NEAR MY BROTHER AGAIN AND I'LL FRY YOU. YOU HEAR...
UNH... UNH...

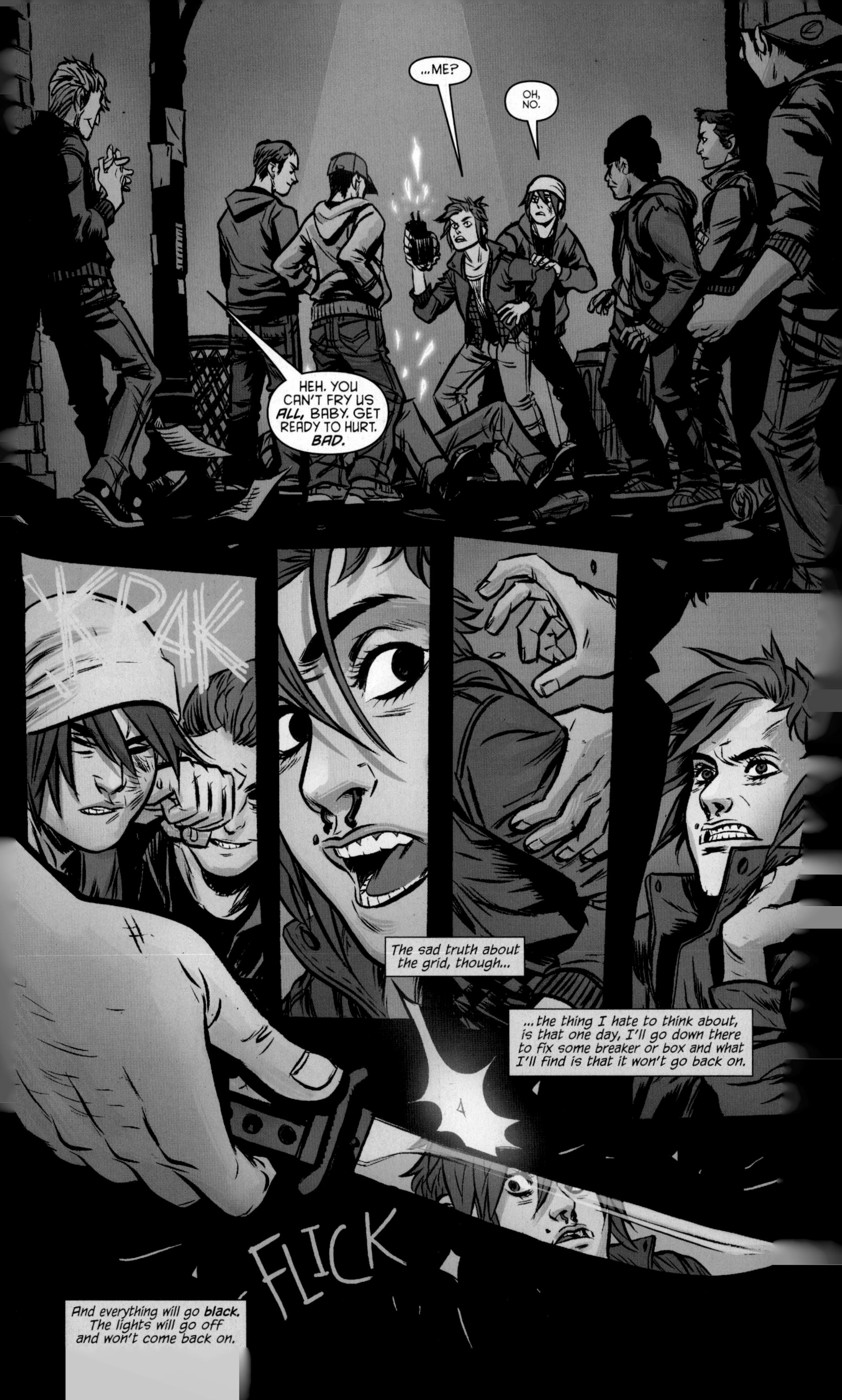
...ME?
OH, NO.
HEH. YOU CAN'T FRY US ALL, BABY. GET READY TO HURT. BAD.
KRAK
The sad truth about the grid, though...
...the thing I hate to think about, is that one day, I'll go down there to fix some breaker or box and what I'll find is that it won't go back on.
FLICK
And everything will go black. The lights will go off and won't come back on.

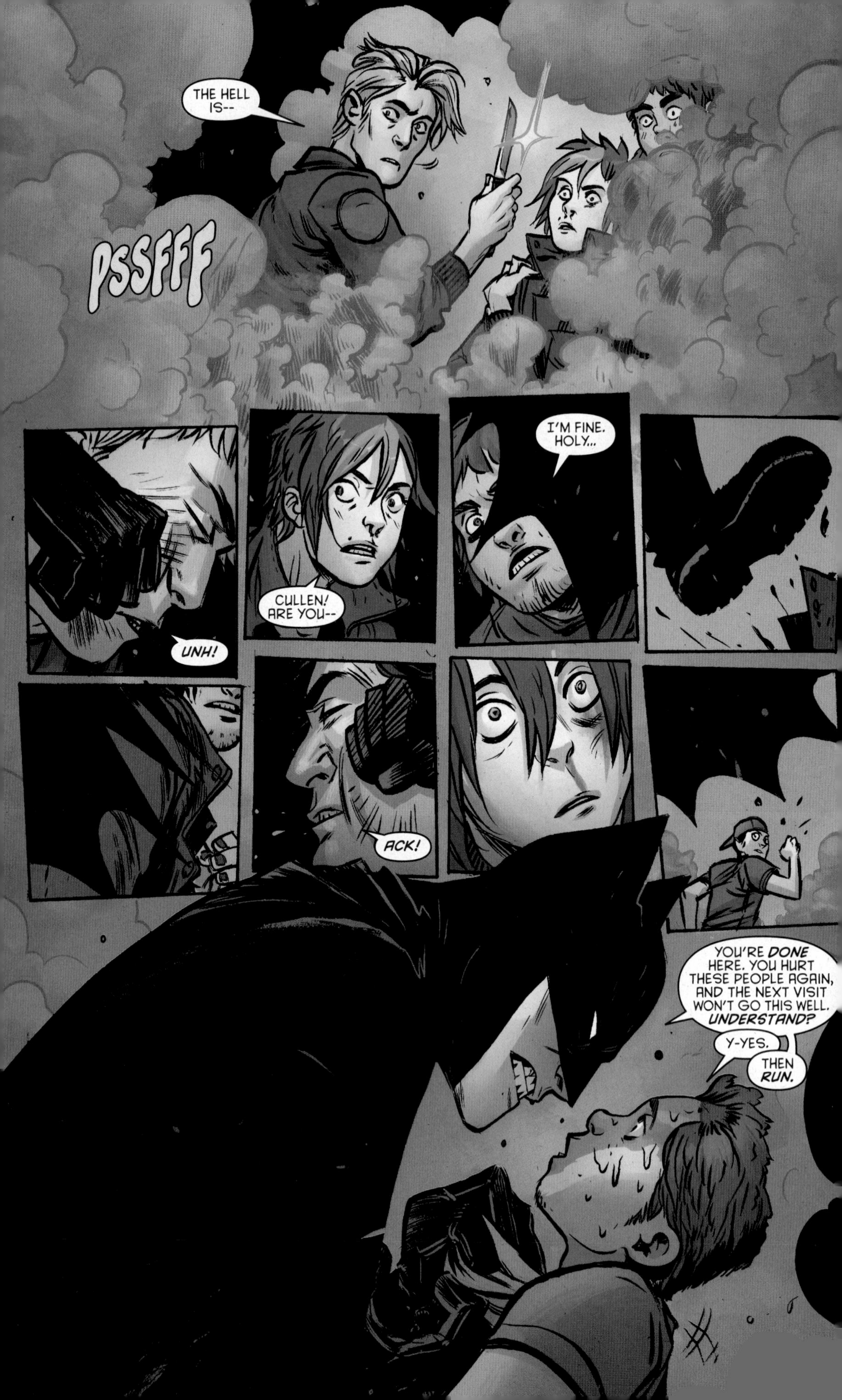
THE HELL IS--
PSSFFF
UNH!
CULLEN! ARE YOU--
I'M FINE. HOLY...
ACK!
YOU'RE *DONE* HERE. YOU HURT THESE PEOPLE AGAIN, AND THE NEXT VISIT WON'T GO THIS WELL. ***UNDERSTAND?***
Y-YES.
THEN ***RUN.***

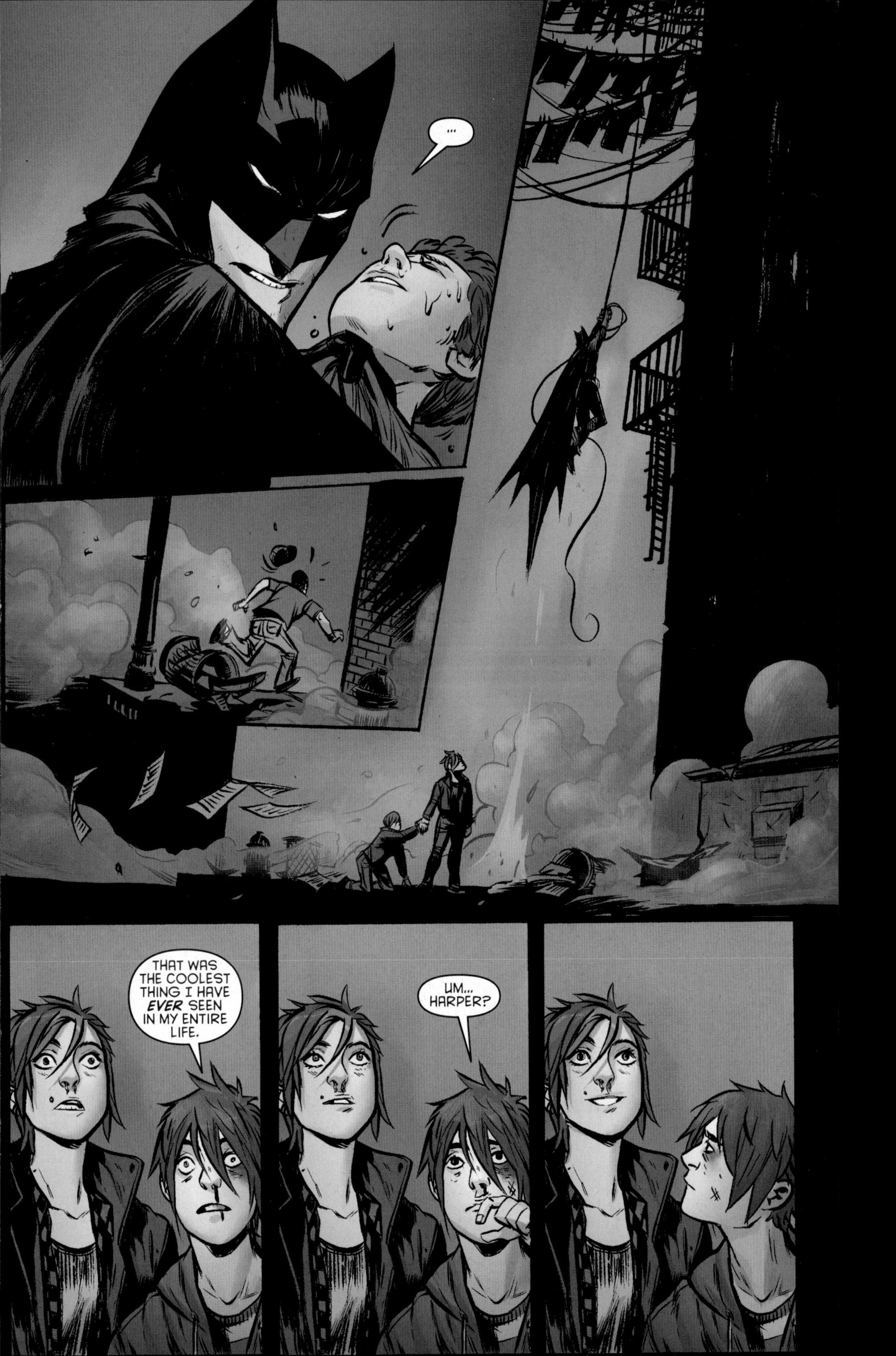
...
THAT WAS THE COOLEST THING I HAVE EVER SEEN IN MY ENTIRE LIFE.
UM... HARPER?

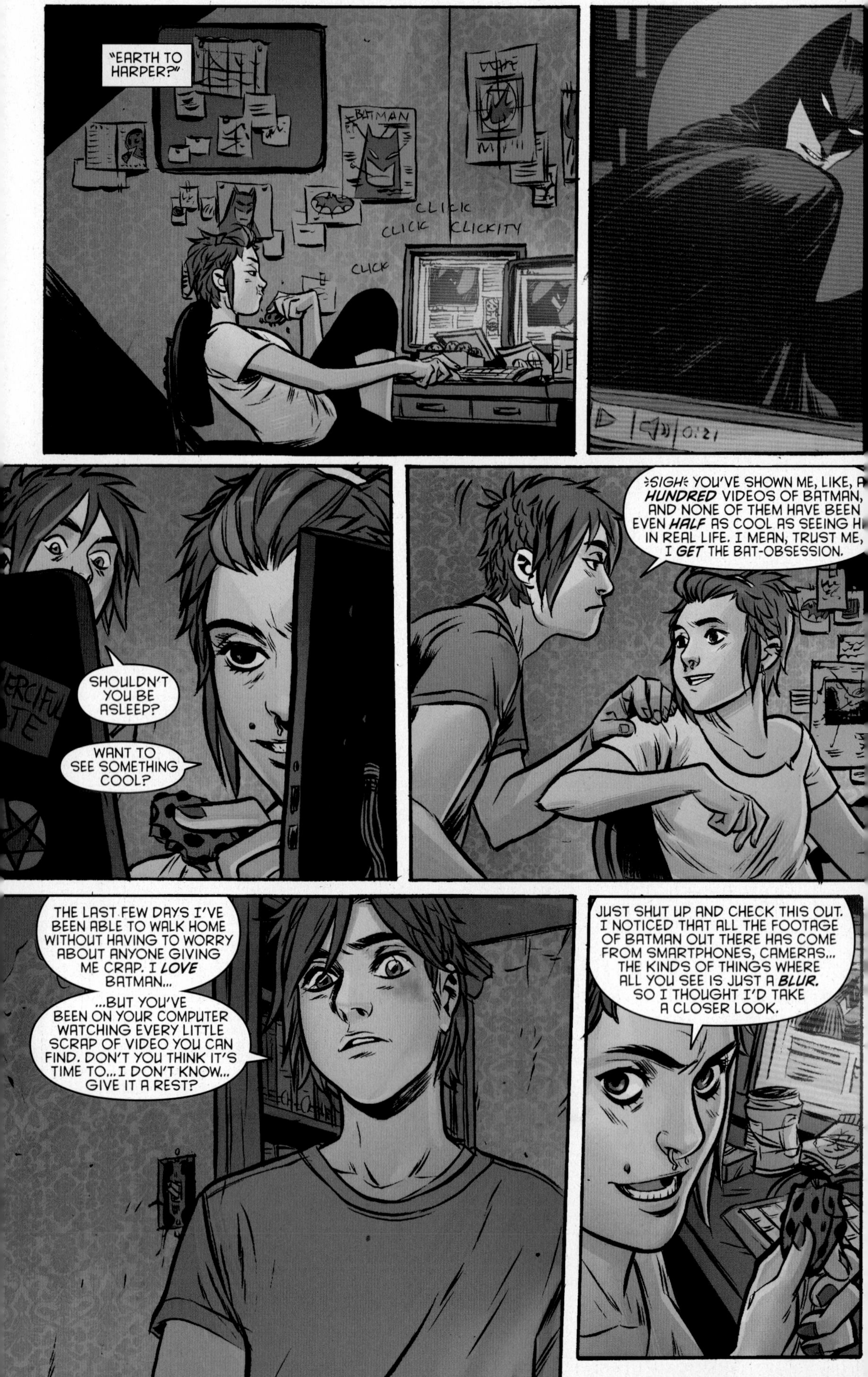

"EARTH TO HARPER?"
CLICK CLICK CLICK CLICKITY CLICK
BATMAN
0:21
SHOULDN'T YOU BE ASLEEP?
WANT TO SEE SOMETHING COOL?
SIGH YOU'VE SHOWN ME, LIKE, A HUNDRED VIDEOS OF BATMAN, AND NONE OF THEM HAVE BEEN EVEN HALF AS COOL AS SEEING HIM IN REAL LIFE. I MEAN, TRUST ME, I GET THE BAT-OBSESSION.
THE LAST FEW DAYS I'VE BEEN ABLE TO WALK HOME WITHOUT HAVING TO WORRY ABOUT ANYONE GIVING ME CRAP. I LOVE BATMAN...
...BUT YOU'VE BEEN ON YOUR COMPUTER WATCHING EVERY LITTLE SCRAP OF VIDEO YOU CAN FIND. DON'T YOU THINK IT'S TIME TO...I DON'T KNOW... GIVE IT A REST?
JUST SHUT UP AND CHECK THIS OUT. I NOTICED THAT ALL THE FOOTAGE OF BATMAN OUT THERE HAS COME FROM SMARTPHONES, CAMERAS... THE KINDS OF THINGS WHERE ALL YOU SEE IS JUST A BLUR. SO I THOUGHT I'D TAKE A CLOSER LOOK.

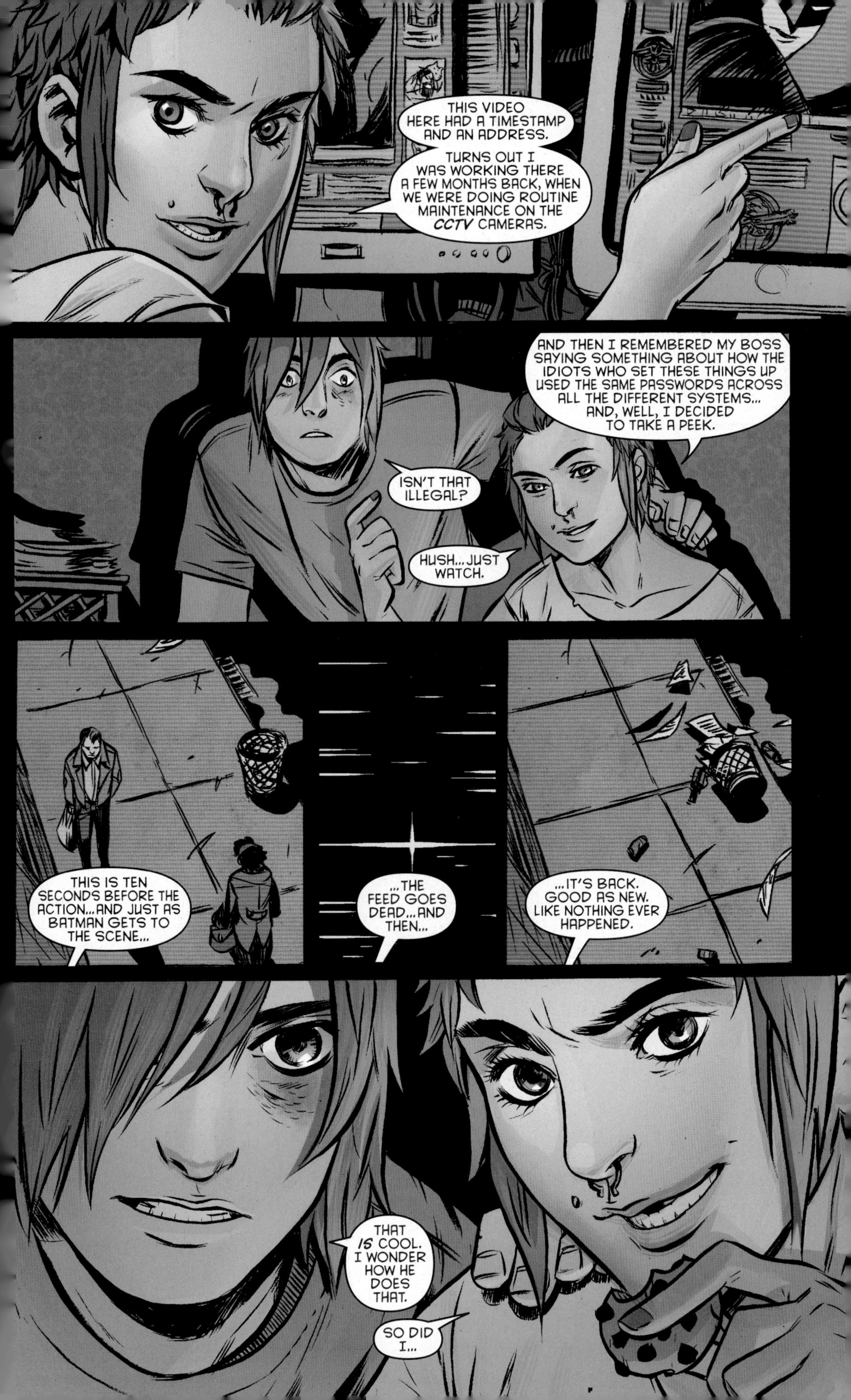
THIS VIDEO HERE HAD A TIMESTAMP AND AN ADDRESS.
TURNS OUT I WAS WORKING THERE A FEW MONTHS BACK, WHEN WE WERE DOING ROUTINE MAINTENANCE ON THE *CCTV* CAMERAS.
AND THEN I REMEMBERED MY BOSS SAYING SOMETHING ABOUT HOW THE IDIOTS WHO SET THESE THINGS UP USED THE SAME PASSWORDS ACROSS ALL THE DIFFERENT SYSTEMS... AND, WELL, I DECIDED TO TAKE A PEEK.
ISN'T THAT ILLEGAL?
HUSH... JUST WATCH.
THIS IS TEN SECONDS BEFORE THE ACTION... AND JUST AS BATMAN GETS TO THE SCENE...
...THE FEED GOES DEAD... AND THEN...
...IT'S BACK. GOOD AS NEW. LIKE NOTHING EVER HAPPENED.
THAT *IS* COOL. I WONDER HOW HE DOES THAT.
SO DID I...

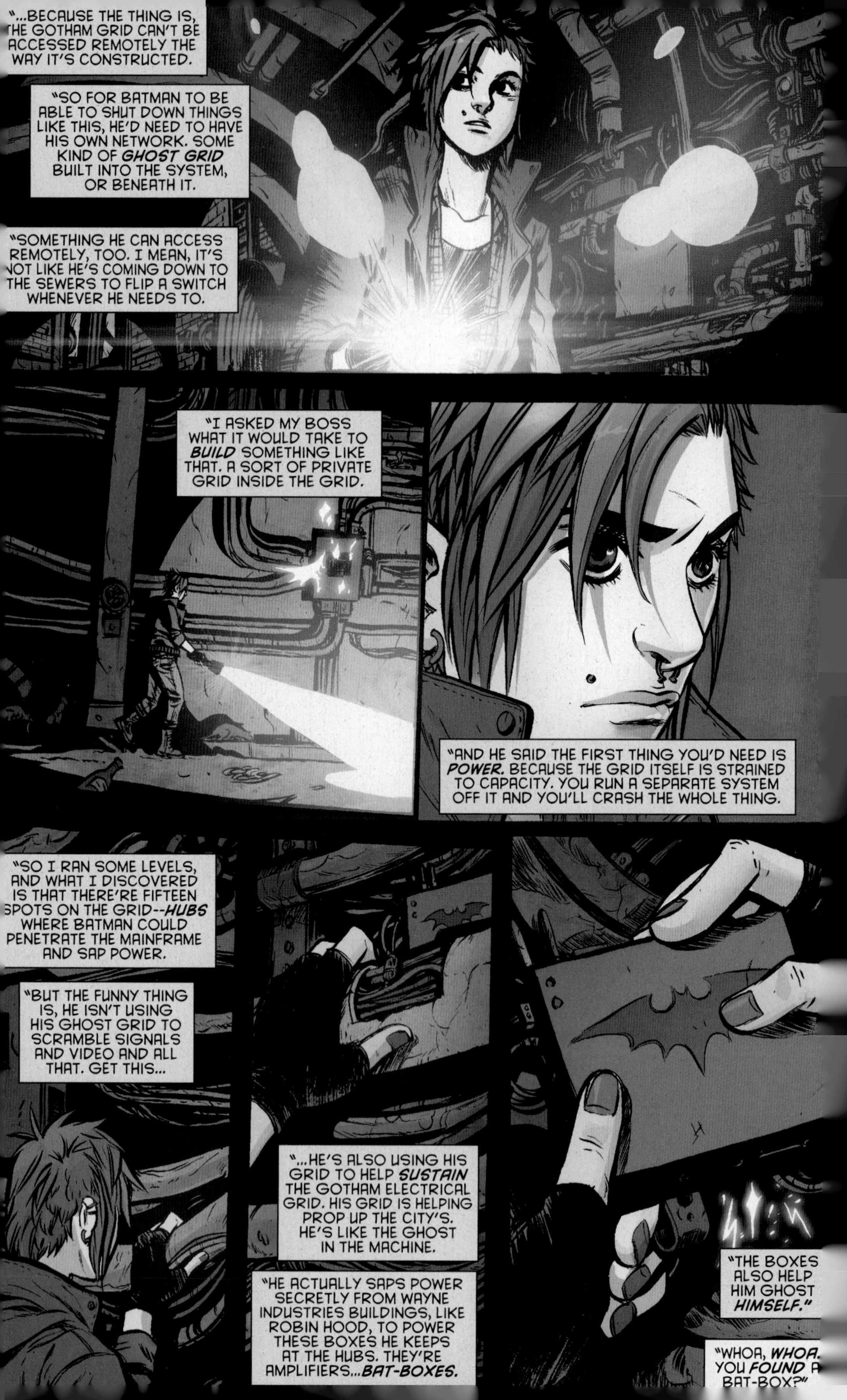
"...BECAUSE THE THING IS, THE GOTHAM GRID CAN'T BE ACCESSED REMOTELY THE WAY IT'S CONSTRUCTED.
"SO FOR BATMAN TO BE ABLE TO SHUT DOWN THINGS LIKE THIS, HE'D NEED TO HAVE HIS OWN NETWORK. SOME KIND OF GHOST GRID BUILT INTO THE SYSTEM, OR BENEATH IT.
"SOMETHING HE CAN ACCESS REMOTELY, TOO. I MEAN, IT'S NOT LIKE HE'S COMING DOWN TO THE SEWERS TO FLIP A SWITCH WHENEVER HE NEEDS TO.
"I ASKED MY BOSS WHAT IT WOULD TAKE TO BUILD SOMETHING LIKE THAT. A SORT OF PRIVATE GRID INSIDE THE GRID.
"AND HE SAID THE FIRST THING YOU'D NEED IS POWER. BECAUSE THE GRID ITSELF IS STRAINED TO CAPACITY. YOU RUN A SEPARATE SYSTEM OFF IT AND YOU'LL CRASH THE WHOLE THING.
"SO I RAN SOME LEVELS, AND WHAT I DISCOVERED IS THAT THERE'RE FIFTEEN SPOTS ON THE GRID--HUBS WHERE BATMAN COULD PENETRATE THE MAINFRAME AND SAP POWER.
"BUT THE FUNNY THING IS, HE ISN'T USING HIS GHOST GRID TO SCRAMBLE SIGNALS AND VIDEO AND ALL THAT. GET THIS...
"...HE'S ALSO USING HIS GRID TO HELP SUSTAIN THE GOTHAM ELECTRICAL GRID. HIS GRID IS HELPING PROP UP THE CITY'S. HE'S LIKE THE GHOST IN THE MACHINE.
"HE ACTUALLY SAPS POWER SECRETLY FROM WAYNE INDUSTRIES BUILDINGS, LIKE ROBIN HOOD, TO POWER THESE BOXES HE KEEPS AT THE HUBS. THEY'RE AMPLIFIERS...BAT-BOXES.
"THE BOXES ALSO HELP HIM GHOST HIMSELF."
"WHOA, WHOA. YOU FOUND A BAT-BOX?"

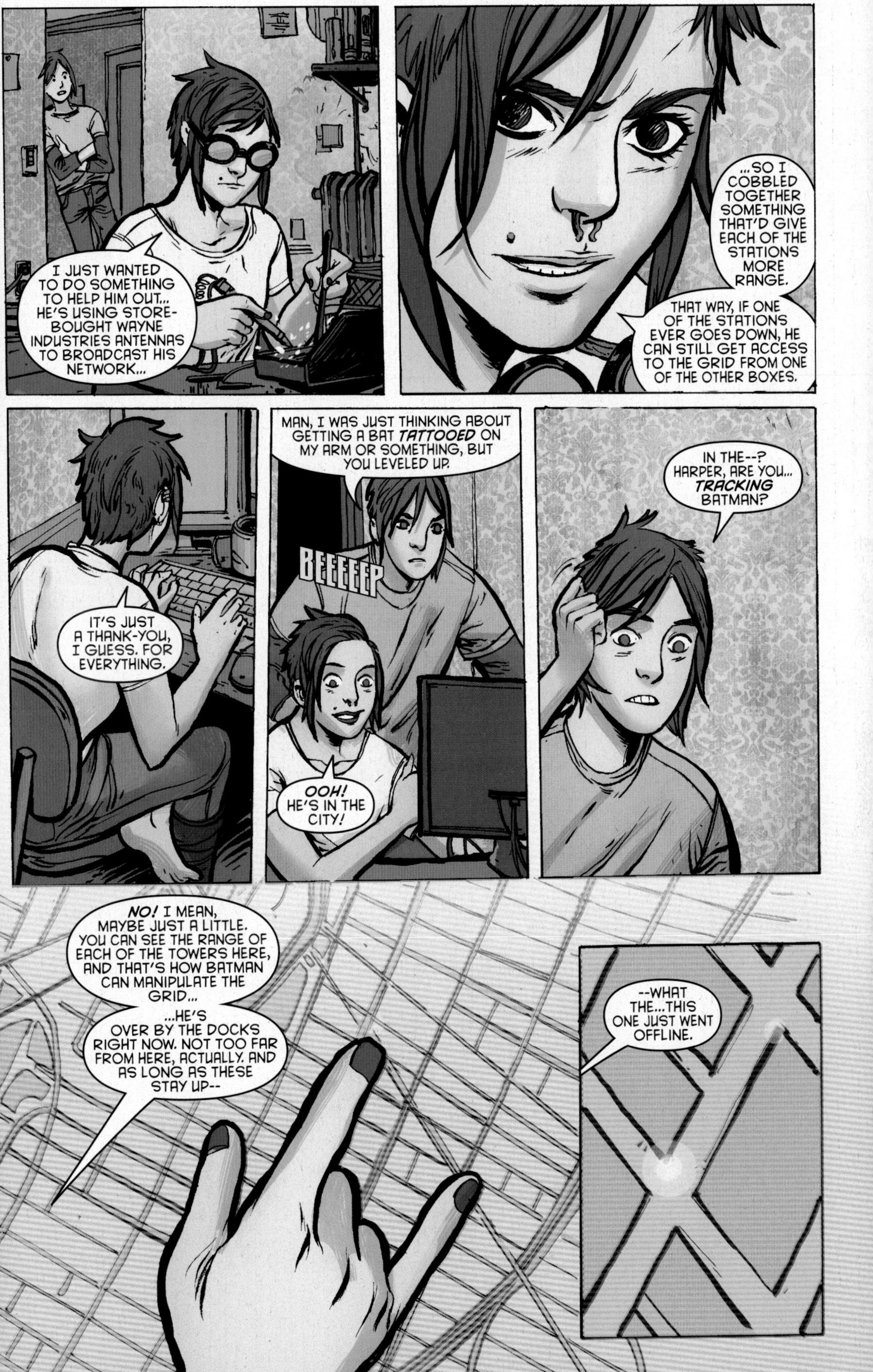
I JUST WANTED TO DO SOMETHING TO HELP HIM OUT... HE'S USING STORE-BOUGHT WAYNE INDUSTRIES ANTENNAS TO BROADCAST HIS NETWORK...
...SO I COBBLED TOGETHER SOMETHING THAT'D GIVE EACH OF THE STATIONS MORE RANGE.
THAT WAY, IF ONE OF THE STATIONS EVER GOES DOWN, HE CAN STILL GET ACCESS TO THE GRID FROM ONE OF THE OTHER BOXES.
IT'S JUST A THANK-YOU, I GUESS. FOR EVERYTHING.
MAN, I WAS JUST THINKING ABOUT GETTING A BAT TATTOOED ON MY ARM OR SOMETHING, BUT YOU LEVELED UP.
BEEEEEP
OOH! HE'S IN THE CITY!
IN THE--? HARPER, ARE YOU... TRACKING BATMAN?
NO! I MEAN, MAYBE JUST A LITTLE. YOU CAN SEE THE RANGE OF EACH OF THE TOWERS HERE, AND THAT'S HOW BATMAN CAN MANIPULATE THE GRID...
...HE'S OVER BY THE DOCKS RIGHT NOW. NOT TOO FAR FROM HERE, ACTUALLY. AND AS LONG AS THESE STAY UP--
--WHAT THE...THIS ONE JUST WENT OFFLINE.

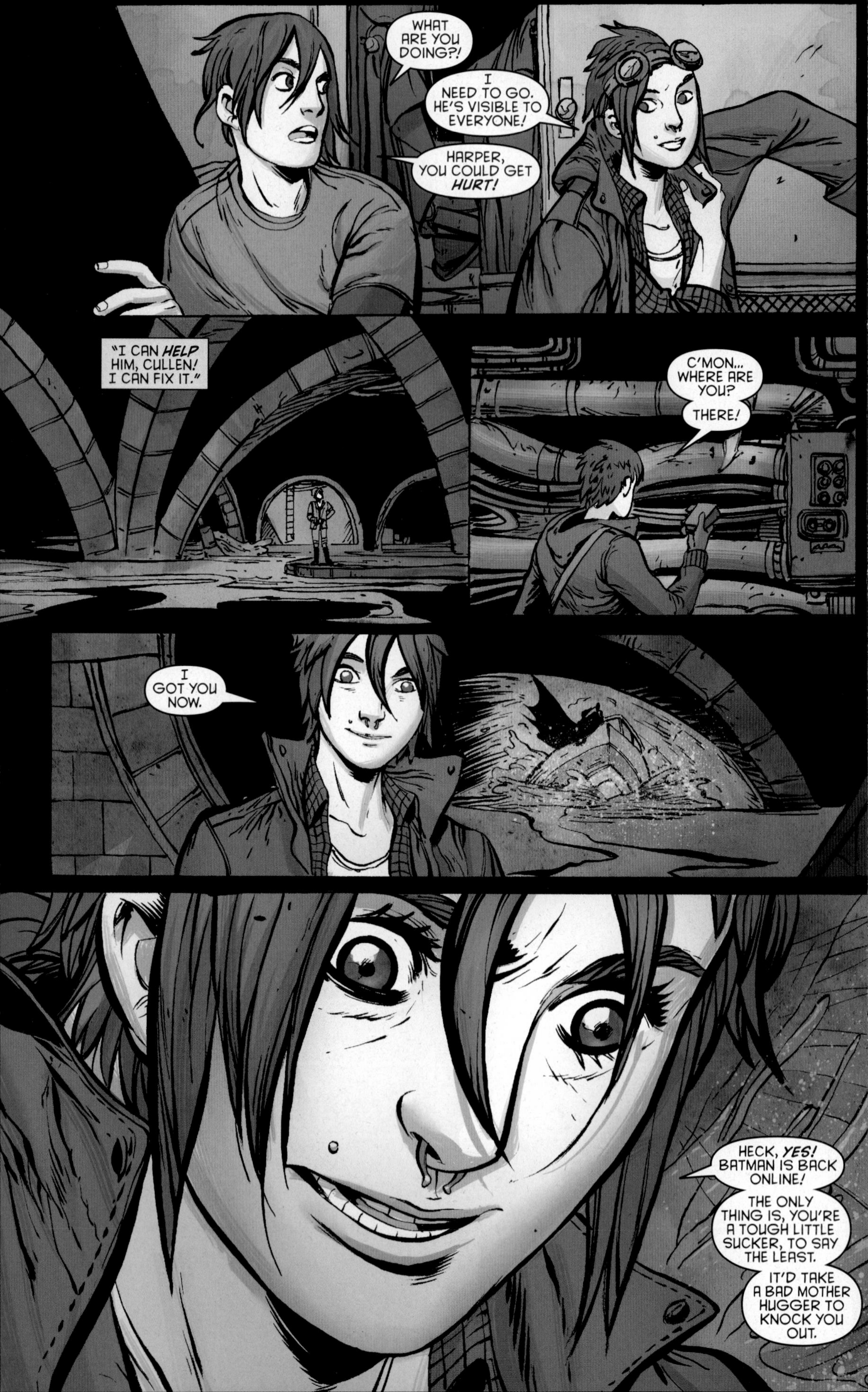

WHAT ARE YOU DOING?!
I NEED TO GO. HE'S VISIBLE TO EVERYONE!
HARPER, YOU COULD GET *HURT!*
"I CAN *HELP* HIM, CULLEN! I CAN FIX IT."
C'MON... WHERE ARE YOU?
THERE!
I GOT YOU NOW.
HECK, *YES!* BATMAN IS BACK ONLINE!
THE ONLY THING IS, YOU'RE A TOUGH LITTLE SUCKER, TO SAY THE LEAST.
IT'D TAKE A BAD MOTHER HUGGER TO KNOCK YOU OUT.

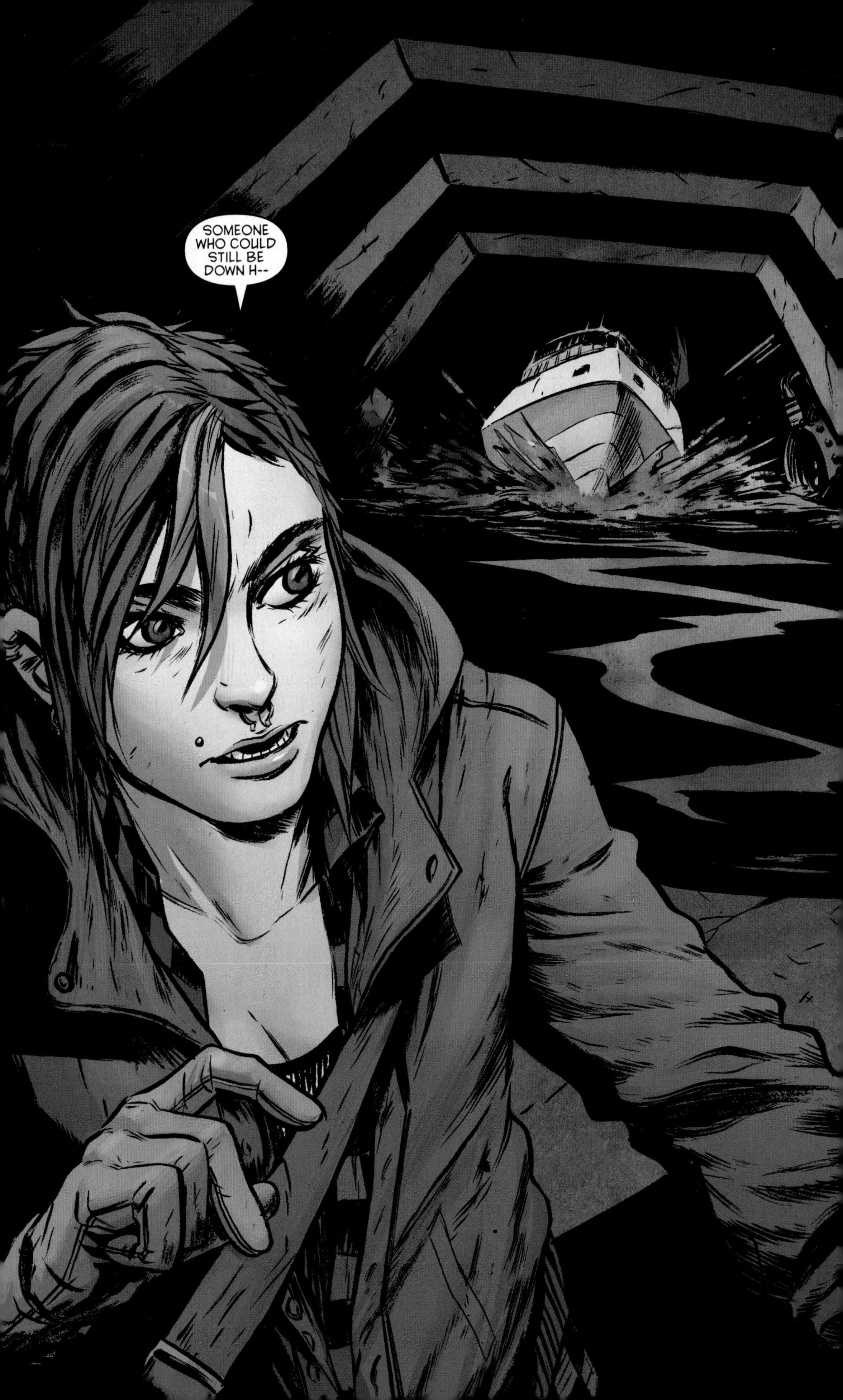
SOMEONE WHO COULD STILL BE DOWN H--

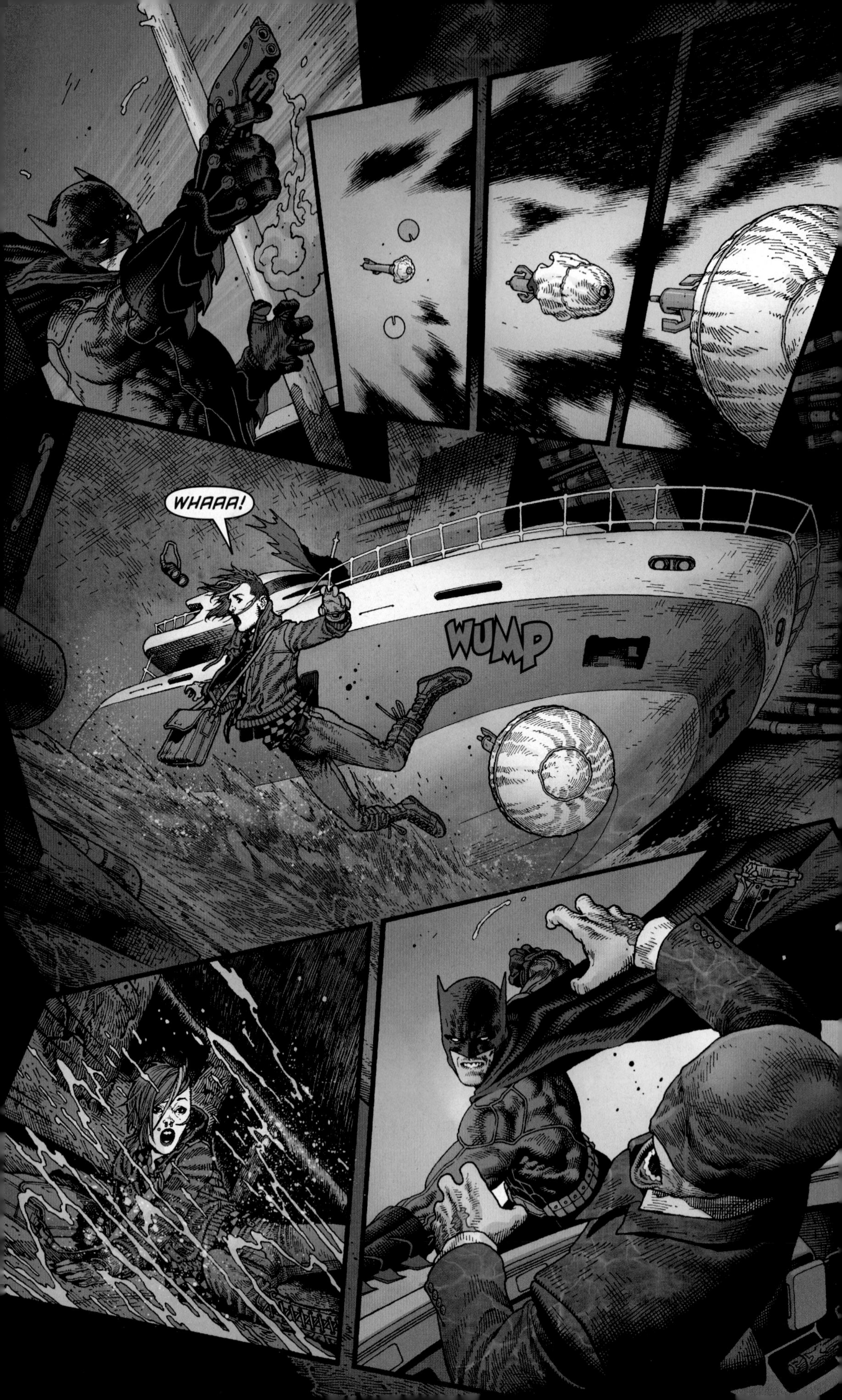

WHAAA!
WUMP

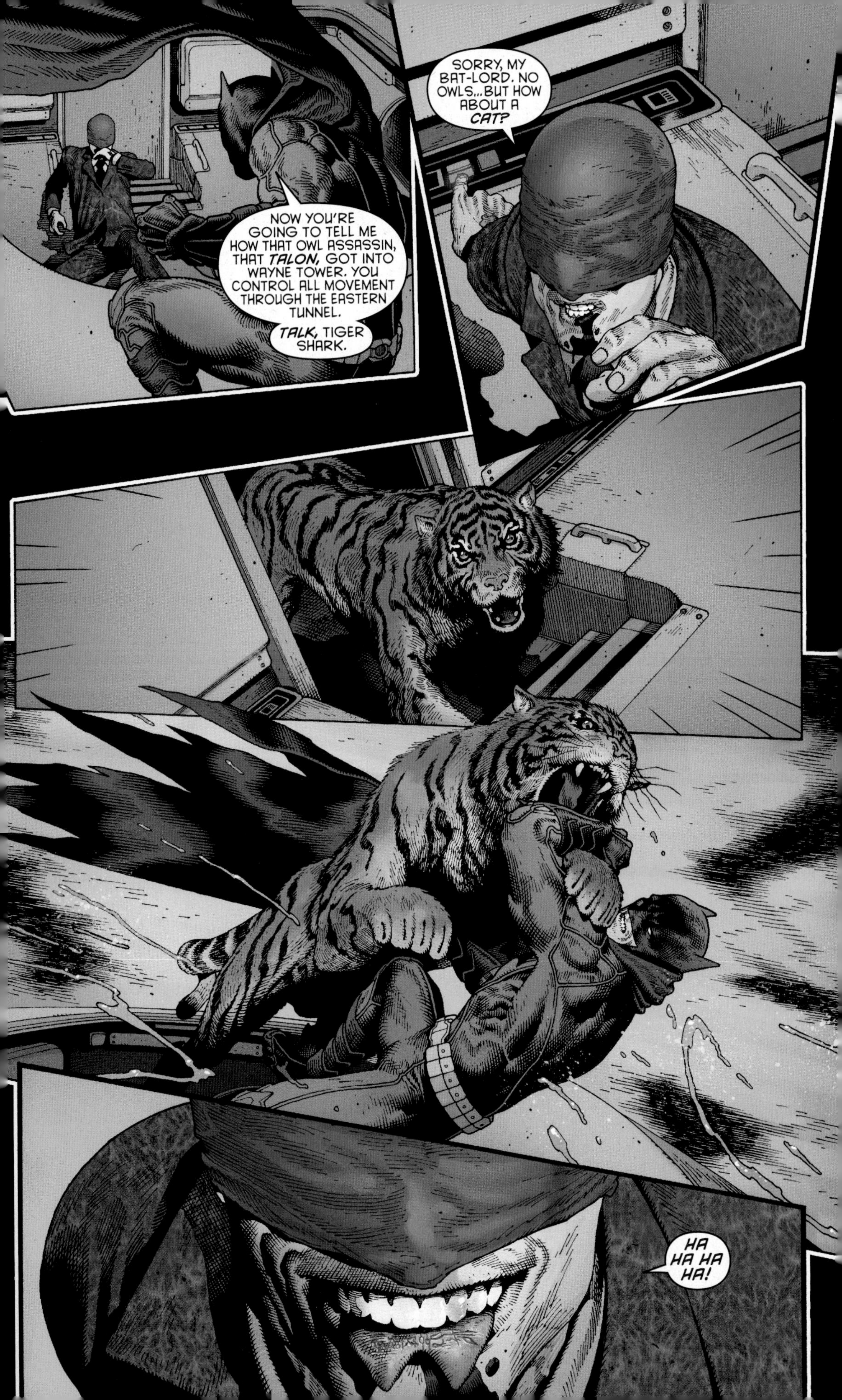
NOW YOU'RE GOING TO TELL ME HOW THAT OWL ASSASSIN, THAT TALON, GOT INTO WAYNE TOWER. YOU CONTROL ALL MOVEMENT THROUGH THE EASTERN TUNNEL.
TALK, TIGER SHARK.
SORRY, MY BAT-LORD. NO OWLS...BUT HOW ABOUT A CAT?
HA HA HA HA!

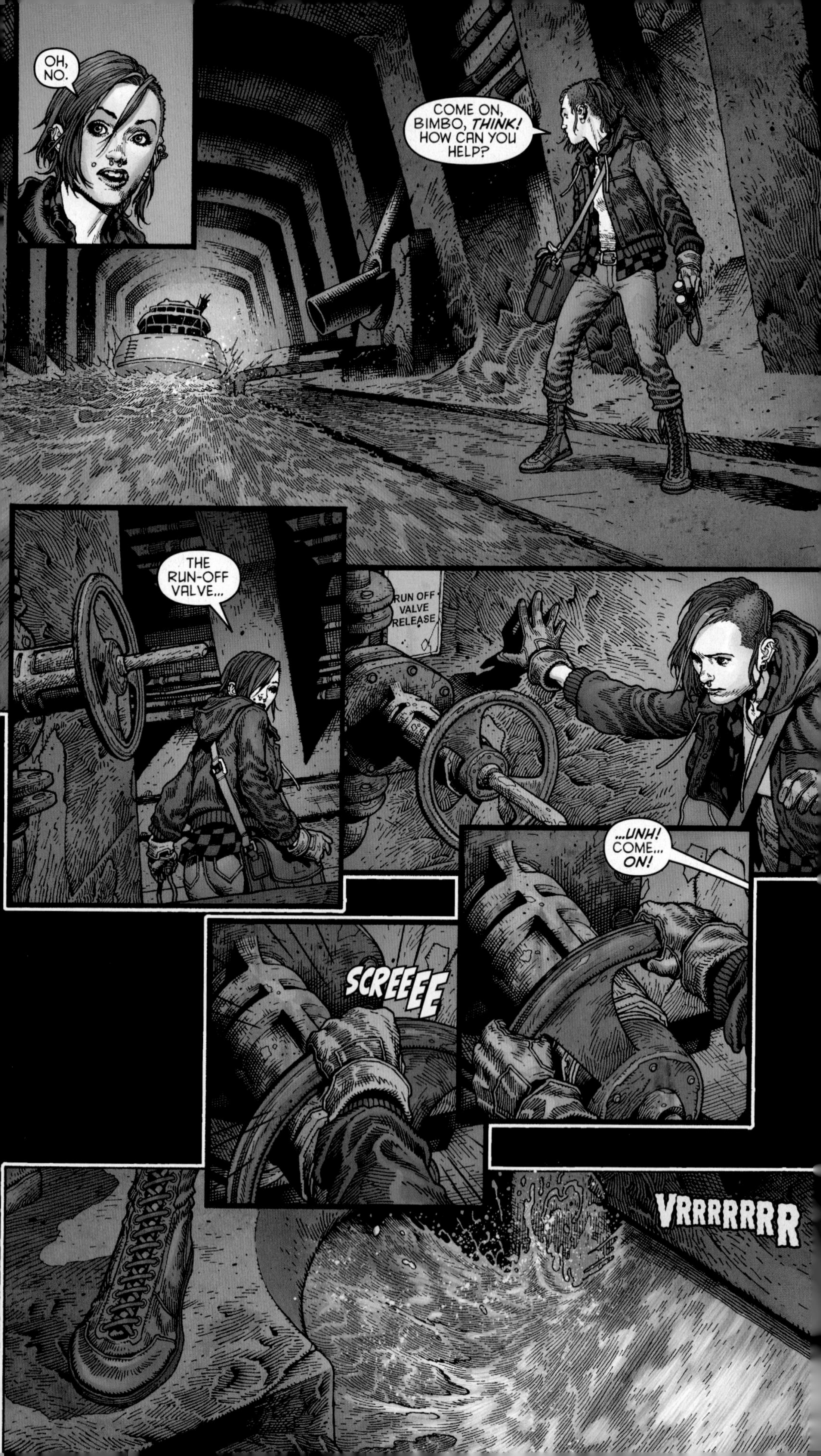
OH, NO.
COME ON, BIMBO, *THINK!* HOW CAN YOU HELP?
THE RUN-OFF VALVE...
RUN OFF VALVE RELEASE
...UNH! COME... *ON!*
SCREEEE
VRRRRRRR

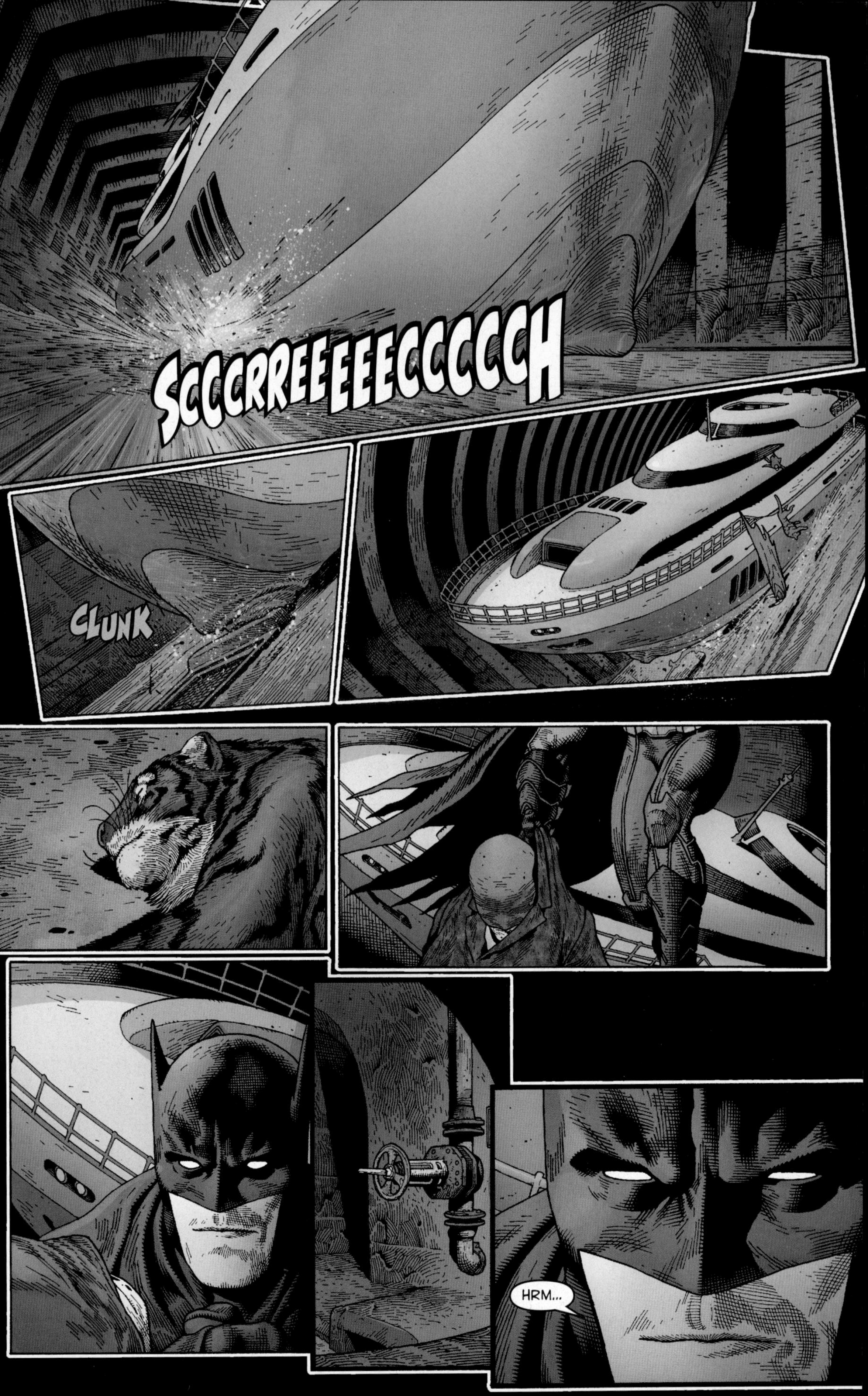
SCCCRREEEEEECCCCCH
CLUNK
HRM...

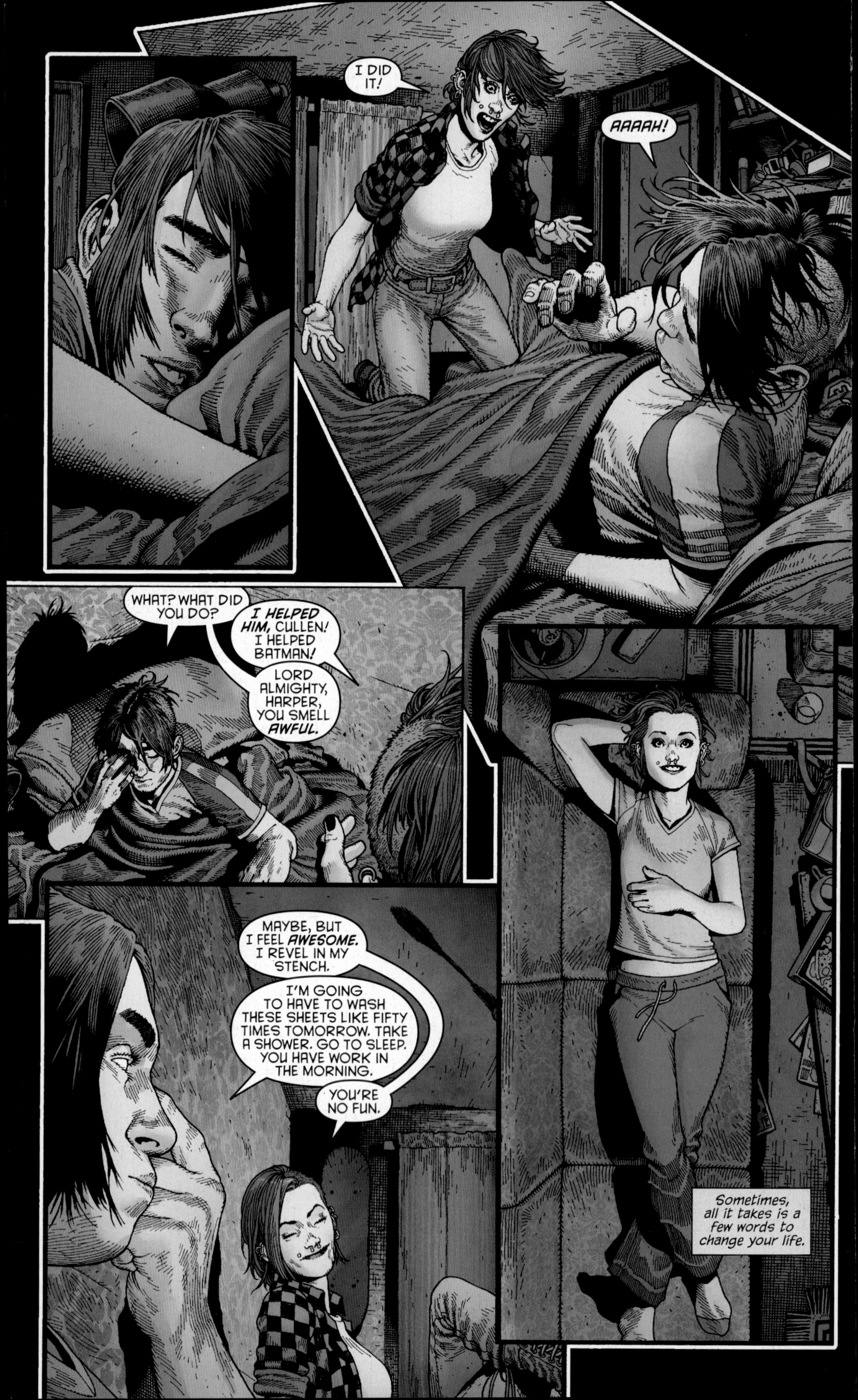
I DID IT!
AAAAH!
WHAT? WHAT DID YOU DO?
I HELPED HIM, CULLEN! I HELPED BATMAN!
LORD ALMIGHTY, HARPER, YOU SMELL AWFUL.
MAYBE, BUT I FEEL AWESOME. I REVEL IN MY STENCH.
I'M GOING TO HAVE TO WASH THESE SHEETS LIKE FIFTY TIMES TOMORROW. TAKE A SHOWER. GO TO SLEEP. YOU HAVE WORK IN THE MORNING.
YOU'RE NO FUN.
Sometimes, all it takes is a few words to change your life.

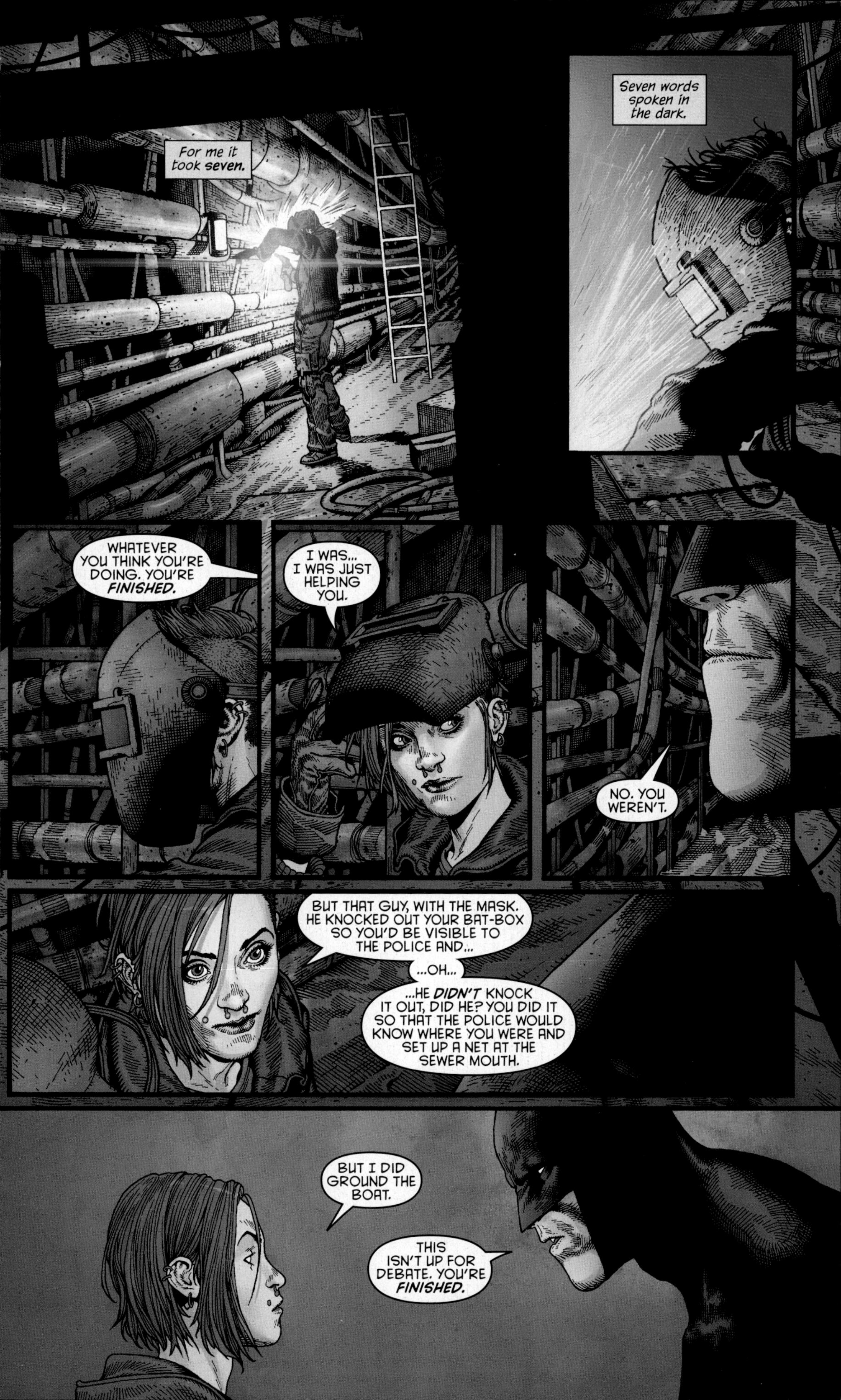
For me it took seven.
Seven words spoken in the dark.
WHATEVER YOU THINK YOU'RE DOING. YOU'RE FINISHED.
I WAS... I WAS JUST HELPING YOU.
NO. YOU WEREN'T.
BUT THAT GUY, WITH THE MASK. HE KNOCKED OUT YOUR BAT-BOX SO YOU'D BE VISIBLE TO THE POLICE AND...
...OH...
...HE DIDN'T KNOCK IT OUT, DID HE? YOU DID IT SO THAT THE POLICE WOULD KNOW WHERE YOU WERE AND SET UP A NET AT THE SEWER MOUTH.
BUT I DID GROUND THE BOAT.
THIS ISN'T UP FOR DEBATE. YOU'RE FINISHED.

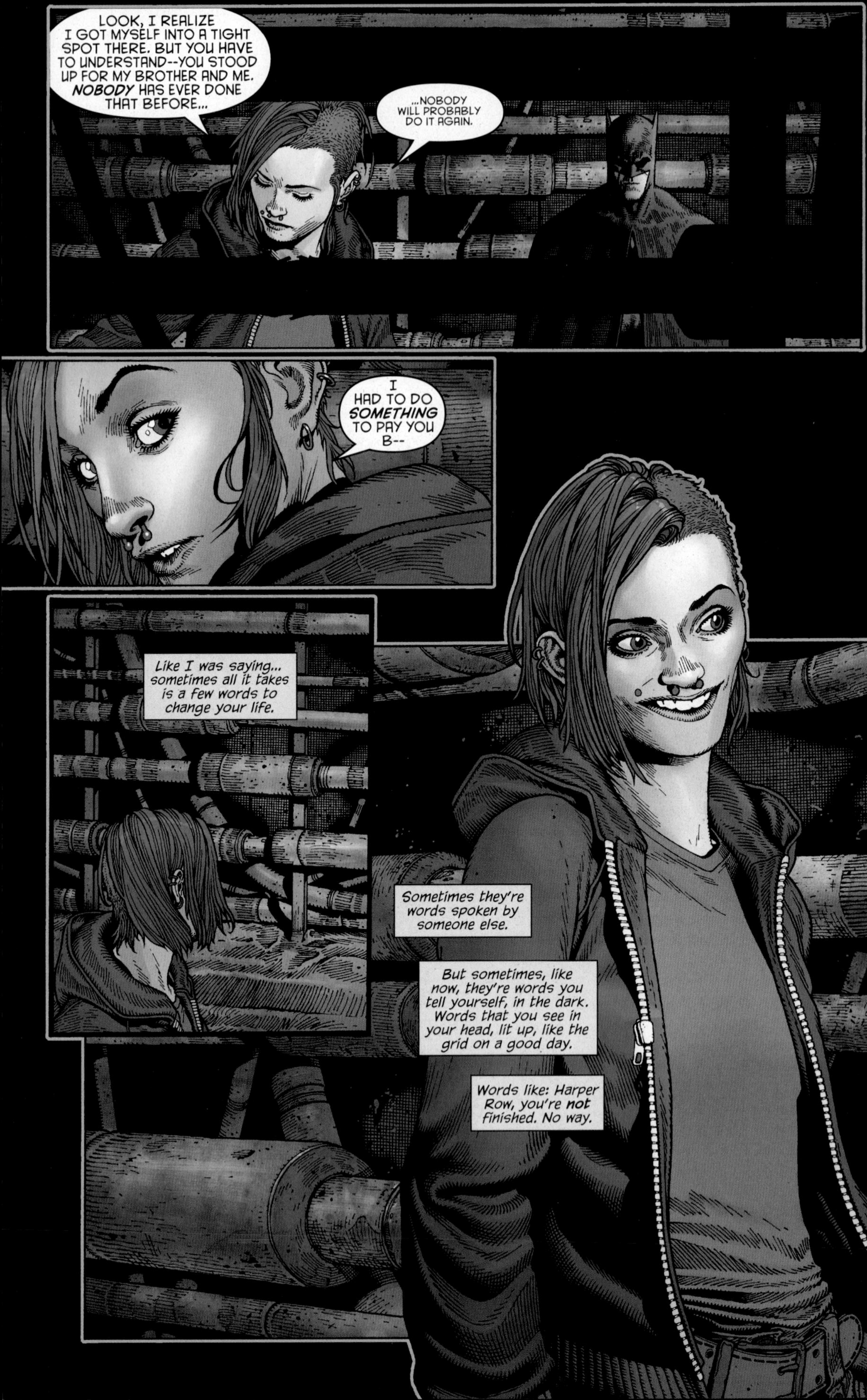
LOOK, I REALIZE I GOT MYSELF INTO A TIGHT SPOT THERE. BUT YOU HAVE TO UNDERSTAND--YOU STOOD UP FOR MY BROTHER AND ME. NOBODY HAS EVER DONE THAT BEFORE...
...NOBODY WILL PROBABLY DO IT AGAIN.
I HAD TO DO SOMETHING TO PAY YOU B--
Like I was saying... sometimes all it takes is a few words to change your life.
Sometimes they're words spoken by someone else.
But sometimes, like now, they're words you tell yourself, in the dark. Words that you see in your head, lit up, like the grid on a good day.
Words like: Harper Row, you're not finished. No way.

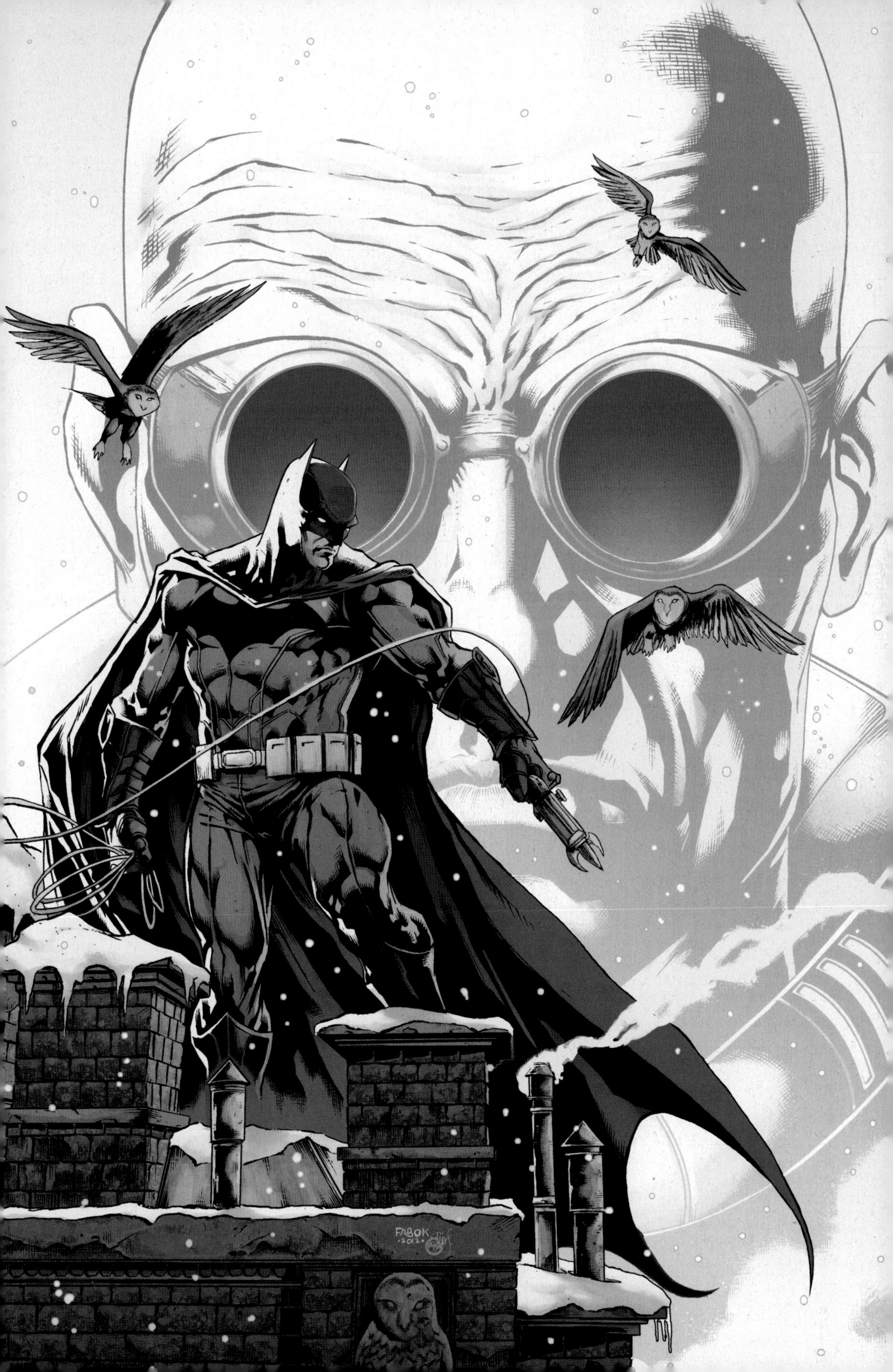
FABOK
·2012·

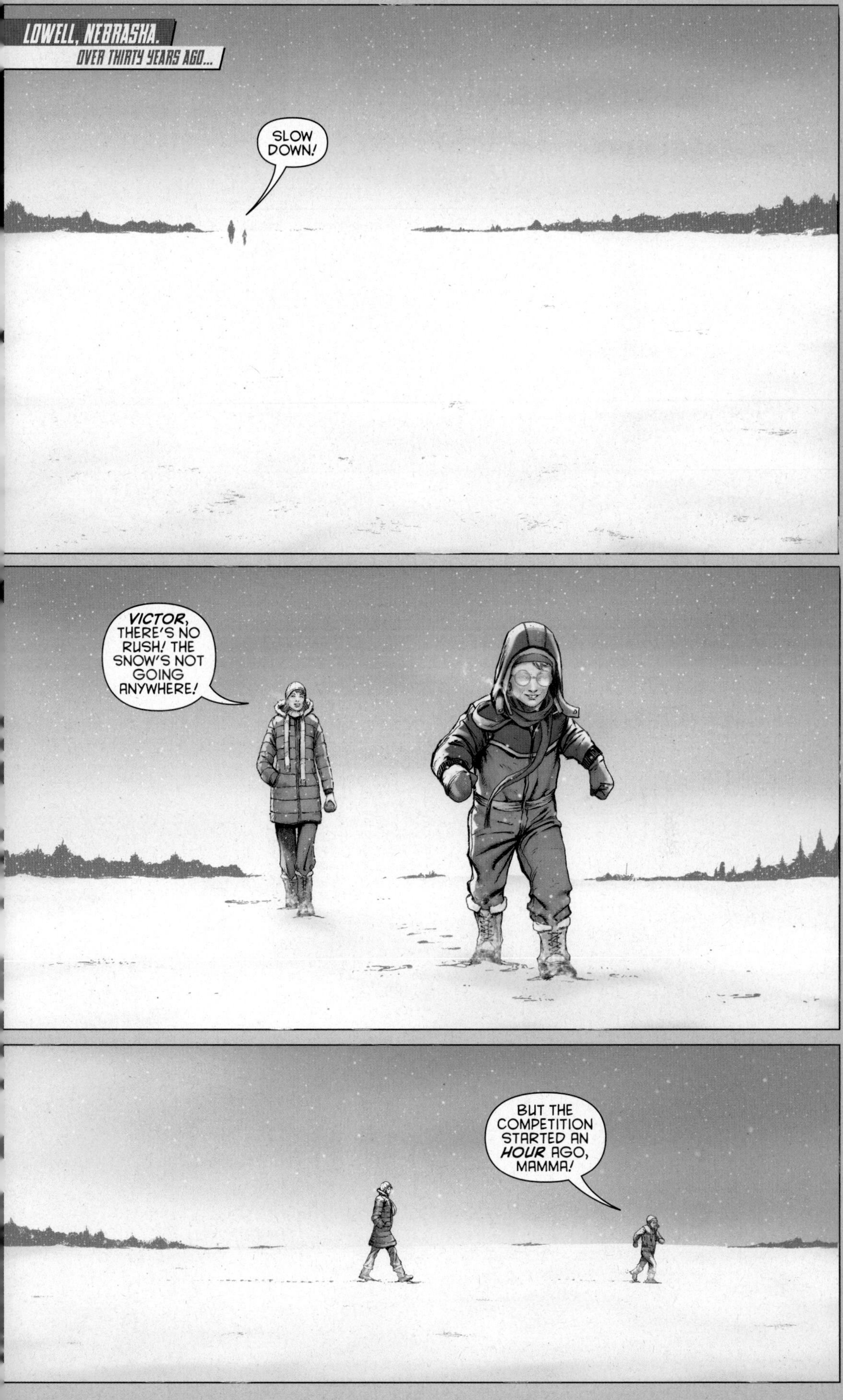
LOWELL, NEBRASKA.
OVER THIRTY YEARS AGO...
SLOW DOWN!
VICTOR, THERE'S NO RUSH! THE SNOW'S NOT GOING ANYWHERE!
BUT THE COMPETITION STARTED AN HOUR AGO, MAMMA!

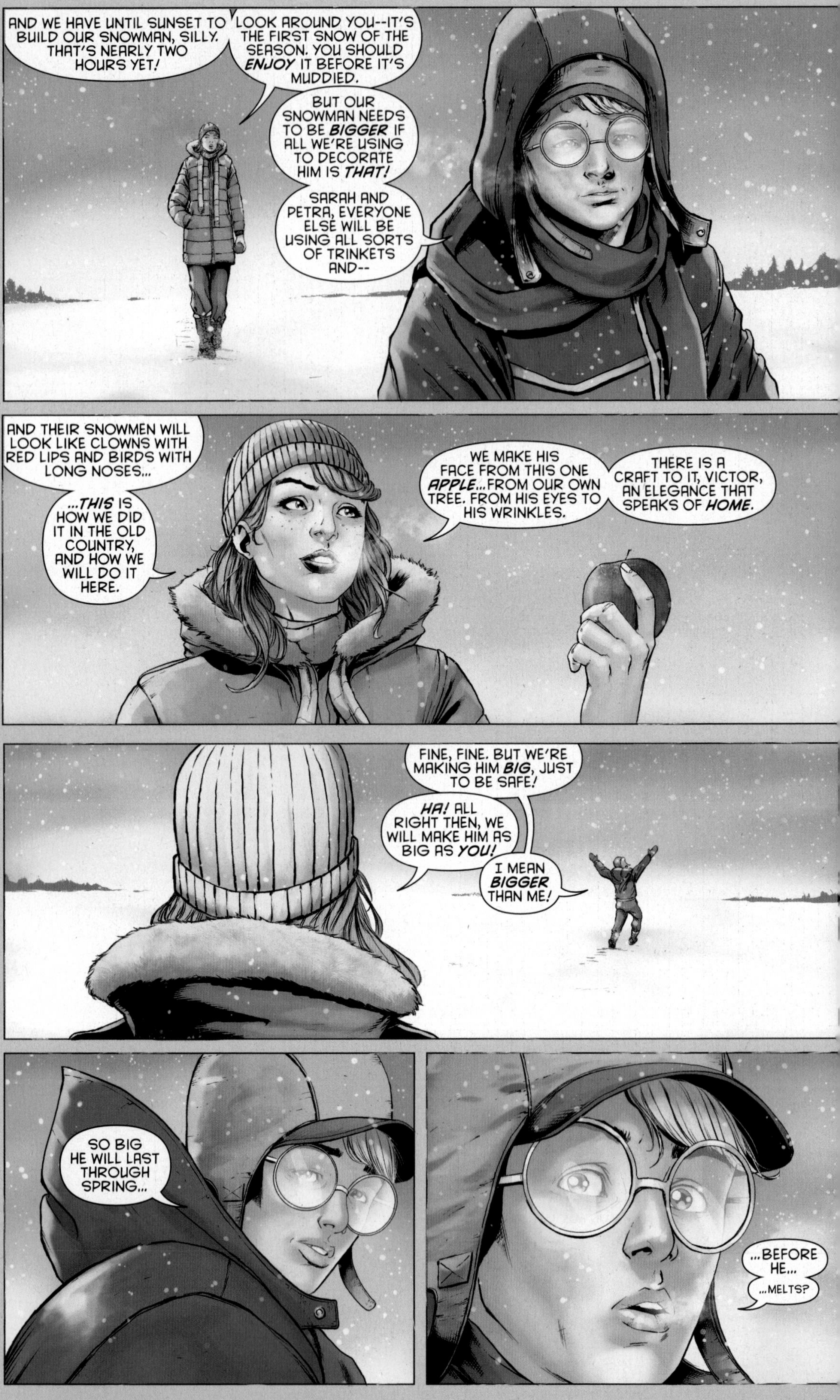
AND WE HAVE UNTIL SUNSET TO BUILD OUR SNOWMAN, SILLY. THAT'S NEARLY TWO HOURS YET!
LOOK AROUND YOU--IT'S THE FIRST SNOW OF THE SEASON. YOU SHOULD ENJOY IT BEFORE IT'S MUDDIED.
BUT OUR SNOWMAN NEEDS TO BE BIGGER IF ALL WE'RE USING TO DECORATE HIM IS THAT!
SARAH AND PETRA, EVERYONE ELSE WILL BE USING ALL SORTS OF TRINKETS AND--
AND THEIR SNOWMEN WILL LOOK LIKE CLOWNS WITH RED LIPS AND BIRDS WITH LONG NOSES...
...THIS IS HOW WE DID IT IN THE OLD COUNTRY, AND HOW WE WILL DO IT HERE.
WE MAKE HIS FACE FROM THIS ONE APPLE...FROM OUR OWN TREE. FROM HIS EYES TO HIS WRINKLES.
THERE IS A CRAFT TO IT, VICTOR, AN ELEGANCE THAT SPEAKS OF HOME.
FINE, FINE. BUT WE'RE MAKING HIM BIG, JUST TO BE SAFE!
HA! ALL RIGHT THEN, WE WILL MAKE HIM AS BIG AS YOU!
I MEAN BIGGER THAN ME!
SO BIG HE WILL LAST THROUGH SPRING...
...BEFORE HE...
...MELTS?

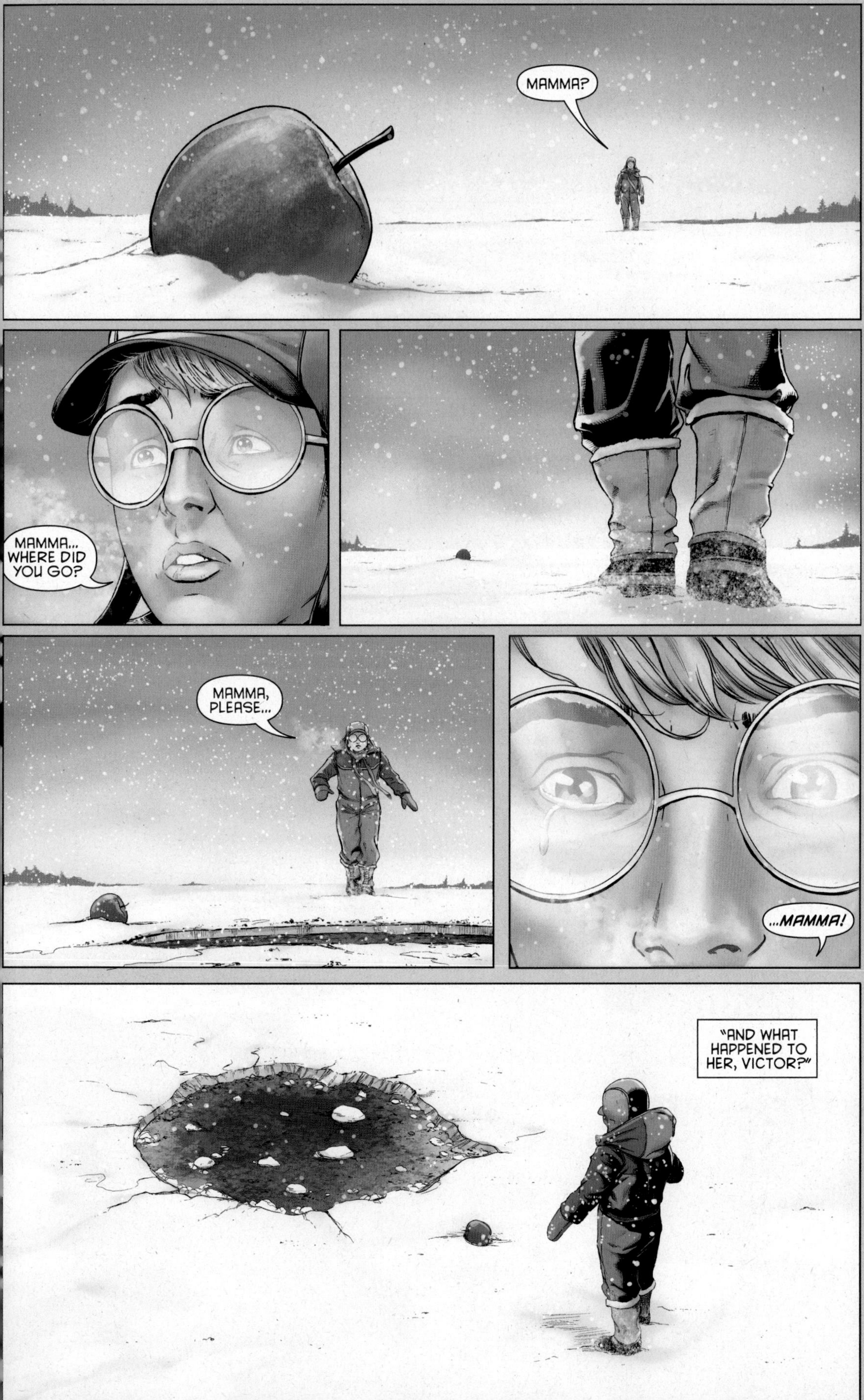
MAMMA?
MAMMA... WHERE DID YOU GO?
MAMMA, PLEASE...
...MAMMA!
"AND WHAT HAPPENED TO HER, VICTOR?"

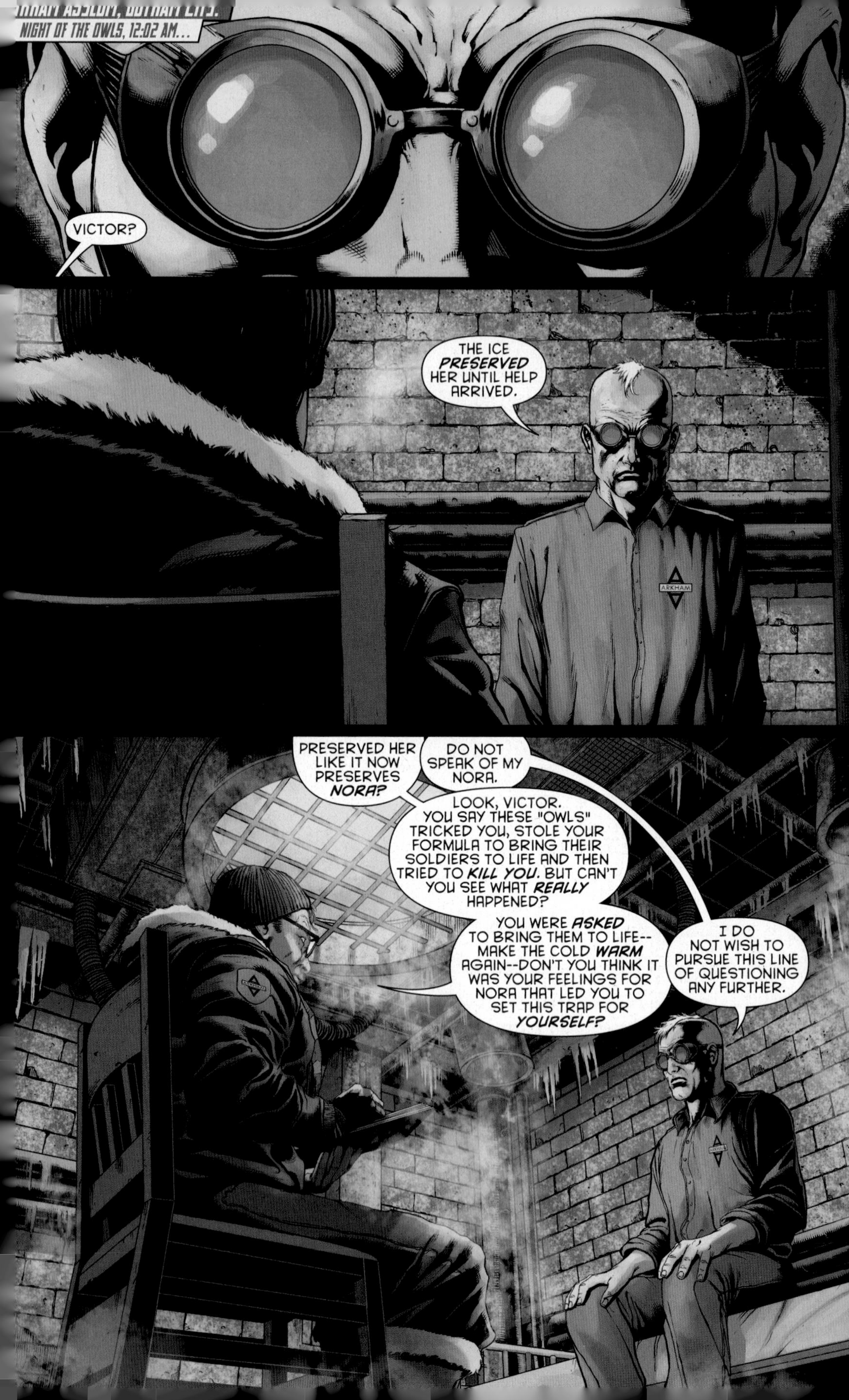
NIGHT OF THE OWLS, 12:02 AM...
VICTOR?
THE ICE PRESERVED HER UNTIL HELP ARRIVED.
PRESERVED HER LIKE IT NOW PRESERVES NORA?
DO NOT SPEAK OF MY NORA.
LOOK, VICTOR. YOU SAY THESE "OWLS" TRICKED YOU, STOLE YOUR FORMULA TO BRING THEIR SOLDIERS TO LIFE AND THEN TRIED TO KILL YOU. BUT CAN'T YOU SEE WHAT REALLY HAPPENED?
YOU WERE ASKED TO BRING THEM TO LIFE--MAKE THE COLD WARM AGAIN--DON'T YOU THINK IT WAS YOUR FEELINGS FOR NORA THAT LED YOU TO SET THIS TRAP FOR YOURSELF?
I DO NOT WISH TO PURSUE THIS LINE OF QUESTIONING ANY FURTHER.
ARKHAM

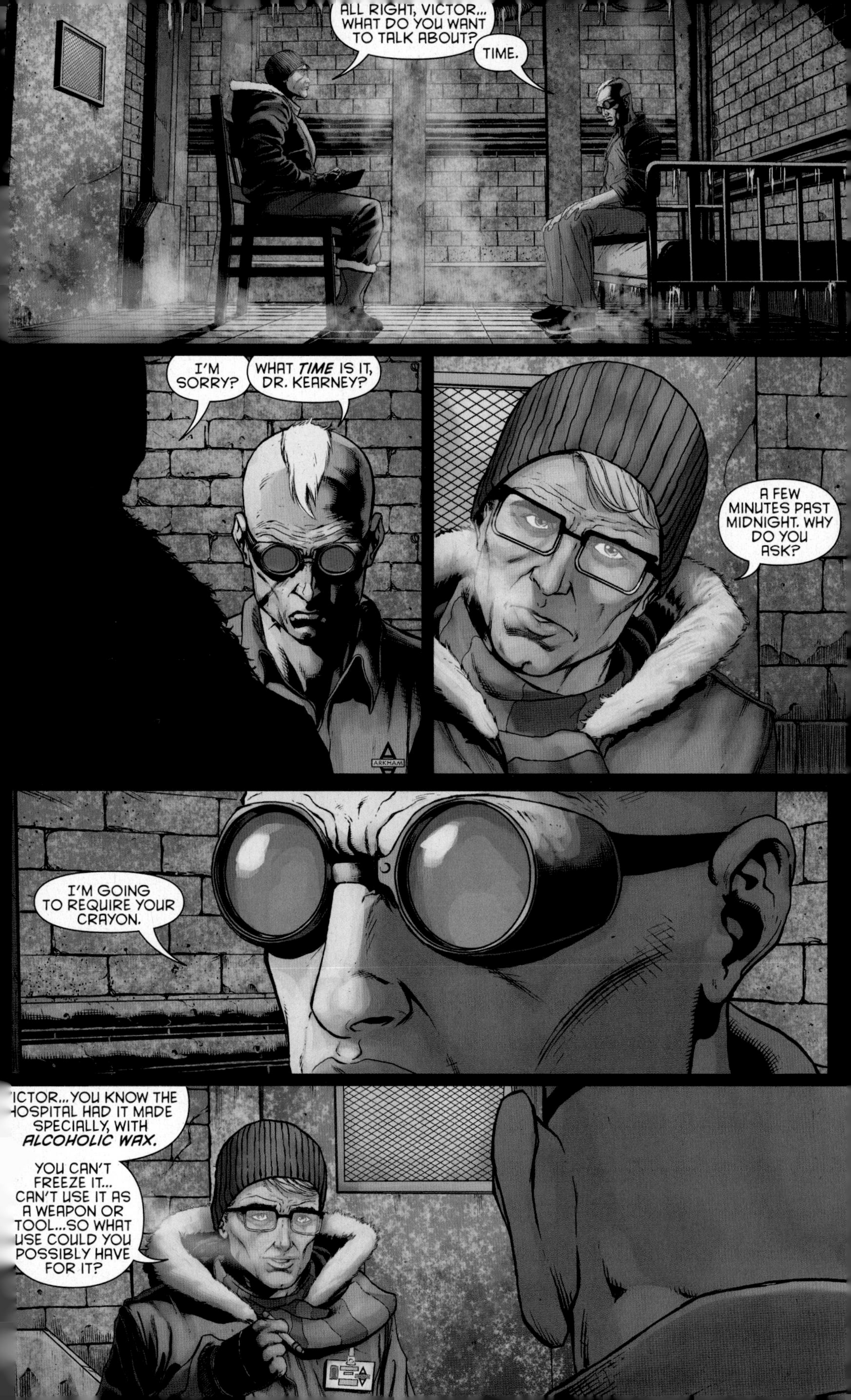
ALL RIGHT, VICTOR... WHAT DO YOU WANT TO TALK ABOUT?
TIME.
I'M SORRY?
WHAT *TIME* IS IT, DR. KEARNEY?
ARKHAM
A FEW MINUTES PAST MIDNIGHT. WHY DO YOU ASK?
I'M GOING TO REQUIRE YOUR CRAYON.
VICTOR...YOU KNOW THE HOSPITAL HAD IT MADE SPECIALLY, WITH ***ALCOHOLIC WAX.***
YOU CAN'T FREEZE IT... CAN'T USE IT AS A WEAPON OR TOOL...SO WHAT USE COULD YOU POSSIBLY HAVE FOR IT?

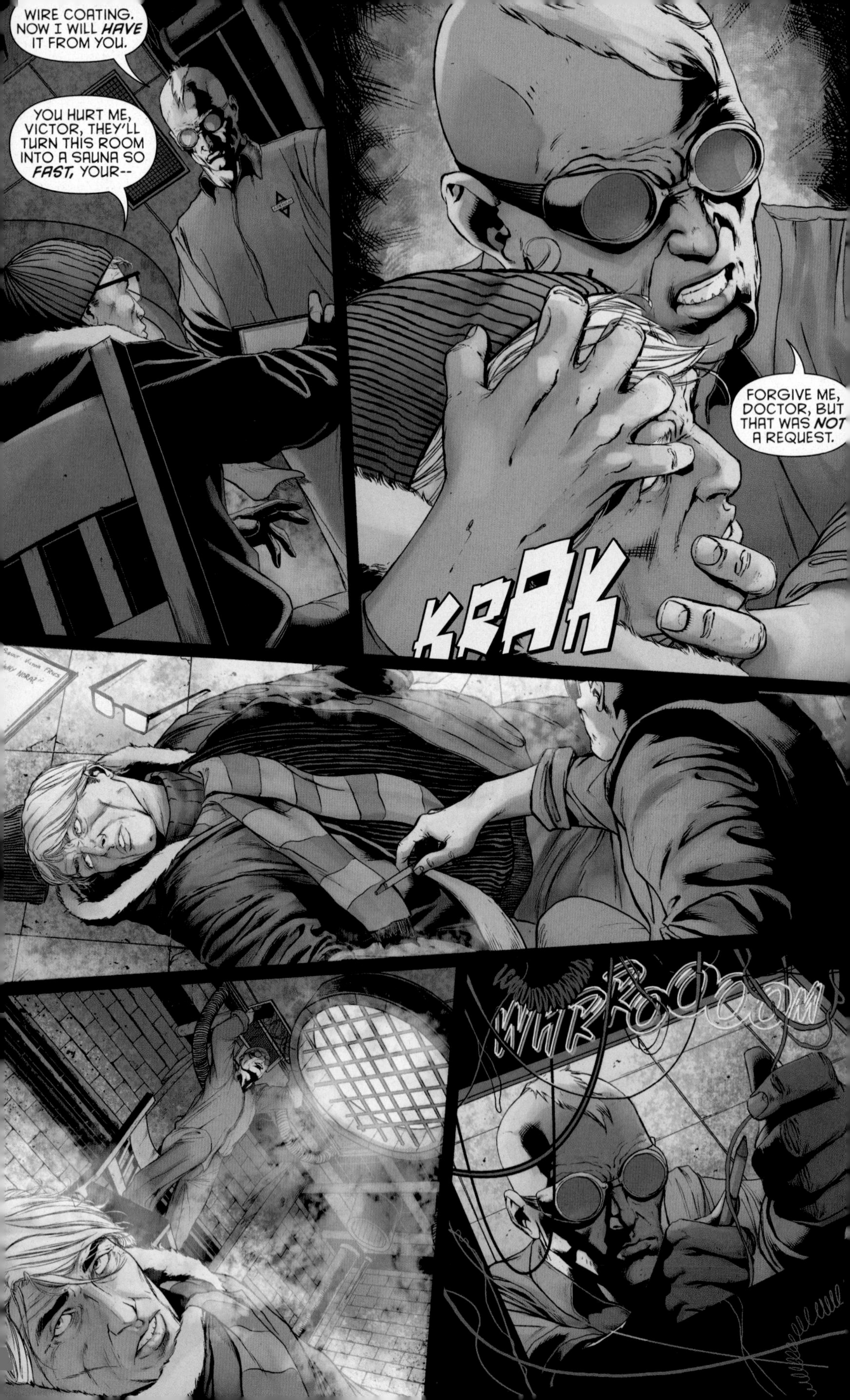
WIRE COATING. NOW I WILL HAVE IT FROM YOU.
YOU HURT ME, VICTOR, THEY'LL TURN THIS ROOM INTO A SAUNA SO FAST, YOUR--
FORGIVE ME, DOCTOR, BUT THAT WAS NOT A REQUEST.
KRAK
WHROOOOOM

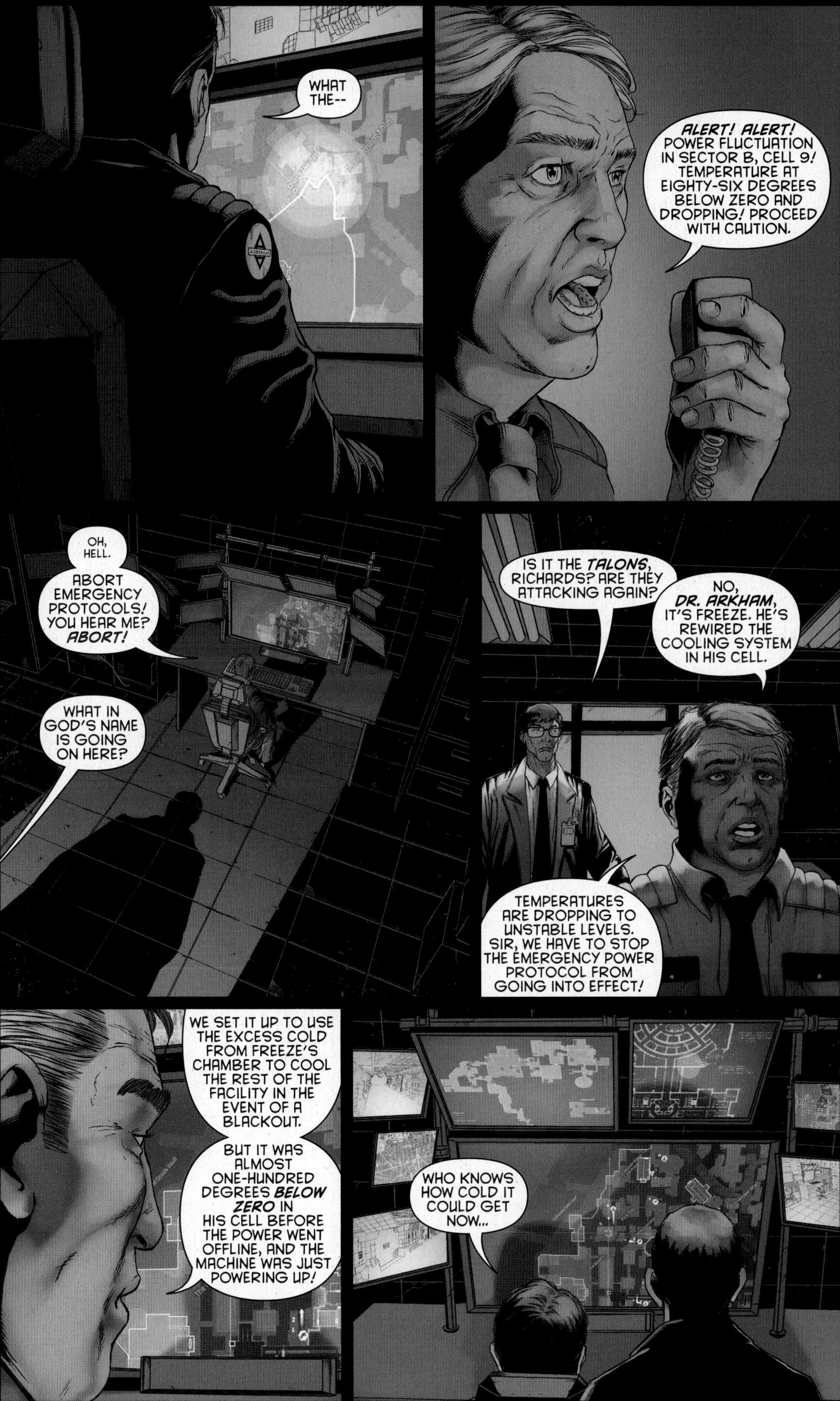
WHAT THE--
ALERT! ALERT! POWER FLUCTUATION IN SECTOR B, CELL 9! TEMPERATURE AT EIGHTY-SIX DEGREES BELOW ZERO AND DROPPING! PROCEED WITH CAUTION.
OH, HELL.
ABORT EMERGENCY PROTOCOLS! YOU HEAR ME? ABORT!
WHAT IN GOD'S NAME IS GOING ON HERE?
IS IT THE TALONS, RICHARDS? ARE THEY ATTACKING AGAIN?
NO, DR. ARKHAM, IT'S FREEZE. HE'S REWIRED THE COOLING SYSTEM IN HIS CELL.
TEMPERATURES ARE DROPPING TO UNSTABLE LEVELS. SIR, WE HAVE TO STOP THE EMERGENCY POWER PROTOCOL FROM GOING INTO EFFECT!
WE SET IT UP TO USE THE EXCESS COLD FROM FREEZE'S CHAMBER TO COOL THE REST OF THE FACILITY IN THE EVENT OF A BLACKOUT.
BUT IT WAS ALMOST ONE-HUNDRED DEGREES BELOW ZERO IN HIS CELL BEFORE THE POWER WENT OFFLINE, AND THE MACHINE WAS JUST POWERING UP!
WHO KNOWS HOW COLD IT COULD GET NOW...

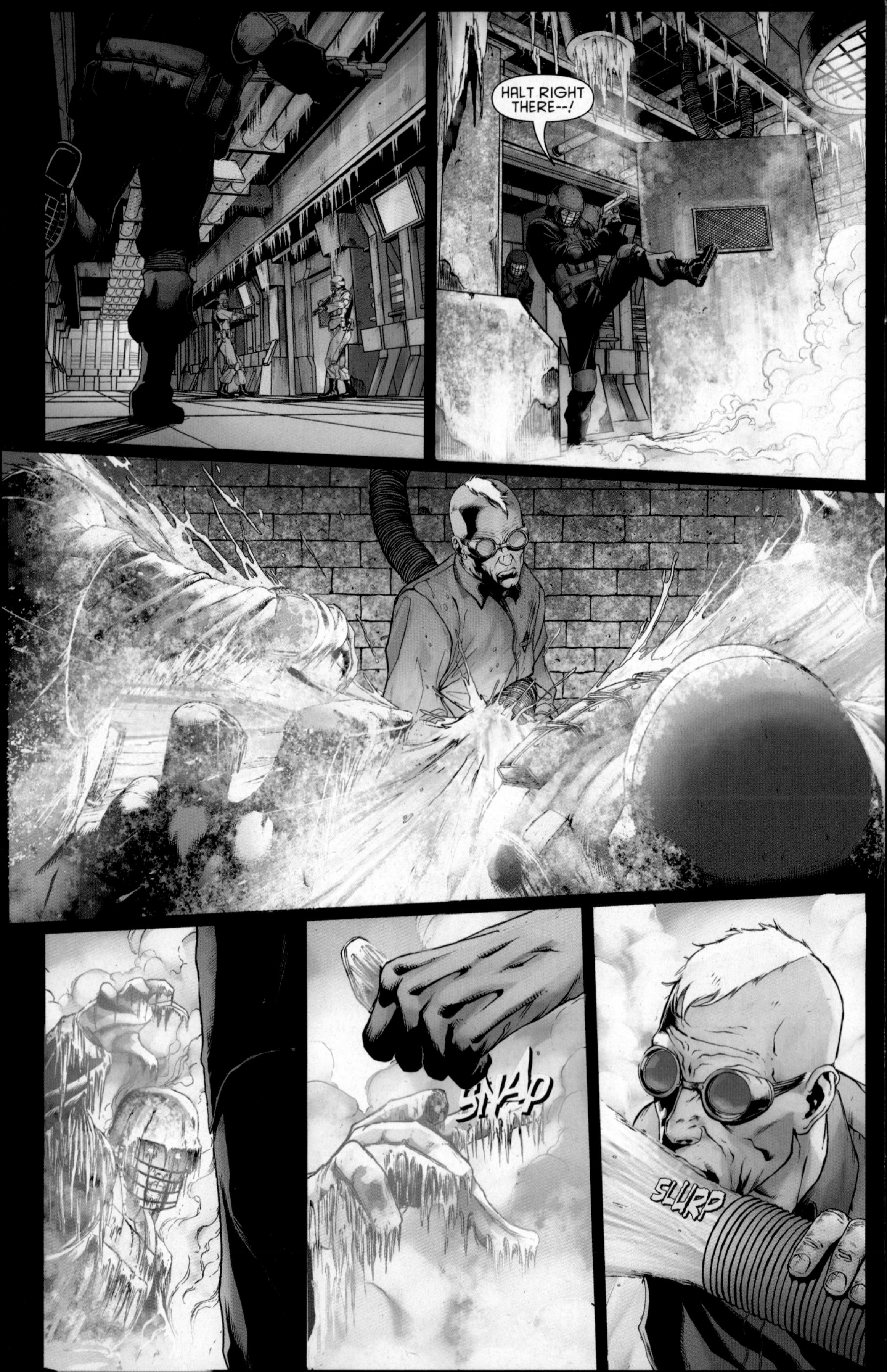
HALT RIGHT THERE--!
SNAP
SLURP

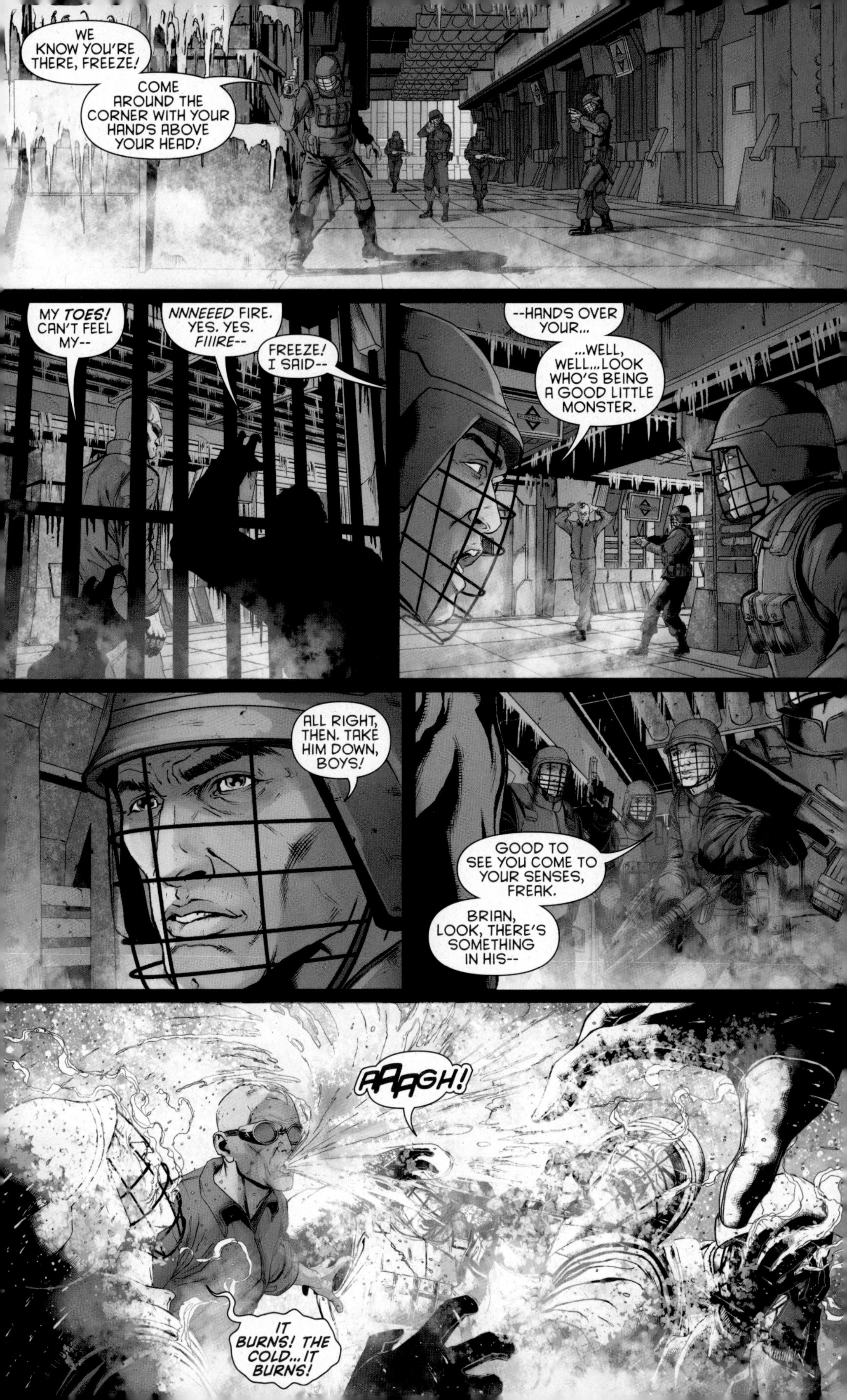
WE KNOW YOU'RE THERE, FREEZE!
COME AROUND THE CORNER WITH YOUR HANDS ABOVE YOUR HEAD!
MY *TOES!* CAN'T FEEL MY--
NNNEEED FIRE. YES. YES. *FIIIRE*--
FREEZE! I SAID--
--HANDS OVER YOUR...
...WELL, WELL...LOOK WHO'S BEING A GOOD LITTLE MONSTER.
ALL RIGHT, THEN. TAKE HIM DOWN, BOYS!
GOOD TO SEE YOU COME TO YOUR SENSES, FREAK.
BRIAN, LOOK, THERE'S SOMETHING IN HIS--
AAAAGH!
IT BURNS! THE COLD...IT BURNS!

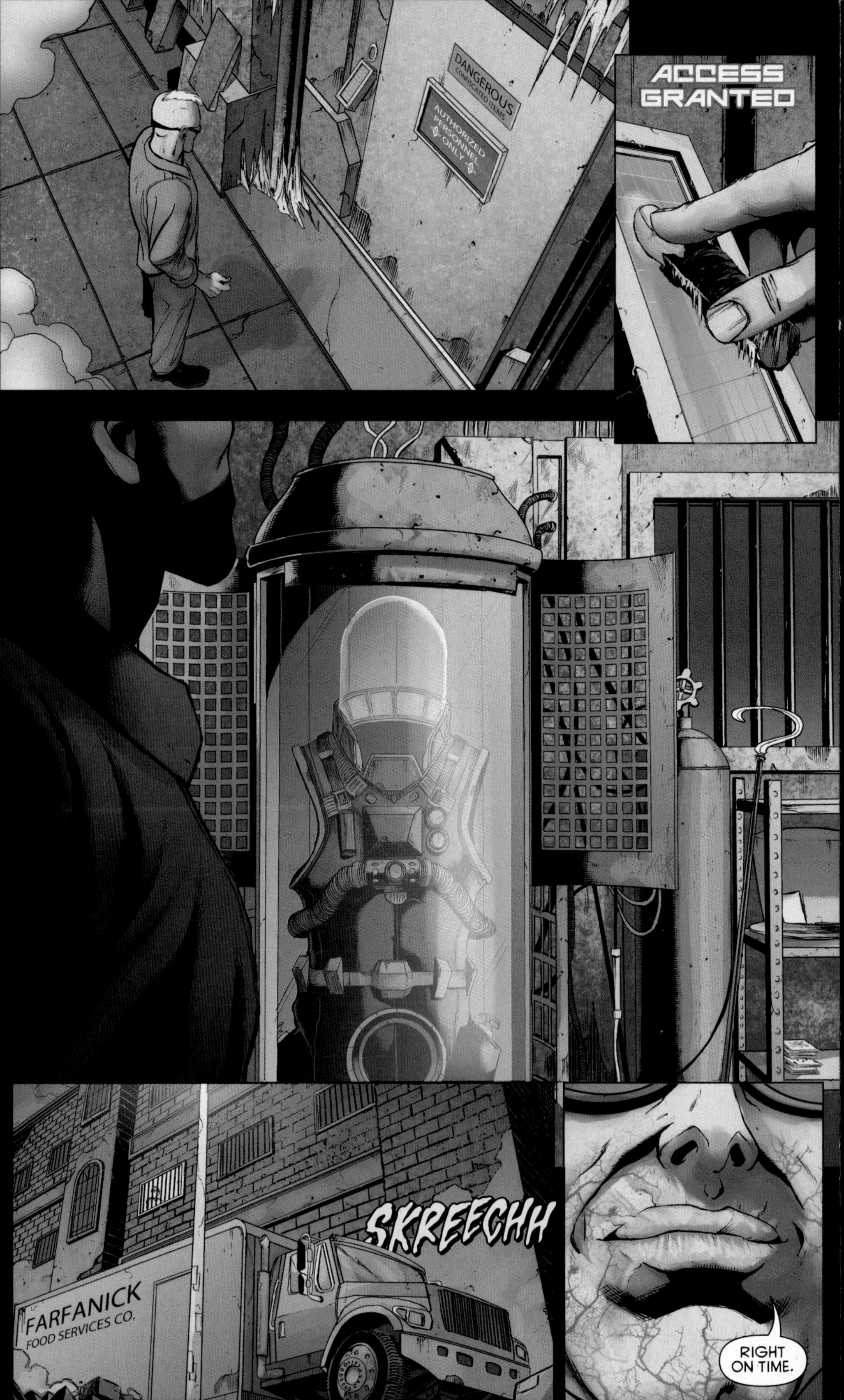
DANGEROUS
CONFISCATED ITEMS
AUTHORIZED PERSONNEL ONLY
ACCESS GRANTED
FARFANICK
FOOD SERVICES CO.
SKREECHH
RIGHT ON TIME.

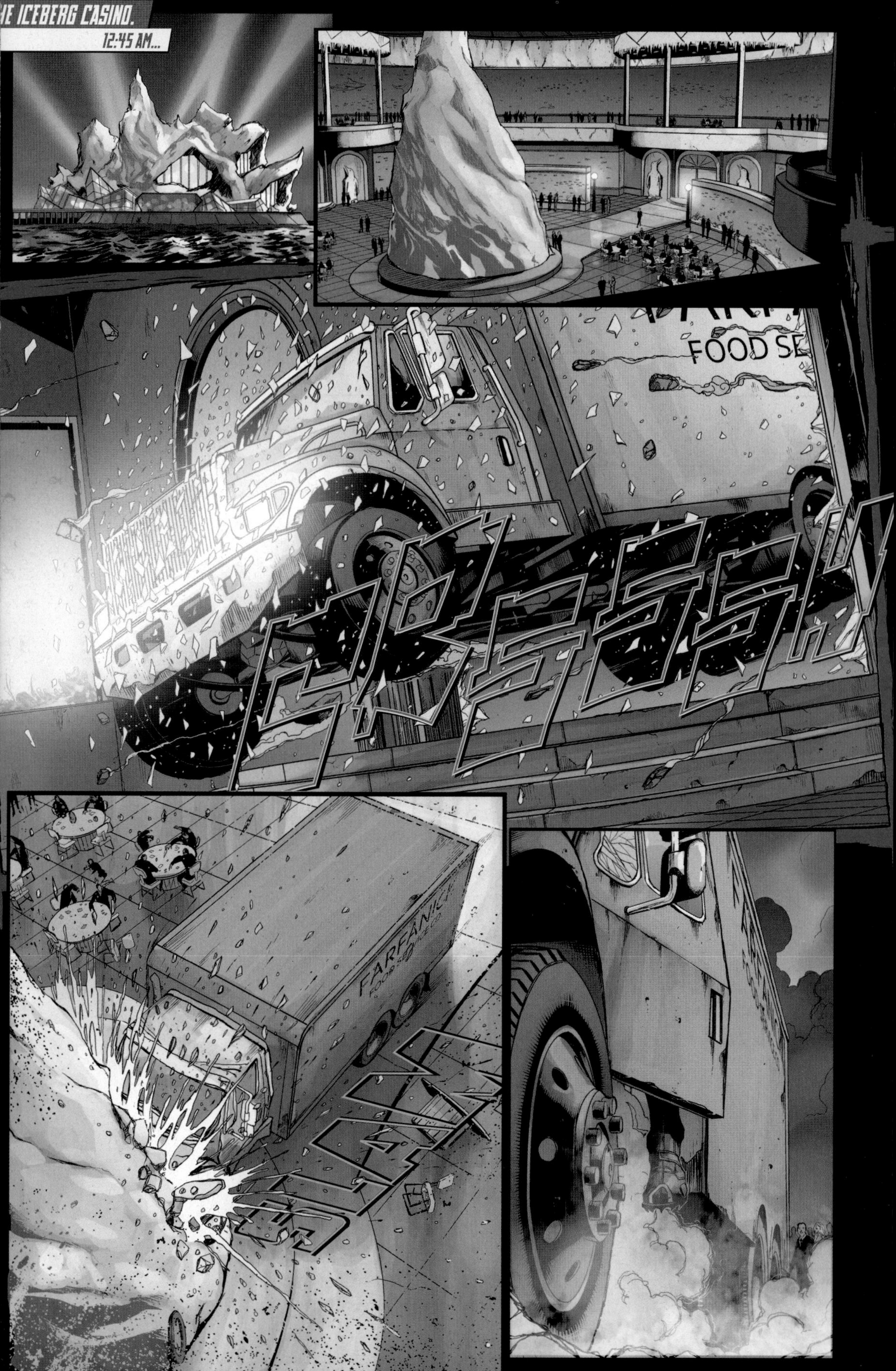
HE ICEBERG CASINO.
12:45 AM...
FOOD SE
FARFANICK

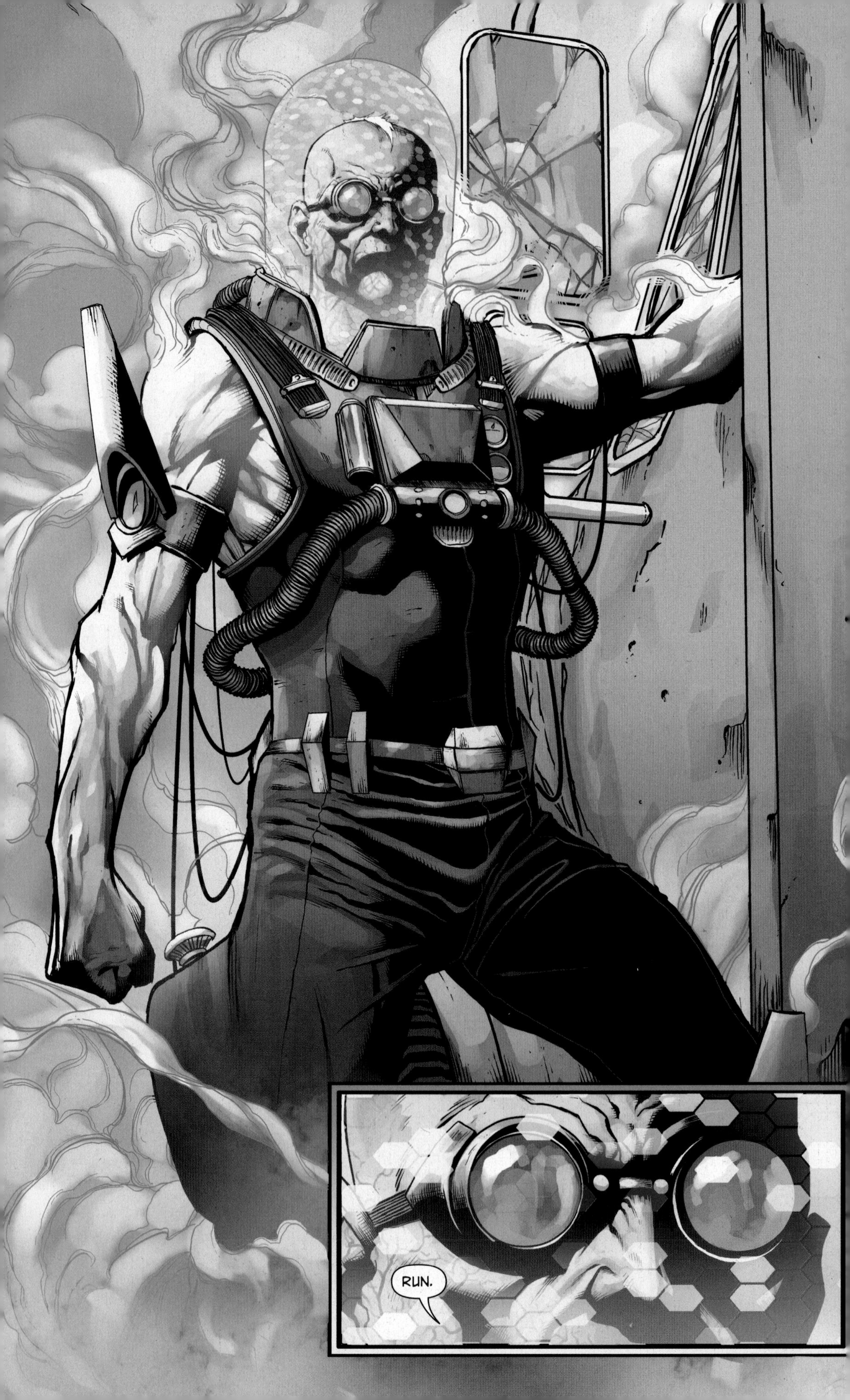
RUN.

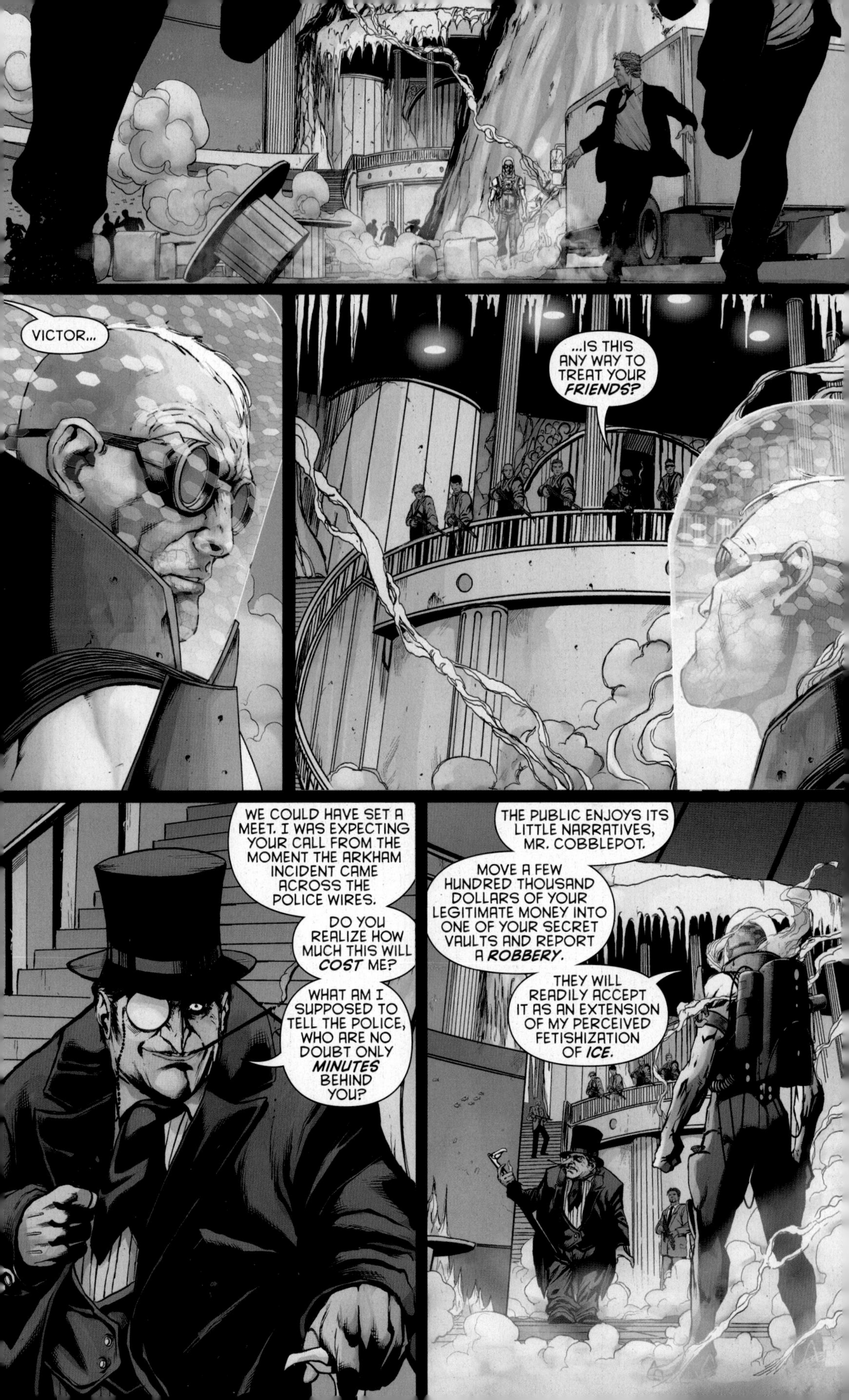
VICTOR...
...IS THIS ANY WAY TO TREAT YOUR FRIENDS?
WE COULD HAVE SET A MEET. I WAS EXPECTING YOUR CALL FROM THE MOMENT THE ARKHAM INCIDENT CAME ACROSS THE POLICE WIRES.
DO YOU REALIZE HOW MUCH THIS WILL COST ME?
WHAT AM I SUPPOSED TO TELL THE POLICE, WHO ARE NO DOUBT ONLY MINUTES BEHIND YOU?
THE PUBLIC ENJOYS ITS LITTLE NARRATIVES, MR. COBBLEPOT.
MOVE A FEW HUNDRED THOUSAND DOLLARS OF YOUR LEGITIMATE MONEY INTO ONE OF YOUR SECRET VAULTS AND REPORT A ROBBERY.
THEY WILL READILY ACCEPT IT AS AN EXTENSION OF MY PERCEIVED FETISHIZATION OF ICE.

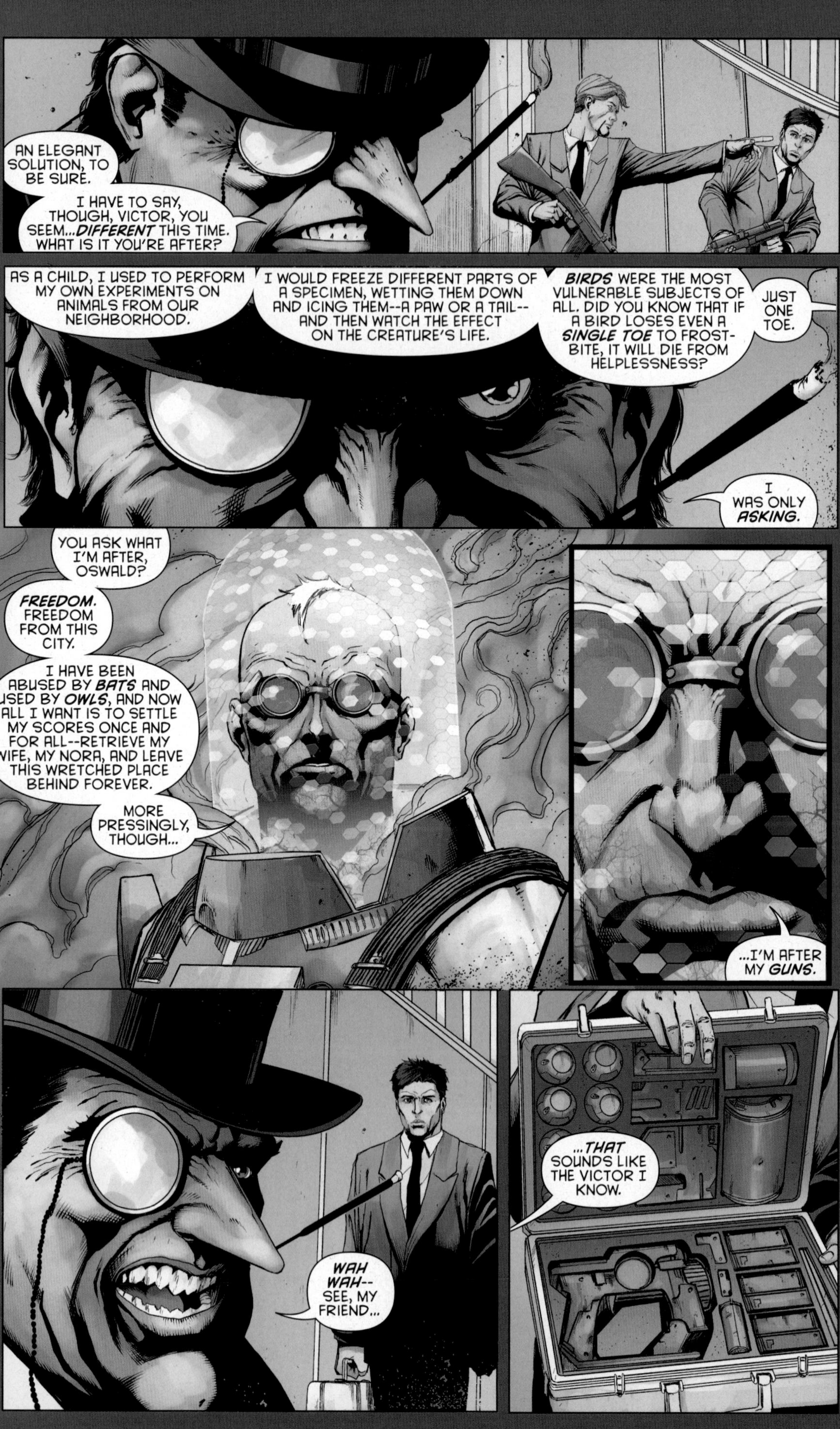
AN ELEGANT SOLUTION, TO BE SURE.
I HAVE TO SAY, THOUGH, VICTOR, YOU SEEM...DIFFERENT THIS TIME. WHAT IS IT YOU'RE AFTER?
AS A CHILD, I USED TO PERFORM MY OWN EXPERIMENTS ON ANIMALS FROM OUR NEIGHBORHOOD.
I WOULD FREEZE DIFFERENT PARTS OF A SPECIMEN, WETTING THEM DOWN AND ICING THEM--A PAW OR A TAIL--AND THEN WATCH THE EFFECT ON THE CREATURE'S LIFE.
BIRDS WERE THE MOST VULNERABLE SUBJECTS OF ALL. DID YOU KNOW THAT IF A BIRD LOSES EVEN A SINGLE TOE TO FROST-BITE, IT WILL DIE FROM HELPLESSNESS?
JUST ONE TOE.
I WAS ONLY ASKING.
YOU ASK WHAT I'M AFTER, OSWALD?
FREEDOM. FREEDOM FROM THIS CITY.
I HAVE BEEN ABUSED BY BATS AND USED BY OWLS, AND NOW ALL I WANT IS TO SETTLE MY SCORES ONCE AND FOR ALL--RETRIEVE MY WIFE, MY NORA, AND LEAVE THIS WRETCHED PLACE BEHIND FOREVER.
MORE PRESSINGLY, THOUGH...
...I'M AFTER MY GUNS.
WAH WAH--SEE, MY FRIEND...
...THAT SOUNDS LIKE THE VICTOR I KNOW.

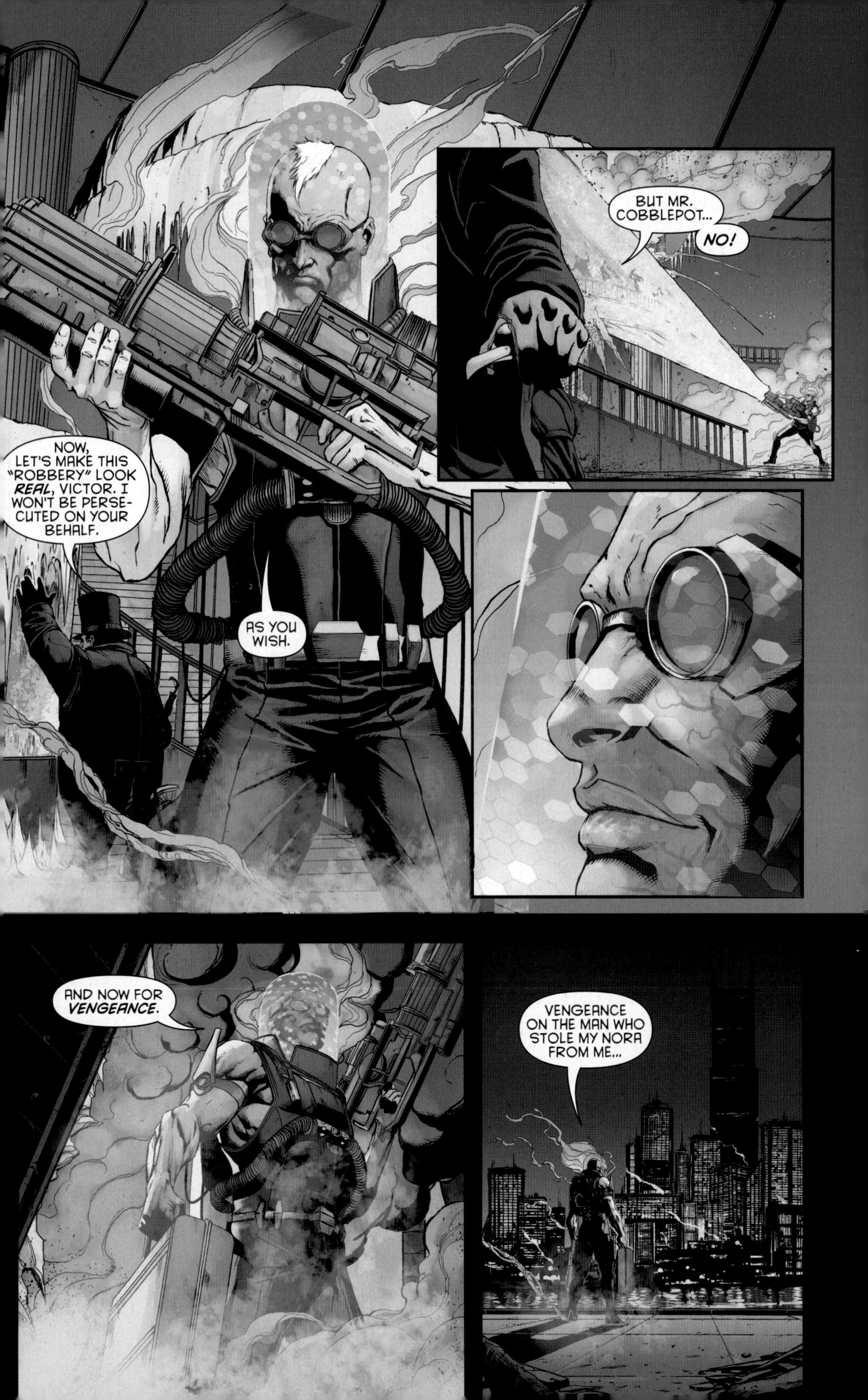
NOW, LET'S MAKE THIS "ROBBERY" LOOK REAL, VICTOR. I WON'T BE PERSECUTED ON YOUR BEHALF.
AS YOU WISH.
BUT MR. COBBLEPOT...
NO!
AND NOW FOR VENGEANCE.
VENGEANCE ON THE MAN WHO STOLE MY NORA FROM ME...

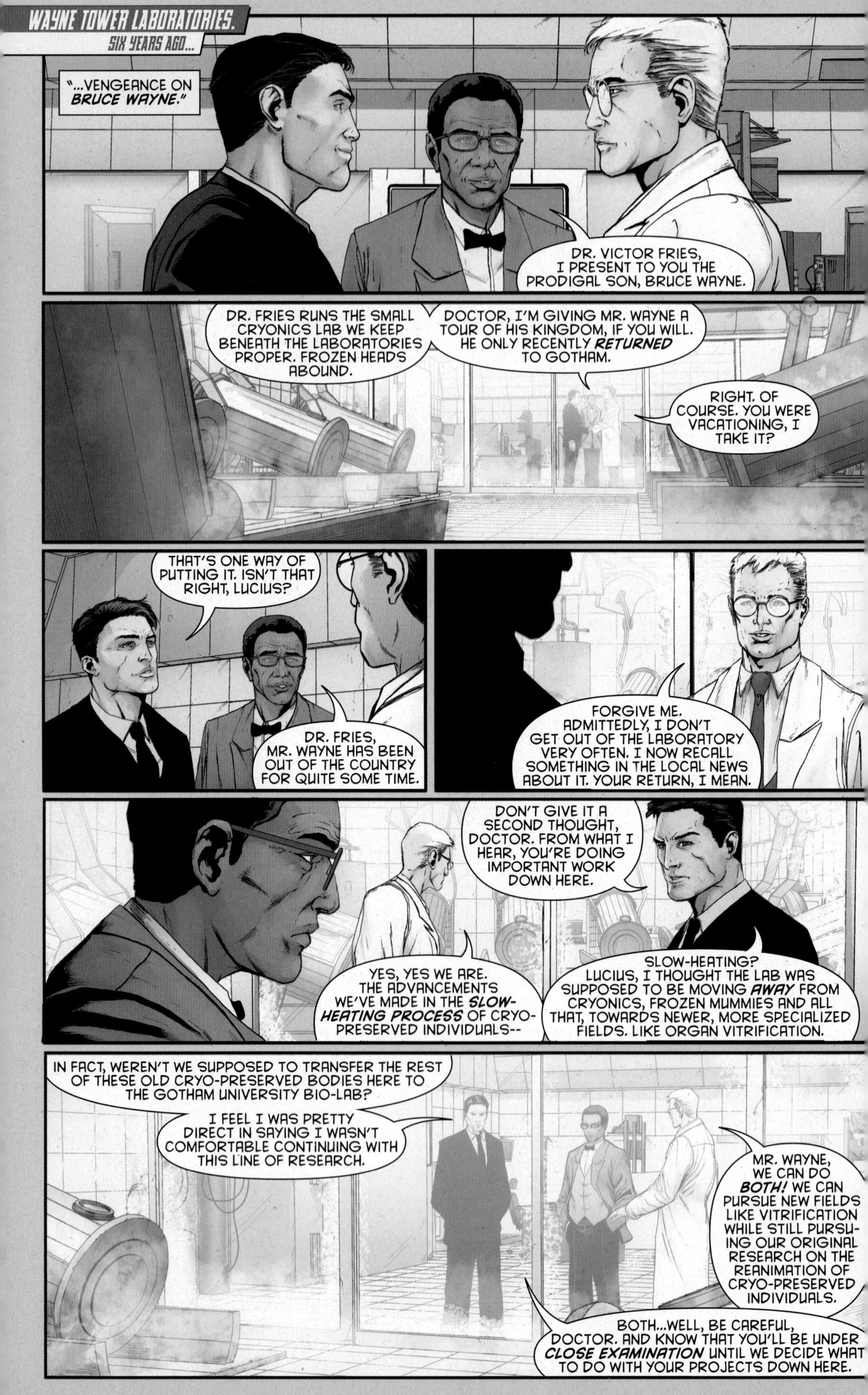
WAYNE TOWER LABORATORIES.
SIX YEARS AGO...
"...VENGEANCE ON BRUCE WAYNE."
DR. VICTOR FRIES, I PRESENT TO YOU THE PRODIGAL SON, BRUCE WAYNE.
DOCTOR, I'M GIVING MR. WAYNE A TOUR OF HIS KINGDOM, IF YOU WILL. HE ONLY RECENTLY RETURNED TO GOTHAM.
DR. FRIES RUNS THE SMALL CRYONICS LAB WE KEEP BENEATH THE LABORATORIES PROPER. FROZEN HEADS ABOUND.
RIGHT. OF COURSE. YOU WERE VACATIONING, I TAKE IT?
THAT'S ONE WAY OF PUTTING IT. ISN'T THAT RIGHT, LUCIUS?
DR. FRIES, MR. WAYNE HAS BEEN OUT OF THE COUNTRY FOR QUITE SOME TIME.
FORGIVE ME. ADMITTEDLY, I DON'T GET OUT OF THE LABORATORY VERY OFTEN. I NOW RECALL SOMETHING IN THE LOCAL NEWS ABOUT IT. YOUR RETURN, I MEAN.
DON'T GIVE IT A SECOND THOUGHT, DOCTOR. FROM WHAT I HEAR, YOU'RE DOING IMPORTANT WORK DOWN HERE.
YES, YES WE ARE. THE ADVANCEMENTS WE'VE MADE IN THE SLOW-HEATING PROCESS OF CRYO-PRESERVED INDIVIDUALS--
SLOW-HEATING? LUCIUS, I THOUGHT THE LAB WAS SUPPOSED TO BE MOVING AWAY FROM CRYONICS, FROZEN MUMMIES AND ALL THAT, TOWARDS NEWER, MORE SPECIALIZED FIELDS. LIKE ORGAN VITRIFICATION.
IN FACT, WEREN'T WE SUPPOSED TO TRANSFER THE REST OF THESE OLD CRYO-PRESERVED BODIES HERE TO THE GOTHAM UNIVERSITY BIO-LAB?
I FEEL I WAS PRETTY DIRECT IN SAYING I WASN'T COMFORTABLE CONTINUING WITH THIS LINE OF RESEARCH.
MR. WAYNE, WE CAN DO BOTH! WE CAN PURSUE NEW FIELDS LIKE VITRIFICATION WHILE STILL PURSUING OUR ORIGINAL RESEARCH ON THE REANIMATION OF CRYO-PRESERVED INDIVIDUALS.
BOTH...WELL, BE CAREFUL, DOCTOR. AND KNOW THAT YOU'LL BE UNDER CLOSE EXAMINATION UNTIL WE DECIDE WHAT TO DO WITH YOUR PROJECTS DOWN HERE.

...I SHOULD GET BACK TO MY WORK.

MR. WAYNE. MR. FOX.

DR. FRIES--

THAT'S OKAY, LUCIUS. DR. FRIES, FORGIVE ME IF I WAS OVER-STEPPING MY BOUNDS.

BEING AWAY SO LONG, MY SOCIAL GRACES NEED A GOOD REFRESHER COURSE. IT WAS A PLEASURE MEETING YOU, AND KEEP UP THE GOOD WORK.

STAY WARM DOWN HERE.

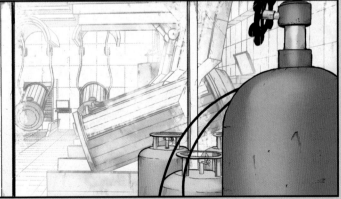

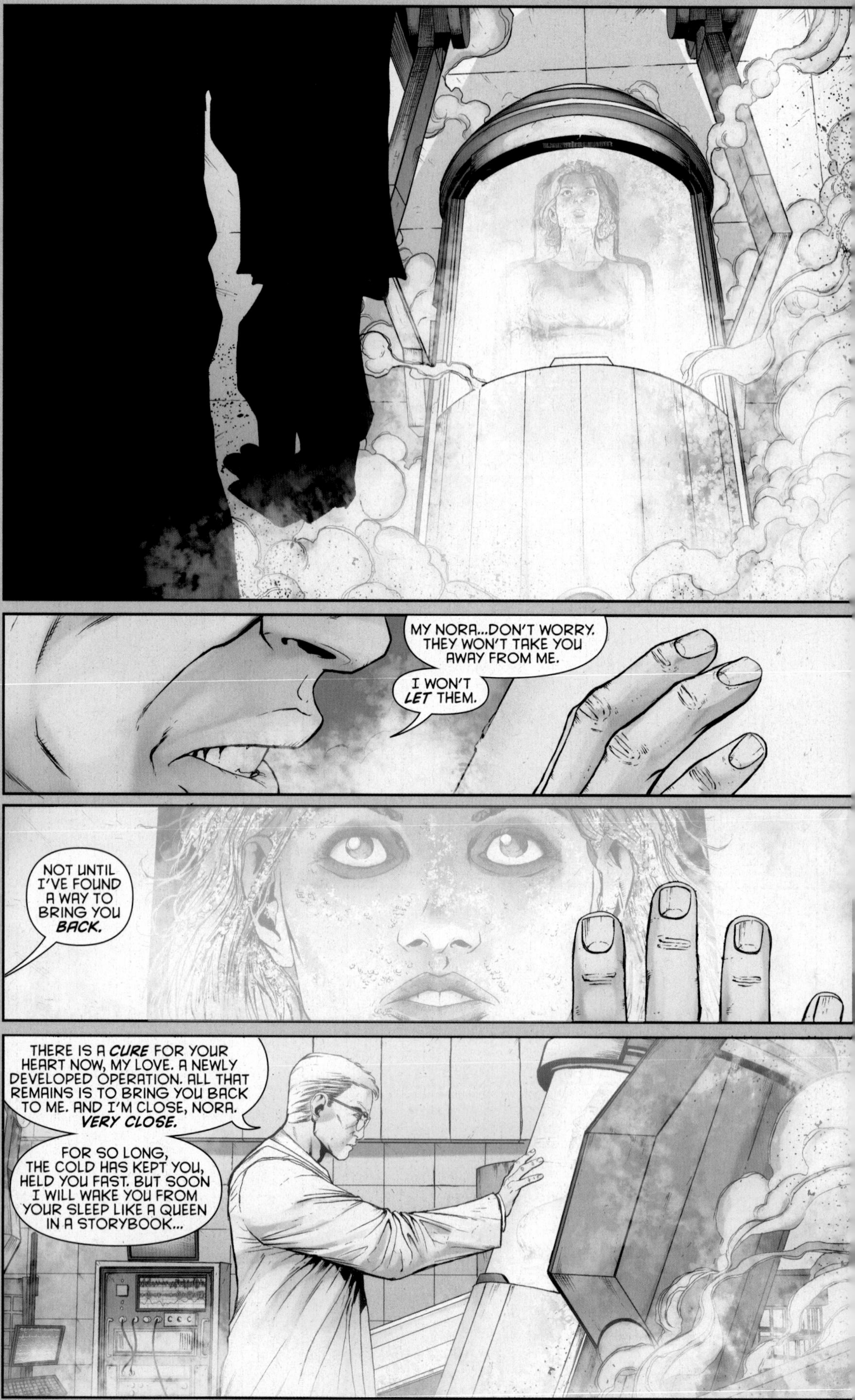

MY NORA...DON'T WORRY. THEY WON'T TAKE YOU AWAY FROM ME.
I WON'T *LET* THEM.
NOT UNTIL I'VE FOUND A WAY TO BRING YOU *BACK.*
THERE IS A *CURE* FOR YOUR HEART NOW, MY LOVE. A NEWLY DEVELOPED OPERATION. ALL THAT REMAINS IS TO BRING YOU BACK TO ME. AND I'M CLOSE, NORA. *VERY CLOSE.*
FOR SO LONG, THE COLD HAS KEPT YOU, HELD YOU FAST. BUT SOON I WILL WAKE YOU FROM YOUR SLEEP LIKE A QUEEN IN A STORYBOOK...

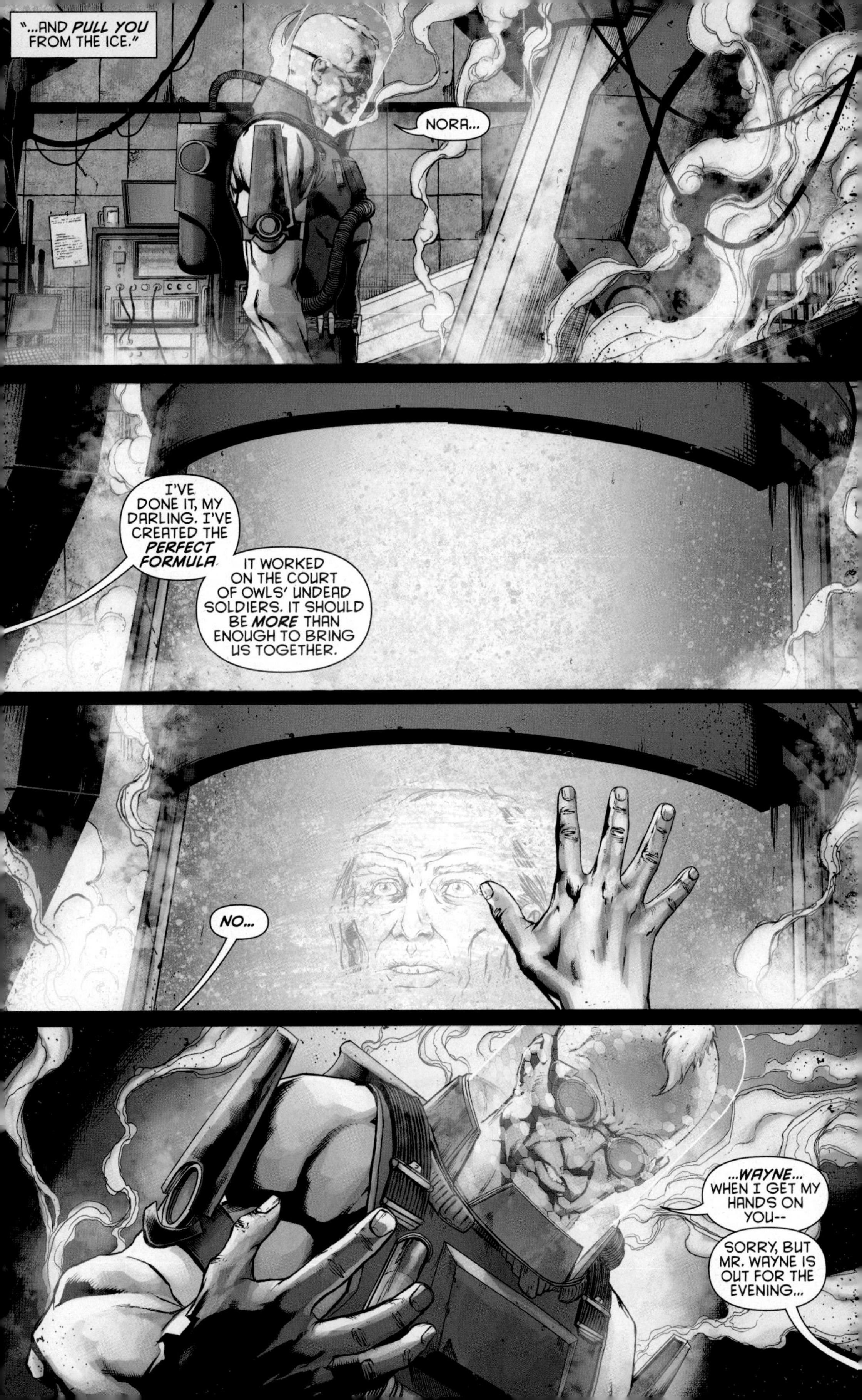
"...AND PULL YOU FROM THE ICE."
NORA...
I'VE DONE IT, MY DARLING. I'VE CREATED THE PERFECT FORMULA.
IT WORKED ON THE COURT OF OWLS' UNDEAD SOLDIERS. IT SHOULD BE MORE THAN ENOUGH TO BRING US TOGETHER.
NO...
...WAYNE... WHEN I GET MY HANDS ON YOU--
SORRY, BUT MR. WAYNE IS OUT FOR THE EVENING...

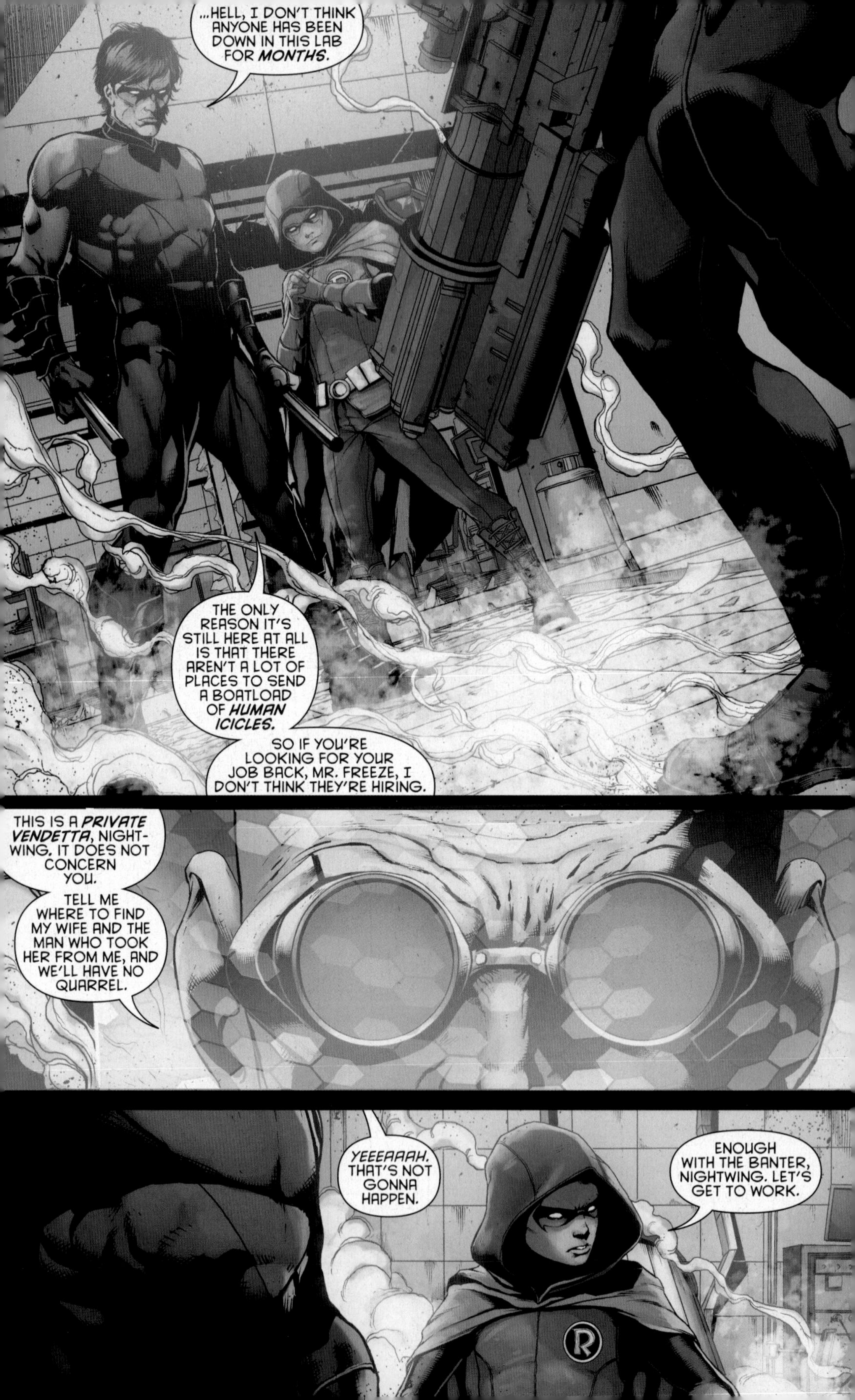
...HELL, I DON'T THINK ANYONE HAS BEEN DOWN IN THIS LAB FOR *MONTHS*.
THE ONLY REASON IT'S STILL HERE AT ALL IS THAT THERE AREN'T A LOT OF PLACES TO SEND A BOATLOAD OF *HUMAN ICICLES*.
SO IF YOU'RE LOOKING FOR YOUR JOB BACK, MR. FREEZE, I DON'T THINK THEY'RE HIRING.
THIS IS A *PRIVATE VENDETTA*, NIGHT-WING. IT DOES NOT CONCERN YOU.
TELL ME WHERE TO FIND MY WIFE AND THE MAN WHO TOOK HER FROM ME, AND WE'LL HAVE NO QUARREL.
YEEEAAAH. THAT'S NOT GONNA HAPPEN.
ENOUGH WITH THE BANTER, NIGHTWING. LET'S GET TO WORK.

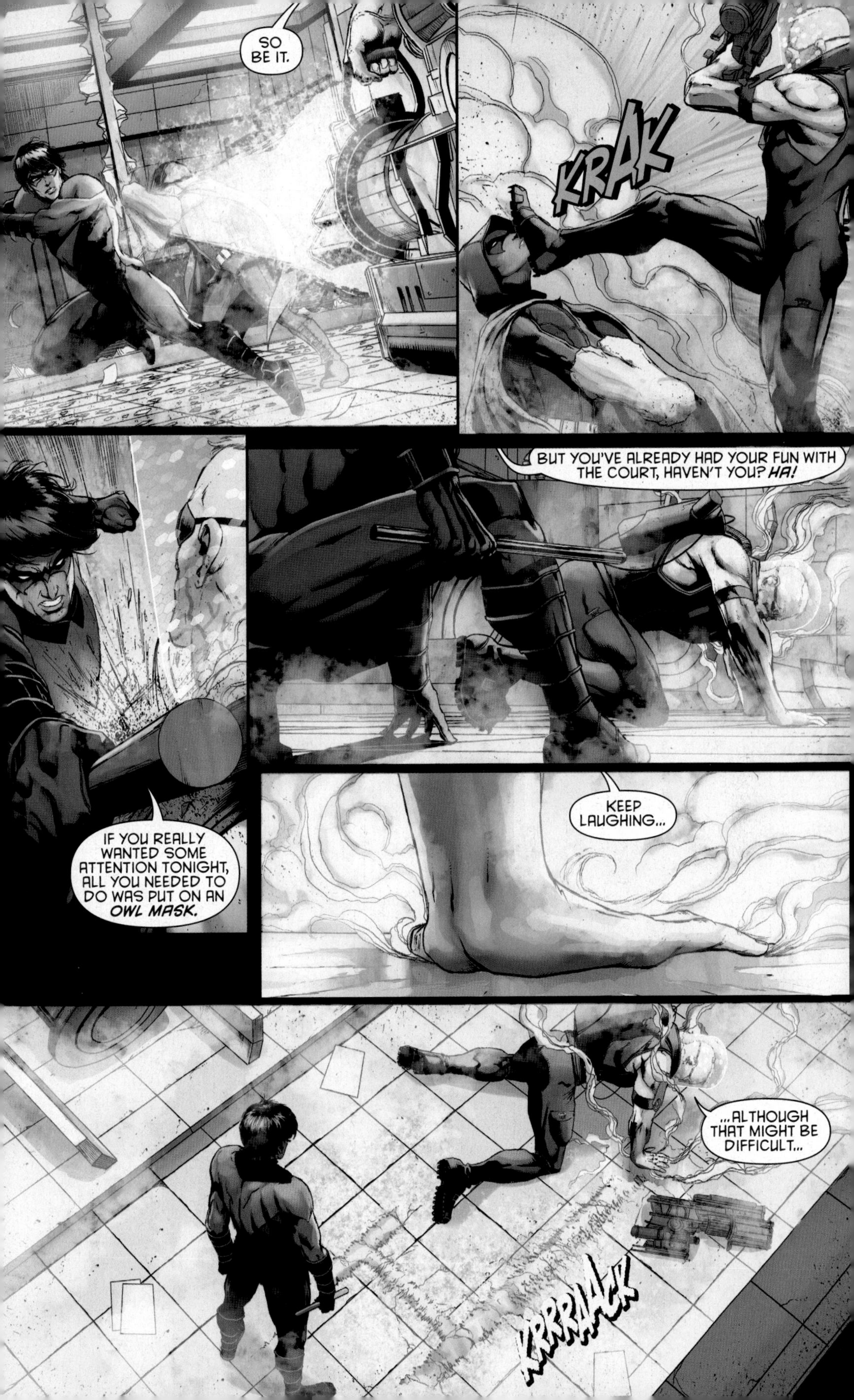
SO BE IT.
KRAK
BUT YOU'VE ALREADY HAD YOUR FUN WITH THE COURT, HAVEN'T YOU? HA!
IF YOU REALLY WANTED SOME ATTENTION TONIGHT, ALL YOU NEEDED TO DO WAS PUT ON AN OWL MASK.
KEEP LAUGHING...
...ALTHOUGH THAT MIGHT BE DIFFICULT...
KRRRAACK

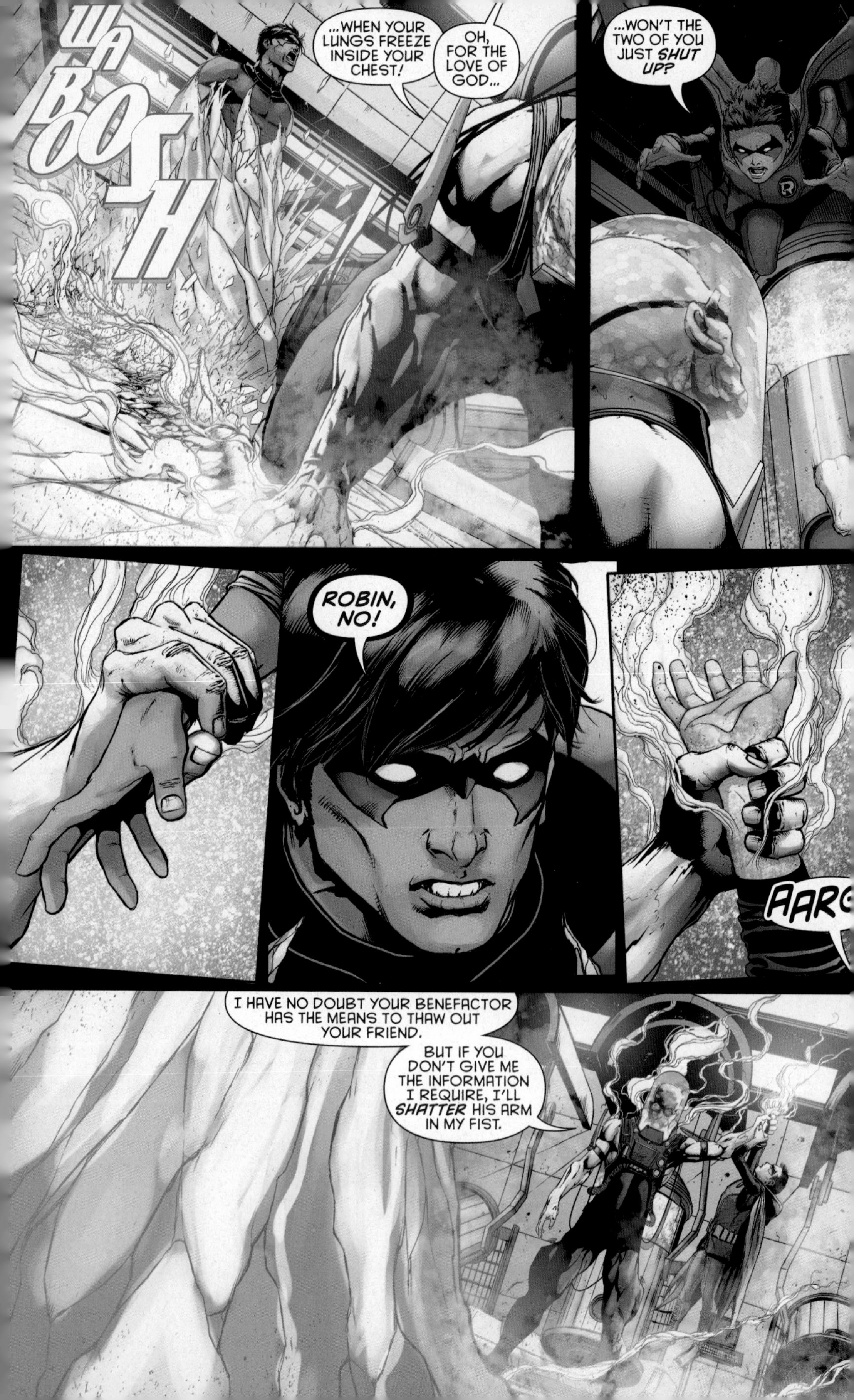
WA
BOOOSH
...WHEN YOUR LUNGS FREEZE INSIDE YOUR CHEST!
OH, FOR THE LOVE OF GOD...
...WON'T THE TWO OF YOU JUST SHUT UP?
ROBIN, NO!
AARG
I HAVE NO DOUBT YOUR BENEFACTOR HAS THE MEANS TO THAW OUT YOUR FRIEND.
BUT IF YOU DON'T GIVE ME THE INFORMATION I REQUIRE, I'LL SHATTER HIS ARM IN MY FIST.

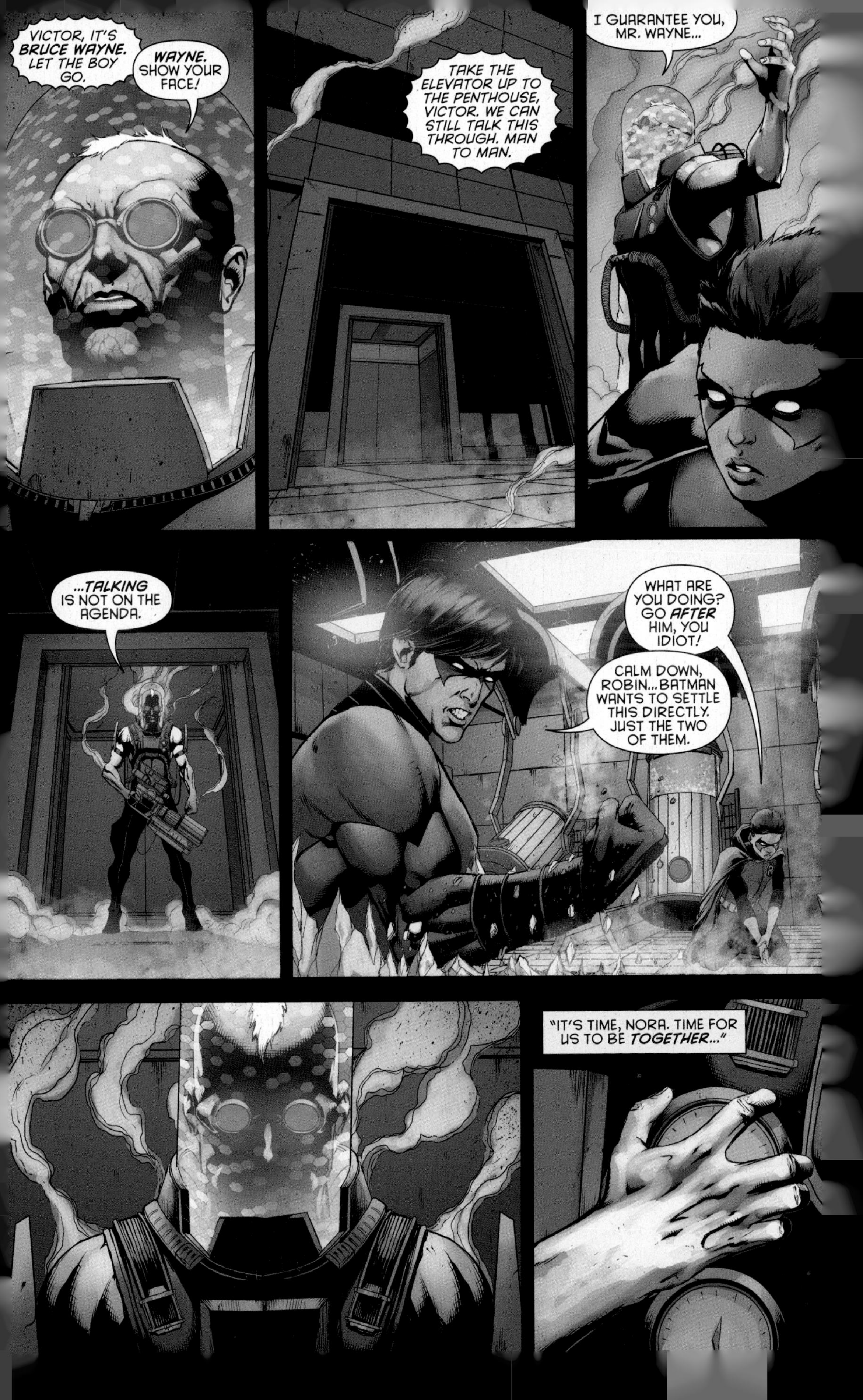

VICTOR, IT'S **BRUCE WAYNE.** LET THE BOY GO.
WAYNE. SHOW YOUR FACE!
TAKE THE ELEVATOR UP TO THE PENTHOUSE, VICTOR. WE CAN STILL TALK THIS THROUGH. MAN TO MAN.
I GUARANTEE YOU, MR. WAYNE...
...**TALKING** IS NOT ON THE AGENDA.
WHAT ARE YOU DOING? GO ***AFTER*** HIM, YOU IDIOT!
CALM DOWN, ROBIN...BATMAN WANTS TO SETTLE THIS DIRECTLY. JUST THE TWO OF THEM.
"IT'S TIME, NORA. TIME FOR US TO BE ***TOGETHER***..."

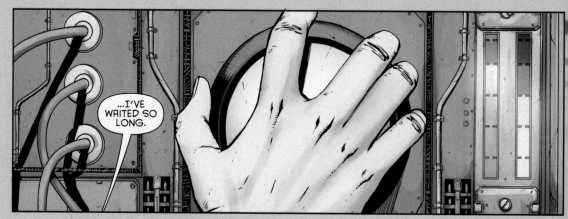

...I'VE WAITED SO LONG.

BUT THIS--THIS *NEW COMPOUND* IS EVERYTHING WE'VE BEEN WAITING FOR, MY LOVE.

AND IT WILL WORK. I *WILL* BRING YOU BACK.

NO, VICTOR...

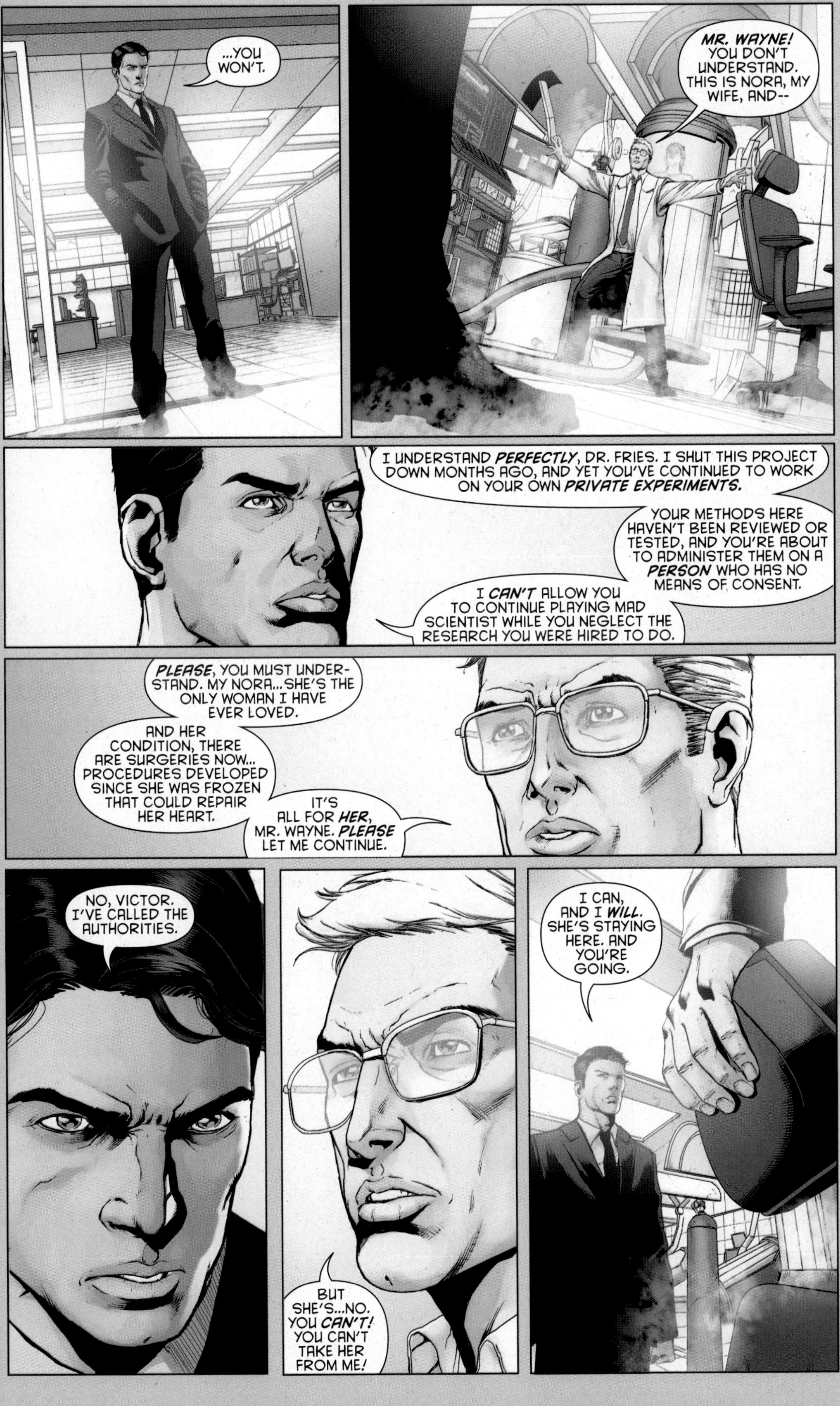
...YOU WON'T.
MR. WAYNE! YOU DON'T UNDERSTAND. THIS IS NORA, MY WIFE, AND--
I UNDERSTAND PERFECTLY, DR. FRIES. I SHUT THIS PROJECT DOWN MONTHS AGO, AND YET YOU'VE CONTINUED TO WORK ON YOUR OWN PRIVATE EXPERIMENTS.
YOUR METHODS HERE HAVEN'T BEEN REVIEWED OR TESTED, AND YOU'RE ABOUT TO ADMINISTER THEM ON A PERSON WHO HAS NO MEANS OF CONSENT.
I CAN'T ALLOW YOU TO CONTINUE PLAYING MAD SCIENTIST WHILE YOU NEGLECT THE RESEARCH YOU WERE HIRED TO DO.
PLEASE, YOU MUST UNDER-STAND. MY NORA...SHE'S THE ONLY WOMAN I HAVE EVER LOVED.
AND HER CONDITION, THERE ARE SURGERIES NOW... PROCEDURES DEVELOPED SINCE SHE WAS FROZEN THAT COULD REPAIR HER HEART.
IT'S ALL FOR HER, MR. WAYNE. PLEASE LET ME CONTINUE.
NO, VICTOR. I'VE CALLED THE AUTHORITIES.
BUT SHE'S...NO. YOU CAN'T! YOU CAN'T TAKE HER FROM ME!
I CAN, AND I WILL. SHE'S STAYING HERE. AND YOU'RE GOING.

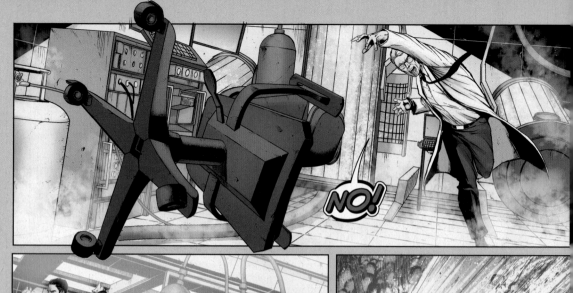

NO!

VICTOR, GET OUT OF THE WAY!

AAAHHH!

NOOO.... RRRAA. NORA....

"THIS IS *INCREDIBLE*, I'VE NEVER SEEN ANYTHING LIKE IT."

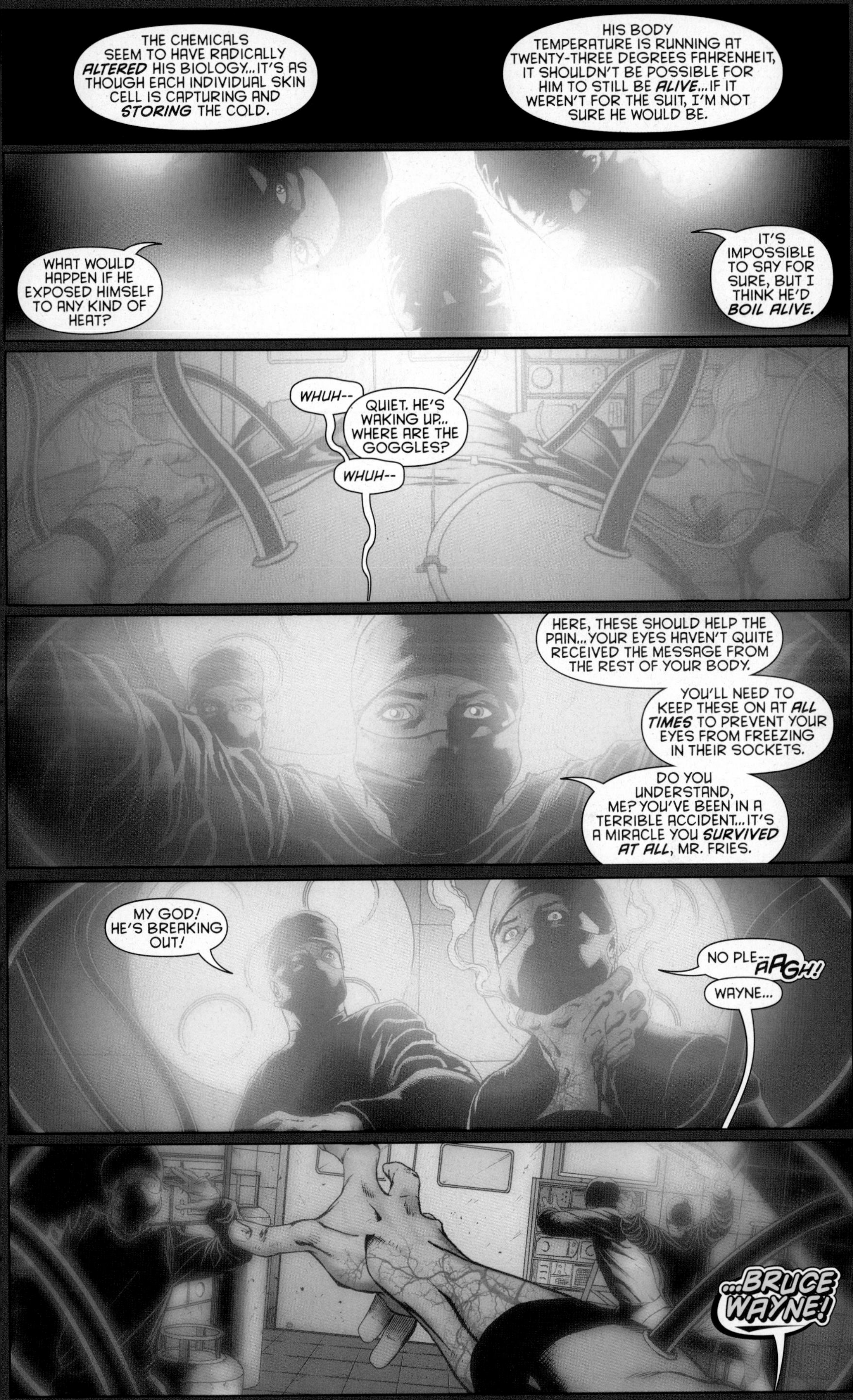
THE CHEMICALS SEEM TO HAVE RADICALLY ALTERED HIS BIOLOGY... IT'S AS THOUGH EACH INDIVIDUAL SKIN CELL IS CAPTURING AND STORING THE COLD.
HIS BODY TEMPERATURE IS RUNNING AT TWENTY-THREE DEGREES FAHRENHEIT, IT SHOULDN'T BE POSSIBLE FOR HIM TO STILL BE ALIVE... IF IT WEREN'T FOR THE SUIT, I'M NOT SURE HE WOULD BE.
WHAT WOULD HAPPEN IF HE EXPOSED HIMSELF TO ANY KIND OF HEAT?
IT'S IMPOSSIBLE TO SAY FOR SURE, BUT I THINK HE'D BOIL ALIVE.
WHUH--
QUIET. HE'S WAKING UP... WHERE ARE THE GOGGLES?
WHUH--
HERE, THESE SHOULD HELP THE PAIN... YOUR EYES HAVEN'T QUITE RECEIVED THE MESSAGE FROM THE REST OF YOUR BODY.
YOU'LL NEED TO KEEP THESE ON AT ALL TIMES TO PREVENT YOUR EYES FROM FREEZING IN THEIR SOCKETS.
DO YOU UNDERSTAND, ME? YOU'VE BEEN IN A TERRIBLE ACCIDENT... IT'S A MIRACLE YOU SURVIVED AT ALL, MR. FRIES.
MY GOD! HE'S BREAKING OUT!
NO PLE--AAGH!
WAYNE...
...BRUCE WAYNE!

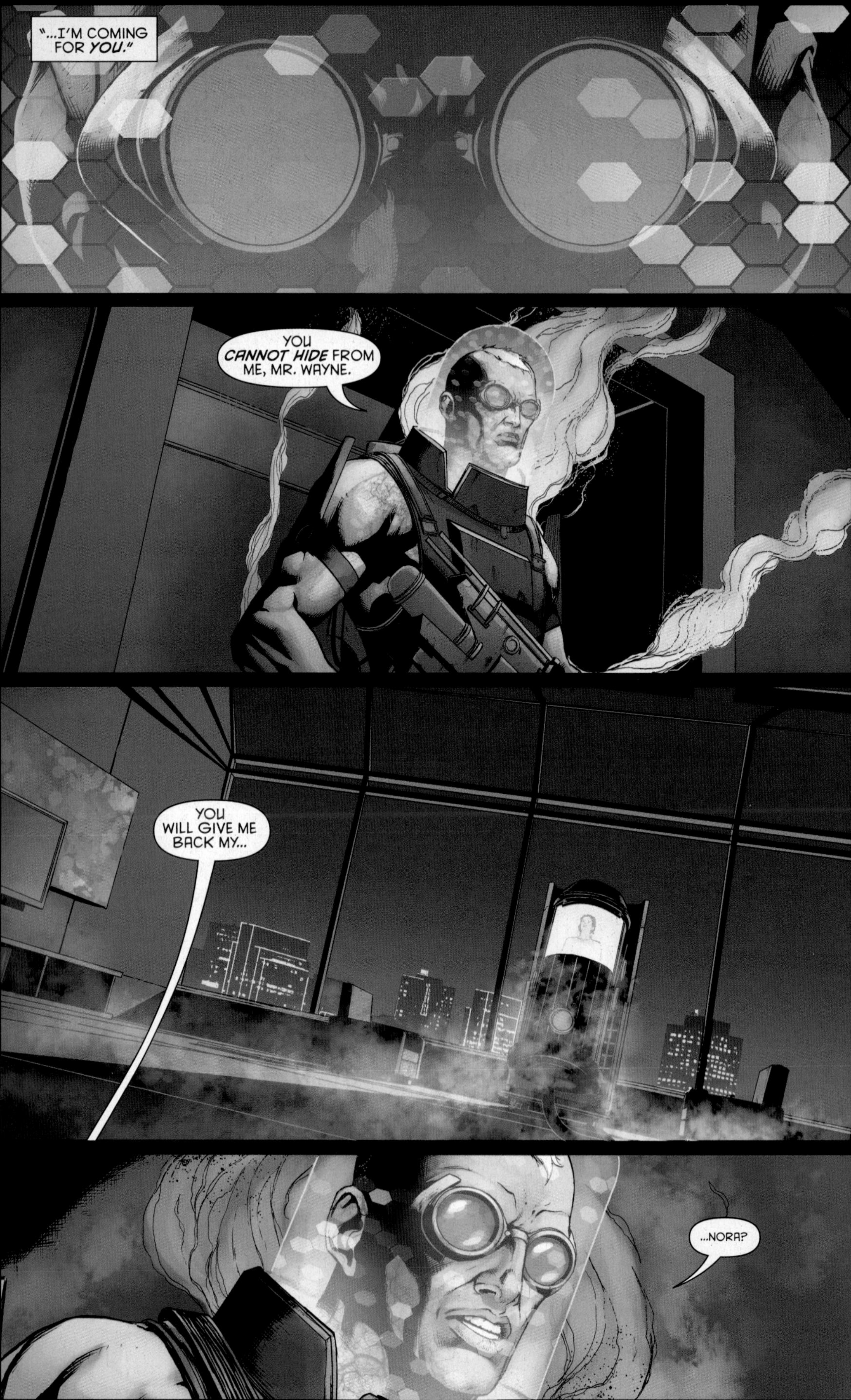
"...I'M COMING FOR *YOU*."
YOU *CANNOT HIDE* FROM ME, MR. WAYNE.
YOU WILL GIVE ME BACK MY...
...NORA?

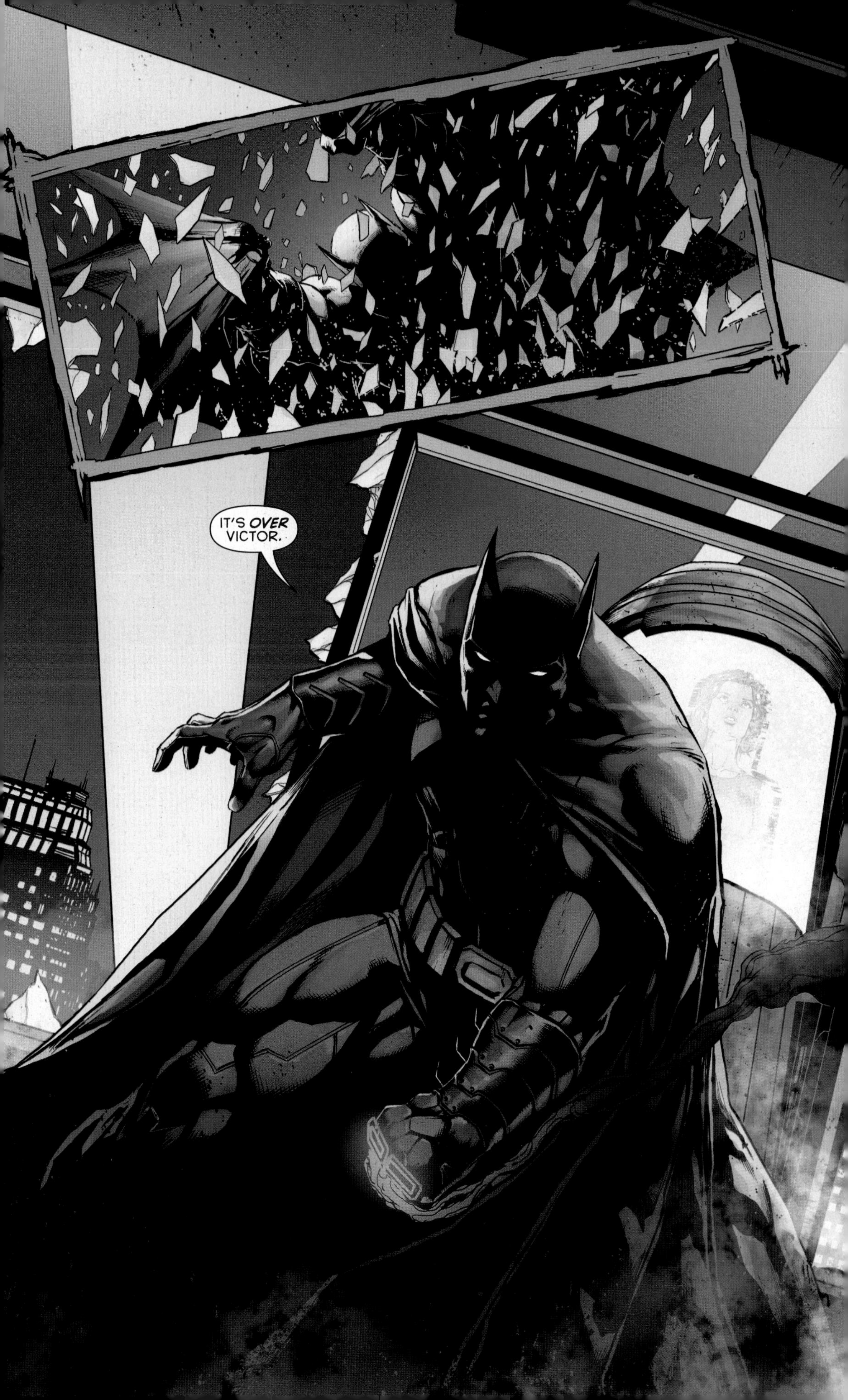
IT'S *OVER* VICTOR.

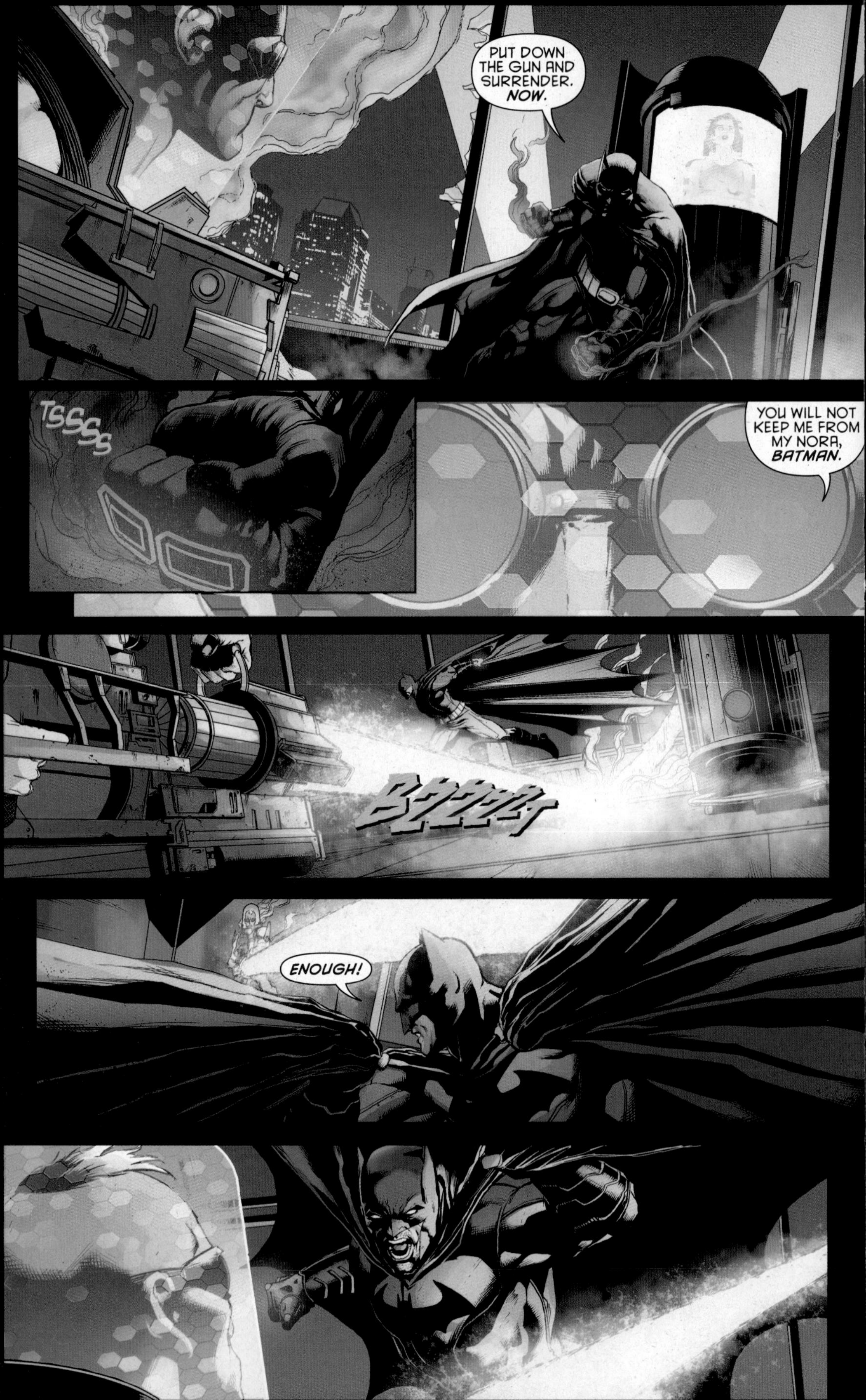
PUT DOWN THE GUN AND SURRENDER. *NOW*.
TSSSS
YOU WILL NOT KEEP ME FROM MY NORA, *BATMAN*.
BZZZZT
ENOUGH!

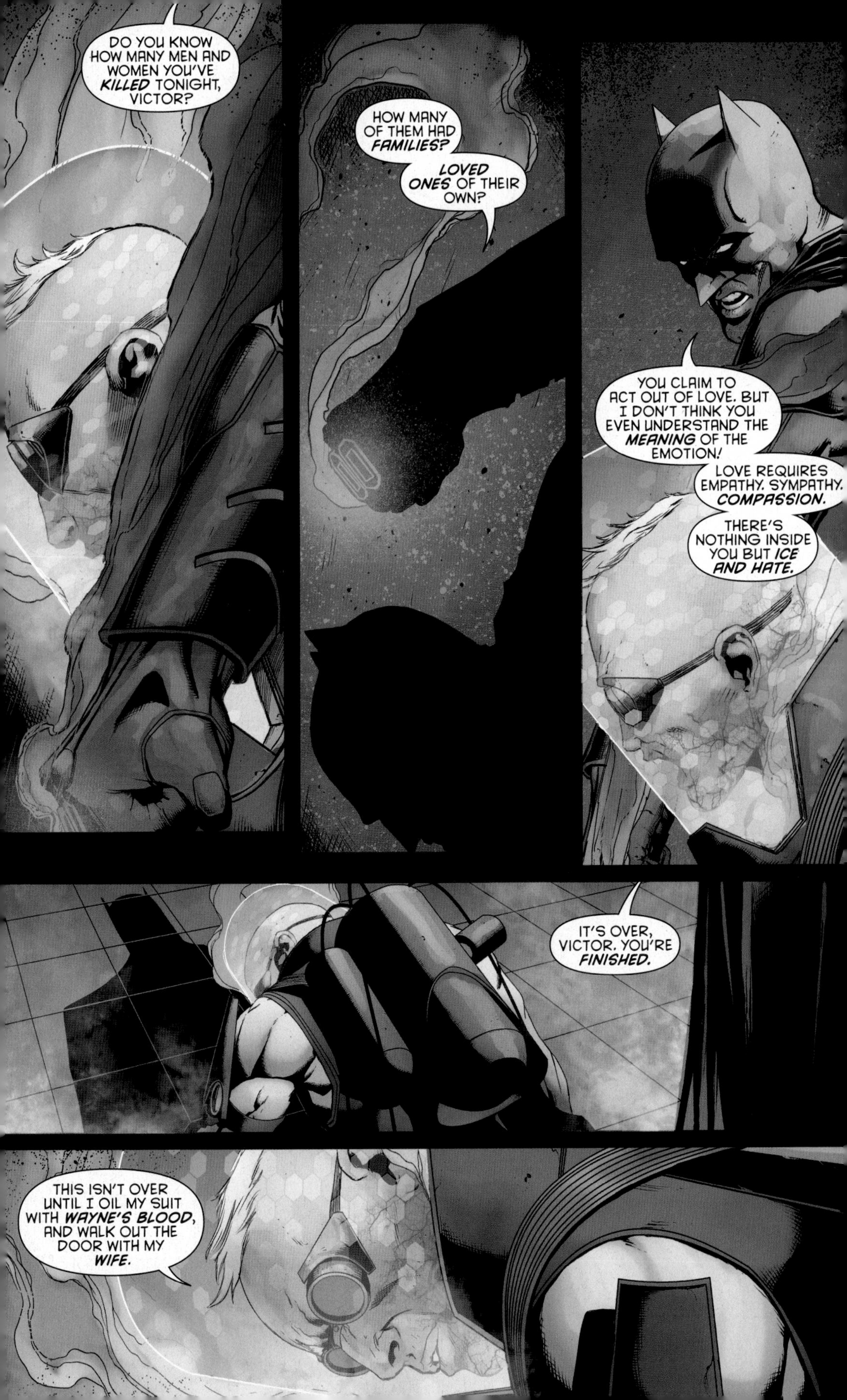
DO YOU KNOW HOW MANY MEN AND WOMEN YOU'VE KILLED TONIGHT, VICTOR?
HOW MANY OF THEM HAD FAMILIES?
LOVED ONES OF THEIR OWN?
YOU CLAIM TO ACT OUT OF LOVE. BUT I DON'T THINK YOU EVEN UNDERSTAND THE MEANING OF THE EMOTION!
LOVE REQUIRES EMPATHY. SYMPATHY. COMPASSION.
THERE'S NOTHING INSIDE YOU BUT ICE AND HATE.
IT'S OVER, VICTOR. YOU'RE FINISHED.
THIS ISN'T OVER UNTIL I OIL MY SUIT WITH WAYNE'S BLOOD, AND WALK OUT THE DOOR WITH MY WIFE.

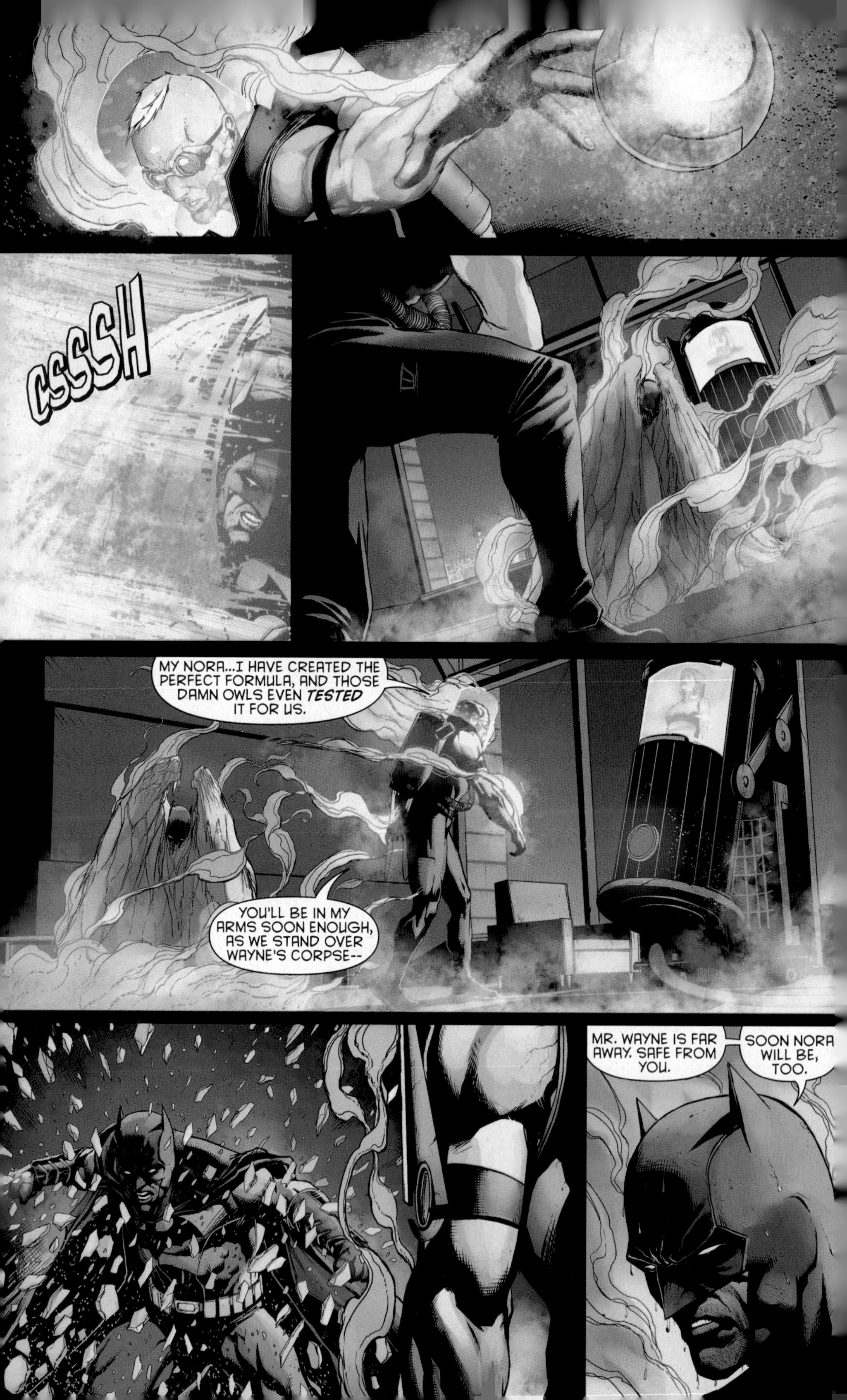

CSSSH
MY NORA...I HAVE CREATED THE PERFECT FORMULA, AND THOSE DAMN OWLS EVEN TESTED IT FOR US.
YOU'LL BE IN MY ARMS SOON ENOUGH, AS WE STAND OVER WAYNE'S CORPSE--
MR. WAYNE IS FAR AWAY. SAFE FROM YOU.
SOON NORA WILL BE, TOO.

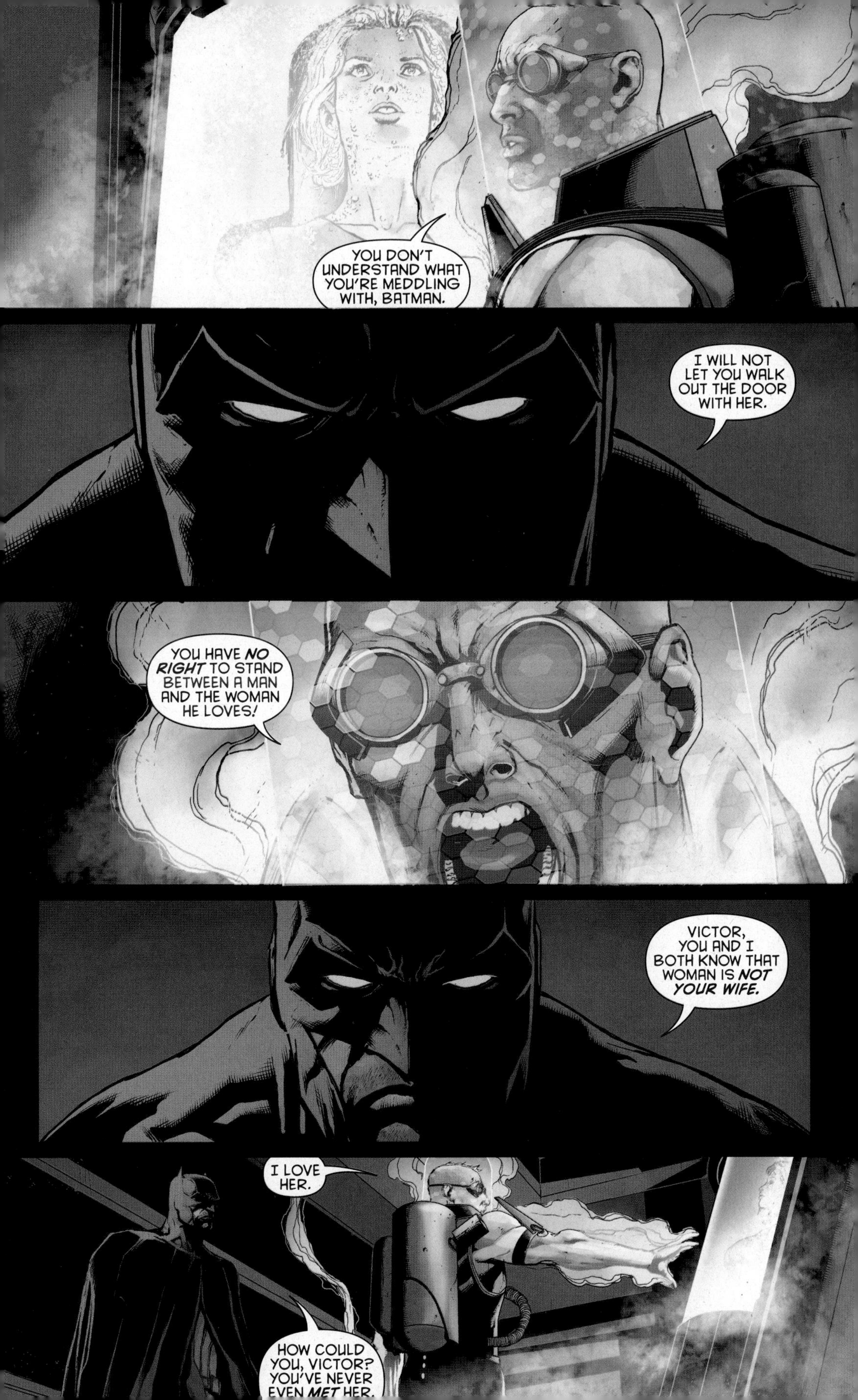
YOU DON'T UNDERSTAND WHAT YOU'RE MEDDLING WITH, BATMAN.
I WILL NOT LET YOU WALK OUT THE DOOR WITH HER.
YOU HAVE ***NO RIGHT*** TO STAND BETWEEN A MAN AND THE WOMAN HE LOVES!
VICTOR, YOU AND I BOTH KNOW THAT WOMAN IS ***NOT YOUR WIFE.***
I LOVE HER.
HOW COULD YOU, VICTOR? YOU'VE NEVER EVEN ***MET*** HER.

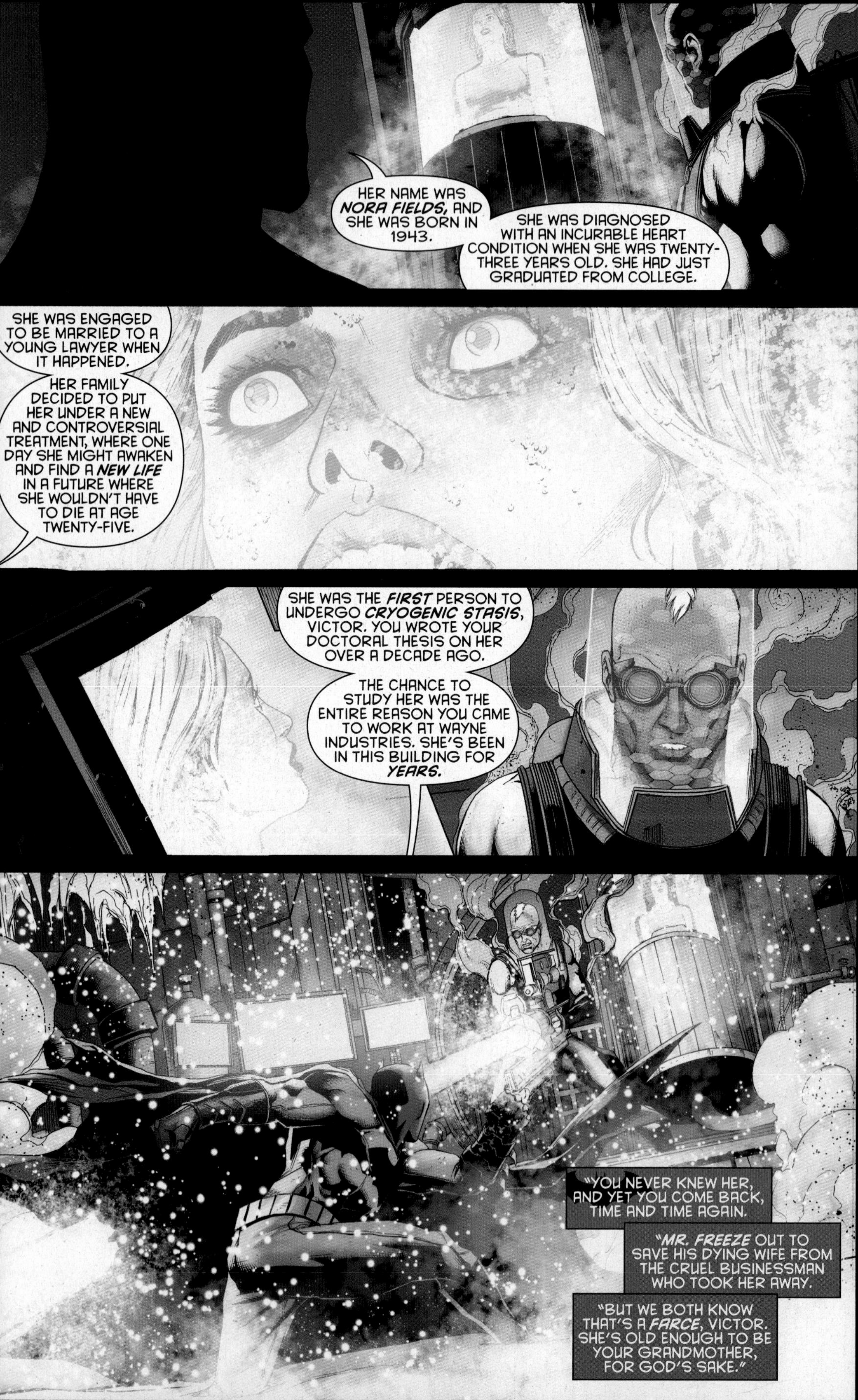
HER NAME WAS NORA FIELDS, AND SHE WAS BORN IN 1943.
SHE WAS DIAGNOSED WITH AN INCURABLE HEART CONDITION WHEN SHE WAS TWENTY-THREE YEARS OLD. SHE HAD JUST GRADUATED FROM COLLEGE.
SHE WAS ENGAGED TO BE MARRIED TO A YOUNG LAWYER WHEN IT HAPPENED.
HER FAMILY DECIDED TO PUT HER UNDER A NEW AND CONTROVERSIAL TREATMENT, WHERE ONE DAY SHE MIGHT AWAKEN AND FIND A NEW LIFE IN A FUTURE WHERE SHE WOULDN'T HAVE TO DIE AT AGE TWENTY-FIVE.
SHE WAS THE FIRST PERSON TO UNDERGO CRYOGENIC STASIS, VICTOR. YOU WROTE YOUR DOCTORAL THESIS ON HER OVER A DECADE AGO.
THE CHANCE TO STUDY HER WAS THE ENTIRE REASON YOU CAME TO WORK AT WAYNE INDUSTRIES. SHE'S BEEN IN THIS BUILDING FOR YEARS.
"YOU NEVER KNEW HER, AND YET YOU COME BACK, TIME AND TIME AGAIN.
"MR. FREEZE OUT TO SAVE HIS DYING WIFE FROM THE CRUEL BUSINESSMAN WHO TOOK HER AWAY.
"BUT WE BOTH KNOW THAT'S A FARCE, VICTOR. SHE'S OLD ENOUGH TO BE YOUR GRANDMOTHER, FOR GOD'S SAKE."

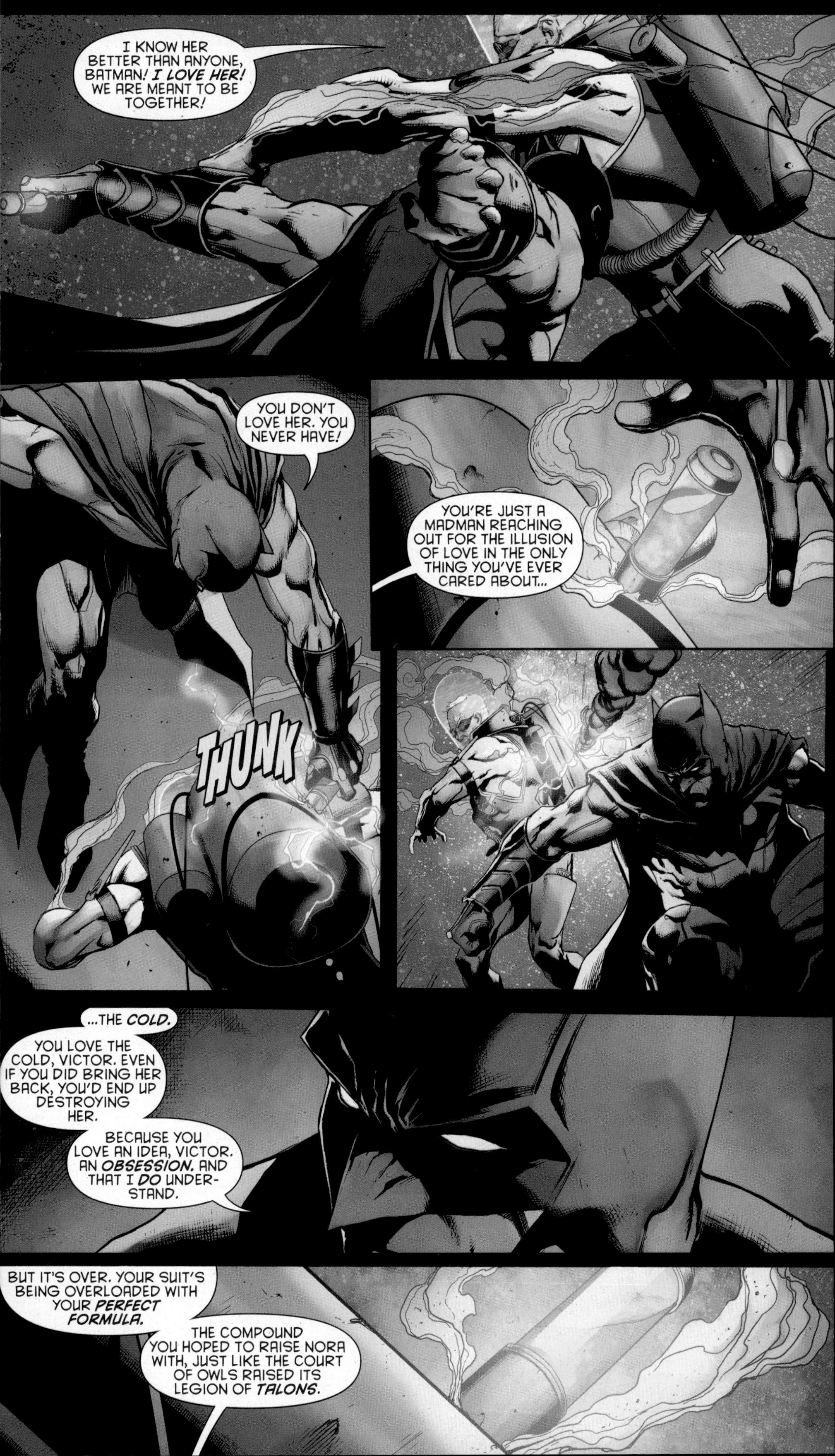
I KNOW HER BETTER THAN ANYONE, BATMAN! *I LOVE HER!* WE ARE MEANT TO BE TOGETHER!
YOU DON'T LOVE HER. YOU NEVER HAVE!
YOU'RE JUST A MADMAN REACHING OUT FOR THE ILLUSION OF LOVE IN THE ONLY THING YOU'VE EVER CARED ABOUT...
THUNK
...THE *COLD.*
YOU LOVE THE COLD, VICTOR. EVEN IF YOU DID BRING HER BACK, YOU'D END UP DESTROYING HER.
BECAUSE YOU LOVE AN IDEA, VICTOR. AN *OBSESSION.* AND THAT I *DO* UNDER-STAND.
BUT IT'S OVER. YOUR SUIT'S BEING OVERLOADED WITH YOUR *PERFECT FORMULA.*
THE COMPOUND YOU HOPED TO RAISE NORA WITH, JUST LIKE THE COURT OF OWLS RAISED ITS LEGION OF *TALONS.*

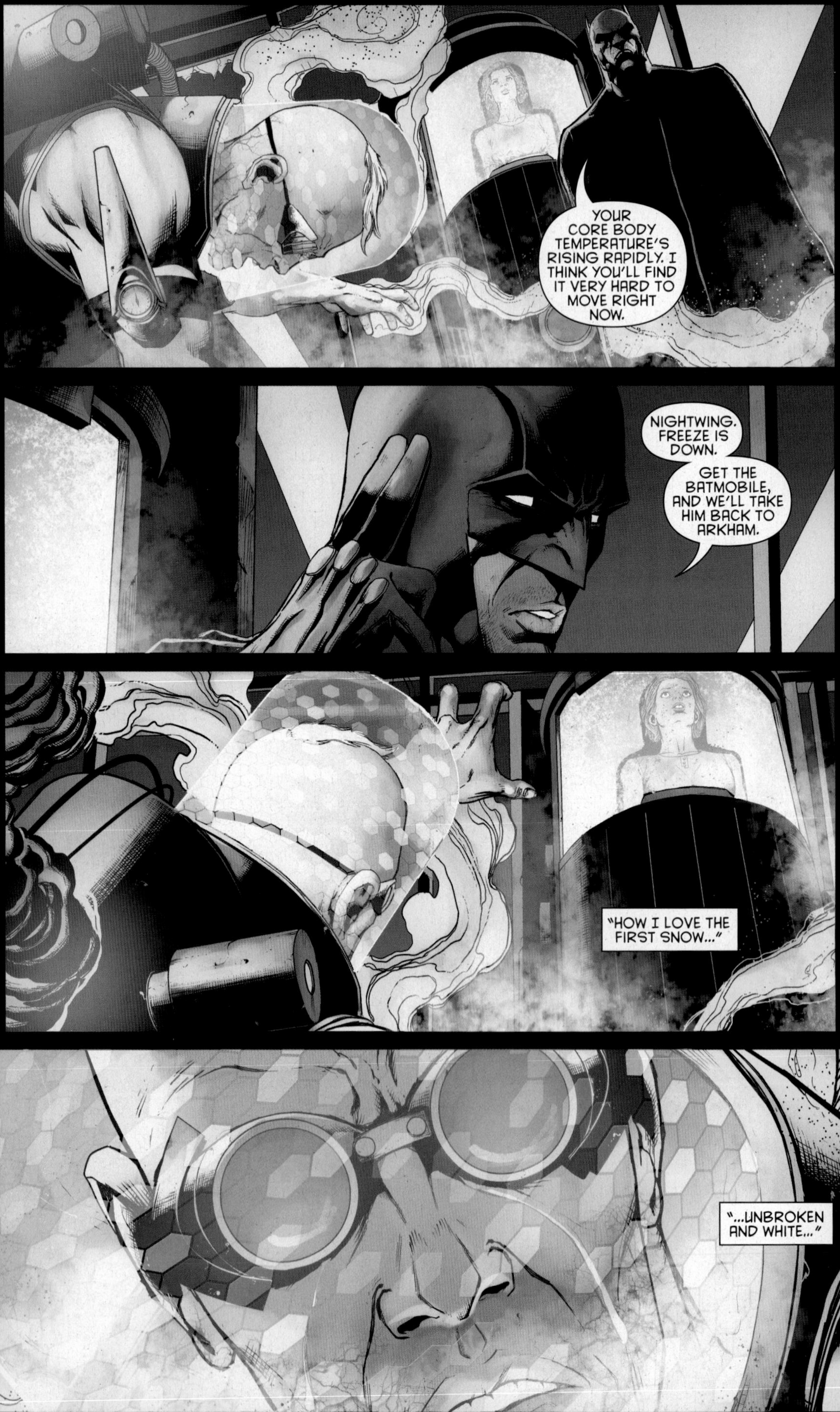
YOUR CORE BODY TEMPERATURE'S RISING RAPIDLY. I THINK YOU'LL FIND IT VERY HARD TO MOVE RIGHT NOW.
NIGHTWING. FREEZE IS DOWN.
GET THE BATMOBILE, AND WE'LL TAKE HIM BACK TO ARKHAM.
"HOW I LOVE THE FIRST SNOW..."
"...UNBROKEN AND WHITE..."

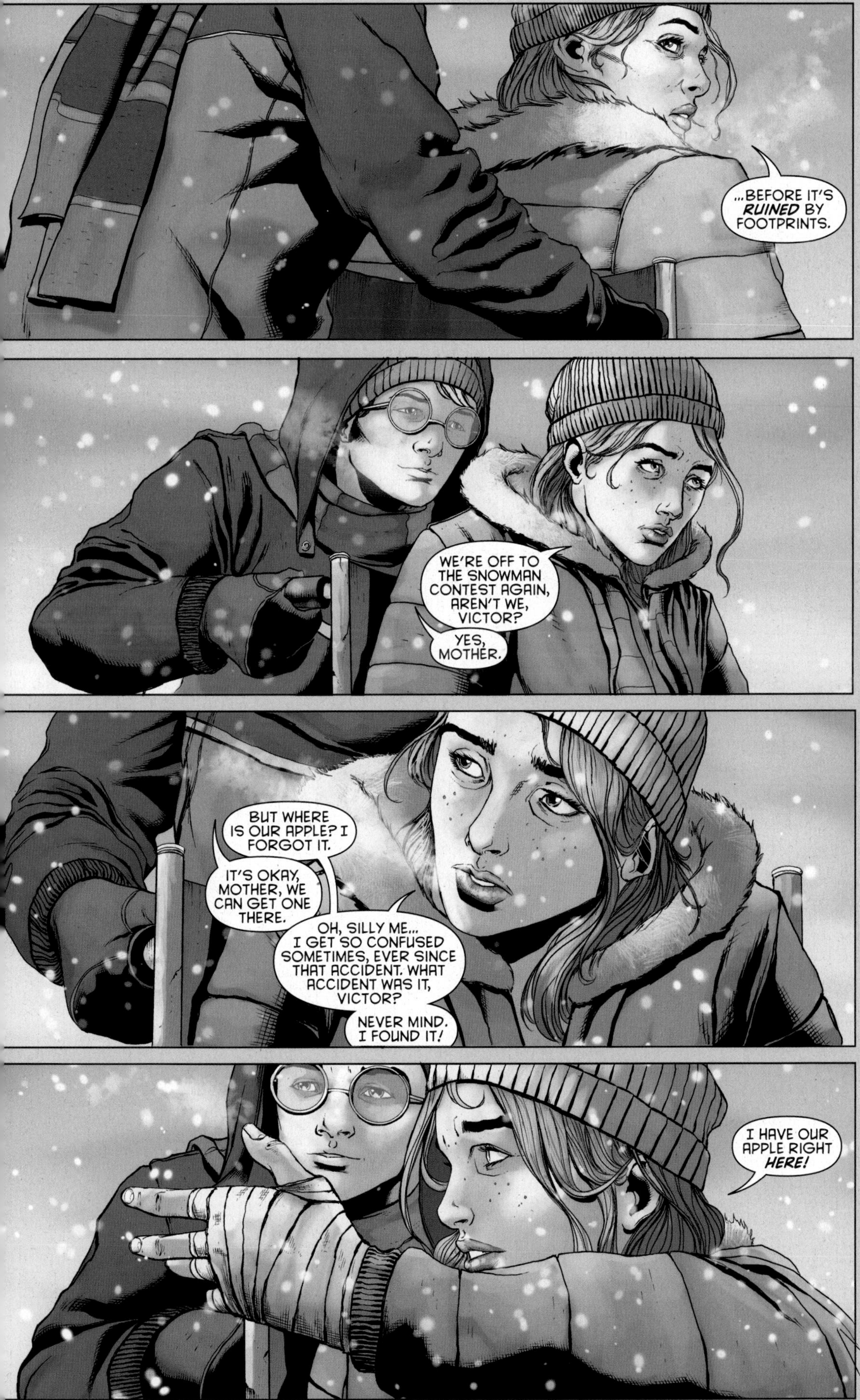
...BEFORE IT'S *RUINED* BY FOOTPRINTS.
WE'RE OFF TO THE SNOWMAN CONTEST AGAIN, AREN'T WE, VICTOR?
YES, MOTHER.
BUT WHERE IS OUR APPLE? I FORGOT IT.
IT'S OKAY, MOTHER, WE CAN GET ONE THERE.
OH, SILLY ME... I GET SO CONFUSED SOMETIMES, EVER SINCE THAT ACCIDENT. WHAT ACCIDENT WAS IT, VICTOR?
NEVER MIND. I FOUND IT!
I HAVE OUR APPLE RIGHT *HERE!*

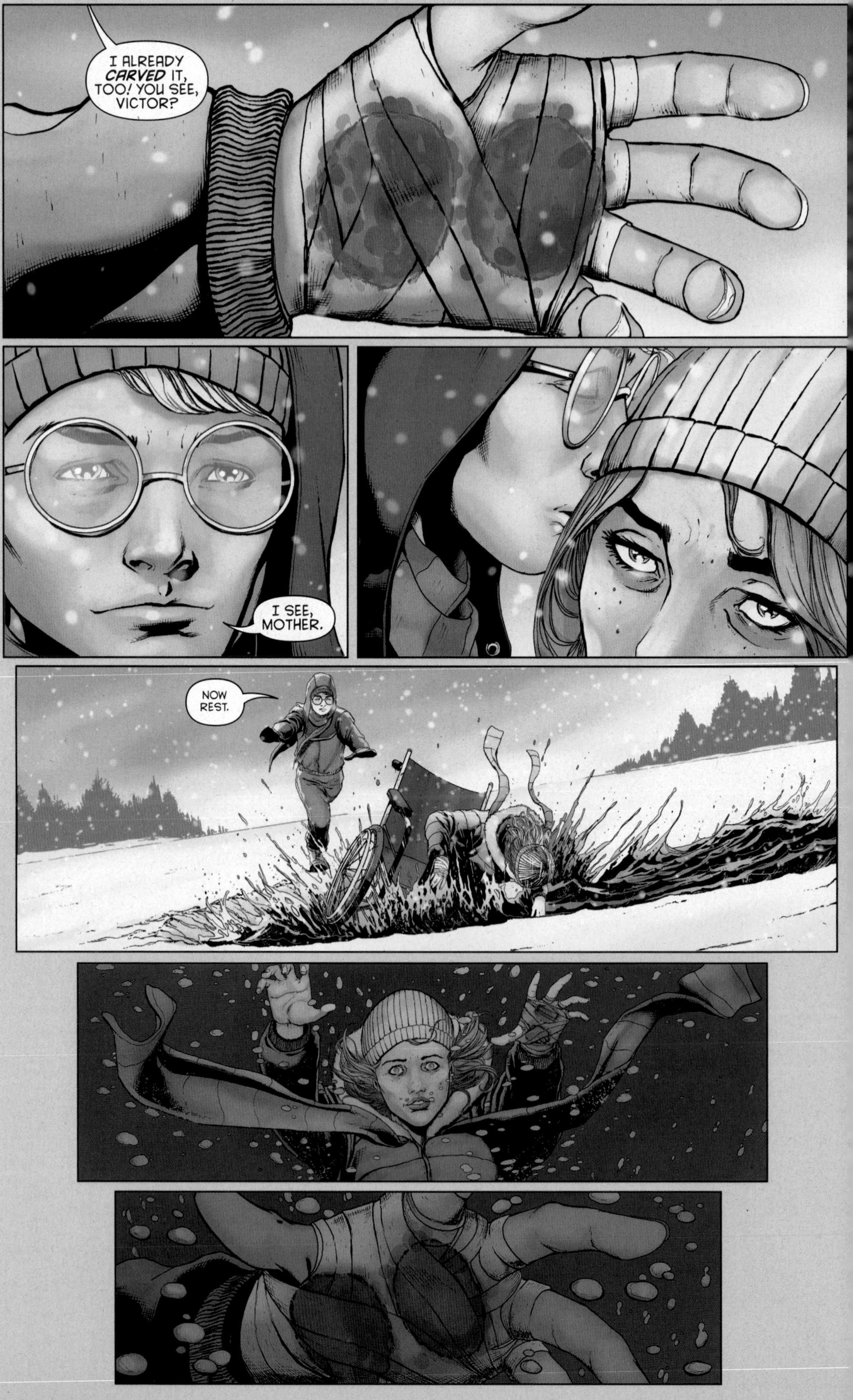
I ALREADY *CARVED* IT, TOO! YOU SEE, VICTOR?
I SEE, MOTHER.
NOW REST.

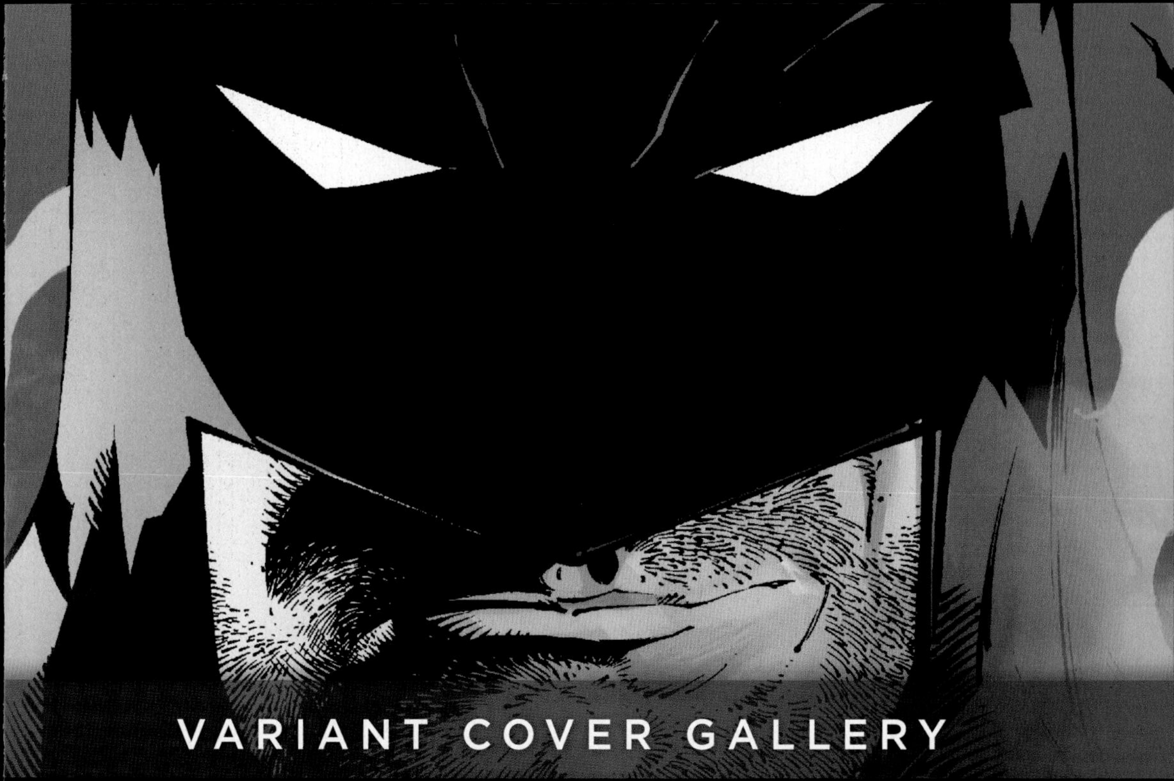

VARIANT COVER GALLERY

BATMAN 8
by Jason Fabok & Peter Steigerwald

BATMAN 9
by Dale Keown & FCO Plascencia

BATMAN 10
by Rafael Albuquerque

BATMAN 11
by Andy Clarke & Tomeu Morey

BATMAN 12
by Bryan Hitch & Nathan Fairbairn

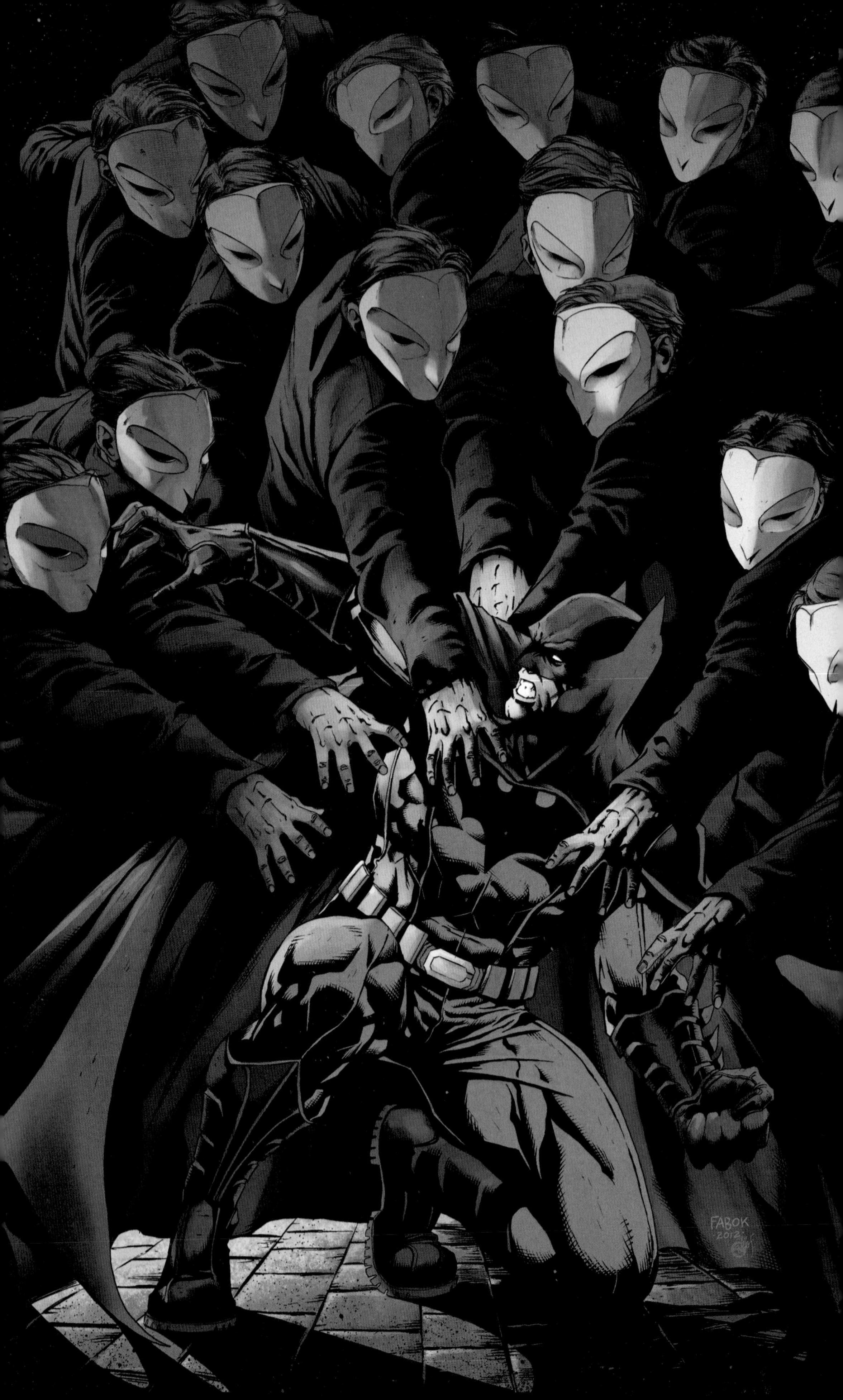
FABOK
2012

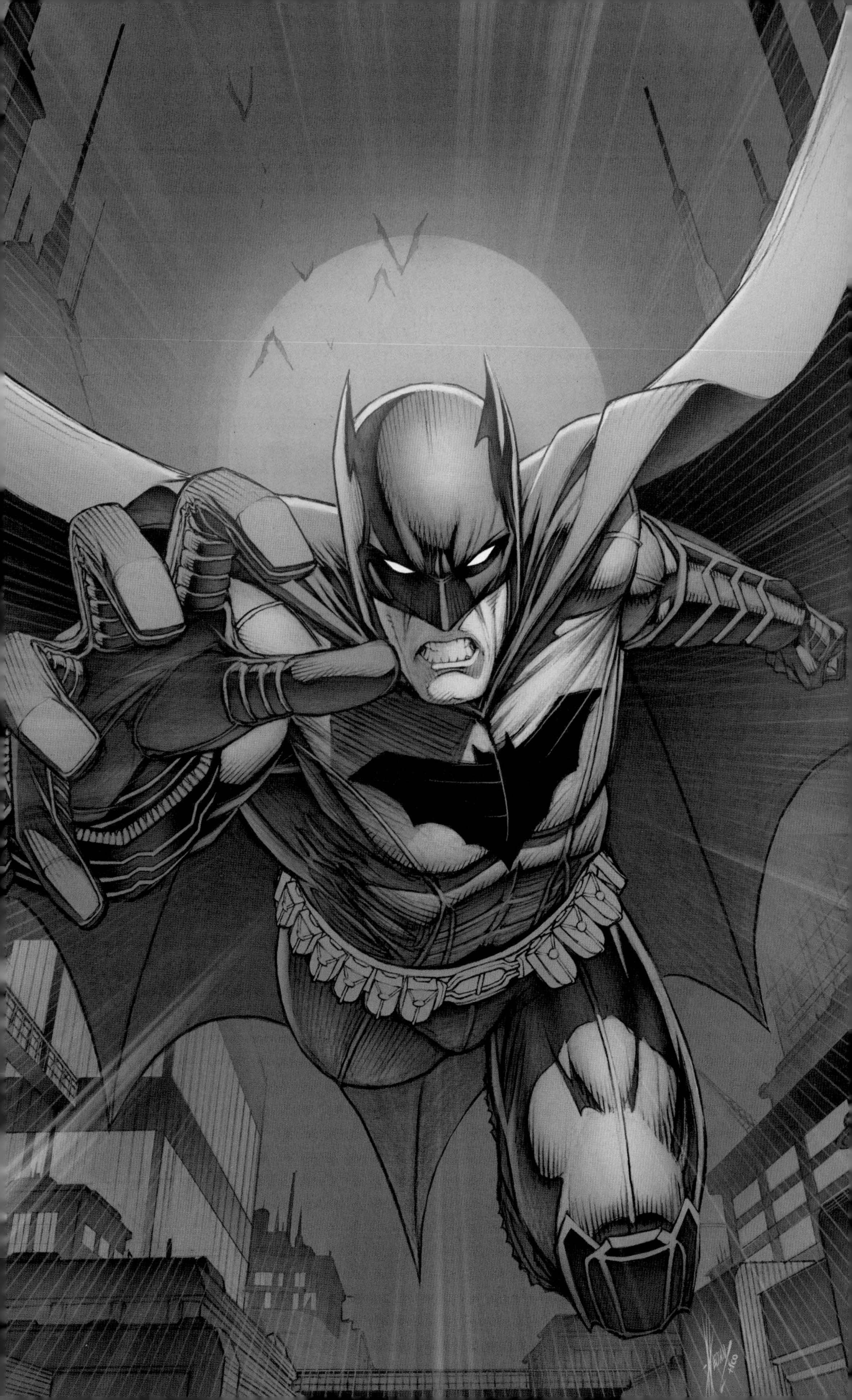

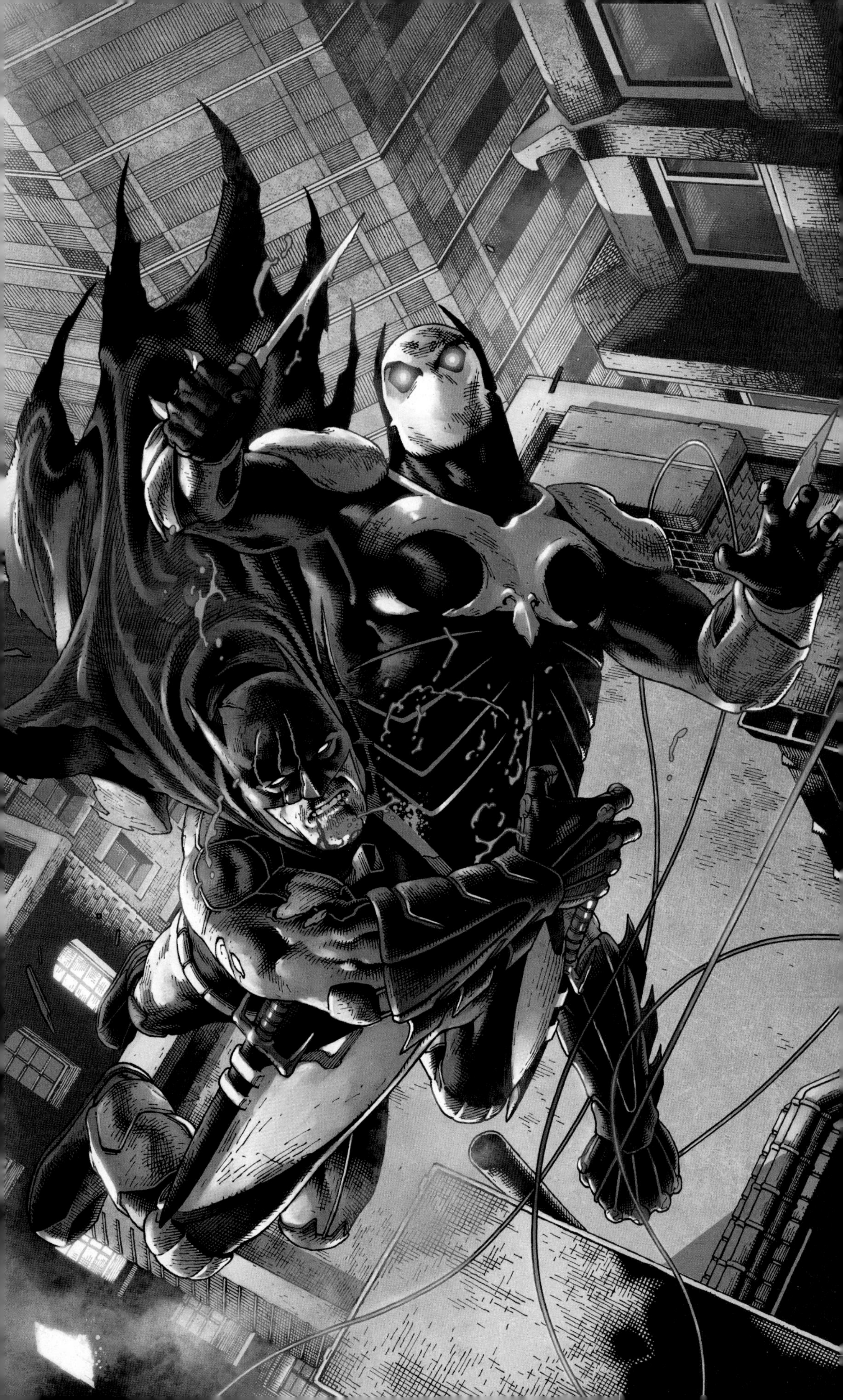

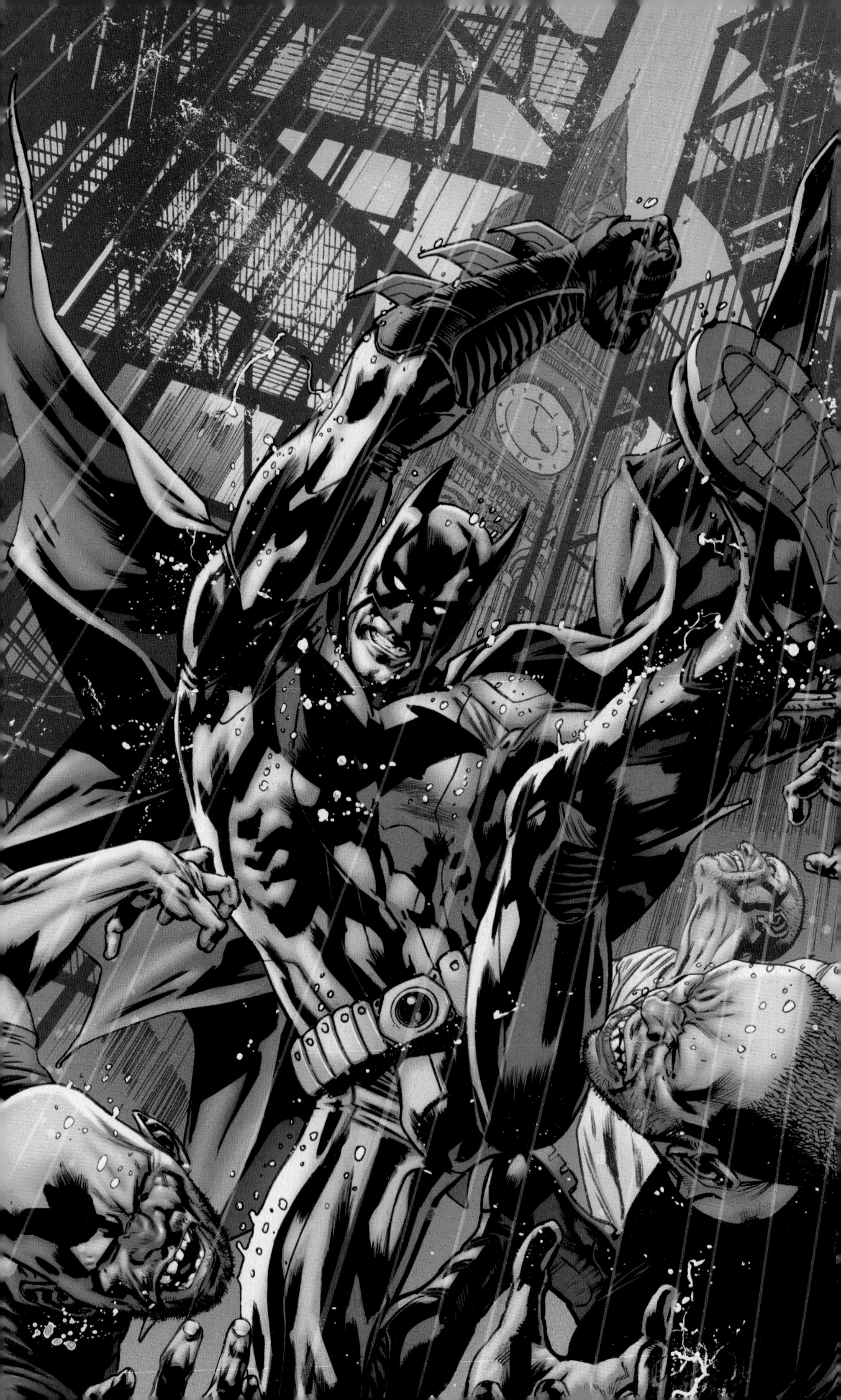